The Aesthetics, Poetics, and Rhetoric of Soccer

Soccer has long been known as 'the beautiful game'. This multi-disciplinary volume explores soccer, soccer culture, and the representation of soccer in art, film, and literature, using the critical tools of aesthetics, poetics, and rhetoric.

Including international contributions from scholars of philosophy, literary and cultural studies, linguistics, art history, and the creative arts, this book begins by investigating the relationship between beauty and soccer and asks what criteria should be used to judge the sport's aesthetic value. Covering topics as diverse as humor, national identity, style, celebrity, and social media, its chapters examine the nature of fandom, the role of language, and the significance of soccer in contemporary popular culture. It also discusses what one might call the 'stylistics' of soccer, analyzing how players, fans, and commentators communicate on and off the pitch, in the press, on social media, and in wider public discourse.

The Aesthetics, Poetics, and Rhetoric of Soccer makes for fascinating reading for anybody with an interest in sport, culture, literature, philosophy, linguistics, and society.

Ridvan Askin is a Postdoctoral Teaching and Research Fellow in American and General Literatures at the University of Basel, Switzerland. He is the author of *Narrative and Becoming* (2016) and the co-editor of *Literature, Ethics, Morality: American Studies Perspectives* (2015) and a special issue of the journal *Speculations* on *Aesthetics in the 21st Century* (2014). His publications include essays on aesthetics, contemporary North American fiction, narrative theory, and Ralph Waldo Emerson. He supports the German Bundesliga team SC Freiburg.

Catherine Diederich is a Teaching and Research Fellow in Linguistics and Language Didactics at the University of Teacher Education in St. Gallen, Switzerland. Her research focuses on the development of pragmatic competence in the foreign language classroom. Her main research areas include cognitive semantics, intercultural pragmatics, and sensory language. She is the author of the book *Sensory Adjectives in the Discourse of Food: A Frame-Semantic Approach to Sensory Language* (2015) in which she explores the interrelation between language and sensory perception. Her interest in the senses and embodied cognition is also what fascinates her about language use in the soccer arena—apart from her passion for soccer since early childhood when she played in the American Youth Soccer Organization. In addition, she is interested in multilingualism in soccer team management, particularly from a didactic perspective.

Aline Bieri is a Research Assistant and Instructor for English Linguistics at the University of Basel, Switzerland. She holds an M.A. in English and Biology from the University of Basel and is currently working on her Ph.D. entitled *Content and Language Integrated Learning (CLIL) in the Swiss Context: The Linguistic Challenges and Implications of Teaching a Subject such as Biology in English*. She is especially interested in the interface of biology as a subject and its linguistic requirements for students and for teachers in a CLIL and non-CLIL environment as well as how this then manifests itself in the classroom discourse in a multilingual context such as that of Switzerland. Her academic research interests cover everything from sociolinguistics to cognitive linguistics (with special emphasis on first and second language acquisition and bi- and multilingualism). Other than being a passionate linguist she is also an enthusiastic soccer aficionado and lifelong supporter of the one and only Swiss soccer club FC Basel.

Routledge Research in Sport, Culture and Society

91 Global Perspectives on Sports and Christianity
Edited by Afe Adogame, Nick J. Watson and Andrew Parker

92 Sporting Capital
Transforming sports development policy and practice
Nicholas F. Rowe

93 Rugby Union and Professionalisation
Elite player perspectives
Mike Rayner

94 International Safeguards for Children in Sport
Developing and embedding a safeguarding culture
Daniel Rhind and Frank Owusu-Sekyere

95 Transforming Sport
Knowledges, practices, structures
Edited by Thomas F. Carter, Daniel Burdsey and Mark Doidge

96 Football Fans, Activism and Social Change
Dino Numerato

97 Rethinking Olympic Legacy
Vassil Girginov

98 Surfing, Sex, Genders and Sexualities
Edited by lisahunter

99 The Aesthetics, Poetics, and Rhetoric of Soccer
Edited by Ridvan Askin, Catherine Diederich, and Aline Bieri

www.routledge.com/sport/series/RRSCS

The Aesthetics, Poetics, and Rhetoric of Soccer

Edited by Ridvan Askin,
Catherine Diederich, and
Aline Bieri

LONDON AND NEW YORK

First published 2018 by Routledge

2 Park Square, Milton Park, Abingdon, Oxfordshire OX14 4RN
52 Vanderbilt Avenue, New York, NY 10017

Routledge is an imprint of the Taylor & Francis Group, an informa business

First issued in paperback 2019

Copyright © 2018 selection and editorial matter, Ridvan Askin, Catherine Diederich, and Aline Bieri; individual chapters, the contributors

The right of Ridvan Askin, Catherine Diederich, and Aline Bieri to be identified as the authors of the editorial matter, and of the authors for their individual chapters, has been asserted in accordance with sections 77 and 78 of the Copyright, Designs and Patents Act 1988.

All rights reserved. No part of this book may be reprinted or reproduced or utilised in any form or by any electronic, mechanical, or other means, now known or hereafter invented, including photocopying and recording, or in any information storage or retrieval system, without permission in writing from the publishers.

Notice:
Product or corporate names may be trademarks or registered trademarks, and are used only for identification and explanation without intent to infringe.

British Library Cataloguing-in-Publication Data
A catalogue record for this book is available from the British Library

Library of Congress Cataloging-in-Publication Data
A catalog record has been requested for this book

ISBN: 978-0-8153-8573-8 (hbk)
ISBN: 978-0-367-89569-3 (pbk)

Typeset in Sabon
by Wearset Ltd, Boldon, Tyne and Wear

Contents

Lists of figures	vii
Acknowledgments	ix

Pep talk — 1

Klopp's Heideggerianism	3
SIMON CRITCHLEY	

Taking the field — 11

Introduction: aesthetics, poetics, rhetoric, soccer	13
RIDVAN ASKIN, CATHERINE DIEDERICH, AND ALINE BIERI	

First half: aesthetics — 25

1 Good games as athletic beauty: why association football is rightly called 'the beautiful game'	27
EMILY RYALL	
2 Appreciating the not-obviously-beautiful game	44
ADAM KADLAC	
3 "England 'til I die": soccer, national identity, and contemporary art	62
DANIEL HAXALL	

vi Contents

4 The messianic manager in novels by David Peace   90
DAVID KILPATRICK

Half time: poetics   107

5 The man in the dugout: fictional football managers and the
politics of resistance   109
CYPRIAN PISKUREK

6 The importance of trivial oppositions in football fandom:
the narcissism of minor differences in derby games   126
KRISTOF K.P. VANHOUTTE

7 Stupidity in football   141
PHILIP SCHAUSS

Second half: rhetoric   161

8 "Caveman stuff": Ireland's soccer struggle with identity,
style, and success   163
MICHAEL O'HARA AND CONNELL VAUGHAN

9 The beautiful and the grim: British cultural discourses of
the Eastern European game   182
BLANKA BLAGOJEVIC

10 "Text sex with Becks": football celebrities, popular press,
and the spectacle of language   200
JAN CHOVANEC

11 Multimodal construction of soccer-related humor on
Twitter and Instagram   227
THOMAS MESSERLI AND DI YU

12 Multilingualism in football teams   256
EVA LAVRIC AND JASMIN STEINER

Notes on contributors   275
Index   279

Figures

1.1	The relationship between open and closed skill and their corresponding value as a skillful interchange	40
3.1	Stuart Roy Clarke, *Three Pillars of Society*, 2015	65
3.2	Chris Steele-Perkins, *England*, 1982	66
3.3	Mark Wallinger, *31 Hayes Court, Camberwell New Road, Camberwell, London, England, Great Britain, Europe, The World, The Solar System, The Galaxy, The Universe*, 1994	67
3.4	Mark Wallinger, *They think it's all over ... it is now*, 1988	69
3.5	Volker Schrank, *Gesammelte Helden: Beckenbauer (A Collection of Heroes: Beckenbauer)*, 2003–2005	72
3.6	Werner Büttner, *Cultural Imperialist Rascals' Trick*, 1987	73
3.7	Albrecht Tübke, *Spieler (Hans-Jürgen Kreische)*, 2006	75
3.8	Thomas Hoepker, *Munich, day before the opening of the Soccer World Cup, scene from downtown. Brochures on newsstand in Kaufingerstrasse*, 2006	76
3.9	Paul Pfeiffer, *The Saints*, 2007	79
3.10	Paul Pfeiffer, *The Saints*, 2007	80
3.11	Esra Ersen, *Im Strafraum (In the Penalty Area)*, 2001	82
3.12	Hassan Hajjaj, *Nike v. Adidas*, 2010/1431	84
3.13	Hassan Hajjaj, *Just Do It*, 2006/1427	85
10.1	Humorous treatment of taboo in the Matt cartoon	220
10.2	A parody of the taboo guessing in the Matt cartoon	221
11.1	Incongruities in pictures	234
11.2	Recontextualizing incongruity	235
11.3	Reinforcing incongruities in pictures	237
11.4	Incongruous action	238
11.5	Juxtaposing incongruities	238
11.6	Incongruous collage	239
11.7	Juxtaposed incongruous pictures	240

11.8	Humorous caption	242
11.9	Humorous recontextualization	243
11.10	Juxtaposed pictures and captions	244
11.11	Breaking the pattern	245
11.12	Crying-laughing emoji	247
11.13	Stranded conversation in comments	249
11.14	Multimodal comment	250
11.15	Multimodal comment	251

Acknowledgments

This book originates in a conference on "The Beautiful Game: The Aesthetics and Poetics of Soccer in Transnational Perspective," organized by the editors under the auspices of the Swiss Association for North American Studies and held at the University of Basel during the 2016 European Championship. The conference was generously funded by the Swiss Academy of Humanities and Social Sciences. Without the many excellent contributions to the conference, this book would not have been possible. Our thanks are also due to the members of staff of Basel's Department of English who provided invaluable help in the preparation of and during the conference: Sixta Quassdorf, Johanna Schüpbach, Rahel Ackermann Hui, and Denise Kaufmann. That this volume is not a mere conference proceedings is due not only to the fact that we asked our contributors to significantly expand on the topics and issues they first raised in their conference papers, but also to the follow-up workshop held at Wake Forest University in the summer of 2017 when most of the contributors came together again to discuss a first version of their articles. We would like to express our gratitude to Adam Kadlac and the Wake Forest Department of Philosophy for making this possible. Adam is unrivalled in his generosity, both in intellectual and in more material terms, his patience, and his—sometimes unrelenting—humor, a most formidable host indeed. We would also like to thank all our contributors for their commitment and their hard work. We feel privileged to have been working with such splendid colleagues.

We gratefully acknowledge the permission to use material from Simon Critchley, *What We Think About When We Think About Football*, London: Profile Books, 2017.

Ridvan Askin, Catherine Diederich, and Aline Bieri
Basel and St. Gallen, November 2017

Pep talk

Klopp's Heideggerianism[1]

Simon Critchley

I would like to talk about Jürgen Klopp. If you are clueless about Klopp, then that's your problem. You can find out all about him on Wikipedia or with a simple Google search. Klopp is a gifted, hard-working, passionate, immensely likeable, and tactically astute football coach, who established himself with huge success at FSV Mainz 05 in Germany before spending seven seasons at Borussia Dortmund and completely changing their fortunes, winning the Bundesliga twice and getting to the final of the Champions League in 2013. Klopp was appointed manager of Liverpool Football Club on October 8, 2015. My son Edward and I were drinking ale in a pub in London's West End when the news broke. He was completely ecstatic. I was rather pleased myself. Klopp inherited a football club in some disarray, lacking confidence in the coaching ability of the increasingly delusional and constantly on-message Brendan—"I once attended a management course and drive a BMW"—Rodgers. Liverpool had also been damaged by a dubious "moneyball" transfer policy that had led to embarrassments like Mario Ballotelli wearing a Liverpool shirt. We had become a club far too preoccupied with past glories (just to remind you, 5 Champions Leagues, 3 UEFA cups, and 18 English league wins) and arguably mired with a sense of its own victimization. The impatience of Liverpool's huge and international legions of fans had declined into a kind of lackluster indifference and the club seemed to have lost direction since the departure of the Promethean Luis Suárez to Barcelona in July 2014. Klopp changed the mood inside and outside the club very quickly, and although Liverpool's form in the Premier League is still patchy and marred by inconsistency, we have reached the finals of two competitions, the Carling Cup and the Europa League. Sadly, we lost on both occasions.

When I was kindly invited to Basel by Ridvan, I felt at my back the forces of fate like a gathering gale force wind. Liverpool had embarked on an improbable Europa League run, defeating historic rivals Manchester United, Klopp's former team Borussia Dortmund (we will come back to that game) and Villarreal in the semi-final. The final took place in St. Jakob's Stadium in Basel on May 18 and I imagined myself coming to

Basel and gloating in glory after beating Sevilla. But instead we lost 3–1. Indeed, we were completely outplayed in the second half. I was in a pub in South London this time, also with my son and two of his mates. A goal up at halftime, we looked comfortable. I was wearing my 1976 V-necked, short-sleeved Liverpool replica shirt, taking a confident piss in the toilet, smiling to myself. I said to the fan standing next to me at the urinal, "I think we've got the measure of Sevilla and we'll win." He was more skeptical. He was also right. Seventeen seconds after the start of the second half, following a defensive error by Moreno, Sevilla scored and we completely lost our shape and confidence. The midfield seemed to implode, Sevilla's Coke scored two more excellent goals, and we never recovered or looked like getting back into the game. It was horrible. My son and I could barely speak after the game, we were so upset, and I flew back to NYC the next morning, defeat weighing heavily on me. It still weighs on me.

So, Basel was a total failure, a humiliation and capitulation to a better-organized, stronger, more effective, and more experienced team. But there is always a lesson in defeat. Football is not just about winning. It is usually about losing. It has to be. But the really strange thing about football is not defeat as such. It's not defeat that kills you. It's the ever-renewed hope. The hope that every new season offers. The hope that comes in to tickle your feet, and then you realize, as Anne Carson says, that your soles are on fire (Carson, 2015, p. 23). Football can often be an experience of righteous injustice, where defeat is experienced as bad refereeing decisions or a bad pitch or even bad weather. But sometimes you can just be outplayed by a superior team. That's a different kind of pain, when you realize that your team just isn't good enough. But still ticklish hope flickers and burns.

There's a lot that can be said about Klopp and it is usually defined by banalities about "heavy metal football," *Vollgas-Fussball*, *Gegenpressing*, being "the normal one" and not "the special one" like José Mourinho with his trademark charismatic smile. Klopp's writings and interviews are not particularly revealing. But there is one recurring word in his lexicon that particularly interests me: *the moment*. Football, for him, is about the creation of the moment. Now, I want to give a Heideggerian inflection to the moment and link it to the idea of the *Augenblick*, the moment of vision or the blink of the eye that is developed in Division II of *Sein und Zeit*. I do this not just because Klopp grew up in the small town of Glatten, which is less than 100 km from Freiburg im Breisgau, where Heidegger worked, nor because Heidegger was a football fan, with a deep respect for the leadership abilities of "Kaiser" Franz Beckenbauer and a TV hidden in his office so that he could watch games. It is more because I'd like to think about the experience of time in relation to football. Football is about temporal shifts. The shift that particularly interests me begins with clock-time, the vulgar time of everyday life that moves ineluctably from the now of the present and the not-yet-now of the future before slipping into the no-longer-now of the past—tick tick tick. Clock-time finds its confirmation in the linear and chronometric time of the 90 minutes of the match, a time assiduously kept by the referee and his assistants. Over against clock-time is what we might call Klopp-time, the ecstatic time of the moment, the moment of vision, when we are lifted up and out of clock-time into some other experience of temporality. In paragraph 68 of *Sein und Zeit*, on the temporality of understanding, Heidegger brings together a series of concepts that have been developed in the previous chapters of Division II. Heidegger writes, in a wonderful passage:

> In resoluteness, the Present is not only brought back from distraction with the objects of one's closest concern, but it gets held in the future and in having been. That *Present* which is held in authentic temporality and which thus is *authentic* itself, we call the "moment of vision". This term must be understood in the active sense as an ecstasis. It means the resolute rapture with which Dasein is carried away to whatever possibilities and circumstances are encountered in the Situation as possible objects of concern, but a rapture which is *held* in resoluteness. The moment of vision is a phenomenon which *in principle* can *not* be clarified in terms of the "*now*" [dem *Jetzt*]. The "now" is a temporal phenomenon which belongs to time as within-time-ness: the "now" 'in which' something arises, passes away, or is present-at-hand. 'In the moment of vision' nothing can occur; but as an authentic Present or waiting-towards, the moment of vision permits us *to encounter for the first time* what can be 'in a time' as ready-to-hand or present-at-hand.
>
> (Heidegger, 1962, pp. 387–388, italics in original)

In the moment of vision, we are carried away in a rapture where we stand outside our immersion in everyday life and encounter that latter for the first time. In the blink of an eye, we are carried away from clock-time or what Heidegger calls the "within-time-ness" of the seemingly endless flow of now-points, into an ecstasy where we encounter the world of the ready-to-hand and the present-at-hand for the first time. To be clear, the ecstasy here is not some sort of Dionysian, drunken intoxication. It is a *resolute* rapture, a sober ecstasy, that sees the indifference of everyday for what it is and accepts it as a Situation full of possibilities. It is not that we leave the world or ourselves behind, as if Heidegger were simply updating Plato's allegory of the cave, but that we see the world and ourselves clearly for what they are and in that moment of vision embrace existence in its many possibilities. The moment does not last longer than a moment. But in that moment, we arrest the flow of clock-time, and open the potential for another experience of time and thereby create the possibility for history, a history of moments.

6 Simon Critchley

To be a fan is to live for a history of moments. It is to create and possess such a history, to be able to recount it with others and to have the possibility of creating new moments. It is this sharing of moments that allows for the possibility of togetherness among fans, what binds them into some kind of collective. In Sartrean terms, it is the passage from the seriality of a line of individuals to a fused group. Let me give an example. In the second leg of Liverpool's game against Dortmund on April 14, 2016, we conceded two goals in the first ten minutes and were 3–1 down in the tie overall. Half-time arrived; Klopp disappeared quickly into the dressing room. He was very calm, very relaxed, because the performance of the team, in his view, was good and Liverpool indeed created a lot of chances. The key to understanding Klopp's approach to football is not to focus on goals conceded or defeats. Every team will be beaten. What he always focuses on—resolutely, soberly—is the performance, because that is the key to the development of the team. It is performance that has to be celebrated, not goal-scoring (when Klopp is analyzing games with his coaching staff and players, he never watches the goals—they are edited out). So, although Liverpool were 3–1 down on aggregate at half-time, Klopp was happy with the performance. He said to the team that they now had the chance to "create a moment to tell our grandchildren about." Namely, the creation of a history, of a heritage. As all football fans know, most games are forgettable and soon forgotten. What one seizes hold of, what gives fans their experience of historicity, shared memory, and collectivity consists in a series of moments: 1977, 1978, 1981, 1984, 2005, when Liverpool won the European Cup and the Champions League. But there are also other moments, like the disgrace of the Heysel Stadium disaster of 1985, which left 39 people dead, nearly all of them fans of the mighty Juventus; or the Hillsborough disaster of 1989, which left 96 Liverpool fans dead at the hands of the South Yorkshire Police. (My cousin David was at the end of the ground with all the fatalities and—in those distant days before cell phones—there was no way he could get in touch for more than 24 hours. We genuinely feared for his life.) The number "96" remains emblazoned on the back collar of the Liverpool shirt between flames of remembrance.

At his first press conference on October 9, 2015, Klopp said with regard to the high expectations that come with managing a big club like Liverpool, "History is only the base for us … but it's not allowed that you take history in your backpack … This is a great team now. This is the perfect moment to do this." Klopp knows a good deal about backpacks, as his 1995 sports thesis was called "Walking—Bestandsaufnahme und Evaluationsstudie einer Sportart für alle." There is a strong strand of Heideggerian resoluteness in Klopp as well as an obsessive work ethic. He continually emphasizes that a team like Liverpool are a great team now, adding the crucial, voluntarist caveat, "If we want … if we want." With regard to the pressure of managing a team like Liverpool, he said in an echo on Heidegger on the Situation, "I feel pressure before each game and between them, of course, but only to develop and improve and as quickly as possible. I have to accept the situation." And again, "Pressure is there but the art is only to feel the pressure to win games." What is also central to Klopp and makes his coaching style different from the orchestrated precision of the great Barcelona teams, or the defensive, ironic cynicism of José Mourinho, is a particular emphasis on emotion, on passion, on what Heidegger calls *Stimmung* and *Grundstimmung*, attunement and fundamental attunement. For Klopp, football is not just about performance, accepting pressure, and embracing the situation. It is not about biometric data or the statistical analysis of each facet of the player's game. It is about playing with and for emotion, with and for passion, where everything is articulated around the attainment of a fundamental attunement. Let me risk another Heideggerian analogy, this time with *Angst* or anxiety. As is well known, anxiety is not fear, say the fear of some fact in the world, like making a mistake or even losing a game. Anxiety is not jitteriness. No, anxiety is that basic mood or fundamental attunement when our entire being is stretched out into the experience of the moment, and when we feel ourselves most alive. Anxiety is, importantly, a kind of joy, or what Heidegger calls in "What Is Metaphysics?," a calm, a kind of entranced calm. At such moments, one is not worried, one is not fearful, one is entirely focused on the situation and on the movement of play. I think this is why Klopp always looks so unusually calm under pressure. As long as everyone is working as hard as they can for the team, controlling and passing, controlling and passing, and showing fighting spirit, then the moment can come. The key thing here is belief. As Klopp says, "If someone wants to help, you have to change from a doubter to a believer. It's a very important thing." Of course, Klopp is a protestant Christian, maybe even some kind of Schwabian pietist like Hölderlin, and it is clear that Heidegger was very close to the Pauline theology of Luther in the 1920s. When Klopp was asked by my friend Roger Bennett how he deals with the cynicism of the football world with a seemingly fathomless optimism and joy, he replied without hesitation, "I believe in God and my only job is to do the best in life. ... My only pressure is to be a good human being."

Talking of divine intervention (and, of course, it would be terrific if Liverpool could get Jesus Christ on a free transfer from FSV Nazareth 00), let's go back to what happened in the second half against Dortmund on April 14. It was indeed a moment. After Divock Origi scored for Liverpool to make it 2–1, Marco Reus of Dortmund scored a sublime goal to make it 3–1, creating space on the left side of the pitch before deliciously curling the ball past the keeper with his right foot. I texted "game over" to my son and slouched back into the couch. But then, nine minutes later, the little master, Philippe Coutinho, scored for Liverpool and the mood in the stadium suddenly seemed to change. Everyone could feel it. A kind of belief spread through the fans and the team, and interchange between them grew second by second into a strange, wild intensity. Dortmund could feel it too. Their hitherto dominant midfield began to contract and shrink, their frightening counter-attacking movement ceased, and Dortmund dropped deeper and deeper into defense. This was possibly going to be one of the great Anfield European nights. Mamadou Sakho scored from a scrappy header on 77 minutes to level the game, but Liverpool still needed an extra goal because of Dortmund's away goals. Then, in the ninety-first minute, Daniel Sturridge received the ball and moved into space, passed to James Milner, who accelerated towards the goal line, crossed the ball expertly to the back post and Dejan Lovren headed the winner. Anfield erupted. Klopp was strangely still. It was a moment. The really odd thing is that the winning goal didn't feel surprising. It felt as if it was destined to happen. It felt like fate or the moment of some *deus ex machina*. Thomas Tuchel, Klopp's former assistant and successor as manager at Dortmund, described the result as "illogical." He was right. Football sometimes defies logic and these are the moments that we live for.

I'd like to finish with Klopp's post-match press conference, as it encapsulates much that I have tried to say in this talk about the moment, about performance, about a certain entranced calm, and about emotion, mood, and basic attunement. What is especially interesting here is the way in which Klopp invokes the memory of the moment in 2005 in the Champions League final in Istanbul when Liverpool came from 3–0 behind to beat AC Milan on penalties after extra-time. The awareness of the history of that moment allows for a repetition or fetching back, a *Wiederholung*, in a new historical moment, which itself provides the potential for the creation of future moments, a new heritage. It simply doesn't matter that none of the current Liverpool players were present in 2005, nor that Klopp himself wasn't there. It is as if the memory of the fans forms a living archive of meaning, a vast historical reservoir that can be drawn from and imbibed. Liverpool's eventual defeat against Sevilla in the Europa League final in Basel is not a refutation of such moments. As I said, there will always be defeats. It is the nature of the game. The question is how one seizes hold of one's history as a way of accepting defeat and trying again, going again, carrying on, together and stronger.

To bring this to an end, I have on many occasions criticized Heidegger's fundamental ontology, and I still stand by those criticisms. They turn in particular on the way the logic of authenticity is worked out in *Sein und Zeit*. As a general account of how human beings are in the world and with others, Heidegger's phenomenology arguably raises as many questions as it solves. As a political ontology, it is without doubt a disaster. But, oddly perhaps, as a philosophy of football, it works rather well. Perhaps Heidegger only really makes sense as a philosophy of football. Perhaps, as a consequence, we should be suspicious of football and more critical than celebratory of the role that it plays in our lives. Perhaps one can love football too much and lose oneself and one's critical faculties in the process. Perhaps we need to approach football as a form of mass psychology that is inherently fascistic and licenses the ugliest nationalisms. I don't know. That would be a story for another occasion. Thank you for listening.

Note

1 The editors wish to point out that the following text is an excerpt from Simon Critchley's keynote lecture delivered at the "The Beautiful Game: The Poetics and Aesthetics of Soccer in Transnational Perspective" conference held at the University of Basel, June 30–July 2, 2016. The at times noticeable oral quality has been deliberately preserved. A slightly different version of this text appears as part of Simon Critchley's recently published *What We Think About When We Think About Football* (Profile Books 2017).

References

Carson, A. 2015. Antigonick. London: New Directions.
Critchley, S. 2017. What we think about when we think about football. London: Profile Books.
Heidegger, M. 1962. Being and time. Oxford: Blackwell.

Taking the field

Introduction

Aesthetics, poetics, rhetoric, soccer

Ridvan Askin, Catherine Diederich, and Aline Bieri

The Aesthetics, Poetics, and Rhetoric of Soccer brings together several closely related discussions that have remained distinct for the most part so far: the philosophical discourse on the aesthetics of sport in general and that of soccer in particular, the cultural studies (broadly conceived) discourse on soccer culture and the politics of its representation, and the discourse on the rhetorical and discursive strategies taken up in and around soccer as predominantly discussed by linguists and literary scholars.[1] In doing so, this book not only wishes to contribute to the respective discussions in these specific discursive fields, but also aims to provide a forum for dialogue and interdisciplinary debate. Accordingly, it provides exemplary discussions of soccer in relation to the book's three titular concepts from a variety of disciplinary perspectives. Contributors to the volume hail from philosophy, cultural studies, literary studies, linguistics, art history, and the creative arts. At the same time, the concepts of the aesthetic, the poetic, and the rhetorical inform each individual essay's argument and provide thematic foci. Let us briefly sketch in which way these central concepts are employed throughout the volume.

Beginning with the concept of the aesthetic, three salient senses in which this notion has been taken up in the context of discussions of sport and, more specifically, soccer can be observed. The first of these is the sense in which the notion of the aesthetic is employed in philosophy or theory of art. Arguably, this is in agreement with the more general discourse on aesthetics ever since, roughly, the end of the nineteenth century, which indeed understands aesthetics as the branch of philosophy concerned with the theorization of art (Georg Friedrich Wilhelm Hegel's *Aesthetics: Lectures on Fine Art* [1975] is the reference point and model here). Ever since the philosophy of sport came into its own as a specific field of study in the mid-1960s (Kretchmar, 1997, pp. 193–196), this is the sense of aesthetics that has been at the forefront in discussions of sport and aesthetics. The central question in this debate focuses on whether sport can be properly understood as art.[2] A related discourse emerged from this debate on sport's relation to art, revolving around whether the aesthetic dimension is in fact central to sport and, by implication, soccer.[3] Those who believe this to be the case but either reject or at least remain agnostic vis-à-vis the stronger claim that sport is art, usually still employ aesthetics in the sense of theory of art. In this vein, these scholars discuss features that make sport and soccer an enjoyable and pleasurable experience, whether they are primarily concerned with the active practice or the passive consumption of sport. Questions of beauty, creativity, genius, imagination, skill, drama, spectacle, and play are at the heart of these discussions.[4] Emily Ryall's and Adam Kadlac's contributions to this volume certainly belong in this category. While Ryall continues and expands her discussion of why soccer is rightly called "the beautiful game,"[5] Kadlac introduces a new angle to the question by taking his cue from youth soccer, scrutinizing what this less orderly and less structured way of playing might tell us about the beauty of the game, ultimately providing us with what one could call a contextualist account of soccer beauty.

In a second sense, aesthetics refers to artistic, filmic, and literary representations of sport and soccer, that is, modes of representing sport and soccer that are deemed to be particularly aesthetic. Scholarship of this kind is legion in cultural studies, covering all kinds of sport from antiquity to today and dealing with a variety of topics and issues ranging from questions of race, class, and gender to national identity, from mythography to the athletic body itself, to name but a few.[6] In the present volume, Daniel Haxall adds to this discourse by engaging with contemporary soccer art and its negotiations of national identity. David Kilpatrick, in turn, addresses the mythographic dimension of literary representations of the soccer manager and how these might be understood as projecting viable models for a future to come.

A third and, to our mind, particularly interesting and promising sense of aesthetics operative in thinking about sport and soccer is that of aesthetics as *aísthēsis*. This sense goes back to Alexander Gottlieb Baumgarten's coinage and definition of aesthetics not merely as theory of art but also and predominantly as "science of perception," "lower-level epistemology," and "science of sensuous cognition" (Baumgarten, 1954, §116; Barnouw, 1988, p. 324).[7] Baumgarten gives the senses their due in our striving for truth: While the senses only allow for clear and confused cognition over and against the clear and distinct cognition of reason—the senses lack the power to make distinctions—they give us the concrete, material plenitude and richness of things, something abstract and rational thought misses out on (Baumgarten, 2007, §617, §560, §564). Basically, *aísthēsis* denotes pure perception or intuition. It seems that scholars are increasingly taking recourse to this sense of the aesthetic in their discussions of the aesthetics of soccer. For example, Kreft has recently argued that "to play a (soccer) game a kind of visionary approach produced by our imagination is needed" (2015, p. 125). Arguably, this sense of the aesthetic is, at least implicitly, also present in the first sense sketched above: Whenever someone discusses skill, creativity, a given player's ability to 'read the game', or—the most blatant example—genius, they are taking implicit recourse to something like Baumgarten's notion of "sensuous cognition" (this, then, is also true of Ryall's and Kadlac's contributions to this volume). Hardly anyone believes that the decisions and choices athletes and soccer players make, often within fractures of seconds, are the result of a deliberate, conscious, and rational weighing of available options; rather, they are bodily, intuitive decisions—sensuous cognition indeed. Given that most (though, depending on one's favorite definition, not necessarily all) sports primarily consist of series of bodily movements in space and time, such accounts promise to get at the heart of the matter. In this vein, the aesthetic becomes not just one aspect among others that might be important for discussions of sport, but the most central and essential issue. Besides Baumgarten, a plethora of theorists and philosophers of perception, intuition, or *aísthēsis* could serve as potentially fruitful resources here. The early Friedrich Nietzsche with his account of the Dionysian in art as presented in the *Birth of Tragedy* (1968) and phenomenological accounts such as Martin Heidegger's and Maurice Merleau-Ponty's have already been proposed by scholars such as Mumford (2012), Gumbrecht (2006), Kilpatrick (2010a), Edgar (2015), and, most recently, Tuncel (2017). In the present volume, Simon Critchley, too, takes recourse to Heidegger in his discussion of the Heideggerian *Augenblick*, the creation of the very moment of vision as it plays out in soccer. Of course, phenomenology with its focus on the body and lived experience has always been a preferred resource for philosophers of sport, at least ever since Drew Hyland's classic *The Philosophy of Sport* (1990). The pragmatist approach as advocated by Elcombe (2012) and approaches based on what has become known as everyday aesthetics as championed by Kreft (2014) also belong here. But many new pathways open up once one understands aesthetics as *aísthēsis*, not the least of which might be a return to thinkers of the late eighteenth and early nineteenth centuries: With its emphasis on intuition, imagination, and genius, the romantic tradition—the *locus classicus* of aesthetics as *aísthēsis*—promises to be a veritable treasure chest in this respect.

Since in the romantic understanding intuition, imagination, and genius invariably denote faculties, capacities, or activities, the aim of which is to tap the very source of the powers of creation, this brief foray into romanticism brings us right to the second concept in our triad: poetics. Etymologically, poetics—derived from the Greek term for "to make," *poiein*—denotes the discipline concerned with the creation, production, and formation of something. Any poetics of soccer must then distinguish and contend with those features that make soccer possible in the first place: What are the constitutive elements of soccer? Asking this question brings us right back to the question of aesthetics we started with, as many of these constitutive elements concern the players' proper employment of their body and their senses. Similarly, whenever we watch soccer with an eye to its constitutive elements, we discern precisely those features that we already pointed out above: players' specific skills in relation to the appropriate command of their body resulting in certain bodily movements, anticipation of the game flow, and the capacity to envision a given situation and act in the blink of an eye, to name but a few. What distinguishes an aesthetics of soccer from a poetics of soccer in this sense is mostly a question of perspective, emphasis, or directionality: While aesthetics is always concerned with questions of *perception*, whether they pertain to a certain set of judgments concerning the beauty or lack of beauty of the game in general, of a particular game, or maybe just a certain play or even just one specific bodily movement, or to the players' own *aisthetic* powers, poetics is concerned with the very same phenomena from the point of view of their *production*. How does a certain player wield their *aisthetic* powers, their vision of the game, in order to create a new situation on the pitch, to set up a goal, or to fool an opponent and dribble past them? Similarly, where aesthetics *qua* discourse of the beautiful or pleasurable focuses on the perception of beauty and the feeling of pleasure, poetics zooms in on their very production. Analogous to how such an aesthetics of soccer might enlarge its categories to include the ugly, the monotonous, the boring, and possibly even the zany (Saito, 2015; Moller, 2014; Ngai, 2012), a correlative poetics of soccer might want to inquire into the very conditions of the emergence of ugliness, boringness,[8] and so on. Steffen Borge and Mike McNamee recently introduced the notion that soccer is a "constructive-destructive sport" (2017, p. 250), a description they suggest best captures soccer's "inherent structure" (2017, p. 253), which comprises both "creating or inventing ways to score" and "preventing or hindering the other team from scoring" (2017, p. 250). Aesthetic judgment of a given game will then depend on the relation and ratio between the constitutive constructive and destructive features and actions it displays. When the destructive capacities of two teams cancel out their respective constructive forces to such a degree that the latter are barely noticeable, the result will arguably be boringness in Moller's sense of the term. But boringness might well also result from too big an asymmetry between the constructive and destructive capacities of two teams, when one team overcomes the other team's destructive efforts too easily while simultaneously succeeding in quenching its constructive attempts. From the point of view of a poetics of soccer, one might then ask how this imbalance or too much balance between the constructive and destructive forces on the pitch came about in the first place. Is it due to a better employment of game vision and the correlative distribution of bodies in space? Or maybe the soccer genius of one or two particular players is responsible? Or the inverse is the case, and the result is due to stupidity rather than genius? This is indeed one of the questions Philip Schauss asks in his contribution to this volume, in which he draws on Erasmus's protagonist goddess in *The Praise of Folly* as an example for the categorization of various forms of stupidity in order to characterize and define stupidity as it occurs in and around the soccer arena. While Schauss is interested in stupidity, Kristof K.P. Vanhoutte turns his attention to narcissism, which he detects as the very condition of possibility of a specific kind of rivalry, namely that between derby fans, subsequently extending this analysis to fandom in general.[9] Drawing on Freud's theory of the 'narcissism of minor differences' and Sara Ahmed's theory of emotions, he singles out derby fans' constant negotiations of love and hate or proximity and distance based on narcissistically cherished minor differences as the source of the overloaded affect that is necessary to sustain their rivalry. Both Schauss and Vanhoutte scrutinize a (potentially) constitutive element for the respective phenomenon in question, soccer and the discourse on soccer in Schauss's, and derby fandom in Vanhoutte's case. While Schauss adds a new angle to the poetics of soccer, Vanhoutte contributes to the discussion of what one might call a poetics of fandom.

A second, narrower but more widespread sense of poetics is that of the discipline engaged in the analysis and categorization of the constitutive elements of literary works and genres. The classical point of reference in this context is of course Aristotle's *Poetics* (2006). While Kilpatrick has already ventured to propose a poetics of soccer in light of the Aristotelian categories of *muthos, ethos, dianoia, lexis, melos,* and *opsis* elsewhere (Kilpatrick, 2010b), casting soccer games as performances analogous to those of drama, poetics in this literary, though not necessarily Aristotelian sense, is taken up in the present volume by Cyprian Piskurek in his discussion of fictional and fictionalized soccer managers that range from the depiction of the veteran manager in Michael Corrente's film *A Shot at Glory* (2000) and in the satirical comedy film *Mike Bassett: England Manager* (2001) to the fictionalization of esteemed managers such as Bill Shankly in David Peace's novel *Red or Dead* (2013) and the fictional manager as private eye in Philip Kerr's literary soccer trilogy *January Window* (2014), *Hand of God* (2015a), and *False Nine* (2015b). Piskurek's analysis of the figure of the soccer manager not only provides a counter-reading to Kilpatrick's interpretation of Peace in our volume. By means of discussing a range of examples, he also presents us with the first steps towards a poetics of the fictional soccer manager.

We could then say that investigations into the poetics of soccer contribute to an understanding of soccer as the product of a certain production process, defining and delimiting inherent constitutive elements and relations. On the one hand, if one follows Kilpatrick in taking Aristotle's classic, which serves to carve out the constitutive elements of literature,[10] as a blueprint for a poetics of soccer, then actual soccer becomes truly poeticized. On the other hand, we have numerous examples of fictionalized soccer in soccer fiction.[11] On a meta-level, this seems to speak to an affinity between the fiction frame and the soccer frame, both of which allow for creativity, dynamism, and unpredictability, but also rely on sets of specific elements that combine to produce the respective whole.

Interestingly enough, Aristotelian *lexis* poses the greatest difficulty for Kilpatrick in his poetics of soccer. Indeed, he writes that "speech-acts aren't an essential aspect of the game, so one might reasonably conclude that the constituent element *lexis* is inapplicable" (2010b, p. 87, italics in original). He goes on to propose tactics as the true "language" of soccer, though this remains metaphorical and a mere analogy (as Kilpatrick himself admits; see also his essay in the present volume). Eva Lavric and Jasmin Steiner in their contribution to this volume, however, show that *lexis*, in the sense of language form, is indeed a fundamental element of soccer as they zoom in on a host of rhetorical and linguistic strategies that players employ when communicating on the pitch. Their work builds on a previous collection of studies on *The Linguistics of Football* (Lavric et al., 2008). Seeing the pitch as a multilingual work place for the players and everyone involved in running a soccer team, Lavric and Steiner provide us with a survey of the diverse linguistic strategies players use to communicate with each other. Specifically intriguing in this context is their examination of multilingualism, as Lavric and Steiner point to the fact that in any multilingual work place the usual linguistic strategies sometimes fail with interactants thus having to find non-verbal, symbolic, and other innovative semiotic strategies to effectively communicate with each other on and off the pitch.

This brings us to our third concept, rhetoric. It is no coincidence that we arrived at this concept by means of a discussion of *lexis* in Aristotle's *Poetics*, as *lexis* is also one of the fundamental terms operative in his *Rhetoric*.[12] That the *Poetics* and *Rhetoric* are closely connected is commonplace in scholarship. Some scholars have even argued that the *Rhetoric* constitutes rhetoric itself as a *poietic* discipline, concerned with the production of persuasive speech.[13] In this vein, both the *Poetics* and the *Rhetoric* are concerned with the artistic composition of a given work, with the difference between them boiling down to one of purpose. This is the line along which the two disciplines of poetics and rhetoric subsequently developed: In poetics, the purpose of the artistic composition lies in the creation of pleasure or enjoyment for the audience, whereas the purpose of rhetoric lies in the persuasion of an audience (Kennedy, 2001, p. 13320). Poetics would then primarily be concerned with how the elements of a given text come together to produce a certain experience, and rhetoric with the effective use of language and argument for the sake of persuasion. In this sense, rhetoric denotes "the systematic practice of persuasive communication strategies" (Ilie, 2006, p. 574).

According to Aristotle, such persuasion can be achieved by appealing to the three means of persuasion, *ethos*, *pathos*, and *logos*: *Ethos* refers to the speaker's character, to what endows them with credibility and authenticity, *pathos* concerns the emotional effect the speaker has on the audience, and *logos* denotes the argument itself (Rapp, 2010; Murphy, 2006, p. 579; Rapp, 2002, pp. 355–366; Aristotle, 1991, I.2, II.1, II.20–22). But the section that is most important for our purposes here, the very section that contains a discussion of *lexis*, only begins when Aristotle turns his attention from content to form, or from argument to style in book three: It is not enough for a speaker to know *what* to say, but the speaker must also know *how* to say it (1991, III.1). This is indeed the aspect that many modern theories of rhetoric build on, including, for example, more pragmatic and semiotic approaches and what has become known as stylistics (Lotman, 2006; Toolan, 1998; Leech and Short, 1981). In the vein of this modern tradition, we understand rhetoric as the function of linguistic strategies in particular and larger semiotic and discursive strategies in general and their effect on a given audience. How is something talked about? What specific techniques are used in communicating certain contents and achieving certain effects? How and to which end is the audience affected?

There is a range of contexts with regard to soccer in which rhetoric in this sense comes into play, for instance the linguistic and semiotic strategies used to talk about the game and its players in the media, the broader public, and, ultimately, overall culture. Considering Kennedy's distinction between "a broader view of rhetoric as a persuasive tool of political speaking and discursive writing ... [and] a narrow view of rhetoric as a linguistic or literary phenomenon, largely limited to the use of tropes and figures in written language" (2001, pp. 13319–13320), the essays in this volume adhere less to the broader notion of a persuasive tool and more to the narrower understanding concerning the specific use of language, with the added caveat that they do not restrict themselves to written language. On the contrary, as the contribution by Thomas Messerli and Di Yu testifies, rhetorical strategies are often multimodal in nature, combining purely linguistic elements with other elements such as the visual and the auditory. But if we substitute Kennedy's understanding of a broader view of rhetoric with that of larger, cultural semiotic strategies, and if we accept soccer as a cultural form of expression, then questions of style in soccer would indeed fall under the rubric of a rhetoric of soccer (in this sense, Kilpatrick's suggestion to understand tactics as the *lexis* of a poetics of soccer no longer seems merely metaphoric).[14] Availing themselves of such a broader notion, Michael O'Hara and Connell Vaughan in their essay in this volume present a historically informed discussion about the notion of style with respect to soccer in Ireland and its relation to the rhetoric of national politics. In other words, they link the rhetoric of Ireland soccer to the rhetoric of Irish politics, showing that the discourse on *how* the national team scores a goal and achieves success is intricately linked to the rhetoric of Irish independence, the Irish national state, and Irish national identity. Kennedy's narrower view on rhetoric, in turn, solicits questions such as: How is soccer talked and written about? What are the functions of specific rhetorical techniques when talking or writing about soccer, especially, but not exclusively in soccer media coverage? What role does language form actually play on the pitch, in the communication among players and, by extension, among players, coaches, and staff?

Apart from Lavric and Steiner, several more contributions to our volume take recourse to rhetoric in this sense. Blanka Blagojevic in her contribution presents a close-analysis of two soccer-themed travel narratives, investigating the function of the rhetorical strategies of *idealization* and *debasement* employed by the two authors Simon Kuper and Jonathan Wilson in order to depict the state of soccer in post-1989 Eastern Europe. By analyzing how soccer in Eastern Europe is written about in the authors' travelogues, Blagojevic also sheds light on British and Western European post-1989 discourses about Eastern Europe more generally.

Jan Chovanec's and Thomas Messerli and Di Yu's essays in this collection are devoted to the media rhetoric surrounding soccer, scrutinizing the function of specific rhetorical means with regard to soccer media coverage.[15] Chovanec focuses on the specific linguistic strategies used to report scandals zooming in on David Beckham's famous text sex affair as covered in online newspapers as a test case. Messerli and Yu are concerned with the rhetoric of soccer-related humor in social media, more specifically with multimodal strategies that are used to create and also react to humor on soccer-themed Twitter and Instagram accounts.

Minimally, these contributions show that *lexis*, that language form and style, indeed plays a crucial role in soccer, both in communication on and off the pitch. But we think they also emphasize that an analysis of soccer language and communication and what could be called a stylistics of soccer significantly enrich the somewhat more wide-ranging discourses on the aesthetics and poetics of soccer. In the end and taken together, the contributions to our volume show that while they remain distinct areas of inquiry, the aesthetics, poetics, and rhetoric of soccer are nevertheless inextricably entwined.

Notes

1 We would like to thank Philipp Schweighauser for his engaging, attentive, and critical feedback on an earlier version of this introduction. We are also grateful for the valuable input we received from the participants at Wake Forest University's Beautiful Game Workshop in July 2017.

2 For an earlier contribution that rebuts this view, see David Best's highly influential monograph (1978). For a more recent paper defending the view, see the article by Dimitris Platchias (2003). Tim L. Elcombe (2012, pp. 202–204) provides a brief historical overview of the debate.

3 Again, Elcombe (2012, pp. 204–206) provides a short and crisp overview of this discussion before presenting his own take on the issue.

Introduction 21

4 Andrew Edgar's and Elcombe's recent articles are pertinent here (Edgar, 2015; 2013a; 2013b; Elcombe, 2012). On the aesthetics of watching sport, see also the books by Stephen Mumford (2012) and Hans Ulrich Gumbrecht (2006), with the former providing a discussion in light of analytic philosophy and the latter working from a continental perspective. Teresa Lacerda and Stephen Mumford (2010) discuss the notion of genius in conjunction with that of creativity in relation to sport in their jointly authored essay on the topic. Lev Kreft provides an account of sport as dramatic spectacle (Kreft, 2012) and argues for the centrality of the imagination with respect to sport and, particularly, soccer (Kreft, 2015). For a sustained discussion of the notion of play in the context of sport see Randolph Feezell's essay and book (2010; 2006). That several of the essays cited in this introduction were actually published in two recent special issues on the aesthetics of sport and soccer in two of the leading journals in the field testifies to the reawakened interest in and the timeliness of the topic.
5 Ryall draws and builds on an earlier essay on the issue (Ryall, 2015).
6 Some recent exemplary publications include an edited volume on the cultural history of sport and literature (Tadié et al., 2014), a historically oriented collection of essays on sport and film (Briley et al., 2008), a book on cricket and literature (Bateman, 2009), a personal account about race, fandom, and soccer (Farred, 2008), a monograph on athletics and literature in the Roman Empire (König, 2005), an edited collection on sport, gender, and rhetoric (Fuller, 2006), a monograph on the portrayal of the athlete in art and literature (Womack, 2003), and a book on soccer and literature in South America (Wood, 2017). The recently diagnosed visual turn in sport history also belongs here (Huggins, 2015; Huggins and O'Mahony, 2011).
7 "Lower-level epistemology" and "science of sensuous cognition" are Barnouw's translations of Baumgarten's original Latin: "AESTHETICA (theoria liberalium artium, gnoseologia inferior, ars pulchre cogitandi, ars analogi rationis) est scientia cognitionis sensitivae" (Baumgarten, 2007, §1).
8 Moller (2014) is keen on distinguishing the property of boringness from the psychological state of boredom.
9 Vanhoutte revisits and builds on an earlier study on the derby in his contribution (Vanhoutte, 2010).
10 While it is true that Aristotle himself only sought to describe the elements and effects of tragedy, his treatise is seen as providing the basis for drama and drama theory, for narrative and narrative theory, and, ultimately, for literature and literary theory at large. No doubt this is due to the fact that Aristotle singles out *muthos* (fable, plot) as the most important element in his classification. This also explains why L.J. Potts in his translation opted to render the *Poetics* under the title *Aristotle on the Art of Fiction* (Potts, 1968).
11 For a recent overview on soccer fiction, see Lee McGowan's essay (2017).
12 Aristotle actually refers back to his discussion of lexis in the *Poetics* at the end of the first chapter of book III of the *Rhetoric*. While the whole of book III, which deals with *lexis* in oratory, is relevant in this context, chapter 1 distinguishes the use of *lexis* in poetry or literature from that in oratory (Aristotle, 1991, III.1).
13 Christof Rapp discusses this issue in his extensive introduction to his German translation of the *Rhetoric* (Rapp, 2002, p. 170). See also his entry on the *Rhetoric* in the *Stanford Encyclopedia of Philosophy* (2010).
14 In such a framework, the rhetoric of soccer would indeed form part of a more encompassing poetics of soccer.

15 While these two contributions deal with two specific aspects of soccer media coverage, another interesting aspect concerns live commentary. Worth mentioning in this regard are the works of Torsten Müller (2007), who focuses on the respective moment an utterance is made in relation to the extra-linguistic event it is commenting on, and Cornelia Gerhardt (2014), who analyzes families' discourses about soccer while watching the FIFA World Cup on TV.

References

A Shot at Glory. 2002. [Film]. Michael Corrente. dir. UK: Butcher's Run Films, Eagle Beach Productions.

Aristotle. 1991. On rhetoric: A theory of civic discourse. New York: Oxford University Press.

Aristotle. 2006. The poetics of Aristotle: Translation and commentary. Chapel Hill: University of North Carolina Press.

Barnouw, J. 1988. Feeling in enlightenment aesthetics. Studies in Eighteenth-Century Culture. **18**, pp. 323–342.

Bateman, A. 2009. Cricket, literature and culture: Symbolising the nation, destabilising empire. Farnham: Ashgate.

Baumgarten, A.G. 1954. Reflections on poetry/Meditationes philosophicae de nonnullis ad poema pertinentibus. Berkeley: University of California Press.

Baumgarten, A.G. 2007. Ästhetik [Aesthetica]. Mirbach, D. ed. Hamburg: Meiner.

Best, D. 1978. Philosophy and human movement. London: George Allen & Unwin.

Borge, S. and McNamee, M. 2017. Football and philosophy. In: Hughson, J., Moore, K., Spaaji, R. and Maguire, J. eds. The Routledge handbook of football studies. London: Routledge, pp. 245–254.

Briley, R., Schoenecke, M.K. and Carmichael, D.A. eds. 2008. All stars and movie stars: Sports in film and history. Lexington: University Press of Kentucky.

Edgar, A. 2013a. The aesthetics of sport. Sport, Ethics and Philosophy. 7(1), pp. 80–99.

Edgar, A. 2013b. The beauty of sport. Sport, Ethics and Philosophy. 7(1), pp. 100–120.

Edgar, A. 2015. Football and the poetics of space. Sport, Ethics and Philosophy. 9(2), pp. 153–165.

Elcombe, T.L. 2012. Sport, aesthetic experience, and art as the ideal embodied metaphor. Journal of the Philosophy of Sport. 39(2), pp. 201–217.

Erasmus, D. 2003. The praise of Folly. New Haven: Yale University Press.

Farred, G. 2008. Long distance love: A passion for football. Philadelphia: Temple University Press.

Feezell, R. 2006. Sport, play and ethical reflection. Urbana: University of Illinois Press.

Feezell, R. 2010. A pluralist conception of play. Journal of the Philosophy of Sport. 37(2), pp. 147–165.

Fuller, L. ed. 2006. Sport, rhetoric, and gender: Historical perspectives and media representations. New York: Palgrave.

Gerhardt, C. 2014. Appropriating live televised football through talk. Leiden: Brill.

Gumbrecht, H.U. 2006. In praise of athletic beauty. Cambridge, MA: Harvard University Press.

Hegel, G.W.F. 1975. Aesthetics: Lectures on fine art, 1835–1838. Oxford: Clarendon Press.

Huggins, M. 2015. The visual in sport history: Approaches, methodologies and sources. The International Journal of the History of Sport. 32(15), pp. 1813–1830.

Huggins, M. and O'Mahony, M. 2011. Prologue: Extending study of the visual in the history of sport. The International Journal of the History of Sport. 28(8–9), pp. 1089–1104.

Hyland, D.A. 1990. The philosophy of sport. New York: Paragon.

Ilie, C. 2006. Rhetoric, classical. In: Brown, K. ed. Encyclopedia of language and linguistics. 2nd ed. Oxford: Elsevier, pp. 573–579.

Kennedy, G.A. 2001. Rhetoric. In: Baltes, P.B. ed. International encyclopedia of the social and behavioral sciences. Oxford: Pergamon, pp. 13317–13323.

Kerr, P. 2014. January window. London: Head of Zeus.

Kerr, P. 2015a. Hand of god. London: Head of Zeus.

Kerr, P. 2015b. False nine. London: Head of Zeus.

Kilpatrick, D. 2010a. Nietzsche's arsenal. In: Richards, T. ed. Soccer and philosophy: Beautiful thoughts on the beautiful game. Chicago: Open Court, pp. 37–46.

Kilpatrick, D. 2010b. Poetics and the beautiful game. Aethlon: The Journal of Sport Literature. 27(1), pp. 79–89.

König, J. 2005. Athletics and literature in the Roman empire. Cambridge, UK: Cambridge University Press.

Kreft, L. 2012. Sport as a drama. Journal of the Philosophy of Sport. 39(2), pp. 219–234.

Kreft, L. 2014. Aesthetics of the beautiful game. Soccer & Society. 15(3), pp. 353–375.

Kreft, L. 2015. Aesthetic imagination in football. Sport, Ethics and Philosophy. 9(2), pp. 124–139.

Kretchmar, R.S. 1997. The philosophy of sport. In: Massengale, J.D. and Swanson, R.A. eds. The history of exercise and sport science. Champaign: Human Kinetics, pp. 181–201.

Lacerda, T. and Mumford, S. 2010. The genius in art and in sport: A contribution to the investigation of aesthetics of sport. Journal of the Philosophy of Sport. 37(2), pp. 182–193.

Lavric, E., Pisek, G., Skinner, A. and Stadler, W. eds. 2008. The linguistics of football. Tübingen: Gunter Narr.

Leech, G. and Short, M.H. 1981. Style in fiction: A linguistic introduction to English fictional prose. London: Longman.

Lotman, M. 2006. Rhetoric: Semiotic approaches. In: Brown, K. ed. Encyclopedia of language and linguistics. 2nd ed. Oxford: Elsevier, pp. 582–589.

McGowan, L. 2017. Football and its fiction. In: Hughson, J., Moore, K., Spaaji, R. and Maguire, J. eds. The Routledge handbook of football studies. London: Routledge, pp. 222–235.

Mike Bassett: England Manager. 2001. [Film]. Steve Barron. dir. UK: Artists Independent Productions, Film Council, Hallmark Entertainment.

Moller, D. 2014. The boring. The Journal of Aesthetics and Art Criticism. 72(2), pp. 181–191.

Müller, T. 2007. Football, language and linguistics: Time-critical utterances in unplanned spoken language, their structure and their relation to non-linguistic situations and events. Tübingen: Gunter Narr.

Mumford, S. 2012. Watching sport: Aesthetics, ethics, and emotion. Abingdon: Routledge.

Murphy, J.J. 2006. Rhetoric: History. In: Brown, K. ed. Encyclopedia of language and linguistics. 2nd ed. Oxford: Elsevier, pp. 579–582.

Ngai, S. 2012. Our aesthetic categories: Zany, cute, interesting. Cambridge, MA: Harvard University Press.

Nietzsche, F. 1968. The birth of tragedy. In: Kaufman, W. ed. The basic writings of Nietzsche. New York: The Modern Library, pp. 1–144.

Peace, D. 2013. Red or dead. London: Faber and Faber.

Platchias, D. 2003. Sport is art. European Journal of Sport Science. 3(4), pp. 1–18.

Potts, L.J. 1968. Aristotle on the art of fiction: An English translation of Aristotle's Poetics with an introductory essay and explanatory notes. Cambridge, UK: Cambridge University Press.

Rapp, C. 2002. Einleitung. In: Aristoteles, Rhetorik. Rapp, C. ed. Darmstadt: Wissenschaftliche Buchgesellschaft, pp. 167–383.

Rapp, C. 2010. Aristotle's rhetoric. In: Zalta, E.N. ed. The Stanford encyclopedia of philosophy. [Online]. Stanford: CSLI. [Accessed October 5, 2017]. Available from: https://plato.stanford.edu/archives/spr2010/entries/aristotle-rhetoric/.

Ryall, E. 2015. Good games and penalty shoot-outs. Sport, Ethics and Philosophy. 9(2), pp. 205–213.

Saito, Y. 2015. Aesthetics of the everyday. In: Zalta, E.N. ed. The Stanford encyclopedia of philosophy. [Online]. Stanford: CSLI. [Accessed October 5, 2017]. Available from: https://plato.stanford.edu/archives/win2015/entries/aesthetics-of-everyday/.

Tadié, A., Mangan, J.A. and Chaudhuri, S. eds. 2014. Sport, literature, society: Cultural historical studies. London: Routledge.

Toolan, M. 1998. Language in literature: An introduction to stylistics. London: Hodder Arnold.

Tuncel, Y. 2017. The aesthetic and ecstatic dimensions of soccer: Towards a philosophy of soccer. Soccer & Society. 18(2–3), pp. 181–187.

Vanhoutte, K.K.P. 2010. Playing the derby. In: Richards, T. ed. Soccer and philosophy: Beautiful thoughts on the beautiful game. Chicago: Open Court, pp. 231–240.

Womack, M. 2003. Sport as symbol: Images of the athlete in art, literature and song. Jefferson: McFarland.

Wood, D. 2017. Football and literature in South America. London: Routledge.

First half

Aesthetics

Chapter 1

Good games as athletic beauty
Why association football is rightly called 'the beautiful game'[1]

Emily Ryall

Introduction

Association football, or soccer, has long been regarded as holding a special place in the sports world for its global reach and accessibility. One of the reasons given for its success is its simplicity; all that is required is a spherical object that can be kicked towards a target. It is parodied as a 'gentleman's game played by thugs', which reflects its history as a working-class sport, but it also tellingly notes football's inherent capacity for beauty. The fact that it is perceived as a 'gentleman's game' suggests an element of refinement and class. As such, it is colloquially called 'the beautiful game'.[2] The question then is whether it deserves such a moniker, and if so, why. There are two supplementary questions that will help to answer this. First, what criteria should be applied to judge the aesthetic value of sport? Second, what is the relationship between these criteria and the sport of football? I will begin by considering the former.

One of the first debates articulated in the academic literature in the philosophy of sport was not about doping or cheating, or the nature of competition or sport itself, but rather whether sport had anything important to say about aesthetics. The American philosopher Paul Ziff (1974) argued philosophers ought not to waste time considering the aesthetics of sport and was notably forthright in his view:

> Research devoted to the aesthetics of sport can accomplish nothing. There is nothing there to be accomplished. Worse, it would not only contribute to the vaunted dreariness of aesthetics, it could serve to delay even impede other possibly significant research.
>
> (Ziff, 1974, p. 93)

Strong stuff indeed. Ziff may have been deliberately provocative but regardless, he was wrong. Aesthetics is at the heart of sport, and is ultimately what gives it its value. The aesthetics of sport, whether via the phenomenological raw-sense it provides us with, or through a more concrete articulation of beauty, is a fundamental reason that sport exists in the lives of many.

Aesthetic and purposive sports

Often, when the aesthetics of sport is considered, the sports that are cited as exemplars are those in which beauty is a central element in determining outcome: sports such as figure skating, gymnastics, and synchronized swimming. As such, sport is often divided into two clear types: sports whereby beauty matters in the outcome, and sports whereby beauty is irrelevant in determining it. The former are known as aesthetic sports, the latter as purposive sports. This distinction was first articulated by David Best (1978) who is largely known for his thesis that sport is not, and cannot be art. Purposive sports are those sports which contain a clear pre-lusory goal[3] which is independent of the means to reach that goal. A pre-lusory goal is effectively the aim of the game; such as putting a ball into a net (e.g., football, hockey, netball), crossing a designated line (e.g., running, sailing, cycling, rowing), or getting a ball or other object into a court (e.g., tennis, badminton, volleyball). The means for attaining the pre-lusory goal specifies how the goal may be achieved, i.e., through the use of the feet, a bicycle, or racquet. Purposive sports, such as football, cricket, and tennis, are often cited as exemplars of sport but they also include track and field and most combat sports. They are the sports where there is a clear measurement for winning. Aesthetic sports, in contrast, are those which focus upon and judge the movement of the body, and where the pre-lusory goal is less clear and is wholly dependent on the means. There is no independent pre-lusory goal of aesthetic sports such as gymnastics, figure skating, high-board diving, and skateboarding. The lusory purpose is only intelligible via the means itself.

This difference can be explained more clearly by considering specific examples. In football, a goal is worth the same amount of points whether it was the result of several pin-point accurate passes and a spectacular half-volley from the edge of the box into the top right-hand corner of the net, or whether it came from a goal mouth scramble and a ricochet off a defending player. What matters in these purposive sports is that the pre-lusory goal is achieved via the accepted means and within the rules; i.e., if the ball has crossed the goal-line without a preceding foul. In contrast, the pre-lusory goal for aesthetic sports is more difficult to establish. In the pommel horse for instance, marks are awarded for swings, holds, and dis-mounts. But, contrary to a goal being scored in football, it is the way in which the competitor achieves these elements that determines how many points are awarded: it matters *how* a competitor gets into a handstand position and how well they hold it, not merely that they managed to orientate themselves in an upside-down position with their weight supported on their hands.

While the distinction between purposive and aesthetic sports might draw our attention to the immediate salient differences between two different types of sporting competition, it must not be over-played. Indeed, when considered more closely the sharpness of the divide starts to disappear. At first glance, it may appear that aesthetic sports are judged subjectively. For we might argue that aesthetics refers to judgments about perceptual stimuli and emotional effect. The subjective view of aesthetics asserts that appreciation of beauty cannot be held to any objective standard. It is merely individual preference in the same way that some people prefer chocolate to cheese. Yet, it is not the case that aesthetic sports are adjudicated by the subjective preferences of the judges. The rules of sport will always dictate objective elements that the competitor needs to adhere to. So for aesthetic sports, such as gymnastics, figure-skating, snowboarding, skateboarding, surfing, and high-board diving, it is the adherence to the rules of the sport that matters, not how beautifully or gracefully the performers carry out those rules. Marks are not awarded on pure subjective preference but rather for carrying out a series of movements in accordance with specified criteria. One could imagine for example, a gymnast using a vault as a prop in a beautiful dance, but this would not score any points since it does not fulfil the rules of vaulting. The rules of gymnastic vaulting specify the points to be deducted for particular actions in take-off and landing as well as the points to be awarded for particular successful actions during performance. It also includes point deduction for auxiliary elements such as starting before a flag is raised and using a spotter.[4] In so-called aesthetic sports, points are not awarded purely for subjective preference or emotional affect, which explains why some performances might leave the crowd in raptures but do not translate to overall competition victory. Ultimately, the rules of the sport are the final arbiter in what constitutes a good or bad performance, even though the development of these rules may originate from an aesthetic judgment.

Athletic skill as beauty

In this respect, we might say that there are objective standards of beauty, and one of these is that beauty equates with skill. The athletes that we often admire the most are the ones that make everything look easy. Such effortless smoothness often disguises a great degree of skill, as novices find out when they attempt to replicate such actions. That there is often an equation between beauty, elegance and simplicity is something that scientists and mathematicians have noted in their considerations of scientific and mathematical theory. The best solutions to problems are those that strip away all unnecessary excess and the pureness that results shows itself in its beauty. Thomas Kuhn (1977), for one, noted how aesthetic considerations are a motivational factor in dismissing or accepting theories and producing paradigm shifts in the way we understand a phenomenon:

> In the sciences [the aesthetic] is ... a tool: a criterion of choice between theories that are in other respects comparable, or a guide to the imagination seeking a key to the solution of an intractable puzzle.
>
> (Kuhn, 1977, p. 342)

This is often the case within sport too; biomechanical efficiency is more likely to lead to successful outcome and this is revealed through an aesthetic appreciation. Whether the reason is one of human nature or human culture, biomechanically efficient actions often match our subjective tastes: efficient, smooth actions are more aesthetically pleasing than jarring, inefficient actions. In order to highlight this further, it is worth considering methods of scoring in 'aesthetic sports'.

In so-called aesthetic sports, points are awarded according to the success of an athlete carrying out proscribed movements (for example, a round-off in gymnastics or a hardflip in skateboarding) yet such movements are valued because of the correlation between skill and beauty. Falling on the floor, no matter how intentional, is not valued because it does not equate with skill. There are obviously difficult judgments to be made between badly executed (ugly) and difficult actions, and perfectly executed (beautiful) but easier actions. This is a judgment that both performers and adjudicators have to make, but generally more points are awarded to the latter—that is, to perfectly executed but slightly less complex actions—than the former. In high-board diving for example, a competitor will state the difficulty of dive that they will attempt, with each dive being worth a pre-set number of points (the greater the difficulty of dive, the more points it is worth). Points are deducted for any detraction from the perfect dive. As such, a diver will generally attempt the most difficult dive that they have perfected in order to gain themselves the most points. In diving, it is better to perform a simple dive perfectly, than a complex dive poorly.

It must be noted however, that there are exceptions to the rule that skill always equates with beauty. Most of these exceptions exist in the so-called purposive sports, since as highlighted earlier, there is a separation between the pre-lusory goal and the means by which it is achieved. The *New York Times* said of the great distance runner, Emil Zatopek:

> Bobbing, weaving, staggering, gyrating, clutching his torso, slinging supplicating glances toward the heavens, he ran like a man with a noose around his neck. He seemed on the verge of strangulation.
>
> (Litsky, 2000)

Zatopek, while certainly a skillful runner as demonstrated by his success, was not an aesthetically beautiful runner by any stretch of the imagination. There are also many footballers who are not renowned for their skill but rather for their brute strength and aggression. The so-called 'hard men' of football are celebrated, not because they demonstrate any great beauty or even skill, but because their success comes from their capacity to intimidate and cause injury to others, thus increasing the likelihood of victory for their team (Davis and Ryall, 2017). However, while the correlation between skill and beauty may appear to be more contingent in the purposive sports, there are occasional athletes in aesthetic sports too, that are renowned for their 'sketchy' style and yet are still considered incredibly skillful. The skateboarder Rodney Mullen belonged to this category. Mullen was lauded for his creativity in developing novel tricks and moves that others went on to aesthetically perfect.

Nevertheless, perhaps it is these exceptions that give the rule its credibility since the athletes that are most celebrated are the ones that make extreme skill appear effortless. The fleeting footwork of Messi, Maradona, Suárez or Cruyff as they weave their way through defenders exemplifies the highest form of skill in football. Keeping a ball in total control with one's feet while others attempt to wrest it away demonstrates a capacity that few possess. The use of a spherical object that can ricochet away at the slightest of touches and feet that are designed to allow us to balance and walk and are not renowned for flexibility or dexterity, highlights the elegant simplicity of the sport itself. To balance, turn, sprint, and navigate moving obstacles while controlling a ball is a feat that few can manage. When it is done well, the grace, rhythm, and fluidity appears as a choreographed dance.

It seems then that there is a correlation between skill and beauty. And while this might manifest itself most clearly in aesthetic sports due to the way in which outcome is determined by the means it occurs, even in purposive sports such as football a skillful goal is appreciated more than a goal that results from a player's mistake or error. Athletic skill then is the first aesthetic category that should form the basis of an aesthetics of sport.

Sport as a meaningful experience

Ziff's sentiments on the philosophical value of sporting aesthetics was a response to Paul Kuntz's (1974) paper "Aesthetics Applies to Sports as Well as to the Arts." In it, Kuntz argued that sports have an important aesthetic value that can be appreciated by both the performer and the spectator. This is found in the beauty, joy, and kinaesthetic empathy that we find in sport. It is the aesthetic element attached to sport that gives it value. Kuntz cites Roger Bannister's account of running to demonstrate how sport mirrors that of other arts, such as music, in providing a deep emotional quality that makes us want to engage with it. Bannister himself pointed to the aesthetic element of sport as the key reason for why he wanted to do it, and his diary reflects this account:

> I was running now, and a fresh rhythm entered my body. No longer conscious of my movement I discovered a new unity with nature. I had found a new source of power and beauty, a source I never dreamed existed. From intense moments like this, love of running can grow.
>
> (Bannister, 1956, pp. 11–12)

This account of sport's aesthetic value for participants demonstrates that although competition is an important element in defining what sport is, it does not fully account for why people do it. A deep phenomenological aesthetic account of the value of sport is exemplified in many sporting biographies like Bannister's. It runs throughout sporting literature and is recorded in sporting memories. Kuntz wished to show that the aesthetic qualities that we ascribe to the arts, such as music, theatre, and fine art, can be equally applied to sport. Sport provides similar meaning, affects our emotions, and creates dramatic spectacle, albeit via different means.

While sport more generally may provide an emotional force for many, football is doubtless *the* global game and arguably there is something that the sport of football captures that other sports do not. The meaningfulness associated with football has been considered by scholars such as Wisnik (2008), Illundáin (2006), and Campos (2010). Illundáin argues that football has an intrinsic and cultural value that transcends other external goods of sport, such as money and prestige. Football holds a narrative that mirrors life itself but in such a way that enables a creative expression that is meaningful to both individuals and entire communities. It allows us to move from the ordinary into the extraordinary and enables "us to find rich meanings at a transcendental level that may be instrumental for confronting life and its problems" (Illundáin, 2006, p. 83). More generally, sport provides a narrative in our lives that both complements and transcends other aspects of our daily activities and is paradoxical in that it is both trivial and of ultimate import. Playing or watching sport makes little sense when isolated from its internal goods—there is no good reason to expend energy in trying to get a ball into the back of a net. And yet, for those that are engaged in this endeavor, it holds immense value. It is part of a good life.

This in itself perhaps points to one of the obvious aesthetic categories that can be applied to sport: the emotional effect and the dramatic spectacle that it provides us with. All sports can induce a powerful aesthetic effect in certain situations. Indeed, it is the competitive nature of sports that gives rise to this. What this means for football in particular as opposed to other sports is a point I will return to later in regard to the concept of drama as a consequence of time-limitedness. Nevertheless, the second aesthetic category that can be formed is that of meaningful experience.

E-games and t-games

Up to now, I have given a general overview of some of the debates that have been considered in the philosophy of sport literature in order to consider some over-arching aesthetic categories. However, while I have attempted to highlight how these categories might apply to football, advocates of other sports could quite easily do the same. As such, there does not seem to be anything particular to football to be deserving of the moniker 'the beautiful game'. To give credence to football above other sports, I will turn to a discussion that is founded on Kretchmar's (2005) paper entitled "Game Flaws." In it, Kretchmar argues that sports such as football are structurally, morally, and aesthetically inferior to games such as golf. The argument rests upon a distinction between what he calls t-games, and what he calls e-games.

The t in t-games signifies time. The e in e-games signifies event. Kretchmar divides sports up in this way to distinguish between those that have a time limit in which to be played, e.g., football being a game of 90 minutes; and those that end when a set amount of actions has taken place, e.g., after 18 holes have been played. According to Kretchmar, any game or sport which is limited by a set time, such as football, rugby, hockey, handball or basketball, is inferior to games that end only after completing a particular number of actions, such as golf, tennis, shooting, high board diving or vaulting.

The flaw that Kretchmar argues is inherent in t-games is related to the notion of skill, which as discussed, is an integral element in the aesthetics of sport. Kretchmar's criticism is based on his claim that t-games are not able to show athletic skill as much as e-games. He argues that event-regulated games are structurally designed to promote a positive and consistent test of the skills that define that game (he calls these 'skillful interchanges' or SIs). In contrast, time-regulated games can reward gamesmanship, which is antithetical to testing the skills inherent to that game. Kretchmar provides the example of golf to illustrate his point: golf is an event-regulated game whereby the result is determined by the number of shots taken to complete 18 holes. It is not constrained by time and therefore it does not matter if you rush around the course as quickly as possible or spend a degree of time assessing the lie of each ball before taking a shot. If golf was time-regulated, it would mean that the result is determined by which player had the lowest score after a set time, say four hours. This could mean that a player who was winning at the 3-hour-15-minute mark could spend the next 45 minutes pretending to line up their next shot while never actually taking it.[5] As such, rather than being a consistent test of game-related skill, i.e., the ability to hit a ball accurately, the last 45 minutes are taken up by time-wasting. Kretchmar concludes that since t-games allow for time-wasting rather than a demonstration of skill, they are inherently flawed.

In support of Kretchmar's view, it does seem to be the case that criticism is often directed towards t-games for the time-wasting behavior they appear to reward, for instance, retreating to a negative defensive strategy in order to hold on to a lead or avoid defeat. In regard to football, for instance, time is often wasted by making unnecessary substitutions, kicking the ball back to the goal-keeper, keeping the ball in the corner, and feigning injury. While the clock ticks down, the skills being tested are arguably not those inherent to the game that is being played. Although such behavior is generally frowned upon, spectators and officials are often resigned to the fact that such behavior is not explicitly against the rules. In this Kretchmar is right, time-wasting does not demonstrate the type of skill that we wish to see in sport and therefore has negligible aesthetic merit.

This leads to Kretchmar's moral criticism of games such as football: because they are limited by time, they provide an incentive to play the game badly. Time-wasting is a way of spoiling not enhancing sport. Yet, the ability to waste time is often contingent to victory. It therefore rewards an instrumental approach to game-playing since stalling and other non-game-related behavior become the most rational action for players to take in order to win. In contrast, in event-regulated games, such actions would never be rational whatever attitude it is played with (whether intrinsic/amateur or instrumental/professional). Kretchmar appears to be right here: there is something morally distasteful about a game which rewards attempts to avoid playing it. Yet, as Paul Davis (2006) notes in his critique, it is doubtful as to whether time-wasting occurs as much in reality as Kretchmar suggests. One of the reasons it may not occur as often as Kretchmar's theory supposes is perhaps due to the phenomenological and lusory desire to 'play the game' and the meaningful experience it gives participants.

Nevertheless, Kretchmar argues that such instrumental attitudes based upon the structural defects of t-games result in behavior that is not aesthetically conducive to a good game. According to Kretchmar, teams and individuals are motivated to take any action that runs down the clock and these actions are antithetical to the qualities that we are attracted to when we play and watch sport. Simply put, Kretchmar asserts that the structural flaws in t-games mean they will also be aesthetically deficient.

The problem with limiting a game by time is that it leads to two equally unsatisfactory outcomes. Either we are left wondering who might have won if the game lasted as long as is necessary for the integral skills to be fully tested (as in the case of score or no-score draws), or we are left with a dull and tedious game that has been decided before the time has expired (since teams will often try to protect leads by time-wasting). As Kretchmar notes:

> In time-regulated games, ... [w]e might experience a full complement of testing opportunities during a set period of time. Or we might not. And when we do not, we might feel cheated. After all, we built the game to be played for, say, 40 minutes—not to be played for 25 or 30, with the remainder spent in relatively nonskillful inactivity. In short, it would be odd to construct an artificial test for the purpose of determining who is better at solving a gratuitous problem, only to have a game structure that (on occasion) favors the individual who refuses to address that very problem.
>
> (Kretchmar, 2005, p. 41)

Kretchmar asserts that in the majority of t-games, the outcome has been decided before full time has elapsed. He contrasts this with event-regulated games, such as golf, tennis, and snooker, whereby it is always logically possible for the opposition to claw their way back into the game; as illustrated by examples such as Ben Ainslie's inspired victory in the 2013 America's Cup which saw Team Oracle turn around an 8–1 deficit to win 9–8, Europe's Ryder Cup victory in 2012, or England's Ashes test win at Headingley in 1981. In contrast to t-games, in e-games, such as tennis or golf, it is not over until it is over.

The limitation with Kretchmar's claim, however, is that although this may be the case in the high-scoring t-games he cites (e.g., rugby or basketball), where it is unlikely that a team will come back from a double figure deficit in the latter stages, it is far from the norm in lower scoring t-games such as football whereby the victor rarely attains more than a two-goal advantage. Such a small deficit as is the case in many games of football can, and does, frequently get overturned in the dying minutes of a game.

Sport as dramatic spectacle

It is at this point where Kretchmar's argument fundamentally fails. Despite the fact that the victory and the end of the game are logically dependent on one another in e-games, it is t-games that allow for a more dramatic spectacle which provides greater aesthetic value. Contrary to Kretchmar's argument that limited time reduces the value of these sports, it is the very restriction of time that enhances its value. It is this aesthetic element of dramatic spectacle that provides a greater value to t-games and is what makes them worthwhile and popular. The discerner of the good game wishes to see the 'sweet-tension of uncertainty of outcome'.[6] But contrary to Kretchmar's assertion, it is a time constraint that can heighten this possibility. Kretchmar's argument that e-games are superior to t-games is based on his assertion that e-games provide a fuller test of integral skills and it is this that primarily determines the good game. However, this assumption is incorrect. Arguably part of the value of a good game lies in the aesthetic element of the 'sweet tension of uncertainty' that each individual game provides. Although a few examples of great sporting comebacks in e-games were illustrated previously, a more empirical analysis (in contrast to Kretchmar's anecdotal evidence) might well demonstrate that this is more, rather than less, common in t-games than e-games. Kretchmar's purism and his focus on the ratio of skillful interchanges to non-skillful interchanges neglects the aesthetic value for which the rationing of time provides. Although he notes the global popularity of football, he dismisses it as an exception and insists that the most popular games for both playing and spectating are event-regulated ones. Such a claim, however, seems doubtful.

Stephen Mumford (2013) draws upon Heidegger to illustrate this point further. Heidegger notes that we are time limited creatures and therefore time is of utmost importance to us in our lives. Sport, Mumford argues, mirrors the structure of our lives. We know that we must 'beat the clock' to get the things we want, and that 'time waits for no man':

> [A] time-limitation also enhances the dynamic of the sport: teams that trail have to play with more urgency and be more adventurous and risk taking. This creates the danger of conceding a goal from a rapid breakaway, which is one of the most exciting things to see in football. There is also a tactical battle to impose your desired pace on the game as the winning team seek to slow it down and the trailing team seek to speed it up. Such a contest can make for high drama as each goal in a game can change the dynamic, teams going from being content with their game situation, and seeking to hold it, to a position where they require a change in the game situation. Contrary to Kretchmar's (2007: 329–31) claim, therefore, it does not seem that all stalling in a sport should be corrected. Some of it may contribute to the spectacle and chime with our time-limited view on the world.
>
> (Mumford, 2013, p. 24)

Kreft (2014; 2012) too argues that drama is at the heart of the aesthetics of sport. Good sport provides a theatre in which human action, constrained by time and space, is worth watching. It is compelling and absorbing. Football in particular allows for this absorption since the drama and tension rises throughout the match. While the game might ebb and flow in its rhythm and advantage, the ticking of the clock and the relative paucity of goals means that the theatre in which it is played makes the prospect of a compelling narrative all the more likely. Pity the spectator that walks out of the stadium five minutes before the final whistle to discover the game has been turned on its head.

Purism or partisanship?

This aspect of drama highlights another debate in the aesthetics of sport: whether it is better to be a purist or partisan. Sports fans are often separated into two types of spectator: those that value particular aspects of sport generally (such as aesthetic beauty or excellence of skill) regardless of who is performing those actions, and those that value particular teams or individuals regardless of their performance. Nicholas Dixon (2007) describes them as follows:

> The 'partisan' is a loyal supporter of a team to which she may have a personal connection or which she may have sworn to support by dint of mere familiarity. The 'purist', in contrast, supports the team that he thinks exemplifies the highest virtues of the game [and virtues here, I think can reasonably encompass, moral, physical and aesthetic virtues], but his allegiance is flexible.
>
> (Dixon, 2007, p. 441)

On this account, Kretchmar appears to be a purist, since he values the aesthetic elements of sport in the number of skillful interchanges that take place, rather than who wins the contest. However, Stephen Mumford argues that Dixon's description of a purist is misleading, and I would agree with him. Dixon's purist seems to make a conscious decision to support a team or an individual based on the style of performance that they give and their allegiance will change according to whether the team or individual continues to uphold these standards. As such, Dixon appears to be describing a fickle partisan with purist tendencies. In contrast, a true purist has no affiliation to a team or individual at all: they will value the action in its entirety regardless of who is carrying it out. As Mumford (2013, p. 16) notes, "A true supporter of the virtues of the sport could have no team allegiance because in any game or passage of play, which team plays virtuously could alternate rapidly."

On first inspection, it appears that purists are the true sports fans since they value the intrinsic goods of sport, namely aesthetic beauty, including pure athletic excellence. Purists have no pre-determined allegiance and merely wish for a good game that demonstrates the highest levels of physical skill and beauty. In contrast, the partisan is merely interested in the result, however it is achieved. Yet this is unacceptable for Dixon on moral grounds, since it reflects an instrumental approach towards the value of sport which leads to all sorts of corrupt practices such as cheating and violence. On this basis, the purist who watches sport for its aesthetic elements is morally superior to the partisan.

Yet ultimately the purist does not and cannot exist. Sport only makes sense in the context of competition, i.e., the desire to beat your opponents in attaining a pre-set goal while adhering to specified rules, and therefore the purist is not watching sport at all—they just watch the movement of bodies with no interest in the purpose or goal of that movement. Without recognizing the competitive purpose behind sport to rank, order, and measure the participants in their physical skill, the concept of sport itself dissolves. While there are dangers of falling into an instrumental (and corrupted) attitude, it is the partisan who can take advantage of the aesthetic categories of meaningful experience and dramatic spectacle. The time constraints of t-games, such as football, mean that as the clock ticks down, the partisan feels the sporting experience all the more intensely. Despite being 'just a game' it matters significantly whether *your* team can hold on to a narrow lead despite the pressure they are under defending attack after attack, or whether *their* team can squeeze back a goal in the dying seconds to take the game to penalties. While the purist might appreciate the sporting skill in isolation, it is the partisan that feels its full effects. The upshot then is that those that enjoy sport are both purists and partisans, and it is a combination of both that provides us with a worthwhile aesthetic experience.

Football as the beautiful game

If we are able to reject part of Kretchmar's argument on the aesthetic value that a restriction of time provides, there may also be a case to reject the premise on which Kretchmar bases his argument: that t-games provide a lesser test of valuable skills that are inherent to the game.

Kretchmar is correct in arguing that one of the key values in sport is the demonstration of athletic skill, and this is one of the aesthetic categories that has been previously identified. He is, however, wrong in his analysis of how skill relates to different types of sport. If we define skill as: "acquired, intentional, and purposeful capacities to negotiate solutions to problematic situations" (Torres, 2000, p. 84), then the problem in football is how to get the ball into the goal using only one's feet (or at least not using the arms, hands or other prohibited means), while remaining in a defined area (the pitch), with only ten other supporting players, while at the same time preventing the opposition from doing likewise. Conversely, the problem in golf is to get the ball into the hole while using a specified club and negotiating hazards between the starting tee and the finishing hole. These skills are both physical and cognitive: the ability to know what to do and to be able to do it. The ability to solve these sporting problems is ultimately what Kretchmar means by 'skillful interchanges' and why

Good games as athletic beauty   39

Kretchmar argues that a game that maximizes the number of skillful interchanges is superior to one that does not. The issue, however, is that Kretchmar under-defines a skillful interchange and this leads to his flawed conclusion that football is inferior to golf.

This can be demonstrated by considering the distinction between closed skills and open skills. Closed skills are those whereby variables can be controlled and the test of skill remains the same. Open skills are more complex (usually a non-predetermined sequence of closed skills) and require adaptation to changing variables. An example of a closed skill is a golf shot from the tee or kicking a ball into an undefended net from the penalty spot. An example of an open skill is dribbling a basketball around an active defender to shoot into the net or passing to a moving player while avoiding a tackle in football. Torres (2000) asserts that open skills are much more valued than closed skills because closed skills tend to be restorative whereas open skills tend to be constitutive. This means that when the game breaks down, say in the case of the ball going out of the field of play, a simple and effective measure to restart the game is required. The simplest and most effective measure is via a closed skill; in the case of football, to throw the ball back on to the pitch. Torres argues that the further away the action is to the central skills required by the game, the simpler and more efficient it is likely to be. A throw-in in football is a perfect example of this. Football is a game that is primarily played with the feet; the skills inherent to the game are those which require the foot to control and manipulate the ball. The use of hands, in contrast, is prohibited with the exception of the goal-keeper who is allowed to use other aspects of her body in a designated area of the pitch in order to reduce the advantage given to the attacking player when shooting at goal. Since the game of football is predicated on the use of the feet, it might be reasonable to ask why, when the ball goes out of play along the sidelines, is the game then restarted with a throw-in rather than a kick-in? The answer, according to Torres, is that a throw-in is one of the most efficient ways of restarting the game and allowing play to continue. While it may be accepted that closed skills may be developed and advanced in technique as is the case for the development of open skills (so techniques of the throw-in have developed in order to maximize range and accuracy in providing an advantage for the team in possession rather than merely an efficient way of restarting the game) the problems that closed and open skills attempt to solve, differ. Moreover, the problems that are solved with open skills are much more interesting and arguably valuable, than those that require closed skills. It is this aspect that points to the flaw in Kretchmar's argument and where he fails with his conception of skillful interchange. As such, the value of a game can be assessed in the opportunities it allows for the use of open skills rather than skills per se. Moreover, the fact that football is a team sport whereby a number of individuals demonstrate skill both concurrently and sequentially means that there is a greater fluidity and depth to the movement involved. Rather than the skill being linear as in the game of golf, the dynamic movement of the team acting together in the passing of a ball provides for a far greater account of skillful interchange than Kretchmar's one-dimensional analysis. The complexity of a team moving together as one body to achieve a goal demonstrates a far greater level of skillful interchange, and thus aesthetic beauty, than one person conducting the closed skill of swinging a club to hit a ball—no matter how accurate the shot.

Football ultimately is an inherently good game because it maximizes the opportunity for a greater number of open skills to be demonstrated. The value of golf, however, is diminished because, in contrast, it is a game which predominantly requires closed skills. This can be illustrated in the types of skill that each game requires as set out in Figure 1.1. When presented in this way, it is clear that the game of football allows for a greater number of the more valuable skillful interchanges to be tested than games such as golf, as the opportunities for unpredictable or novel situations requiring the use of more valuable open skills arise to a much greater extent.

Genius as an aesthetic value

The reason that open skills are more valuable than closed skills is that they allow for a greater range of aesthetic qualities to be demonstrated, including that of genius. While skill often correlates with that which we find beautiful, if the skill also contains pure originality, it is this which makes the performance notable. This consideration of novel skill has led Teresa Lacerda and Stephen Mumford (2010) to argue that genius should be considered a valid aesthetic category in sport. It comprises five characteristics: creativity, innovation, originality, freedom, and inspiration for others to follow. They argue:

> Seeing something allows us to experience its aesthetic features but seeing it for the first time gives us something that is not in the subsequent encounters. The genius at work provides us with such

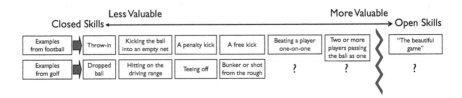

Figure 1.1 The relationship between open and closed skill and their corresponding value as a skillful interchange.

experiences when few others would be able to do so. This appreciation of the new—of novel successful strategies—is what rationally grounds our fascination with genius.

(Lacerda and Mumford, 2010, p. 192)

Ultimately, they argue "the genius is one who is able to break out from the existing chains of convention" (Lacerda and Mumford, 2010, p. 192). For example, Maradona demonstrated a vision and awareness in football that was unsurpassed. He was able to negotiate his way, seemingly effortlessly, past opposition players while continuing to keep control of the ball as in his infamous second goal against England in the 1986 World Cup when he received the ball in his own half and with his back to the opponent's goal just to shake off two England players, run down the right wing evading two more players, and finally fooling England goalkeeper Peter Shilton before nimbly putting the ball in the back of the net. In gymnastics, Schuschunova developed new linking movements between set gymnastic moves which brought a grace and fluidity to a routine that had not been seen before, while in ski-jump and high-jump, Boklöv and Fosbury developed new techniques in sport that enabled previous limits of human ability to be surpassed: Boklöv with the v-shape and Fosbury with his novel backward jumping technique. While Lacerda and Mumford cite a variety of sporting geniuses in a range of different types of sport, there are arguably far more opportunities for the demonstration of genius in open and fluid sports such as football than in closed and static sports such as high-jumping. The scope for genius may well be dependent on whether the sports fundamentally are a test for open or closed skills. As noted in Figure 1.1, the nature of football as a fluid, multi-directional team game has far more scope for aesthetic beauty than static, linear individual sports such as golf: the possibility for original skill, meaningful experience, and dramatic spectacle is so much greater.

Conclusion

To return to our initial questions, the aesthetic categories of sport can be summarized as follows. Sport provides us with a meaningful experience which can be a raw phenomenological experience, or is dependent on the narrative it provides as a dramatic spectacle. Having a partisan preference for who succeeds adds to this drama since good sport is ultimately the sweet tension of uncertainty of outcome whereby the victor is unknown no matter how unequal the competition may at first seem. Furthermore, in contrast to Kretchmar's assertion, this dramatic spectacle is often enhanced, not diminished, by the constraint of time because as self-conscious creatures, the passing of time plays a fundamental part in understanding deeper philosophical questions about the meaning of life. Finally, it is athletic skill which underpins an aesthetics of sport, and within this, the scope for originality and creativity that is exemplified by sporting genius.

The particular sport of football allows for all of these qualities to flourish. With regard to the demonstration of athletic skill, its rules provide for a variety of skills to be demonstrated—speed, deftness, deception, power, agility, guile. Moreover, these skills are open skills that allow for a far greater creativity and originality compared to the relatively closed skills required by golf, snooker or other e-games. Lastly, football seems to be the sport that has its drama enhanced to the greatest extent by a restriction of time. Last minute goals that change the outcome are far more likely than in many other sports. The nature of football, and its relative paucity in goals, means that the aesthetic partisan is sitting on the edge of her seat waiting for a moment of release. It is these things together that demonstrate why football is rightly called 'the beautiful game'.

Notes

1 Some of the content for this chapter has been taken and adapted from previously published work in Ryall (2015).
2 The origin of the phrase 'the beautiful game' is contested but since the latter half of the twentieth century it has become common vernacular for soccer.
3 The term pre-lusory goal was coined by Bernard Suits (1973) to distinguish the particular goal of a specific game from more general motivational goals, such as: to win, have fun or make friends.
4 The Fédération Internationale de Gymnastique (2017) for instance, provides very detailed guidance as to how to award and when to deduct points.
5 Kretchmar uses the example of (pretending) to look for a lost ball in the rough for 45 minutes but the laws of golf have since been changed so that a player is only able to spend five minutes looking for a ball.
6 This phrase has been attributed to Warren Fraleigh and developed further by Sigmund Loland (2002).

References

Bannister, R. 1956. The four-minute mile. New York: Dodd, Mead & Co.
Best, D. 1978. Philosophy and human movement. London: George Allen & Unwin.
Campos, D. 2010. On the value and meaning of football: Recent philosophical perspectives in Latin America. Journal of the Philosophy of Sport. 37(1), pp. 69–87.
Davis, P. 2006. Game strengths. Journal of the Philosophy of Sport. 33(1), pp. 50–66.
Davis, P. and Ryall, E. 2017. Evaluating violent conduct in sport: A hierarchy of vice. Sport, Ethics and Philosophy. 11(2), pp. 207–218.
Dixon, N. 2007. The ethics of supporting sports teams. In: Morgan, W.J. ed. Ethics in sport. 2nd ed. Leeds: Human Kinetics, pp. 441–449.
Fédération Internationale de Gymnastique. 2017. Technical regulations 2017. [Online]. [Accessed October 11, 2017]. Available from: www.fig-gymnastics. com/site/rules/main.

Illundáin, J. 2006. Goles transcendentales. In: Torres, T.R. and Campos, D.G. eds. La pelota no dobla? Ensayos filosóficos entorna al fútbol. Buenos Aires: Libros del Zorzal, pp. 25–57.

Kreft, L. 2012. Sport as a drama. Journal of the Philosophy of Sport. 39(2), pp. 219–234.

Kreft, L. 2014. Aesthetics of the beautiful game. Soccer & Society. 15(3), pp. 353–375.

Kretchmar, R.S. 2005. Game flaws. Journal of the Philosophy of Sport. 32(1), pp. 36–48.

Kuhn, T.S. 1977. Comment on the relations between science and art. In: Kuhn, T.S. ed. The essential tension. Chicago: University of Chicago Press, pp. 340–351.

Kuntz, P. 1974. Aesthetics applies to sports as well as to the arts. Journal of the Philosophy of Sport. 1(1), pp. 6–35.

Lacerda, T. and Mumford, S. 2010. The genius in art and in sport: A contribution to the investigation of aesthetics of sport. Journal of the Philosophy of Sport. 37(2), pp. 182–193.

Litsky, F. 2000. Emil Zatopek, 78, ungainly running star, dies. The New York Times. [Online]. November 23. [Accessed January 15, 2017]. Available from: www.nytimes.com/2000/11/23/sports/23ZATO.html.

Loland, S. 2002. Fair play in sport: A moral norm system. London: Routledge.

Mumford, S. 2013. Watching sport: Aesthetics, ethics and emotion. London: Routledge.

Ryall, E. 2015. Good games and penalty shoot-outs. Sport, Ethics and Philosophy. 9(2), pp. 205–213.

Suits, B. 1973. The elements of sport. In: Osterhoudt, R.D. ed. The philosophy of sport: A collection of original essays. Springfield, IL: Charles C. Thomas, pp. 48–63.

Torres, C. 2000. What counts as part of a game? A look at skill. Journal of the Philosophy of Sport. 27(1), pp. 81–92.

Wisnik, J.M. 2008. Veneno remédio: O futebol e o Brasil [Poison remedy: Football and Brazil]. São Paulo: Companhia das Letras.

Ziff, P. 1974. A fine forehand. Journal of the Philosophy of Sport. 1(1), pp. 92–109.

Chapter 2

Appreciating the not-obviously-beautiful game

Adam Kadlac

Introduction

Despite its reputation as 'the beautiful game', I suspect that most people who watch soccer can recall many instances where the product on the field has been far from aesthetically pleasing. Think, for example, of youth soccer. Anyone who has watched young children play the game is familiar with the sight of kids clustered around the ball, kicking furiously in the hopes that they might emerge from the pack and make a break for goal. Such a scene calls many things to mind, but beauty is not likely to be foremost among them.

Even when we contemplate the soccer that is played at the highest levels of competition, many of us will be somewhat stingy with our attributions of beauty. The flowing, attacking approach of Barcelona contrasts sharply with the stout defensiveness of Atlético Madrid, and the aesthetic juxtaposition of Dutch *totaalvoetbal* ('total football') and Italian *catenaccio* ('door-bolt') has historically been striking. While these characterizations are obviously fluid, as teams change their style of play over time, most soccer fans will have in mind their own examples of teams that play attractively and those that do not. The latter may be effective in securing results, but beautiful soccer and winning soccer need not be the same thing.

What I want to do in the discussion that follows is examine these kinds of aesthetic judgments. For my contention is that even if the soccer being played on the field is decidedly unattractive, there are a number of other things occurring in the context of a football match that can nevertheless be regarded as beautiful: exerting maximum effort, being a good teammate, demonstrating sportsmanship, and the like. If this analysis is correct, we would seem to have a more nuanced way of appreciating the aesthetic dimensions of soccer than a simple division between 'ugly soccer' and 'beautiful soccer' would allow. Put differently, the view on offer suggests that we can see beautiful things while watching soccer even if the soccer we are watching is not especially beautiful.

In the first section, I lay the groundwork for this conclusion by examining Alasdair MacIntyre's (1984) account of "intelligible action." According to MacIntyre, characterizing any instance of human behavior as an action requires that we appeal to the settings in which that behavior occurs. And since our behavior may take place in many different settings at once, there are likely to be a number of different answers to the question of what an individual is doing at any given time. Focusing on the example of youth soccer, I thus show how this analysis entails that an individual can be performing multiple intelligible actions even though she may seem to simply be trying to play a game with her teammates.

In the second section, I consider how this account bears on our aesthetic judgments. Here, my basic contention is that judgments of beauty are often informed by our sense of what we are seeing. And if, as I argue, we may be seeing many different things happening at one time when individuals are playing soccer, a number of different aesthetic judgments may therefore be justified regarding what is happening on the field.

In making this case, I do not intend to be taking a firm stand on what constitutes beautiful soccer or, indeed, what the most plausible account of beauty might be. My focus is instead on what might serve as plausible objects of aesthetic judgment. Thus, if the discussion is compelling, the soccer we are watching might be beautiful, or it might be ugly. But either way, there will be plenty of other candidates for beauty in the vicinity.

Doing many things at once

"What is he doing?" seems like a straightforward question that deserves a straightforward answer. After all, in most cases, "He is walking the dog" or "He is jumping rope" or "He is going to the store" are answers likely to satisfy anyone posing such a query. One may, therefore, be tempted to think that all of our behavior is subject to similarly basic characterizations and that there is one unique answer to the question of what one is doing at any given moment.

In his seminal book *After Virtue* (1984), Alasdair MacIntyre points out that such an impulse does not, in fact, square with the way that either philosophers or ordinary agents think about questions regarding what one is doing. Suppose, for example, that you look into the yard next door and see your neighbor moving around. Perplexed, you might ask your spouse what the neighbor in question is doing. MacIntyre suggests that in this scenario, a variety of answers may be given: "'Digging', 'Gardening', 'Taking exercise', 'Preparing for winter' or 'Pleasing his wife'" (MacIntyre, 1984, p. 206). While you might have some background information that would lead you to be skeptical about some of these answers, none would strike you as nonsensical. You might know that your neighbor's sedentary lifestyle makes it unlikely that he is really trying to get exercise, and the absence of any vegetable plants in his yard for the past 20 years may make you question whether he could possibly be gardening. However, this skepticism does not result from any fundamental unintelligibility in the responses. Maybe you doubt that your neighbor is taking exercise because of some specific background knowledge you have about your neighbor. But that belief is consistent with the notion that someone else exhibiting similar bodily movements may very well be taking exercise.

For MacIntyre, it is crucial to recognize that the settings that render our behavior intelligible are essentially historically oriented. He writes:

> [I]t is central to the notion of a setting as I am going to understand it that a setting has a history, a history within which the histories of individual agents not only are, but have to be, situated, just because without the setting and its changes through time the history of the individual agent and his changes through time will be unintelligible.
>
> (MacIntyre, 1984, pp. 206–207)

Thus, the context of gardening has a history, and any individual instance of gardening takes its place within that temporally extended story. Similarly, marriage as an institution has a history, as does every particular marriage. In this way, our actions are constituted as the particular actions they are by the place they occupy in these various narratives. To conclude that your neighbor is gardening is, therefore, to see his digging in the dirt in the context of the historically developing practice of various kinds of agriculture. And if you think that your neighbor is doing something that will make his wife happy, such a conclusion will make sense not only because you understand something about the broader history of marriage but also because you have some sense of the particular history of your neighbor's relationship to his wife.

Importantly, MacIntyre points out that *all* of the possible answers to the question of what your neighbor is doing might be correct. He may be digging, gardening, taking exercise, preparing for winter, and pleasing his wife all at the same time. Moreover, his intentions may match what it is that he is doing—in the sense that he is, in fact, doing what he is trying to do—or they may not. As MacIntyre notes, "Some of these answers will characterize the agent's intentions, others unintended consequences of his actions, and of those unintended consequences some may be such that the agent is aware of them and others not" (1984, p. 206). Maybe your neighbor is not explicitly trying to take exercise or make his wife happy but is instead simply trying to get the garden planted; the exercise and marital benefits are simply unintentional byproducts of getting the seeds in the ground. Nevertheless, it would not be correct to say that he is not, in fact, getting exercise or pleasing his wife. The various settings in which he is operating determine that he is doing those things whether or not he is explicitly trying to do them.

The notion that what we are doing is subject to factors beyond our control may seem counterintuitive. After all, how can one be doing something that one is not trying to do? The very idea might seem to violate the Western sensibility that we are masters of our own destiny. However, I think the basic idea here should be familiar to anyone who has tried to do something and failed. For example, I am trying to write an interesting chapter on the aesthetics of soccer, but I might not succeed. If the chapter ends up being rubbish, what I will have done is write a rubbish chapter on the aesthetics of soccer, and that fact will not be changed by my earnest attempt to write a good one. If I try to repair my car, but actually make the problem worse, the mechanic who has to remedy my mistakes is not going to be interested in what I have tried to do. And if I make a joke in a good-natured attempt to lighten the mood at a party that ends up offending everyone in the room, what I have done is offend everyone in the room rather than lighten the mood.

What MacIntyre's analysis adds to this familiar experience is that very often, the factors beyond our control—factors which make it the case that what we are trying to do is not always what we end up doing—are the settings in which we act. Your neighbor working in his backyard may be in direct control of his bodily movements as he digs in the dirt and puts seeds in the ground. But there are many settings in which he is acting over which he does not exercise complete control. To begin with, he is not in control of his wife's expectations, and so he cannot ever *guarantee* that what he does will please his wife. He is not in control of the history of human agriculture, so he cannot be in complete control over how his movements are intelligible as a part of that context. And he is not in control of human physiology, so he cannot be in complete control over whether his bodily movements constitute exercise. Thus, insofar as the settings in which he is acting are beyond his control, his intentions will only play one part in determining what it is that he is doing.

More important than the role of intentionality in determining what one is doing is MacIntyre's claim that we can see individuals doing multiple things at once when we try to interpret their bodily movements. The point here is not that one can be doing many different things at once in the sense that one can multitask. For example, right now, I am writing a chapter while drinking coffee and listening to music (and periodically checking my e-mail and looking out my office window). As a result, one observing my behavior could sensibly allege that I am doing many different things— probably too many different things—at once. At any given moment, I might be performing one action and then quickly transitioning to another and then another.

But this is not the sense of doing many things at once to which MacIntyre draws our attention. Rather, what he highlights is that understanding any piece of human behavior requires that we locate that behavior in some broader context and that "one and the same piece of behavior may belong to more than one setting" (MacIntyre, 1984, p. 207). Thus, you might locate your neighbor's actions "in an annual cycle of domestic activity" which "presupposes a particular type of household-cum-garden setting" and at the same time see it as part of "the narrative history of a marriage" (MacIntyre, 1984, p. 206). In so doing, you will see that he is both gardening and making his wife happy even though—unlike me, as I struggle to focus on writing my chapter—he is wholly absorbed in what he is doing.

If we turn our attention from gardening back to soccer, I think it becomes apparent how many settings are in play—that is, how many different narratives are unfolding—when we watch individuals run around kicking after a ball on an expanse of grass. Consider, as a particularly illustrative example, a youth soccer game. Watching such an event from the sidelines, we can contemplate what we are seeing in the context of soccer itself—a game with a long and nuanced history that is informed by the more particular histories of the game around the world: England, Europe, South America, and the United States, to say nothing of the more particular locales of Manchester, London, Rio De Janeiro, Mexico City, Los Angeles, or Winston-Salem, North Carolina. We can, therefore, consider the setting of the game writ large or view it from a more locally oriented perspective. The kids might be playing soccer, but they might also be attempting to play soccer in a style that reflects the game's local history.

Narrowing our scope somewhat, we can see the kids' actions as part of the narrative of various organizations or teams. Perhaps those organizations have a long and storied past, or perhaps they are brand new. Maybe two teams are longstanding rivals from neighboring communities, or maybe they have never played each other before. In the United States, it is not at all uncommon for different youth teams from the same club to face off against each other and for those teams to be made up of players who have been teammates in the past but now find themselves on opposing sides of the field. Given these various settings, children might be squaring off against friends at the same time they are playing their first game for a new club.

Within teams, there are the settings constituted by the histories of individual players. Some kids will have played the game as long as they can remember (even if that is only a couple of years). Others might be trying it out for the first time. Some will come from soccer-playing families and have soccer-playing parents and siblings. Others will have parents who are themselves new to the sport they are watching their kids play. Some kids will want to be on the field and be focused intently on what they are doing; others will look like they want to be anywhere else but where they are; and some will look like they do not have a clue what is going on around them. Some children will immediately exhibit skill with the ball at their feet; others will struggle for a while before finding their way; and still others may never quite get the hang of it.

Appreciating the game   49

I do not intend for this list of settings to be at all exhaustive, and there are clearly other settings that will be relevant to any soccer match, not just the youth game. For example, our personal histories are also bound up with broader narratives concerning race, gender, and class, and these settings certainly inform our understanding of all sorts of behavior. In this way, what someone is doing will often depend on one's ethnic background, whether it is a woman or a man who is doing it, and perhaps the socio-economic status of that person or that person's family. A woman who seems to be performing the same action as a man may also be doing things that the man could not do—for example, breaking down barriers or inspiring other girls to pursue athletics. Similarly, racial minorities may be able to challenge stereotypes in ways that other players are unable to do because their actions are part of different narratives.

What is important for my purposes is that no matter how we fill out the list of possible settings, the range of intelligible actions being performed by individuals running around after a ball is expansive. A single player may, at the same time, be kicking a ball, playing soccer, striving to play the possession-oriented game of her local community, engaged in a heated rivalry, surprising her non-soccer-playing parents with her tenacity and skillfulness, representing her club, challenging cultural assumptions about girls of color, and any number of other things. And if spectators are witnessing all of these actions happening at the same time, then it seems that any plausible understanding of the aesthetic features of that experience should account for the multiplicity of actions being observed.

Beautiful and not-so-beautiful at the same time

If I exclaim, "That's beautiful," the appropriate response is likely to be one of perplexity. Without some further specification of the referent of my comment, one has nowhere to focus one's attention. The natural reply is thus to ask, "What are you talking about? What is beautiful?" If we are sitting on the sidelines of a soccer game, I might be referring to the sunset in the distance, a majestic bird flying overhead, the evocative scene of my wife and young child walking towards me hand in hand, or some aspect of the game being played on the field. After all, everyday claims invoking beauty are not generally abstract claims about the mere existence of beauty. They instead tend to be claims that some particular thing—some X—is beautiful: a sunset, a bird, the image of loved ones together, or soccer-related movements in the context of a game.

Moreover, as I have argued, even if our attention is clearly focused on the field of play, we will find many different candidates for intelligible attributions of beauty since there are many different things happening on the field at any given time. Maybe the occasion for my comment is a particular bit of skill displayed by a player on the team I am supporting or a sequence of passes involving several different players that leads to a goal. Or perhaps I recognize the players on the field attempting to implement a technique or strategy that the coach has been emphasizing throughout the season. In these cases, the relevant beautiful actions would seem to be framed by the general setting of soccer or, focusing a bit more narrowly, the particular style of soccer being encouraged at the players' club.

There are, however, numerous other settings that might frame actions in ways that draw forth explicitly aesthetic reactions. For example, I might recognize a player who is new to the game as starting to master some basic technical and tactical skills. Knowing her lack of experience, I might be particularly engaged by actions that would not draw my attention if they were performed by more experienced players. A stretch of gritty defending by an undersized player against much larger opponents may impress me to the point that I regard the display of courage as beautiful. The fact that the team on the field is made up of players from a variety of different ethnic backgrounds may strike me as a particularly attractive picture of what society can be. Watching a girls' game, I might be struck by the opportunities that participating in sports offers to young women—opportunities that might not have been available to previous generations.

In all of these cases, the actions being performed cannot be identified simply as 'playing soccer' or even something more basic, such as 'closing down an attacker' or 'kicking a ball'. The beauty is instead being attributed to kids who are 'learning the game', 'fighting like hell', 'celebrating diversity', and 'learning important life lessons'. The different settings that frame these actions come together on the soccer field, but it is not the act of playing soccer itself that occasions an aesthetic response. That response is tied to some of the other things that the kids are doing at the same time they are playing soccer. Indeed, the soccer may not be especially beautiful *qua* soccer. But different aesthetic judgments may nevertheless be appropriate when the same piece of behavior is considered as part of a different setting.

To be clear, I am not arguing that ugly soccer is, contrary to appearances, actually beautiful. For present purposes, I am happy to accept whatever account of soccer beauty turns out to be most plausible. If it turns out that according to such criteria, a great deal of soccer is not aesthetically pleasing *qua* soccer, then so be it. By the same token, it is consistent with the view on offer that those who regard many forms of soccer playing as unattractive are mistaken in that judgment. As I note above, I think what I have to say here is consistent with any number of different views about what constitutes beautiful soccer.

What I want to highlight instead is the multiplicity of actions that are being performed at the same time a soccer game is being played and the attendant complexity and nuance that might characterize the aesthetic experience of watching all the various actions on the field. Viewers should, therefore, be comfortable with mixed aesthetic judgments of what they are

Appreciating the game 51

seeing and use the ambiguity of their responses to direct their attention in different ways. Indeed, I contend that by watching soccer with a variety of different settings and narratives in mind, our aesthetic experience of watching sports can be deepened and enriched. We do not have to confine ourselves to questions about whether the soccer conforms to some ideal standard of beauty. Maybe it does, and maybe it does not. But either way, there can still be plenty of beauty to enjoy.

At this point, three sorts of objection might arise to the view I have been developing. First, one might suggest that in identifying displays of courage or the celebration of diversity as beautiful, I have equivocated on the term 'beauty'. According to this line of thought, courage and diversity may be inspiring or compelling in various ways, but they cannot, strictly speaking, be beautiful. To invoke the term in such contexts is, therefore, to commit a kind of category mistake.

However, it is not at all obvious why we should deny that attributions of beauty to displays of courage or diversity can be legitimate. They may be false, in that one might be wrong to claim that the display is beautiful. But it does not follow that one is systematically mistaken about what sorts of things are capable of being beautiful. To begin with, in popular usage, 'beauty' seems to refer to "a *generic* sort of aesthetic excellence" rather than a more substantive aesthetic property that can be distinguished from other aesthetic properties (Zangwill, 2003, p. 327, italics in original). Few people make fine-grained distinctions between, for example, beauty and elegance (Zangwill, 2003, p. 327). Rather, they employ the notion of beauty to register their aesthetic approval, and this is part of the reason why we do not question people when they declare that such varied phenomena as paintings, sunsets, horses, novels, films, and music are beautiful. When one attributes beauty to a display of courage, one might, therefore, simply be highlighting that it is appropriate to think of the display in aesthetic terms and to render a positive appraisal.[1]

Even if one presses a more specified notion of beauty, it is not obvious why we should deny that displays of courage or diversity can be beautiful. For example, Alexander Nehamas writes that beauty is:

> the emblem of what we lack, the mark of an art that speaks to our desire ... [and that] [b]eautiful things don't stand aloof, but direct our attention and our desire to everything else we must learn or acquire in order to understand and possess, and they quicken the sense of life, giving it new shape and direction.
>
> (Nehamas, 2007, p. 77)

Witnessing a display of courage could, quite clearly, direct our attention and desires in the ways that Nehamas suggests and point to things—qualities of character, perhaps, or life experiences and opportunities—that speak to various of our desires. As such, it would seem to be a legitimate object of aesthetic appraisal.

Explicitly hedonist accounts of beauty would quite clearly allow that displays of courage or diversity can be beautiful. David Hume thus writes that beauty "is such an order and construction of parts as, either by the primary constitution of our nature, by custom, or by caprice, is fitted to give a pleasure and satisfaction to the soul" (1988, p. 299). Insofar as we might be incredibly pleased when we see someone behaving courageously or witness individuals from a variety of different backgrounds working together to achieve a common goal, the Humean would seem open to the possibility that our souls could be satisfied in such circumstances and that it is appropriate to attribute beauty to what we are seeing.

Even accounts of beauty which prominently appeal more directly to ideals of balance and symmetry would seem to allow that displays of courage and diversity could be beautiful.[2] Recognizing the balance in view when a variety of different cultural backgrounds are represented on the field may elicit a distinctly aesthetic response. And a display of courage might lend a particular kind of balance to the life narrative of the individuals who are acting. For example, one might exhibit remarkable courage in returning from a serious injury, and that return might complete a narrative arc in which the player has finally returned to where they started. They have completed their comeback and restored a kind of balance to their athletic career. To see the display of courage as beautiful is, perhaps, to recognize the role such actions play in providing a measure of symmetry to their life story as it plays its way out on the field.

It is obviously beyond the scope of this chapter to show how every account of beauty would support the claim that displays of courage could, in principle, be beautiful, and there will clearly be views that rule out such a possibility. Nevertheless, I think this representative list demonstrates that the idea has some minimal credibility.[3]

A second line of objection might focus on the idea that the view on offer fundamentally misrepresents the structure of our aesthetic experience—an experience in which our sense of beauty generally *precedes* any clear sense of what it is that we are seeing. On this view, we do not see something, identify it as the particular thing it is, and then respond to it aesthetically. On the contrary, we simply have an aesthetic reaction to whatever it is we are experiencing such that we need not characterize the object of that experience with any specificity. In the context of a soccer game, then, we watch the game being played, and in the course of watching, find ourselves responding in a particular way. We may not be able to characterize what it is we are seeing, or even know exactly what aspect of the events unfolding before us are eliciting any given reaction.

One might see this sort of response as broadly Kantian in emphasizing "that aesthetic judgment 'is neither *grounded* in concepts nor *aimed* at them'" (Gumbrecht, 2006, p. 42, italics in original).[4] Without getting too deep into the weeds of Kant interpretation, Eli Friedlander thus gives a helpful explanation of what this means in practice:

> We of course identify a painting, say, as a material object having certain properties. But our aesthetic experience does not take the form of identifying such and such properties in the object whose presence would then justify calling it beautiful (even though it is as if we locate beauty wholly in the object). Beauty exists only in the space opened by the subject in being responsive to the object, and such space of possibilities of advance must be distinguished from any collection of actual objective properties of an existing object.
>
> (Friedlander, 2015, p. 21)

If we apply this analysis to a soccer match, we might say that while individuals who are watching what is happening on the pitch are certainly aware of various things happening, their aesthetic experience does not consist in the identification of particular actions that justify attributions of beauty. Rather, if I understand Friedlander's Kant accurately here, we experience the game as beautiful by attending *to our response* to what we are witnessing.

I do not want to deny the possibility of experiences of beauty that precede a refined understanding of the object of our experience. Indeed, the sense I have of my own response to a lot of abstract art very much fits the pattern laid out by Friedlander. I do not necessarily understand what I am seeing when I look at an abstract painting or sculpture, but I nevertheless have a fairly immediate aesthetic response to it. Nevertheless, I do not think the existence (and legitimacy) of these kinds of experiences undermines the basic view I am putting forward. Thus, even if it is the case that someone might experience beauty while watching a soccer game in the way a Kantian might suggest, I think other instances of aesthetic experience very clearly involve a more refined sense of the objects of those experiences.

To begin with, one cannot regard a particular passage of play *as a beautiful passage of play* without understanding the rules of the game being played—that is, without understanding the setting that constitutes the movements of multiple human bodies *as a passage of play in a game of soccer* rather than something else. And surely this is the way in which the overwhelming majority of people watch sports. We see the left winger making an overlapping run, the center forward laying the ball off for him, and the back proceeding to launch a cross into the box. Indeed, as one grows more familiar with the rules and structure of the game, one cannot help but see these things. They become irreducible features of our experience. It would, therefore, be rather surprising if they did not figure prominently in the aesthetic dimensions of that experience.

54   Adam Kadlac

Kantians might respond by insisting that while it is true that we often see the various passages of play or the movements of players on the field *as* movements of players on the field, these factors of our experience do not figure into our aesthetic judgments. Such judgments attach solely to the movement of certain patterns and shapes and therefore are not determined by concepts like 'left back' or 'launching a cross into the box'. Indeed, to invoke such concepts is to undermine the purity of aesthetic judgment—judgments which, by definition, cannot be brought under concepts.[5]

The problem with this approach, as I see it, is that the Kantian position fundamentally mischaracterizes not only aesthetic experience, but the conceptually loaded nature of human perception more generally. In other words, human beings bring something to our perceptual experiences—what Daniel Dennett calls "excess baggage"—in ways that affect not only our aesthetic judgments, but what it is that we see. Dennett thus offers the following example of how this works in practice:

> [I]magine that musicologists unearthed a heretofore unknown Bach cantata, definitely by the great man, but hidden in a desk and probably never yet heard even by the composer himself. Everyone would be aching to hear it, to experience for the first time the 'qualia' that the Leipzigers would have known, had they only heard it, but this turns out to be impossible, for the theme of the cantata, by an ugly coincidence, is the first seven notes of "Rudolf the Red-Nosed Reindeer"! We who are burdened with that tune would never be able to hear Bach's version as he intended it or as the Leipzigers would have received it.
>
> (Dennett, 1991, p. 388, cited in Mumford, 2012, p. 65)

The point here is not that we will judge the newly discovered cantata as less beautiful because it resembles a children's Christmas song. It is the much more fundamental point that knowing the tune of "Rudolph the Red-Nosed Reindeer" means that we cannot but hear the opening lines of the new Bach as a mimicry of that song. Similarly, knowing what it is for a right back to make an overlapping run, we will not be able to see soccer players moving in various patterns as anything but a right back making an overlapping run, whatever aesthetic judgment we then make about what we are seeing. The concepts are, as it were, baked into the perceptions from the very start.

An advantage of rejecting the Kantian picture on this point is that it enables us to see the ways in which individuals who have knowledge of all the various narratives at play in a given sporting event might also be aware of more instances of beauty than someone who acknowledges only the formal arrangement of players on the field. If I see a player make a soccer-related move and know nothing about her background, I might respond in one way. But my response may be very different if I know that she is playing her first game back from a year's long battle with cancer. Possessing that knowledge, I can respond not only to her behavior regarded narrowly in the context of soccer. I can also see someone persevering in the face of a significant challenge, and witnessing an action of this sort is likely to produce a different response in me than simply seeing a girl playing soccer. Indeed, I may be moved to tears by the beauty of a girl persevering after a cancer fight even if her soccer playing is kind of rubbish. Thus, even if our aesthetic responses sometimes precede any understanding of what we are seeing, it is equally clear that sometimes that understanding very much informs our responses.

A third objection to the view on offer might be that I have made intentionality figure too prominently in the aesthetic experience of watching sports. Hans Ulrich Gumbrecht has advanced a version of this view in arguing that we primarily view sports in the dimension of "presence" as opposed to the dimension of "meaning." Central to this distinction is the idea of a separation between "meaning and the material objects that articulate meaning" (Gumbrecht, 2006, p. 68). When people view things in the dimension of meaning, they "conceive of themselves primarily as mind" and "necessarily see the world of objects from a position of distance" (Gumbrecht, 2006, p. 62). People in the presence dimension, however, "feel that they are part of and contiguous with objects in the physical world" (Gumbrecht, 2006, p. 62).

For Gumbrecht, what follows from an appreciation of this distinction is that we can see "any human body movement as a performance," and, hence, as a legitimate candidate for aesthetic experience, "as long as we see it, predominantly at least, in the presence dimension. For I believe that we hardly ever watch sports from any other angle" (2006, p. 69). Gumbrecht is careful to qualify this claim, noting that there are clearly actions taking place on any field of play. Nevertheless, he thinks "that seeing the athlete's movements as transformations of his world—that is, asking ourselves what a player's intention may possibly be while he throws or kicks the ball—is not what we mainly do when we become sports spectators" (2006, p. 69).

To be sure, as I have noted, many of the actions we perform do not depend on our intentionality of performing them. Thus, the neighbor digging in his garden may not be explicitly attempting to make his wife happy. He may simply be trying to get the spring planting in the ground. Whether he, in fact, ends up making his wife happy will depend on facts about his wife's expectations, the emotional state of their relationship as he works in the yard, and whether she is even aware of what he is doing. Similarly, a girl returning to the soccer field after a fight with cancer may not be explicitly trying to display great resilience in the face of her illness. She may just be trying to score a goal.

Nevertheless, I find it difficult to think of the experience of watching sports absent a backdrop of intentionality—that is, absent the basic assumption that players on the field are trying to do something. To begin with, I am quite sure that many sports fans do exactly what Gumbrecht attempts to marginalize as an aberration. In my experience, one of the more common exclamations to be heard at sports bars is "What was he thinking?!" This is followed closely in frequency by "What is he doing?!" Many fans want nothing more than to get into the heads of the athletes they are watching, and fans are quick to criticize various actions precisely on the grounds that the wrong decision was made.

Moreover, experienced viewers—perhaps especially those who have some experience playing the sport they are watching—will often be highly attuned to all of the particular actions that are happening on the field of play. In this vein, Randolph Feezell writes of all the actions that are occurring during a baseball game:

> The pitcher attempts to establish his fastball, probes the weaknesses of certain hitters, and attempts to gain a sense of the umpire's strike zone. Fielders position themselves according to their judgment of the swing and strength of the hitters; they must remember previous at bats. Coaches learn and respond as the game proceeds. The pitcher has a poor move to first; the catcher's arm is strong but his release is slow and his feet are plodding. The pitcher never throws breaking balls when he's behind in the count. A decision is made to steal second base. And so on. ... From the fan's perspective, attention is intensely focused on the actions, decisions, and meanings inside the world of the game. If one knows baseball well, the complexity of a particular game is quite amazing.
>
> (Feezell, 2006, p. 39)

The stop-and-start nature of baseball may make it particularly well-suited to this kind of viewing. But even in a game as fluid as soccer, observers frequently key in on the specific actions of specific players—the aforementioned winger making an overlapping run; the center forward holding up play; one's favorite player returning from injury; the much maligned goalkeeper trying to keep a clean sheet. And when fans observe the game in this way, it is perfectly natural for them to think about what the players on the pitch are trying to do.

Indeed, Gumbrecht's account suggests that there would be very little difference, from the viewer's perspective, if sports were played by sophisticated robots. The aesthetic dimensions of the experience would not be at all affected because the movements of the robots would be indistinguishable from those of human beings. If these moments are beautiful, then it does not particularly matter what it is that is moving. However, this seems a mistake. Robotic movements can certainly be beautiful in their own way. But whatever else informs the way in which we watch sports, I suggest that we are almost always aware that we are watching human beings who are trying to accomplish things on the field of play. We would not be captivated by a robot Olympics or robot World Cup that looked outwardly just like an actual (human) Olympics or actual (human) World Cup. And because we are acutely aware of the intentionality of the athletes involved, I think any plausible aesthetic should make room for this aspect of our experience of watching sports.

Conclusion

I have tried to highlight the way in which multiple settings can come together to constitute one set of bodily movements as any number of different intelligible actions. As such, our attributions of beauty may be appropriate in one setting even as they are somewhat questionable in another. Soccer playing *qua* soccer playing may be fairly unattractive even as the exhibitions of teamwork and bravery going on simultaneously are quite stirring. What emerges is thus a framework for thinking about the aesthetics of various events that resists straightforward binary judgments: beautiful/ugly, attractive/unattractive, and so on. Rather, when considering the aesthetic qualities of what we are seeing, or reflecting on our own aesthetic experience, we should think instead of the more specific objects of our aesthetic judgments. Are we responding to the soccer playing *qua* soccer playing? Or are we drawn instead to something else that is happening on the field?

Because children do not tend to play a version of the game that many people would be inclined to count as beautiful, my central example to this point has been youth soccer. Indeed, anyone who has watched young kids on the pitch may wonder whether many of them are so much as *trying* to play soccer. For this reason, the importance of contexts for parsing our experience of watching the youth game strikes me as particularly relevant and, perhaps, a source of some aesthetic comfort for those who find themselves on the sideline as a pack of eight-year-olds chase after a ball on a hot and humid Saturday afternoon.

Nevertheless, the implications of what I have been arguing seem to extend well beyond the youth level. Anyone who has followed professional soccer for any length of time is familiar with the sort of fan who is quick to dismiss the performance of certain teams on the grounds that they do not play sufficiently attractive football. More than in any other sport—at least any team sport—many soccer fans (to say nothing of coaches and players) think that it is not enough for a team to win the game; they must also play 'in the right way' and secure their results by playing the appropriate style of soccer. In this vein, a certain kind of soccer purist could be heard disparaging the 2016 Premier League title campaign of Leicester City or the recent Champions League performances of Atlético Madrid (or, for that matter, a great deal of the soccer played in the 2016 European Championships) on the grounds that such football was too defensive, pragmatic, cynical, ugly, or any number of other epithets. And with perhaps slightly different motivations, the soccer played in the 2015 Women's World Cup was frequently discussed in direct comparison with the men's game—a comparison that assumed the women's game was clearly deficient in both its aesthetic and athletic qualities.

I have my doubts about the plausibility of some of these judgments, but for present purposes, let us grant that they are correct. If what I have argued above is plausible, then even if the soccer in these cases is unattractive—even downright ugly—there may still be other candidates for beauty on the field. For example, whatever else Leicester City did in the 2015–2016 season, they certainly triumphed against the odds (5000–1 odds, to be exact) (Rayner and Brown, 2016). One might, therefore, see a fair bit of beauty in the improbability of their achievement, no matter how many defensively oriented 1–0 wins it involved. Many pundits regarded the soccer played in Euro 2016 as decidedly subpar.[6] But the narrative of Iceland's improbable progression to the quarterfinals captivated people around the world: the David vs. Goliath storyline involved in every game they played was certainly a beautiful thing in the eyes of many. Portugal's victory in the final was, no doubt, a thing of beauty for the Portuguese, and fans of Cristiano Ronaldo might also have been moved by scenes of him, injured and unable to play, cheering on his teammates from the sideline in the final against France.

And whether or not the appropriate standard to employ in judging the athletic and aesthetic quality of women's soccer is how it compares to the men's game—a view which, for various reasons, strikes me as exceedingly questionable—it is clear that female soccer players are just as capable as men of doing any number of things on the field that might be regarded as beautiful: representing their country, overcoming adversity, fighting like hell, demonstrating teamwork, and so on. Indeed, as I suggested above, because of their gender, they are probably able to do some things that men are simply not able to do because their actions are constituted by different narratives. For example, they are able to "demonstrate progress for women" in ways that are unavailable to male athletes. Thus, wherever exactly one comes down on the ideal aesthetic of soccer *qua* soccer, it seems that any discussion of the aesthetic experience of watching the game should account for these additional objects of appreciation.

It is an interesting question whether sports are more effective at drawing together various settings than other human endeavors in ways that bear on our aesthetic experience. I am inclined to think that they are, largely because sports are so thoroughly narrative in their structure. We can write stories of games and seasons, and those games and seasons intersect with the stories of individual athletes' playing performances and careers.

Those stories further intersect with the histories of various teams, communities, schools, and nations. So when we watch a sporting contest, we are seeing the confluence of these intersecting narratives all of which have the potential to add texture to our viewing experience.

To point out this feature of sports is not to deny that narratives can come together in similar ways in other human activities. For example, one can easily imagine watching a high school stage production of *Hamlet* and having reactions that are aesthetically mixed in the way that reactions to youth soccer might be aesthetically mixed. Perhaps, *qua* production of *Hamlet*, the play is fairly bad—it might even be fairly bad *qua* high school production of *Hamlet*. Nevertheless, there may be narrative settings that constitute various aspects of the performance as cogent objects of aesthetic approval. Perhaps the play is the product of an entirely new theater program at the school and represents a triumph over various kinds of adversity for the student actors. In such a scenario, one might be compelled by the various narratives that have converged in the performance.

But even if sports are not unique in their ability to draw together various settings, I want to suggest that their power to captivate us is, at least in part, due to the multiplicity of settings that come together on the field of play. Numerous storylines mean that our gaze can be drawn in any number of different directions at any given time. For the interested observer, the multiplicity of narratives creates a seemingly inexhaustible number of objects for one's attention. And if the foregoing discussion has been compelling, it also means that sports offer us numerous chances to see beauty that might not be obvious to others.[7]

Notes

1 Employing aesthetic terms to describe displays of sportsmanship is not at all unusual. For example, bad displays of sportsmanship are often described as ugly, and I would argue that employing the notion of ugliness here does not simply register our ethical disapproval; it signals an aesthetic disapproval as well. For a defense of the idea that the aesthetic and ethical features of sport can affect each other, see Mumford (2012, ch. 8).

2 Thus, Aristotle writes in the *Metaphysics*: "The chief forms of beauty are order and symmetry and definiteness, which the mathematical sciences demonstrate in a special degree" (1984, p. 1075).

3 For a concise overview of various accounts of beauty, see Sartwell (2016).

4 The original quote can be found in Kant (2000, p. 95).

5 In Section 16 of *The Critique of Judgment* (2000), Kant does make a distinction between free and dependent (or adherent) beauty. Free beauty, according to this distinction, "does not presuppose a concept of what the object is meant to be, whereas adherent beauty does presuppose such a concept" (Allison, 2001, p. 139). Thus, Kant writes that, for example, the

> beauty of a human being (and in this species that of a man, a woman, or a child), the beauty of a horse, or a building (such as a church, a palace, an

arsenal, or a garden house) presuppose a concept of the end that determines what the thing should be, hence a concept of its perfection, and is thus merely adherent beauty.

(2000, p. 114)

But Kant clearly thinks that adherent beauty is a muddled kind of beauty, since "the combination of the good (that is, the way in which the manifold is good for the thing itself, in accordance with its end) with beauty does damage to its purity" (2000, p. 115). If we apply this distinction to the examples I have been considering, then it seems that Kant could allow that a sense of what we are seeing figures into some of our judgments about beauty, even if that sense also undermines the purity of such judgments. A judgment that what I am seeing is beautiful *qua* soccer playing may, therefore, be accurate but not a pure aesthetic judgment, in Kant's rarified sense. I am deeply skeptical about whether the notion of a pure aesthetic judgment is coherent. At the very least, I am deeply skeptical that any judgments that actual human beings make would qualify as pure in the sense that Kant seems to advocate. But even if such judgments are possible, then I would be content to take Kant's point on board and grant that I am giving an account of the muddled and impure aesthetic judgments that many of us employ frequently.

6 For a representative statement of this view, see Darke (2016).

7 Many thanks to the editors for their very helpful suggestions and to various participants in the "The Beautiful Game" conference in Basel (2016) for their challenging questions on this chapter.

References

Allison, H. 2001. Kant's theory of taste. Cambridge, UK: Cambridge University Press.

Aristotle. 1984. Metaphysics. In: Barnes, J. ed. The complete works of Aristotle: The revised Oxford translation. Volume 2. Princeton: Princeton University Press.

Darke, I. 2016. Euro 2016 the worst international tournament since Italia '90. ESPNFC. [Online]. July 11. [Accessed November 7, 2017]. Available from: www.espnfc.us/european-championship/74/blog/post/2911368/euro-2016-was-not-a-success-as-negative-football-takes-hold-in-france.

Dennett, D. 1991. Consciousness explained. New York: Penguin.

Feezell, R. 2006. Sport, play, and ethical reflection. Urbana: University of Illinois Press.

Friedlander, E. 2015. Expressions of judgment: An essay on Kant's aesthetics. Cambridge, MA: Harvard University Press.

Gumbrecht, H. 2006. In praise of athletic beauty. Cambridge, MA: Harvard University Press.

Hume, D. 1988. A treatise of human nature. Oxford: Oxford University Press.

Kant, I. 2000. The critique of the power of judgment. Cambridge, UK: Cambridge University Press.

MacIntyre, A. 1984. After virtue. 2nd ed. Notre Dame: University of Notre Dame Press.

Mumford, S. 2012. Watching sports: Aesthetics, ethics, and emotion. New York: Routledge.

Nehamas, A. 2007. *Only a promise of happiness: The place of beauty in a world of art.* Princeton: Princeton University Press.

Rayner, G. and Brown, O. 2016. Leicester City win Premier League and cost bookies biggest ever payout. *The Telegraph.* [Online]. May 2. [Accessed November 7, 2017]. Available from: www.telegraph.co.uk/news/2016/05/02/leicester-city-win-premier-league-and-cost-bookies-biggest-ever/.

Sartwell, C. 2016. Beauty. In: Zalta, E.N. ed. *The Stanford encyclopedia of philosophy.* [Online]. Winter 2016 ed. Stanford: CSLI. [Accessed November 7, 2017]. Available from: https://plato.stanford.edu/archives/win2016/entries/beauty/.

Zangwill, N. 2003. Beauty. In: Levinson, J. ed. *Oxford handbook of aesthetics.* Oxford: Oxford University Press, pp. 325–343.

Chapter 3

"England 'til I die"

Soccer, national identity, and contemporary art[1]

Daniel Haxall

The sport of soccer has long been celebrated as 'the beautiful game' to reference its artistry and aesthetic appeal. This visual quality includes the fine arts, with the world's most popular sport recurring as a subject in art since the nineteenth century. More recently, contemporary artists utilize the game's iconographic potential to contest the identities projected through soccer, including those of inheritance and citizenry. This essay considers visual representations of soccer and their relationship to nationhood, focusing on England and Germany due to their historical significance and popularity as subjects. While some depict their country's supremacy on the pitch or primacy as custodians of the sport, others examine the embedment of soccer within the character and rituals of their compatriots. Across diverse mediums, artists portray the socialization of fans, place of collective memory in commemorating footballing success, and cultural traditions usurped and reinforced by soccer. Immigration and globalization often disrupt these narratives, complicating the local character or cultural specificity projected onto soccer. Ultimately, by deconstructing the national assumptions built into soccer and its legacy, today's artists illustrate the complexities of identity and role of the sport in its formulation.

Introduction

In 2000, Scottish artist Roderick Buchanan created *Endless Column*, a 15-minute video of teams competing in that summer's European soccer championship. He spliced together television feeds of the contestants lined up to sing their respective national anthems before each match, creating a continuous loop of footballers along a horizontal roll. The camera pans across athletes wearing their country's crest over their hearts while pledging allegiance to their homeland, a ritual that symbolically renders competition a vehicle for nationalism. This aspect of sport has been much discussed by historians, with E.J. Hobsbawm (1990, p. 143) famously writing: "The imagined community of millions seems more real as a team of eleven named people." Indeed, tournaments such as the World Cup reinforce the role of sport in fostering national identity by offering outlets for patriotic display and partisan divide. Like Buchanan, many artists depict this aspect of soccer, rendering the game emblematic of communal pride and jingoism. While some depict their country's supremacy on the pitch or primacy as custodians of the sport, others examine the embedment of soccer within the psyche and rituals of their compatriots.

This chapter will consider contemporary artists who engage the socialization of the body politic as citizens and fans of soccer, the place of collective memory in commemorating footballing success, and the cultural traditions usurped and reinforced by soccer in contemporary life. Artistic representations of soccer in England and Germany provide case studies for exploring the game's semiotic potential, particularly the pitch as extension of the nation. Both countries play central roles in the history of the sport through successful soccer associations and thriving domestic leagues, and each invests heavily in the heritage and academic study of the game through soccer-related museums and arts initiatives. The sport featured prominently in both countries' reconception of nationhood following the world wars and collapse of former empires, influencing artists who affirm and contest such rhetoric. Recent political developments suggest a revival of nativism that complicates definitions of state identity, with populist movements setting nationalism against globalization and the collectivism of the European Union and NATO threatened by the departure of its members. As such, this study examines projections of nationhood through representations of soccer by artists from England and Germany as well as immigrants from abroad, elucidating the complexities of identity and role of soccer in its contemporary formulations.

The 'home of football': soccer and English identity

England prides itself as the 'home of football', a distinction rooted in the sport's origins. The English Football Association codified the first rules of the game in 1863 and history's earliest international match featured England against Scotland in 1872.[2] While England would nurture the game throughout the nineteenth and twentieth centuries, amending its laws and providing some of the most fabled club teams in the world, the national team often fails to match its historical significance. England won the men's World Cup on only one occasion, in 1966 when it also hosted the tournament, and it has never won the European championship. Yet despite failing to win a major international competition for over 50 years, England remains one of the world's major footballing nations thanks to global interest in its Premier League and the game's status within the country's cultural heritage. As such, England plays a major role as custodian of the game, preserving its history and significance through museum initiatives and academic study.

In 1995, a joint endeavor by the English Football Association, Football League, FIFA, and other agencies created the framework for the National Football Museum. Originally opened at Preston's Deepdale Stadium in 2001, the museum relocated to Manchester ten years later. The institution grew to become the biggest soccer museum in the world, attracting approximately 500,000 visitors a year and boasting a massive collection of over 140,000 objects. While the National Football Museum features the artifacts and memorabilia expected of a sports museum, it also owns a diverse selection of artworks and often stages temporary exhibitions to critically reflect on the game and its cultural influence. One of the major collections housed within the National Football Museum is Stuart Roy Clarke's *Homes of Football*, a career-long photo-essay about the game and its place in English culture.[3] Comprising thousands of images, this body of work has appeared across Great Britain, with Clarke (1999, jacket notes) attempting to capture what he considers: "the enduring appeal of the game … football fans in love with their club and the passion of a nation." While this project takes him to varied club levels and grounds, his photographs of international competitions capture the unique forms of patriotism engendered by soccer. In many instances, fans don attire culturally specific to their country's history, such as Italian fans wearing Renaissance costumes while "building up their team" during the European championship, or French supporters painting their faces the colors of their national flag and wearing eighteenth-century musketeer hats.

As an Englishman, Clarke often shoots his national team and their fans as they travel across the globe. For example, in several images from 2004 the English draped Lisbon's Estádio da Luz in the red and white of St. George's Cross, the national flag of England that regained currency in 1996 despite its previous association with far-right politics (Kassimeris, 2010, pp. 225–226; Winner, 2005, pp. 86–87). As hosts of the European championship that summer, England celebrated their role as inventors of the modern game by employing the slogan "Football Comes Home" to advertise the tournament. In addition to marketing the significance of soccer to England's cultural heritage, the competition provided an outlet for promoting an English identity distinct from the 'Celtic fringe' of Northern Ireland, Scotland, and Wales (Heyck, 2002; Weight, 2002; Hechter, 1999). Despite maintaining separate soccer associations and national teams since the nineteenth century, England and Scotland competed each other in a major international tournament for the first time in 1996.[4] As such, the 'Union Jack' flag of the United Kingdom, previously flown by England during sporting events such as the World Cup and Olympics, no longer provided the appropriate specificity, prompting England's return to St. George's Cross that remains in place today (Dunmore, 2010; King, 2006). In fact, some advocate the adoption of a new national anthem to further differentiate England from its neighbors and a majority now identify as

'English' rather than the broader 'British' (Perryman, 2016; Gibbons, 2011). While the concept of 'Englishness' remains contested, scholars consider soccer a symbolic component of the United Kingdom's devolution and the subsequent shift towards nativism (Gibbons and Malcolm, 2017; Perryman, 2008; Kumar, 2003). With increased emphasis on political and economic separatism throughout the United Kingdom over the past few decades—including recent votes for Scottish independence and Britain's exit from the European Union—the projection of identities captured by Clarke reinforces the performative nationalism frequently rehearsed at soccer stadiums.

Regardless of the outcome in derbies or rivalry matches, British nations often consider soccer at the heart of their cultural life. Clarke attests to this position in *Three Pillars of Society* (2015, Figure 3.1), a shot of a recent non-league match between Belper Town FC and FC United of Manchester. The game unfolds in a ground flanked by a church and factory, and Clarke's image incorporates what he called the three "traditional cornerstones of British society" (Clarke, 2015) into one frame: soccer, industry, and religion. While Clarke employed the term 'British' to include places like Scotland where he shoots regularly, the earliest soccer clubs were founded in England through schools, churches, and factories; thus the photograph condenses the origins of the game into its contemporary reality. Over 1000 fans attended the match won by FC United 3–1 that

Figure 3.1 Stuart Roy Clarke, *Three Pillars of Society*, 2015. Courtesy of the artist. Shot on film, part of the *Homes of Football* collection.

day, and Clarke adopts a fan's perspective among those standing in the terraces lining the pitch. The setting, plain advertising hoardings, and traditional stadium configuration establish the quaintness of non-league soccer, a far cry from the spectacle of the Premier League. The historic architecture providing the backdrop for the game suggests the retention of age-old rituals, with Christ Church dating to 1850 and the adjacent East Mill building constructed in 1912, reminding spectators that industry fueled Belper's economy throughout its heyday as a center for textile production. Religion and soccer provided respite from factory work, a triad of labor, leisure, and faith continued through match days at the stadium.

Clarke is not alone in representing the centrality of soccer to English domesticity, with photographer Chris Steele-Perkins elucidating this notion in an image of suburban leisure from 1982 (Figure 3.2). Here, a mother reads the newspaper on a lounger while her daughter circles nearby on a bicycle. Further back in the yard, a father commands a soccer goal as his son practices shooting. This snapshot of everyday life captures the gendered avenues for bonding within English society, with girls only recently encouraged to play soccer and sexism persistent in the sport. In Steele-Perkins's work, the soccer practice occurs alongside the ubiquitous English garden shed, a space traditionally reserved for masculine leisure under the purview of do-it-yourself projects, while the two female subjects remain in the lower register of the photograph. This image also captures the

Figure 3.2 Chris Steele-Perkins, *England*, 1982. © Chris Steele-Perkins/Magnum Photos.

enculturation of children into soccer fandom, where support for club and country becomes socially engrained at home. As Pål Kolstø (2006, p. 676) argues, "[n]ational identity is not an innate quality in human beings, neither is it acquired naturally as one grows up. Like any other identity, national identity has to be learnt."

Where Clarke and Steele-Perkins approach soccer as England's national pastime, Turner Prize-winning artist Mark Wallinger often questions the nostalgia and jingoism attached to the game. In this photograph from 1994 (Figure 3.3), the artist and a friend hold aloft the 'Union Jack' along 'Wembley Way', the approach to London's Wembley Stadium where the English national team plays home matches. This banner bears the artist's name, and the lengthy title of the work establishes Wallinger's precise location: *31 Hayes Court, Camberwell New Road, Camberwell, London, England, Great Britain, Europe, The World, The Solar System, The Galaxy, The Universe* (1994). This Joycean maneuver—Stephen Dedalus similarly established his coordinates in James Joyce's *A Portrait of the Artist as Young Man* (1916)—reveals the degrees of identification established by place, whether local environ or country allegiance. The staging of this existential declaration at a soccer match is significant—it was a World

Figure 3.3 Mark Wallinger, *31 Hayes Court, Camberwell New Road, Camberwell, London, England, Great Britain, Europe, The World, The Solar System, The Galaxy, The Universe*, 1994. Color photograph mounted on aluminum, 320 × 480 cm/126 × 189 in. Courtesy of the artist and Hauser & Wirth.

68 Daniel Haxall

Cup qualifier between England and Poland after all—because Wembley Stadium was originally known as the 'Empire Stadium' when opened by King George V in 1924 to inaugurate the British Empire Exhibition. This ode to England's colonial network became a hallowed ground and eventually a "living museum" in the 1990s, marketed as "the venue of legends" with stadium tours and the opportunity to pose for photographs with memorabilia (Winner, 2005, p. 94). Although replaced by a new stadium in 2007, Wembley was called "the church of football" by Pelé (Sheard, 2005, p. 29) and "mecca of stadiums" by Sir Bobby Moore (Sheard, 2005, p. 32), and continues to host significant cup finals and international matches.

In addition to marking his existence, Wallinger's photograph provides a glimpse into English fandom during the 1990s. Throngs of people navigate Wembley Way, many of them wearing England replica kits with the 'three lions' badge above their heart. This crest dates to the 'Lionheart' King Richard I and his military exploits in the twelfth century, providing the 'Three Lions' nickname for the national team who—by extension—is expected to maintain the courage and ferocity associated with their heraldic emblems. A fan wearing the UMBRO jersey, itself a British sportswear brand, 'photo bombs' the image, staring directly at the camera with outstretched arms while others ascend the ramps to the stadium concourse. White men provide nearly the entire crowd, with women and people of color scarce among those gathered to celebrate England's sporting pastime. Wallinger's banner does not seem out of place in this context since similar *tifos* have become common at soccer matches, and the appearance of his name across the middle of the 'Union Jack' is not unusual either as English fans often include their club allegiance or name on the flags they hang in stadiums. While this artwork predates the emergence of St. George's Cross to represent the English national soccer team, the conflation of British history—whether nostalgia for the British Empire or terrace chants about victories in the world wars—with their nation's unique achievements is common among the English, who frequently link past British accomplishments to contemporary England. In this way, symbols of lineage, however undefined and contradictory, allow for the construction of an identity rooted in historical greatness, with soccer a major outlet for such public declarations (Gibbons, 2014; 2010; Maguire and Poulton, 1999).

Among the famous matches staged at the original Wembley Stadium was the 1966 men's World Cup final, won by the hosts over West Germany. This match remains entrenched within England's national consciousness as the country's lone international championship, even if debates about the winning goal persist until today.[5] This triumph has, according to David Goldblatt (2006, p. 453), "allowed the nation to live more comfortably with its post-imperial decline," and the magazine *When Saturday Comes* (Lyons and Ronay, 2006, p. 442) considers the 1966

World Cup "an object of fetishist nostalgia." While this nostalgia colors "English perceptions of the game and their own status in it" (Winner, 2005, pp. 104–105), the victory owes much to the linesman officiating the game. With the game tied in extra time, English striker Geoff Hurst fired a shot off the crossbar that ricocheted down and bounced off the goal line. After conferring with the side judge, the referee ruled the ball had crossed the line, resulting in an England goal despite the protestation of their German opponents. Hurst went on to score an insurance goal late in extra time, his third of the day, to deliver a 4–2 win and the World Cup trophy.

Wallinger, who grew up a West Ham United fan, watched this famous match on television as a child, in fact the 1966 World Cup bears distinction as the first time the tournament had been broadcast live globally (Chisari, 2006). In honor of the momentous, albeit controversial victory, he created, *They think it's all over ... it is now!* (1988, Figure 3.4). Titled after Kenneth Wolstenholme's famous account of Hurst's final goal for BBC television, this work consists of a Subbuteo game placed atop a simulated stone plinth. Here, Wallinger recreated the final goal of the match, preserving a sporting moment in the language of statuary and memorials.

Figure 3.4 Mark Wallinger, *They think it's all over ... it is now*, 1988. Paint, MDF, Subbuteo football game, 131.5 × 148.5 × 109.5 cm/51 3/4 × 58 1/2 × 43 in. Courtesy of the artist and private collection, Nottingham.

70   Daniel Haxall

For him, the final was "the last time that patriotism was an innocent feeling" (Herbert, 2011, p. 41), a naïveté evoked through his appropriation of a popular children's game. Such nostalgia, both for the World Cup victory and youthful play, offered Wallinger escape from the politics that corrupted displays of nationalism in the Thatcher years and subsequent decades. "It was a memorializing of my own memory," he noted (Herbert, 2011, p. 41), one that represented the decline of England as much as its apogee. The dark pedestal evokes funerary monuments rather than triumphant sporting statues, and its coffered panels provide an unexpectedly severe base for the setting of a children's game. Does the conclusion suggested by the title refer to the football match, the British Empire, or postwar affluence and peace? Wallinger finds the jingoism attached to sporting triumphs problematic and fraught with contradiction, a critique he continued in other paintings that reference class struggles and exploitation through football.[6]

Wallinger returned to the 1966 World Cup with his exhibition *The Russian Linesman* (2009), which featured *They think it's all over ... it is now!* among other works that explore the limits of memory and knowledge. The title stems from the misidentification of Tofik Bakhramov, the official from Azerbaijan who ruled Hurst's shot a goal in 1966. As Wallinger (2009, p. 7) explained, "In the West, the adjective 'Russian' was a blanket of ignorance thrown over the whole USSR." Thus, to German fans, the 'Russian' Bakhramov erred on the call, providing Wallinger with an exhibition title rooted in flawed perception and contested perspectives. When he exhibited, *They think it's all over ... it is now!* in Hamburg, Germany, in November 1989, audiences immediately understood the artwork's reference, repeatedly asking him if the Subbuteo game reenacted Hurst's controversial goal (Wallinger, 2009, p. 119). To Wallinger, the sculpture evoked a loss of innocence during a moment of national triumph, while German museum goers viewed the same event with contempt and questioned its legitimacy.

"We are great again": soccer and the rebirth of Germany

Whereas English fans credit themselves for inventing the modern game, Germany stands out as the most successful footballing nation in Europe. Their record of four men's World Cup titles and three European championships is unmatched, yet the fragmentation of Germany lends it a unique character and history. Parts of the country have been skeptical of the game, with soccer prohibited in Bavaria until 1913 and some opposing football because of the emphasis placed on sport and physicality by the Nazi regime (Eisenberg, 1999; Gebauer, 1999). Yet the 1954 men's World Cup produced the 'Miracle of Berne', when the Federal Republic of Germany

(FRG) upset Hungary 3–2 to win the title. This victory galvanized a sense of nationalism with the newspaper *Bild* proclaiming "We Are Great Again" and many associating footballing success with the 'miraculous' socioeconomic rebuilding of West Germany following World War II. As Crolley and Hand (2006, p. 71) suggest, the everyday "working-class" character of the team became celebrated and soccer allowed Germany to boast of the "discipline, collective effort, industriousness and speedy, ruthless efficiency" that had been corrupted by the Nazi party. Industrial and economic prosperity, coupled with innovative approaches to player development and league regulations, propelled Germany to their current position as geopolitical and footballing leaders, inspiring many attempts to replicate their success on and off the pitch (Honigstein, 2015).

While Germany founded their national soccer museum later than England—the Deutsches Fussball Museum opened in Dortmund in 2015— the country launched an unprecedented program of cultural events to coincide with the men's World Cup when it hosted the tournament in 2006. The government invested over €30 million on an extensive series of concerts, films, theatrical productions, and art exhibitions throughout the country. Over a half dozen museum shows appeared in the cities of Berlin, Leipzig, Hamburg, Cologne, Munich, and Nuremberg, all of which hosted tournament matches. The focus of these shows varied—including global icons, referees, and information systems—and two in particular concentrated on art. *Rundlederwelten* (or "round leather worlds"), staged at the Martin-Gropius-Bau in Berlin, featured several works celebrating the West German team led by Franz Beckenbauer that won the 1974 men's World Cup. Despite controversy surrounding player bonuses, the squad captivated artists like Volker Schrank, who photographed the team as *Gesammelte Helden [A Collection of Heroes]* (2003–2005, Figure 3.5) 30 years after their victory. He created individual portraits of his childhood idols wearing their national team kit or warmup, with the *Deutscher Fussball Bund* logo prominent on their chest. Shot from below eye level, the shallow depth of field somewhat obscures the margins of each photo, with the blurred perimeter drawing our attention to the countenance of these middle-aged icons. Despite the large format of the portraits, Schrank was inspired by trading cards and wanted to capture the mythmaking and hero worship generated by media and popular culture (Bullinger, 2005). Indeed, these men are larger than life with no identifying traits beyond their football jersey. While portrayed separately, the stars of the 1974 men's World Cup winners will forever be identified as members of the team and—by extension—the re-emergent German state.

Werner Büttner also celebrated the triumphant 1974 squad in his *Cultural Imperialist Rascals' Trick* (1987, Figure 3.6). The artist was 20 years old when he watched the final on television, and he dubbed the heroics of the "wonder team" a "rascals' trick" for their victory over the much-fancied

Figure 3.5 Volker Schrank, *Gesammelte Helden: Beckenbauer (A Collection of Heroes: Beckenbauer)*, 2003–2005. Ditone print on copperplate paper, 130×100 cm. Courtesy of the artist.

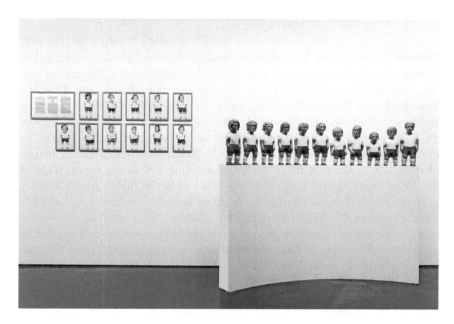

Figure 3.6 Werner Büttner, *Cultural Imperialist Rascals' Trick*, 1987. Eleven figures made of rosewood, painting, each 45 × 10 × 10 cm. Courtesy of the artist and Marlborough Gallery.

Dutch. In a statement accompanying this work, Büttner (2005, pp. 82–85) praised the "iron will" of his "fast and disciplined" compatriots and explained how the inspiration for the piece stemmed from a friend's research trip to the Marquesas Islands in the Pacific Ocean. Büttner sketched 11 members of the West German team and asked his friend to commission a wood carver from the Marquesas to sculpt work based on the drawings. Both the original sketches and completed statues evince a loose, naïve quality, producing stylized portraits distinct from Schrank's high-resolution digital prints. Small in scale, 45 cm or just under 18 inches tall, and placed on a tall plinth, these portraits commemorate the *Mannschaft* albeit in an intimate and nearly innocent manner. By commissioning a self-taught artist and providing him with unrefined drawings, Büttner creates an expressionistic homage rooted in the modernist ideals of primitivism. This maneuver eschews the grand rhetoric and neoclassical idealism embraced by the Third Reich, thereby connecting Büttner's heroes to a pre-Nazi trajectory of expressionism, woodcarving, and folk art. In this way, the artist links Germany's art history with its footballing legacy, aligning Beckenbauer, Müller, and their teammates with Kirchner, Riemenschneider, and the pantheon of great German artists. The 'cultural imperialism' referenced in the title clearly refers to his employment of the

74   Daniel Haxall

Marquesan sculptor, but it also acknowledges the national identity born of Germany's artistic and sporting traditions.

Another art exhibition staged for the 2006 men's World Cup was *Ballkünstler* ("ball artist"), which opened in Leipzig, the city where the German Football Association was founded in 1900. While the nation had been unified for over 15 years by the time of the World Cup, Leipzig's location in the former German Democratic Republic (GDR) presented a challenge for artists and curators hoping to acknowledge the footballers of the East German national teams without being divisive. For example, in his *Player* series (2006, Figure 3.7), Albrecht Tübke photographed the heroes of the GDR squad that defeated West Germany 1–0 in the group stage of the 1974 men's World Cup. Shot 30 years after the match like Schrank's portraits of the FRG team, Tübke diverged from his compatriot by depicting the men at full-length in their own clothes. No jerseys or accessories identify the men as athletes beyond the series' title, instead they appear as everyday individuals. In fact, the word *spieler* remains ambiguous and can mean "gambler" as well as "player." The photographs were staged near Leipzig's stadium that hosted World Cup matches, yet the propaganda associated with the GDR's famous victory remains absent. The stadium is not directly visible and these men have entered the latter stages of their lives. They are no longer youthful footballers, but Germans who witnessed reconstruction and unification, and their humanized depiction removes the political rhetoric attached to their athletic performance. Tübke honors their achievements on the pitch but only as a referent, instead the series suggests how events of the past, even those celebrated as significant, eventually become consigned to history.

Similarly, Wiebke Grösch commemorates the scorer of the winning goal in that fateful East–West Germany contest, Jürgen Sparwasser. In 2006, Grösch arranged to have Sparwasser reenact his famous strike, kicking a muddy football against a goal-shaped panel within the Leipzig Museum of Art. The imprint of the shot remains on the surface of the panel, interrupting the minimalist white painting with the smudge of the ball's impact. However, unlike most paintings constructed and preserved for permanence, this mark appears tenuous and unlikely to maintain longevity. A gesture that carried such profound political implications for both sides of the German state ends up but residue of a game. Although Grösch's celebration of Sparwasser could be read as a contentious maneuver, rehearsing discord and animosity through its performance, the context establishes the goal as a part of a shared history. The World Cup was staged across a unified country after all, and Grösch and Tübke created inclusive narratives appropriate for the realities of contemporary Germany.

These realities, and the embedment of football within German identity, constitute Thomas Hoepker's portfolio of photographs created at the 2006 men's World Cup. A member of the celebrated photographic collective

Figure 3.7 Albrecht Tübke, *Spieler (Hans-Jürgen Kreische)*, 2006. C-print, 38 × 47 cm. Courtesy of the artist.

Magnum, Hoepker has shot soccer across the globe since the 1960s, ranging from boys juggling a ball on the beaches of Rio de Janeiro to international matches in the United Arab Emirates. In 1963, he photographed five children playing with a soccer ball in front of the Berlin Wall. Shot from a low angle to accentuate the height of the imposing barrier, Hoepker set the innocence of play against the severe restrictions of Cold War Germany. Yet the work he produced during the summer of 2006 captured celebrations of patriotism unthinkable in the decades following World War II with the segregation of the German state.

In Munich, he shot a postcard display stand advertising German culture to tourists (Figure 3.8), including Munich's architectural landmarks, Pope Benedict XVI wrapped in a soccer scarf adorned with Germany's colors while holding aloft two balls, merchandise featuring the stadiums built to host the World Cup, a *Hofbräuhaus* image of bratwursts, pretzels, and beer. German identity, this image suggests, hinges upon food and drink, history, religion, and soccer. Further images elucidate this point while centering on the intense nationalism generated by the World Cup and other such competitions. At one of Munich's famous beer gardens, a man in lederhosen and *Gamsbart* hat shakes hands with a compatriot clad in the national team kit, scarf, and flag. The contemporary fan dons a faux Mohawk colored red, yellow, and black, paralleling the extravagant

Figure 3.8 Thomas Hoepker, *Munich, Day before the opening of the Soccer World Cup, scene from downtown. Brochures on newsstand in Kaufingerstrasse,* 2006. © Thomas Hoepker/Magnum Photos.

plumage from the traditional headpiece worn by the older gentleman, suggesting the contemporizing of native fashions. In public viewing parties, fans, again decorated with the German tricolor and other patriotic emblems, cover their hearts as they watch the anthem sung on television, reflecting the 'new patriotism' that emerged during the *Sommermärchen* (or "summer fairy tale") that was the 2006 World Cup. As Uli Hesse claimed, the country's ability to stage a major international sporting event, as well as field a squad of diverse ethnicities united as one nation, changed its perception of selfhood: "More than six decades after the war, Germany was not only reunified, modern, friendly and peaceful, it was also a normal western European society in that it had become truly multi-cultural" (Hesse, 2015, p. 295). While the images of soccer-viewing parties filled with thousands of fans before the Brandenburg Gate suggested the birth of a *new* Germany, the recent emergence of far-right organizations such as the terroristic National Socialist Underground and populist Alternative for Germany, indicates how the concept of German nationhood remains contested.

Outside perspectives: immigration and the globalized field

Despite the widespread multiculturalism of today's globalized age, nativism retains prevalence in many regions with immigration increasingly restricted by lawmakers. However, artists born outside England and Germany offer unique perspectives on the footballing cultures and national identity of both countries, depicting the global impact of soccer from the expatriate's point of view. For example, in 2007 Paul Pfeiffer staged *The Saints*, a multimedia installation comprising footage of the 1966 World Cup which he considered a "very loaded, sacred, nationalist text" (Lingwood, 2009, p. 52). Known for manipulating video of sporting events to comment upon the sport spectacle and its ramifications, Pfeiffer developed *The Saints* to inaugurate the construction of the new Wembley Stadium. Although American, Pfeiffer gravitated towards the project because of the multivalent significance attached to the World Cup final and its place within the collective imagination of both England and Germany:

> There are different ways of looking at the match. So many layers of meaning are already condensed into it. Of course, some aspects are only meaningful to serious football fans. There's also the history of the British Empire in it, and the ghosts of World War II, and the history of video becoming a global medium. There are definite religious overtones as well.
>
> (Pfeiffer, cited in Lingwood, 2009, p. 50)

He originally hoped to install the project in the new Wembley itself; however, his proposal was denied by stadium authorities so Pfeiffer utilized a warehouse adjacent to the arena. As visitors entered the banal industrial building they were greeted by a cavernous, empty space with 16 speakers suspended from the ceiling trellis above. The roar of a crowd filled the warehouse with the songs and chants performed by fans at the World Cup in 1966. The looping soundtrack included the national anthems for both England (*God Save the Queen*) and Germany (*Deutschlandlied*), as well as *Rule Britannia, When the Saints Go Marching In, Jerusalem*, and others. These declarations of allegiance linked fandom with citizenry, thereby structuring identity through sporting terms, an aspect of sporting events like the World Cup that fascinates Pfeiffer. "Within our lifetime our general awareness has gone global, but in our day-to-day lives I think we're still reliant on 20th century categories like national identity to understand our place in the world," he explained, "[i]t still feels right to say I know who I am because I belong to this nation or because I'm a fan of that team" (Lingwood, 2009, pp. 54–56). Indeed, the media rhetoric surrounding international soccer tournaments often reinforces national values through historical or cultural references.

While visitors to Pfeiffer's installation would understand its proximity to a revered sporting site, the building itself lacked the modern flourishes of the new Wembley, ranging from its towering arch to first-class amenities. The only feature that interrupts the otherwise empty warehouse is a self-contained room at the structure's far end. Here, a small monitor projects from the unadorned white wall, playing a television broadcast of the 1966 match (Figure 3.9). The video feed maintains its proper black-and-white format; however, Pfeiffer manipulated the footage and removed the commentary announcing the game as well as the ball, referees, and every athlete on the pitch except for one: Geoff Hurst, the scorer of the infamous winning goal as well as the final tally immortalized in Wolstenholme's now absent call. The resulting video confuses audiences because Hurst's movements lack the context of the game to frame his performance. At times, he seems to walk aimlessly at the periphery of the screen, in other instances he sprints towards objectives that no longer remain knowable. The absence of the ball further confounds traditional soccer spectatorship and the occasional fall or gesticulation renders Hurst's activities absurd, particularly as they occur within a rowdy stadium filled to capacity (White, 2009, p. 28). The disconnect between the crowd chants echoing throughout the warehouse and the behavior on screen furthers the feeling of estrangement, as Pfeiffer ruptures the visual and auditory frames that make athletic competition comprehensible and, by extension, meaningful.

After encountering the Hurst footage, viewers enter a smaller enclosed room with a large split-screen airing two different films: on the left, a contemporary theater filled with 1000 Filipinos chanting in unison, and on the

Figure 3.9 Paul Pfeiffer, *The Saints*, 2007. Installation views by Thierry Bal and video stills courtesy of the artist. Commissioned and produced by Artangel, London.

right, the original television broadcast of the 1966 final (Figure 3.10). The two feeds contrast greatly in image quality and color, while the room's audio remains devoid of commentary and derives from archival recordings of the Wembley crowd. Pfeiffer recorded the Filipino audience in an IMAX theater in Manila, teaching them how to recreate the noise from the original match, including singing the national anthems. Afterwards, he combined the historical English and current Philippine soundtracks into the singular "score" playing throughout the warehouse. Four decades separated these crowds and Pfeiffer decided to use the contemporary performers to ground this event in the present as well as the past. He combatted nostalgia for the old Wembley by reinventing match day rituals and rewriting footballing history, hiring fans with no allegiance to England or rooting interest in the World Cup final to provide its pageantry. In this way, *The Saints* reconsiders the motivations behind fan behavior, with Pfeiffer questioning if the desire to belong to a community influences supporter culture as much as participation in the sport spectacle itself.

Figure 3.10 Paul Pfeiffer, *The Saints*, 2007. Installation views by Thierry Bal and video stills courtesy of the artist. Commissioned and produced by Artangel, London.

Pfeiffer elected to record the contemporary soundtrack in Manila because of financial considerations and his personal background. Born in Honolulu, Hawaii, but raised in the Philippines, he wanted to address the state's history of supporting cheap mass labor. Thus, *The Saints* not only engages the patriotism attached to mass sport but also its colonizing power in the age of globalization. While never a British protectorate, the Philippines were governed by the Spanish for centuries before periods of American and Japanese rule. The act of teaching Filipinos about soccer history parallels the global branding of 'the beautiful game', as the English Premier League broadcasts its matches worldwide for billions of dollars and clubs play exhibitions in emerging markets such as the United States and Asia. While the British Empire represented by the old Wembley no longer exists, a new form of economic imperialism remains in place through soccer, one represented by the modernized Wembley and its retractable roof and corporate suites. England might not return to its former glory, yet nostalgia preserves the event as testimony to English exceptionalism. "I'm fascinated with old myths," Pfeiffer explained, "the way they become obsolete and yet continue to live in people's minds" (Lingwood, 2009, p. 56).

Whether athletic competitions, fictional dramas, or news reports, television remains a major propagator of today's mythologies. As such, Pfeiffer utilizes this medium as a 'found object', exploring how knowledge and memory are shaped by the media. His edits to the World Cup lay bare the constructed nature of reality as well as its shortcomings and manipulations. Video footage and slow-motion replays fail to settle longstanding disputes surrounding Hurst's goal, and Pfeiffer exploits the limitations of technology to critique what Eduardo Galeano (2014) called the "telecracy," our mediated consumption of soccer through television. Viewers' experience of the game depends upon network demand, ranging from kickoff time and advertising intervals to commentary and transmission quality, and our knowledge of the game derives entirely from the broadcast. A replay might prove that a player was offside or the ball crossed the touchline, yet the perspective of the camera could miss an event away from the ball or the network might cut away from a pitch invasion. Ultimately, Pfeiffer reminds viewers of the fabricated nature of spectatorial knowledge by removing players from videos and erasing commentary from television feeds.

In addition to confronting us with the absence of the forces structuring our realities, these acts of negation heighten the power of images and sounds, or what Pfeiffer calls the "aura" of media events like the World Cup. Rather than suppressing or reducing the potency of the sport spectacle, Pfeiffer attempts to "intensify the affective power of images, to intensify the fetish" (Lingwood, 2009, p. 58). Indeed, the fragmented video feeds resemble Jean Baudrillard's (1981, pp. 94–97) description of the "fetish-beauty," the abstraction of a sought-after object into a system of representation. Since the fetish refers to a surrogate, or proxy for that which is desired, techniques of fragmentation and assemblage are often employed to strip the object of its totality and power, thereby rendering it safe for consumption. The transferal of power or agency provided by the fetish perhaps explains how patriotism becomes attached to the soccer pitch, because a victory for the national team could bolster the nation and in the case of the 1966 World Cup, the British Empire symbolically sails again.

In 2007, the National Gallery of Germany acquired *The Saints*, putting the installation on display in Berlin. Where the presentation of *The Saints* prompted German museum goers to consider nationalism and collective memory, Esra Ersen's *Im Strafraum (In the Penalty Area)* (2001, Figure 3.11) confronted them with immigration and the Turkish diaspora through soccer. Featured in the exhibition *Rundlederwelten* as part of the cultural programming for the 2006 men's World Cup, the installation also appeared in two shows in Austria, with these sites of display amplifying the work's meaning. Originally from Ankara and now based in Berlin, Ersen has exhibited regularly in Germany and her experiences inspired *Im Strafraum*, a work rooted in the perspectives of the marginalized and displaced. A video is projected onto the far end of a gallery wall that chronicles "three young women of Mediterranean origin" (Kosova, 2005, pp. 90–91) as they work with an oversized German flag in a room with artificial turf floor. The film follows the women as they unfurl the banner and cut away the black panel of the tricolor standard with scissors.

Figure 3.11 Esra Ersen, *Im Strafraum (In the Penalty Area)*, 2001. Video installation, mixed media, variable dimensions. Installation view, OK Center for Contemporary Art, Linz, Austria, 2005. Photo: Otto Saxinger.

As Erden Kosova (2005, pp. 90–91) notes, this gesture initially "seems militant" as an affront to German nationalism, yet as the process unfolds, we watch the women carefully reconstruct a new flag with only the red and yellow stripes. After piecing together this new standard with a sewing machine, the women stretch the flag across the floor and lie down on it. This banner refers to the soccer club Galatasaray, Turkey's most successful team who won a remarkable 'quadruple' of UEFA Europa League, UEFA Super Cup, Turkish Süper Lig, and Turkish Cup during the 1999–2000 season. Ersen was moved by the way Turkish immigrants across Europe celebrated the team's accomplishments and how sporting success validated the identity of this diaspora. An audio feed accompanying the video consists of Ersen interviewing Turkish emigres based in Germany, and their experiences provide a poignant soundtrack to the construction of a *tifo* connected to both their ancestral and adopted homes.

Ersen erected a faux soccer pitch as part of the installation, complete with artificial turf and goals. However, the two nets do not face each other in typical formation, instead they are stacked with one goal inside the other. Rather than oppositional frames, these goals are interconnected, symbolizing the duality of immigrant identity. The touchline furthers this projection of doubled selfhood, printed with three words describing states of itinerancy: *deplasman*, a Turkish expression for "away" used within soccer to designate an away match; *displacement*, the English word for removal or departure; and *deplaziert*, a Germanic term for being misplaced. This meditation on belonging continued through a scoreboard with clearly demarcated 'home' and 'guest' categories, making viewers consider their origins and loyalties as well as sites of exclusion. For her exhibition at the Offenes Kulturhaus in Linz, Austria (2005–2006), Ersen hung the reconstructed Galatasaray *tifo* above the museum's main entry, marking a national cultural site with an outsider's flag as if staging a military or political occupation. The huge scale of the banner, it cascaded down multiple stories of the façade, recalls the behavior of fans who hang their club's colors on their homes or vehicles, as well as the celebration of patriotic holidays through similar acts of display. While *Im Strafraum* explores the problematic relationship between Germany and its Turkish immigrants, its exhibition in Austrian museums adds a further twist to the project, positioning Turkish footballing success within histories of Ottoman and Habsburg rivalry as well as contemporary migration patterns that include Austria.

Where Ersen reflects upon the Turkish diaspora in Germany, the Moroccan-born, London-based artist Hassan Hajjaj draws upon the collision of cultures that occurs via globalization, especially in international cities like London populated by diverse peoples. In particular, he utilizes soccer references to revise histories of colonialism, Orientalism, and Islamophobia. In recent photographs, he juxtaposed the logos of sportswear manufacturers Nike and Adidas with clothing evocative of Islamic cultures, representing the intersection of consumption and tradition that occurs via soccer and its branded empires. In *Nike v. Adidas* (2010, Figure 3.12), Hajjaj created custom soccer kits, adding the iconic Nike swoosh and Adidas three stripe pattern to the *djellaba*, or hooded gown, and *niqab*, or face veil, characteristic of the Arab world. While such attire has been stereotyped and demonized by the West, Hajjaj fashions it into stylish sportswear that might appeal to broader consumer desire. The idea of opposing Nike and Adidas soccer teams also acknowledges the rivalry among the American and German companies as they vie for control of the marketplace. In *Feet Ball* (2006), Hajjaj emblazons the Nike logo on the *babouche*, or Moroccan slipper, while the competing athletes wear Adidas socks. Framed by Arabic script and the date of the artwork rendered according to the Muslim calendar, 1427, the work presents a colorful intermingling of cultural trends brought together by sport.

In photographs from 2007 Hajjaj juxtaposed sportswear with couture, depicting someone kicking a Louis Vuitton ball. Vuitton created a limited-edition soccer ball for the 1998 men's World Cup hosted in France that came with a leather shoulder strap and currently sells for approximately €1,000 at auction. Considering the price and rarity of these objects—a limited run of 3000 were produced—only the affluent would dare play with such an opulent ball. Perhaps the subject of Hajjaj's photographs is a

Figure 3.12 Hassan Hajjaj, *Nike v. Adidas*, 2010/1431. © Hassan Hajjaj. Courtesy of The Third Line Gallery, Dubai, U.A.E.

footballer, as Louis Vuitton remains a brand coveted by athletes as evidenced by a photo essay published on *The Telegraph*'s website (2013) featuring star players including David Beckham, Gareth Bale, Cristiano Ronaldo, and Wayne Rooney carrying their Louis Vuitton luggage. Yet the *babouches* and patterned setting of the photograph establish a North African or Middle Eastern locale, a possible allusion to the investment in soccer by Qatar and the United Arab Emirates, countries who employ soccer as a form of "soft power" to enhance their international prominence (East, 2015). In this context, owning Manchester City or Paris Saint-Germain functions like a Louis Vuitton handbag in rendering prestige—albeit on a far larger scale. However, the photographs potentially carry a different implication for Africa, as the act of kicking a French luxury good could project anti-colonial animosity wherein Morocco rejects the Treaty of Fez and other spheres of European influence.

In fact, much of Hajjaj's work contests histories of subjugation, and *Just Do It* (2006, Figure 3.13) challenges the conventions of European

Figure 3.13 Hassan Hajjaj, *Just Do It*, 2006/1427. C-type, 109 × 84 cm/42 7/8 × 33 1/8 in. Edition of ten plus three AP. © Hassan Hajjaj. Courtesy of The Third Line Gallery, Dubai, U.A.E.

portraiture that represented the North African female body as available, satisfying the desires and fantasies of the colonizing West. Here, Hajjaj prevents the Orientalizing of the portrait, veiling his subject before a plain backdrop rather than exposing her in an exotic interior. The role of this woman changes from Odalisque or sexual object to athlete, as she wears a jacket and *djellaba* with the badge of the Royal Moroccan Football Federation and *niqab* adorned with Nike's trademark and "Just Do It" slogan. The Morocco women's national team debuted in 1998, and despite struggling continentally and only twice qualifying for the African championships, they advanced to the Arab Cup final in 2006. While systemic sexism persists in hindering the growth of women's soccer, particularly in the Arab world (Matuska, 2010), Hajjaj's work suggests how Islam no longer provides the basis for banning female participation. In fact, sportswear manufacturer Hummel recently released jersey designs for the Afghanistan women's national team, complete with hijab. The press release (Hummel, 2016) announcing this kit connected it to the "brand's mission to Change the World through Sport," and in a similar way, soccer provides the platform for Hajjaj, Ersen, and others to deconstruct the ideas of identity built into the game, especially in places like England and Germany where soccer defines national character.

Conclusion

Before the 2006 World Cup in Germany, news agencies and public service campaigns implored English fans to refrain from invoking World War II at matches (Craven, 2005). These concerns were fueled not only by the countries' contentious political and footballing histories, but the songs chanted by English fans celebrating military victories over Germany, including "Ten German Bombers." The legacy of war perhaps explains artists' fascination with this soccer rivalry, while their contemporary differences further intensify the nationalistic sentiment attached to sport. England recently voted to leave the European Union that Germany helps lead, and both countries continue to negotiate new identities following decades of military, industrial, and economic upheaval. As evidenced in contemporary art, the soccer pitch often serves as a site for expressions of patriotism and the aspirations of the state, while its history sustains cultures deeply invested in sport. However, immigration and globalization often disrupt these narratives, complicating the local character or cultural specificity projected onto soccer. Ultimately, by deconstructing the national assumptions built into soccer and its legacy, today's artists illustrate the complexities of identity and role of soccer in its formulation.

Notes

1 This essay was supported by the Office of Grants and Sponsored Projects and Department of Art and Art History at Kutztown University of Pennsylvania.
2 Many versions of the game predated the 1863 London-based Football Association, for example a set of laws were published in Sheffield in 1858. However, earlier efforts to organize the game failed to maintain the longevity and influence of the FA, therefore 1863 stands as the commonly accepted date for the "creation" of modern soccer (Goldblatt, 2006, pp. 20–49).
3 While Clarke shoots in Scotland as well, the vast majority of his oeuvre focuses on England.
4 While England regularly played Scotland, Wales, and Northern Ireland in the annual British Home Championships from 1884–1984, the 1996 European Championship marked the first major FIFA or UEFA tournament in which they met.
5 For more on the cultural significance of the 1966 men's World Cup, see Hughson (2016) or Perryman (2016).
6 For a discussion of Wallinger's paintings that address football violence and class issues, see Haxall (2017).

References

Baudrillard, J. 1981. For a critique of the political economy of the sign. Candor: Telos Press.
Bullinger, M. ed. 2005. Gesammelte Helden. Die Fußballweltmeister 1974—und in uns glühen die Erinnerungen. Heidelberg: Edition Braus.
Büttner, W. 2005. The rascals' trick. Rundlederwelten [Special issue]. Anstoss (3), pp. 82–85.
Chisari, F. 2006. When football went global: Televising the 1966 World Cup. Historical Social Research. 31(1), pp. 42–54.
Clarke, S.R. 1999. The homes of football: The passion of a nation. London: Little, Brown and Company.
Clarke, S.R. 2015. Caption for: Three pillars of society, Belper Town vs FC United, England, 2015. [Online]. [Accessed January 28, 2017]. Available from: http://homesoffootball.co.uk/items/three-pillars-of-society/.
Craven, N. 2005. Don't mention the war! The Daily Mail. [Online]. December 10. [Accessed January 28, 2017]. Available from: www.dailymail.co.uk/news/article-371234/Dont-mention-war.html.
Crolley, L. and Hand, D. 2006. Football and European identity: Historical narratives through the press. London: Routledge.
Dunmore, T. 2010. England and the St George's Cross: Writing English identity on the flag. Pitch Invasion. [Online]. June 30. [Accessed January 28, 2017]. Available from: https://pitchinvasion.net/england-and-the-st-georges-cross-writing-english-identity-on-the-flag/.
East, S. 2015. Middle East millions fueling European football. CNN. [Online]. January 12. [Accessed October 8, 2017]. Available from: http://edition.cnn.com/2015/01/12/football/qatar-uae-sponsor-football-europe/.
Eisenberg, C. 1999. Histoire du football professional en Allemagne. In: Hélal, H. and Mignon, P. eds. Football: Jeu et société. Paris: INSEP, pp. 163–188.

Galeano, E. 2014. Soccer in sun and shadow. 4th ed. [e-book]. New York: Open Road.

Gebauer, G. 1999. Les trois dates de l'équipe d'Allemagne de football. In: Hélal, H. and Mignon, P. eds. Football: Jeu et société. Paris: INSEP, pp. 101–111.

Gibbons, T. 2010. Contrasting representations of Englishness during FIFA World Cup finals. Sport in History. 30(3), pp. 422–446.

Gibbons, T. 2011. English national identity and the national football team: The view of contemporary English fans. Soccer & Society. 12(6), pp. 865–879.

Gibbons, T. 2014. English national identity and football fan culture: Who are ya? Farnham, Surrey: Ashgate.

Gibbons, T. and Malcolm, D. eds. 2017. Sport and English national identity in a "disunited kingdom." London: Routledge.

Goldblatt, D. 2006. The ball is round: A global history of football. London: Penguin.

Haxall, D. 2017. The ugly side of the beautiful game: Picturing violence in soccer. In: Hovey, C., White, J. and Werntz, M. eds. Sports and violence: History, theory, practice. Newcastle upon Tyne: Cambridge Scholars, pp. 2–21.

Hechter, M. 1999. Internal colonialism: The Celtic fringe in British national development. Piscataway: Transaction.

Herbert, M. 2011. Mark Wallinger. London: Thames & Hudson.

Hesse, U. 2015. Tor! The story of German football. 3rd ed. London: When Saturday Comes Books.

Heyck, W.T. 2002. A history of the peoples of the British Isles: From 1870 to the present. London: Routledge.

Hobsbawm, E.J. 1990. Nations and nationalism since 1780: Programme, myth, reality. Cambridge, UK: Cambridge University Press.

Honigstein, R. 2015. Das Reboot: How German soccer reinvented itself and conquered the world. New York: Nation.

Hughson, J. 2016. England and the 1966 World Cup: A cultural history. Manchester: Manchester University Press.

Hummel. 2016. Hummel presents new Afghanistan football shirt with Hijab. [Online]. March 8. [Accessed January 28, 2017]. Available from: www.hummel.net/US/news/hummel-presents-new-afghanistan-football-shirt-with-hijab.

Joyce, J. 1916. A portrait of the artist as young man. New York: B.W. Huebsch.

Kassimeris, C. 2010. Football comes home: Symbolic identities in European football. Lanham: Lexington Books.

King, A. 2006. Nationalism and sport. In: Delanty, G. and Kumar, K. eds. The Sage handbook of nations and nationalism. London: Sage, pp. 249–259.

Kolstø, P. 2006. National symbols as signs of unity and division. Ethnic and Racial Studies. 29(4), pp. 676–701.

Kosova, E. 2005. Esra Ersen. Rundlederwelten. [Special issue]. Anstoss (3), pp. 90–91.

Kumar, K. 2003. The making of English identity. Cambridge, UK: Cambridge University Press.

Lingwood, J. 2009. Paul Pfeiffer in conversation with James Lingwood. In: Schmitz, B. ed. Paul Pfeiffer: The Saints. Berlin: Staatliche Museen zu Berlin, pp. 49–58.

Lyons, A. and Ronay, B. eds. 2006. When Saturday comes: The half decent football book. London: Penguin.

Maguire, J. and Poulton, E. 1999. European identity politics in Euro 96: Invented traditions and national habitus codes. International Review for the Sociology of Sport. 34(1), pp. 17–29.

Matuska, N. 2010. The development of women's football in Morocco. Middle East Institute. [Online]. May 2. [Accessed January 28, 2017]. Available from: www.mei.edu/content/development-womens-football-morocco.

Perryman, M. ed. 2008. Imagined nation: England after Britain. London: Lawrence & Wishart.

Perryman, M. 2016. They thought it was all over. In: Perryman, M. ed. 1966 and not all that. London: Repeater, pp. 62–106.

Sheard, R. 2005. Stadium: architecture for the new global culture. Singapore: Periplus.

The Telegraph. 2013. Football's love affair with Louis Vuitton. [Online]. July 31. [Accessed January 28, 2017]. Available from: http://fashion.telegraph.co.uk/galleries/TMG10213612/Footballs-love-affair-with-Louis-Vuitton.html.

Wallinger, M. 2009. The Russian linesman. London: Hayward.

Weight, R. 2002. Patriots: National identity in Britain 1940–2000. London: Macmillan.

White, I. 2009. Situation cinema: Models of spectacle, empty spaces and The Saints. In: Schmitz, B. ed. Paul Pfeiffer: The Saints. Berlin: Staatliche Museen zu Berlin, pp. 23–36.

Winner, D. 2005. Those feet: A sensual history of English football. London: Bloomsbury.

Chapter 4

The messianic manager in novels by David Peace

David Kilpatrick

The quotable sportsman and the football lexicon

> Some people believe football is a matter of life and death, I am very disappointed with that attitude. I can assure you it is much, much more important than that.
>
> (Bill Shankly)

> If God had wanted us to play football in the clouds, he'd have put grass up there (or: If God had meant football to be played in the air he would have put grass on the clouds, or: If God had wanted us to play football in the sky, He'd have put grass up there).
>
> (Brian Clough[1])

The sportsman as aphorist, master of the *bon mot*, the quotable quip: two eminently quotable managers, Bill Shankly and Brian Clough, both famous for their gift of gab, used clever word-play to preach the Gospel of the Beautiful Game. These quotes attributed to Bill Shankly and Brian Clough—the most famous, often-repeated examples of Shanklyisms and Cloughisms—are part of the game's folklore, its legends, its word-of-mouth wisdom passed along from pitch-to-pitch and down from generation-to-generation, with any alternate versions of these famous quotes in the game's oral tradition retaining a synoptic sense of a clear sporting aesthetic advocated with fanatical conviction and evangelical fervor.

Noting the controversy over the quote's origins, Geoff Nicholson (2014) suggests that Shankly may be best known as the author of that phrase, those words being better remembered than any of his accomplishments as manager or player. How could it be that the words of a sportsman would be better recalled than their actions, their successes and failures at sport?

In the preface to their *Football Lexicon* (2006) Leigh and Woodhouse note the evolution from brief factual reportage to the non-stop opinionated babble of sport talk. Citing the "relatively recent discovery of the talking footballer or talking football manager," interviews pre-and-post-match have "introduced us to a new vocabulary" (Leigh and Woodhouse, 2006, p. 7). This may appear contradictory to the prevailing notion that "sport is marked down as a natural, taken-for-granted activity. You don't need to talk or write about it. You just do it," as put by Garry Whannel (2008, p. 39). Yet, here we are,[2] responding to the ephemeral phenomenon of the sporting activity with words.

What role does language play in soccer? If one applies the constituent elements of tragedy identified by Aristotle in *Poetics* to the sporting event, *muthos*, *ethos*, *dianoia*, and then *melos* and *opsis* are readily identifiable to greater or lesser degrees while *lexis* may seem initially inapplicable.[3] Yet like a mystic relating the ineffable, we cannot shut up before, during, and after matches. "Football is a game of opinion," Clough once said to David Frost (1974). And what is it we most often express our opinions on, whether we are in the game as players, directing the play as coaches, or critiquing the game as spectators? I would argue that *lexis* is best identified with tactics, "the intelligent deployment of players, and their movement within that deployment," as defined by Jonathan Wilson in *Inverting the Pyramid* as "a combination of formation and style" (2008, p. 1). Then what we talk about before we play, as we play, and what we represent and analyze after we play, comes down to the tactical.

The argument: beauty v cynicism

Jonathan Wilson argues the history of association football tactics may be understood as a dialectic between "two interlinked tensions: aesthetics versus results on the one side and technique versus physique on the other" (2008, p. 6). This conflict between those who would play beautifully and those who would work cynically may be easily identified with the Clough quote(s), but some may mistake Shankly's quote as paraphrasing American (gridiron) football's coaching legend Vince Lombardi's most famous apocryphal quote: "Winning isn't everything, it is the only thing." Playing like it is a matter of life or death would mean that winning or losing is all that matters. But there is something more than just winning or losing, Shankly suggests, something more than just life or death at stake when association football is played.

This is a sporting application of the principle offered by Nietzsche, in *The Birth of Tragedy*, that "it is only as an *aesthetic phenomenon* that existence and the world are eternally *justified*" (1968, p. 52, italics in original).[4] Football in its brutish utilitarian mode is an unjustifiable imposition of work in the realm of play, corrupting play by dragging it into the profane realm of the secular. Playing soccer with an artistic, aesthetic concern, to play poetically rather than merely prosaically, is the ideal, the credo that is shared by the two factional[5] protagonists of David Peace's hagiographic soccer novels, Clough in *The Damned United* (2006) and Shankly in *Red or Dead* (2013). Building upon quotes and anecdotes from both celebrity-managers, Peace concentrates this shared sense of tactics as ideology, making both figures exemplars of a ludic ideal. United by this thematic concern, Peace's novels advocate a distinct philosophy of football and canonize both managers as martyrs for this cause.

Britishness/Englishness and Reepism

Beginning with the codification of the Laws of the Game and the formation of the Football Association at London's Freemason's Tavern in 1863, England's claim as the birthplace of association football and the British Empire's leading role in the global dissemination of the association code as the most popular modern game is undeniable. But as David Winner describes in *Those Feet*:

> [T]he English game was always longish ball. The classic way to switch from defence to attack was to play a long diagonal to the wing. And the objective of classical wing play was to produce crosses for Roy-of-the-Rovers forwards to crash in with thumping shots and bullet headers.
>
> (Winner, 2013, p. 65)

The English may have given us soccer but they did not give us the Beautiful Game. Winner links this with a militarized imperialism that follows like a thread from the arrows at Agincourt to the artillery at Waterloo to the aerial bombardment of Berlin. This preferred military strategy, evolving with the technologies of warfare, is represented in the tactics of English football, as most clearly formulated by former Royal Air Force Wing Commander Charles Reep, with his influential theory of direct-football as an ostensibly scientific method of producing results. Reepism and its proponents look cynically on the sophisticated complexity of 'Continental' possession-based play. The *jogo bonito* of Pelé's Santos and Brazil, the *totaalvoetbal* of Cruyff's Ajax and Holland, and more recently the *tiki-taka* of Messi's Barcelona are antithetical to Reepism and its emphasis on direct-play, which became institutionalized by Charles Hughes as director of education and coaching at the Football Association (FA) from 1983 to 1994.

Archetypal managers

While these three examples cite players and teams, it is of course the manager's responsibility to select the players and assign their positions or roles, choosing the tactics or formation and style of play. In his popular history of the evolution of the manager's role, with special emphasis on English football, Barney Ronay identifies Liverpool's Bill Shankly as "the first football manager to earn the accolade of pop star-style single-name status," citing his "unique personal electricity" (2009, p. 102). In his 15 years at Anfield from 1959 to 1974, he transformed the club from Second Division also-rans into not only a dynasty but a worldwide phenomenon. Ronay attributes Shankly's success to his linking soccer with the sociopolitical. "Shankly often talked about socialism and football, not just as an expression of working-class solidarity but as a means of playing the game, the perfect socialism of the perfect team," says Ronay (2009, p. 103). And this extends beyond the team itself to its supporters: Ronay sees Shankly as "a founding father of the popular notion of fan culture, of a mass communion between supporters, team and geographical place" (2009, p. 103).

Ronay identifies Brian Clough as "the first pop manager" (2009, p. 121), the first manager to cultivate a multimedia cult of personality mimicked and parodied as a pop-culture icon. Like Shankly, Clough took over a Second Division club, Derby County, in 1967, leading them to the First Division title in three years before abruptly resigning in 1973. He repeated the feat with Nottingham Forest, not only taking them from the Second Division to the First Division title in three years, but also to two consecutive European Cup triumphs. And like Shankly, Clough was an outspoken socialist who railed against the prevailing domestic ideology of direct-football, saying in response to the Reepism of the FA's Charles Hughes:

> I want to establish without any shadow of a doubt that Charles Hughes is totally wrong in his approach to football. ... He believes that footballs should come down with icicles on them.
>
> (Wilson, 2008, p. 297)

And such an aerial assault, of course, is not how Clough claimed God intended the game to be played (or there would be grass in the sky).

Shankly and Clough shared not only their socialist ideals and their love for possession-based soccer; they also shared an archrival in Don Revie, whom Ronay describes as a "super-villain" (2009, p. 144) employing the dark arts of football with his Leeds United side, ranging from excessive fouling and feigning injury to superstitious rituals, their anti-football antics earning the side the derisory nickname 'Dirty Leeds'.

If Revie is reviled as a representation of sporting evil, Shankly and Clough were celebrated as soccer's miracle-workers, revered as what Ronay calls soccer's "number-one narrative archetype" (2009, p. 246), the messianic manager. These archetypal roles are readily identifiable in the two novels by David Peace that feature these historical figures.

The Damned Utd

David Peace's sixth novel, *The Damned Utd*, was published by Faber & Faber in 2006. Subtitled "An English Fairy Story" and set from Wednesday July 31–Thursday September 12, 1974, covering Clough's disastrous 44 days at the helm of Leeds United as Revie's replacement, Peace uses flash-backs and -forwards from the perspective of Clough's consciousness to treat the episode of failure within the broader context of Clough's triumphant managerial career.

The novel's title is a nod to questions of damnation or salvation. But if anyone seems destined for damnation, one might assume it would be the arrogant and brash protagonist who sets himself up as a self-reliant antidote to his superstitious predecessor Revie. Taking over the champions (Revie leaving to manage the English national team), Peace has his protagonist utter the exact words he spoke live on Yorkshire Television, saying that although he is taking over the current league champions, "they've not been good Champions" (2006, p. 15). In an attack on Revie and his infamous lucky blue suit, Peace ends day one of the 44-day novel with Clough insisting he is not superstitious because he is a "socialist" (2006, p. 16).

Peace's Clough begins day two at his Elland Road office with a brandy (2006, p. 19) and the alcohol begins to fuel the protagonist's fire, and like a crime-novel convention it begins to provide a Dionysian distortion to the phenomenological, meditative attention to detail. Day two ends with Clough smashing up Revie's desk and burning it along with his files.

Any notion of Clough as a secularized atheist is complicated when Peace dramatizes the infamous day three meeting where Clough tells the Leeds players to chuck their medals in the dustbins. Peace intersperses the "Prayer to be said before a fight at sea against any enemy" from the 1789 *Book of Common Prayer* as Clough insults player after player in the Elland Road dressing room. It is unclear if Peace is claiming Clough read the prayer and then tore into them or if the prayer is being said by Clough silently in his own mind while he speaks (2006, pp. 26–29). But then Peace ends day three with Clough saying to himself: "I don't believe in God. But I do believe in doubt. I do believe in fear" (2006, p. 30).

Day four is the first Saturday of the novel and it is Clough's first match, a friendly at Huddersfield Town. Leeds come from behind to win 1–2 but Clough recognizes, "they are not my team. Not mine. Not this team, and they never will be—They are his team. *His Leeds*" (2006, p. 34, italics in original), the figure of Revie haunting Clough. At the risk of overemphasizing the author-function, Peace disclosed in an interview that this was the first match he ever attended: "I can distinctly remember Clough getting off the coach … [a]nd it was that match that gave me the germ of the idea for the book" (Shaw, 2011, p. 90). The novelist bears witness, mythologizing the charismatic, archetypal messianic manager he saw at this historic moment.

The manager in novels by David Peace   95

Day five, Clough is alone away from his family (he had taken at least one of his sons to work each of the prior days), and he begins to lament the absence of his former sidekick, Peter Taylor, whom he calls "Judas" (2006, p. 35), revealing his own Christocentric identity.

In a flashback scene in day 13, Clough recalls November 1, 1969, when he managed Derby County to a win against Liverpool, a team he admires so much he considers them "a poem" and "their manager a poet" (Peace, 2006, p. 98). Shankly's gracious post-match quote praising Clough's winning team shows him to be the polar opposite of the inconsiderate and graceless Revie.

By day 42, the downward spiral has spun out of control, the players—dressed in black mourning suits for the funeral of Harry Reynolds but Clough sees it as his own—in a meeting with the board chairman, ask for their manager to leave so they might speak their minds freely over what has transpired. They play Third Division Huddersfield Town again, this time not in a friendly but in the League Cup, an 89th minute goal rescuing Leeds for a replay, and with Don Revie dressed in funereal black watching in the stands, Clough knows he will not be managing the rematch. And on day 43, an apologetic board chairman Manny Cussins explains that while he agrees Clough has not had enough time, "the board have made a decision and Leeds United is a democratic institution" (Peace, 2006, p. 333) so Clough is fired.

The next day, the last day of the novel, Clough negotiates a modicum of financial security as compensation for his humiliation from the Leeds board. Bravely embracing the new era of televised scrutiny, he agrees to appear once again on Yorkshire Television to explain his side of things for a special entitled *Goodbye Mr. Clough,* only to be seated next to none other than Revie. Their contentious debate is re-presented by Peace almost like a transcription of the broadcast. Almost. Clough tries to explain to Revie how he wanted to improve upon Leeds, and when Revie dismisses this as an impossibility, Clough says he wanted to win the European Cup. Peace gives Clough the last word and he drives away with two friends, swigging champagne in the back of the Mercedes he negotiated from the board and a check for £25,000—a relieved if not triumphant Clough telling himself, "*I don't believe in God. I don't believe in luck. I believe in football—I believe in family and I believe in me; Brian Howard Clough*" (2006, p. 342, italics in original). Like a post-script, with the final page Peace notes that in May 1979, Margaret Thatcher is elected Prime Minister and Clough's Nottingham Forest win the European Cup.

Leeds are left damned but Clough emerges resurrected. Clough took over the 'Leeds machine' with the design to humanize them, purify them, save their damned sporting souls. Instead, they crucified him. But Clough has already risen from the grave of Elland Road.

Red or Dead

The title of *Red or Dead*, published by Faber & Faber in 2013, plays on the color worn by Liverpool Football Club as well as the color associated with socialism. Divided like minutes of a football match into 90 chapters, it begins on October 17, 1959 at Leeds Road, home of Huddersfield Town, when Shankly is lured away back to the prospect of managing Liverpool. At the risk once more of over-emphasizing the author-function, that Peace is a lifelong Huddersfield Town supporter may be relevant. Peace begins when Shankly leaves Huddersfield Town, where Peace's engagement with football is grounded, the same location that appears twice in *The Damned Utd*. Recognizing the directors of Liverpool Football Club, Shankly initially fears they want to steal away some of his players and is shocked to learn they want him. Although his wife and family do not want to leave, Shankly negotiates "total control" and agrees to join Liverpool in secrecy until his predecessor Phil Taylor is sacked (Peace, 2013, pp. 7–8).

By chapter 18, Shankly has taken Liverpool up the food chain of English football to the hallowed pitch of Wembley to face Revie's Leeds on May Day, 1965. The chapter begins with Bill checking in on overwhelmed and exhausted ticketing manager, Jimmy McInnes, consumed by the incessant ring of the telephone and the piles and piles of letters pleading for tickets to the final (Peace, 2013, pp. 163–164). When Shankly leads his squad out on the fabled pitch, he imagines the eyes of the world upon them:

> And Bill led the players of Liverpool Football Club down the tunnel, the Wembley tunnel, out onto the pitch, the Wembley pitch, and out into a sea of red, a world of red. LI-VER-POOL. A sea so deafening, a world so bright that the whole of London, the whole of England heard that sea and saw that world. LI-VER-POOL. On their radios and on their televisions. LI-VER-POOL. People might have read about the supporters of Liverpool Football Club, but today, on their television, live on their television, in black and white, now people saw the supporters of Liverpool Football Club. LI-VER-POOL. Their scarves and their flags, their banners and their songs. LI-VER-POOL. Now people saw the supporters of Liverpool Football Club and now people heard the supporters of Liverpool Football Club. LI-VER-POOL. This sea of red, this world of red. LI-VER-POOL. In black and white. LI-VER-POOL. And Bill knew people would never forget Liverpool Football Club. LI-VER-POOL. Their sea of red, their world of red. LI-VER-POOL. Not black, not white. LI-VER-POOL. But red, all in red. Their LI-VER-POOL. Not black, not white. LI-VER-POOL. But red, all in red. Their LI-VER-POOL, their LI-VER-POOL, their LI-VER-POOL ... In red, all in red. On the first of May.
>
> (Peace, 2013, pp. 166–167)

The socialist significance of the date is an ideal factional coincidence. Here we clearly see the community cultivated by the protagonist—his methodical, monk-like devotion to detail, his leadership an act of selflessness in service to this community. Three syllables, like a simple anthem or sacred chant, unite the club's supporters.

The phrase 'In agony and in pain' depicts the crushing physicality suffered by Shankly's Reds inflicted by Revie's Dirty Leeds. Overcoming their brutishness, after a scoreless 90 minutes, Liverpool triumph 2–1 in extra-time to claim the club's first FA Cup. When the triumphant Shankly returns to the office at Anfield, he finds the body of Jimmy McInnes, the ticket manager having hung himself under the Spion Kop stand. The building of this Red community has come at great expense, as McInnes becomes the tribe's sacrificial victim, his life the cost of their success.

Shankly's Liverpool defeat Revie's Leeds again in chapter 23, 5–0 at Anfield on November 19, 1966. Revie says to Shankly, "I have to say we were unlucky, very unlucky today. And you were lucky, very lucky today." Shankly responds, "You were not beaten by bad luck, Don. You were beaten by the best team in England. The best-ever team in England. And in Europe, Don. In Europe" (Peace, 2013, p. 214). But facing Ajax in the heavy fog of Amsterdam a month later, Shankly realizes the boast is premature as his Reds lose 5–1. A 2–2 draw in the return leg sends Liverpool out of the European Cup and Shankly into a rage:

> After the whistle, that final, final whistle. In the corridors and the tunnels, the Anfield corridors and the Anfield tunnels. Bill Shankly raged and Bill Shankly ranted. Against defensive football, against negative football. Against European football, against foreign football. And against luck. Against the luck of the Dutch.
>
> (Peace, 2013, p. 221)

Clough appears in chapter 32, when Peace re-presents the same match between Liverpool and Derby County recalled in *Damned Utd* (2006, pp. 98–99), this time from Shankly's perspective:

> Bill had admired Brian Clough as a player. Bill had tried to buy Brian Clough as a player. And Bill admired Brian Clough as a manager. Bill admired the things he had achieved with Derby County. The players he had bought, the way they played the game.
>
> (Peace, 2013, p. 305)

Just as Peace had represented Shankly's post-match praise in the prior novel, in *Red or Dead* he has his current protagonist praise his former protagonist, congratulating Clough by saying: "Well played. Very well played indeed, son" (2013, p. 306), reinforcing a sense of the two

98 David Kilpatrick

managers as allies, sharing a common vision or belief in how the game should be played.

The theme of luck comes up again in chapter 35. After a 1–1 draw in December 1970 with Leeds, again Revie tells Shankly his Reds were "lucky" (Peace, 2013, p. 332). Shankly dismisses Revie by saying, "My advice if you want to win a game of football. Would be to attack, Don. And not simply to defend" (Peace, 2013, p. 332). Later in the chapter, down to Everton in the FA Cup semi-final at Old Trafford, Bill tells his squad:

> You're playing too many high balls, boys. Keep the ball on the grass, the ball on the pitch. Where football is meant to be played, boys. Where God wants it played. On the grass and on the pitch, boys. You'd need a ladder to get to some of these balls. So come on, boys. Come on. Play to your strengths, boys. Play to your talents. On the grass and on the pitch, boys. And so keep the ball down. On the grass and on the pitch, boys. Where it belongs. Where God wants it played, boys. And where I want it played!
>
> (Peace, 2013, p. 348)

Inspired by this theological appeal to technique, they win.

Later in the chapter, Revie's Leeds knock Liverpool out of the Inter-Cities Fair Cup. Shankly congratulates Revie but admonishes him, if Leeds are to find success in Europe, "you'll have to try and attack" (Peace, 2013, p. 353). So while Peace's Clough criticizes Leeds for their brutishness and foul play, Shankly criticizes their cynical defensive tactics.

On New Year's Day 1972 in chapter 39, the two sides meet again, Shankly in the process of rebuilding his squad. "And the new Liverpool Football Club attacked and attacked and attacked. And the old Leeds United defended and defended and defended" (Peace, 2013, p. 388). But Leeds snap Liverpool's streak of 34 League matches unbeaten at Anfield. The defensive negativity of Revie's Leeds disrupts a winning streak achieved with Shankly's positive, attacking tactics. As Shankly tries to rebuild, Revie tries to knock down. Shankly's forward-thinking is spoiled by Revie's conservatism, Liverpool's art countered by the cynical utility of Leeds—the old Leeds Clough briefly inherits and fails to redeem in *The Damned Utd*. In *Red or Dead*, Revie is once more cast as the nemesis, his tactics the antithesis to the aesthetic idealism of the novel's hero, the cynical pragmatism Revie embodies, the greatest threat to the messianic manager's puritanical ambitions.

But unlike Clough in 44 days of *The Damned Utd*, Shankly is allowed to continue his club's rebuilding process, and achieves a greater mani-festation of his sporting ideal. By chapter 42, Shankly can brag to the media in the away dressing room at Upton Park in 1973:

What you gentlemen saw today, what you were lucky enough to watch, what you were privileged enough to witness, was total commitment. Total dedication. Total enthusiasm. Total self-belief. And total skill. And so that is what I call 'Total Football', gentlemen. Total Liverpool football.

(Peace, 2013, p. 423)

But the real test of this boast is continental. Facing Borussia Mönchengladbach in the UEFA Cup Final, Hennes Weisweiler congratulates Shankly, saying "You are easily the best team we have ever played. You are full of power, you are full of strength. But you are also very attractive when you attack. Very skillful" (Peace, 2013, p. 446). After another FA Cup triumph in 1974 in chapter 44, Shankly takes pride in what he has rebuilt, "A young side playing great football, playing pure football. *Pure* football. And so there is no end to it" (Peace, 2013, p. 492). But *Red or Dead* is, like a match, in two halves. And having reached this pinnacle of success, a sustainable success for his community, at the beginning of chapter 46, Shankly decides to leave the Reds and retire. And for the rest of the novel, Shankly walks around like Lazarus, already dead so no longer Red. The remaining 45 chapters are an extended meditation on the awkwardness of a successful transition in leadership as he watches his successor pull off what Clough could not at Leeds, to win better.

In chapter 89, Shankly congratulates Bob Paisley on having won his third consecutive European Cup: "And so you are immortal, Bob. More than immortal!" Paisley responds, "There is only one immortal at Liverpool Football Club, Bill. And that immortal is you. That man is you, Bill. Because none of this, none of these cups. None of it could have happened without you, Bill." But the humble Shankly insists, "Very kind of you to say that. But I know I'm not immortal, Bob. I know I'm mortal. Very mortal" (Peace, 2013, p. 713). And in chapter 90, Shankly closes his eyes for the last time.

A post-script has Shankly on a train with former Prime Minister Harold Wilson. Wilson shows him a postcard. Shankly recognizes the Huddersfield Town side that won three consecutive league championships from 1924 to 1926. But Wilson has him flip the postcard to reveal it is signed "Up the Town, Nikita Khrushchev" (Peace, 2013, p. 715). Like the end of *The Damned Utd*, which links Clough with the rise of Thatcherism, Peace once again ends his novel linking football with geopolitics, if not without ambiguity—especially when one considers the long-standing accusations that the former Labour leader Wilson was a Soviet spy.

Death and damnation: overlaps and omissions

This ending, like other stylistic choices, links the two novels. Both begin with Biblical quotes as epigraphs, *The Damned Utd* with *Jeremiah* 12: 7–9 and *Red or Dead* with *Revelation* 3:20. Both Clough and Shankly figure as products of Protestantism (Anglicanism and Presbyterianism biographically, but post-theologically through the refracted factional prism of Peace's prose), Peace casting them both as twentieth-century embodiments of a reformist Puritanism as Football Purists. Both novels may be read as sharing in a nostalgia for a lost game, a lost Britain.[6]

In both novels, Revie appears as the arch-villain, representing Reepism, excessive aggressivity, and cheating. For both Clough and Shankly, their philosophy of football is rooted in socialism, but for both football is the sacred. Clough is sacrificed (in a pattern akin to the mimetic-scapegoat effect identified by René Girard in *Violence and the Sacred* [1977]), replacing the king. Shankly witnesses the flourishing of the community under his successor as he has willfully converted himself from a subject to an object, conjured with a quote or a black-and-white image frozen in time.

Sins of omission may be detected with a source-studies critical methodology. We might turn to the source material, match and especially interview footage, grainy color images of the emergence of the talking football manager. For instance, Shankly's gracious praise of Derby as worthy champions (Wilson, 2011, p. 228) or Shankly's guest halftime speech to Clough's Nottingham Forest in the locker room at Everton, beginning their league title run for the 1977–1978 season (Taylor, 2015). Why did Peace not use either scene? Or the Clough–Frost unemployed interview (1974), in which, when asked whom he respects, Clough praises Shankly as a "one-off" and compares him to God?

Perhaps the most revealing sin of omission is found with Clough's "I believe in fairies" statement from his exit interview by Austin Mitchell on the Yorkshire Television special *Goodbye Mr. Clough*, with surprise guest Don Revie, which explains the novel's subtitle, "An English Fairy Tale":

> I believe in a different concept of football to Don. I think. I believe that it can be played, it can be played slightly different to the way that Don plays it and get the same results. Now that may be airy-fairy utopia. And it might mean being a little bit stupid. But that is the way I am. I'm a little bit stupid regarding this type of thing. I'm a little bit of an idealist. I do believe in fairies. And that is my, you know, outlook. Now, Don is slightly different. And his record proves, over results, that he, perhaps, is right. But having said that. I want to be like me. And he obviously wants to be like him.
>
> (Goodbye Mr. Clough, 1974)

Revie responded by calling Clough "a fool to himself," the phrase thrown by Peace into the middle of a Revie attack, rather than the point of attack it was when actually uttered.

Triggered by the paratextual enticement of the novel's subtitle, one is led to go outside the text to decode its belief system, its utopian vision. Fairy belief is a lost local pre-Christian mythology. This type of worship, this type of play, is in fidelity to the sacralized Earth, an antidote to the modern condition.

The novel drives us to the interview footage, the inexact-transcription ending of the novel, exposing itself, its fiction, its modification of the truth—the original spoken words, mediated through the medium of live television—Peace modifies the sequence of the conversation and omits much of their dialogue, the odd word, often repetitions and interruptions. The postmodern novel serves as a provocation, bouncing us back and forth from truth to faction to fiction and back or beyond. The novel omits but directs us to the core text/belief, the (televised) speech act, the dogma mythologized by the factional narrative.

Verisimilitude in faction: hagiography and the historical (sport) novel

Peace has claimed that since *The Damned Utd* is based upon his being an eyewitness as a child and especially his thorough research of primary texts, the novel is "*true*, but filtered through my imagination" (*Brian Clough*, 2011, my italics). If this is more explanation than defense, while speaking with Andrew Anthony, Peace confessed, "The fallout from *The Damned United* [sic] wasn't particularly pleasant. ... I never imagined that the most controversial thing I would write would be a book about football" (Anthony, 2013). As the novel became a surprise best-seller, it came to the attention of Clough's family, who took exception to the depiction of the deceased manager. His widow, Barbara Clough, was especially hurt and perplexed by what she read, strongly disputing the characterization as untrue:

> Have you read a novel with a real person's name in it? I keep asking people and they say, "no I haven't really." ... I dismissed it at first as just another book. I got it and read it and I was quite horrified. ... The language was absolutely ... I mean Brian just ... he didn't need that language to express himself. I'm sure you're aware of that. And they had him chain-smoking and he'd given up smoking years before. And they had him with a drink constantly there, and he barely drank in those days. ... He's just taken it on himself to write this book, this awful book. ... He's not here to defend himself, is he? You know, you can't ... that was the legal thing, you can't libel the dead.
>
> (*Clough*, 2009)

While the Clough family protested the literary liberties of the novel and worried over whether the cinematic adaptation would further distort the manager's legacy without legal recourse, former Leeds midfielder Johnny Giles filed a lawsuit against Peace and the novel's publisher, Faber & Faber. Resentful of the way he was depicted as a disrespectful trouble-maker, Giles dismissed the novel as "arty-farty stuff but using real names" (*The Yorkshire Post*, 2010). Defending his disgraced former preferred manager Revie, Giles claims "the perception of him as purely cynical is a myth" (*Independent*, 2010). Claiming damage to his reputation for being falsely depicted as contributing to Clough's dismissal at Leeds, Giles won a financial settlement with the publisher, along with an agreement to delete portions of the novel representing Giles in subsequent editions (Lacey, 2009). It is perhaps ironic that Giles does not fully appreciate how Peace's depiction of Revie should be understood as myth-making, failing to comprehend how adapting the biographical figure to the literary space often works to transform the 'real' person into an archetype, a mode of truth far different from the everyday.

While Giles and the Clough family should be excused for lack of familiarity with the conventions of historical fiction or literature in general, it is perhaps most sad that Clough's family choose to interpret *The Damned Utd* as anything but hagiography, enhancing the mythical status of its subject rather than disparaging the man. Their argument for authenticity, understandable as it may be, misses the point of the mythologizing power of the novel.

No such protests over *Red or Dead* came from Shankly's family, perhaps in no small part due to Peace's insistence in promotional interviews for the novel that he saw his subject "as close to a saint as you could really get" (Anthony, 2013), the hagiography with the second novel perhaps more overt, with less 'antihero' traits explored with Shankly than with Clough.

At the end of each novel, Peace appends "Sources and Acknowledgements," including the primary texts that served as source material. At the end of *The Damned Utd* he writes, "[t]his novel is another fiction, based on another fact" (2006, p. 345) and at the end of *Red or Dead* he writes, "[t]his book is a work of fiction. And so this book is a novel" (2013, p. 717). Despite this literary conceit, with both books we are left questioning what is truth, what is fiction, and how fiction might reveal more meaningful truths. Just as we do with (any) sacred texts.

The novel in sport studies and coaching pedagogy

With Peace's selection of two of the game's canonical figures, Clough and Shankly serve as prophets of a more cosmopolitan, socialist aesthetic approach to the global game—glocal socialists, promoting the football club as an authentic community, with suspicious distance from if not outright detestation for club directors/capitalists.

These novels suggest that literature has a place in sport studies, perhaps even in the somewhat alien realm of coaching education and sport management training programs that tend to ignore the humanities altogether. The myth-making of the novels explores truths about the game far more powerfully than the verifiable facts of biography, and while they advocate a certain approach to playing the game, like the most powerful myths, the novels offer models for behavior, for heroic conduct in the face of intense public scrutiny and conflict.

Brexit and the philosophy of football

Soccer is sacred, ultimately religious—*re-ligio*; it is what binds us, defines us, gives us meaning. We find the sacred in the ludic. I should acknowledge here an affinity with the application of "radical orthodoxy" for sport history advocated by Synthia Sydnor. "Radical orthodoxy though," Sydnor claims:

> holds that a theological sensibility and a sense of the sacred lie at the root of all knowledge work and that the task of understanding and revitalizing such relationships is part of postmodernism's project that has yet to be fulfilled.
>
> (2006, p. 203)

If we are to take such an approach to the figures of Clough and Shankly,[7] as fostered by their messianic treatment by Peace, the historical novel, the text of faction, becomes an ideal genre for such a postmodern analysis of sport.

Revie's goal was domestic. His Leeds never triumphed in Europe. Myopically provincial, when he took over the English national team, his lack of vision and corrupt nature were revealed on the global stage. Ultimately and ironically, he left England for Mideast oil money. The canonization of Clough and Shankly corresponds with a demonization of Revie by Peace.

Enhancing and promoting the canonization (if not deification) of Clough and Shankly, Peace builds upon the cult of the messianic manager in this mythologized futbology—mythologized in that it has its sacred stories, allowing us to see them as neo-Biblical figurations that grant meaning. Peace categorizes himself as "a historical novelist" (Faber, 2013) but his writing in these two novels is essentially apostolic.

This reveals the politics of an aesthetic approach to sport, the sociopolitical implications of this Gospel of the Beautiful Game. As the people of England undergo their period of self-examination in the aftermath of the

Nice Euro 2016 exit defeat to Iceland and the 'Brexit' from the European Union, they will do well to include the soccer novels of David Peace as sacred texts, offering an alternative to the solipsism of nationalism. Both Shankly and Clough were open to continental influence with success in Europe the ultimate barometer of sporting success. Perhaps the game they taught the world will help bring England round. If the global game is to offer humanity a pathway towards a liberating cosmopolitanism, we must understand the question concerning the Home of Football and its sporting destiny as our own. The ideological implication of Peace's messianic managers is that their shared philosophy of football is essentially socialist, guiding us towards a more meaningful existence harmonically true to the Earth. This lusory promise with its hope of deliverance, the prospect of redemption, may be found with the Gospel of the Beautiful Game. Peace has given us two sacred texts that share this Gospel and spread this belief. Without this hierophantic hope, the global game is irrevocably corrupt and unjust.

Notes

1 I do not cite either quote since the origins of both are themselves subject to speculation and debate. The point is their passage into an oral tradition in a physical culture that rarely reads books of any kind, the culture of professional football.

2 By "here" I refer to the Grosser Hörsaal, University of Basel, on July 2, 2016, when the original version of this chapter was read at "The Beautiful Game: The Poetics and Aesthetics of Soccer in Transnational Perspective" conference. My thanks to those who attended the presentation and offered their responses to the ideas addressed by this essay. Now "here" shifts from the live space of the speech act to the written space of the book, still in that tension between the abstraction of language and the action of association football.

3 I attempt an application of the constituent elements identified in Aristotle's *Poetics* to the 2010 FIFA World Cup Final in "Poetics and the Beautiful Game" (Kilpatrick, 2010b). For other detailed analyses of a variety of aspects of this relation, see also Eva Lavric and Jasmin Steiner's, Jan Chovanec's, and Thomas Messerli and Di Yu's contributions to this volume, which all scrutinize the relation between language and soccer in one way or another.

4 In "Nietzsche's Arsenal" (Kilpatrick, 2010a) I attempt to think through what Nietzsche's ontological assertion might mean in terms of an affinity for contemporary elite club football.

5 By "factional" I mean the deliberate blurring of fact and fiction in literature.

6 Indeed, Cyprian Piskurek, in his contribution to this volume, reads Peace's novels in precisely this way.

7 While I appreciate the sacred sensibility advocated by such radical orthodoxy, I do not share with any regressive pre-modern theology, but instead hope to suggest that these texts are post-theologically sacred, perhaps symptomatic if not prescriptive for the modern condition. Football is itself a means of communicating shared religious experience in the wake of the onto-theo-logical (see Kilpatrick, 2010b). Yet, as Peace's novels demonstrate, dogma and puritanical efforts at reform emerge with the new religion of sport.

References

Anthony, A. 2013. David Peace: "Bill Shankly was a good man, as close to a saint as you could get." The Guardian. [Online]. August 11. [Accessed August 10, 2017]. Available from: www.theguardian.com/theobserver/2013/aug/11/david-peace-interview-bill-shankly.

Brian Clough—The greatest manager England never had? 2011. BBC 2. June 5, 23:45.

Clough. 2009. [Film]. Gabriel Clarke, John McKenna and James Williams. dirs. UK: ITV Productions.

Faber. 2013. David Peace: A novel life. Faber & Faber Blog. [Online]. September 1. [Accessed November 8, 2017]. Available from: www.faber.co.uk/blog/david-peace-a-novel-life/.

Girard, R. 1977. Violence and the sacred. Baltimore: Johns Hopkins University Press.

Goodbye Mr. Clough. 1974. Yorkshire Television. [Online]. September 13. [Accessed November 8, 2017]. Available from: www.youtube.com/watch?v=7SQbLb4vFtg.

Independent. 2010. Publish and be damned: Giles fights back for Revie and Clough. [Online]. November 13. [Accessed November 8, 2017]. Available from: www.independent.co.uk/sport/football/news-and-comment/publish-and-be-damned-giles-fights-back-for-revie-and-clough-2132719.html.

Kilpatrick, D. 2010a. Nietzsche's arsenal. In: Richards, T. ed. Soccer and philosophy: Beautiful thoughts on the beautiful game. Chicago: Open Court, pp. 37–46.

Kilpatrick, D. 2010b. Poetics and the beautiful game. Aethlon: The Journal of Sport Literature. 27(1), pp. 79–89.

Lacey, D. 2009. The genius and demons of Brian Clough. The Guardian. [Online]. March 10. [Accessed November 11, 2017]. Available from: www.theguardian.com/football/2009/mar/11/brian-clough-film.

Leigh, J. and Woodhouse, D. 2006. Football lexicon. London: Faber & Faber.

Nicholson, G. 2014. League of his own: Red or dead, David Peace's novel about Bill Shankly. The New York Times. [Online]. June 25. [Accessed November 8, 2017]. Available from: www.nytimes.com/2014/06/29/books/review/red-or-dead-david-peaces-novel-about-bill-shankly.html?_r=0.

Nietzsche, F. 1968. The birth of tragedy. In: Kaufman, W. ed. The basic writings of Nietzsche. New York: The Modern Library, pp. 1–144.

Peace, D. 2006. The Damned Utd. London: Faber & Faber.

Peace, D. 2013. Red or dead. London: Faber & Faber.

Ronay, B. 2009. The manager: The absurd ascent of the most important man in football. London: Sphere.

Shaw, K. 2011. David Peace: Texts and contexts. Eastbourne: Sussex Academic Press.

Sydnor, S. 2006. Contact with God, body, and soul: Sport history and the radical orthodoxy project. In: Philips, M.G. ed. Deconstructing sport history: A postmodern analysis. Albany: State University of New York Press, pp. 203–226.

Taylor, D. 2015. Signing 'a hooligan' and a Shankly team talk: How Clough set up Forest for title. The Guardian. [Online]. November 11. [Accessed November 8,

2017]. Available from: www.theguardian.com/football/2015/nov/11/nottingham-forest-brian-clough-i-believe-in-miracles.

Whannel, G. 2008. Culture, politics and sport: Blowing the whistle, revisited. New York: Routledge.

Wilson, J. 2008. Inverting the pyramid: A history of football tactics. London: Orion.

Wilson, J. 2011. Brian Clough: Nobody ever says thank you. The biography. London: Orion.

Winner, D. 2013. Those feet: A sensual history of English soccer. New York: Overlook.

The Yorkshire Post. 2010. Exclusive: Clough portrayal helped drive Giles's libel bid. [Online]. November 12. [Accessed November 8, 2017]. Available from: www.yorkshirepost.co.uk/sport/exclusive-clough-portrayal-helped-drive-giles-s-libel-bid-1-3025001.

Half time

Poetics

Chapter 5

The man in the dugout

Fictional football managers and the politics of resistance

Cyprian Piskurek

Introduction

In a poignant quip against the managing profession, Colin Shindler has asked: "Who needs a manager? No spectator pays to watch a man gesticulating in a dugout or even kicking water bottles in the technical area" (2013, p. 143). In an age where a few managing stars like Pep Guardiola, Sir Alex Ferguson or José Mourinho have elevated the status of this role, this may not be completely true. These managers' stardom rests of course on their significant success, but also on 'signature tactics' or the media's readiness to identify successful teams via their manager personae. Yet, the different degrees of attention awarded to the man (as is almost always the case) on the sideline and his players on the pitch make it clear that "the job of a football manager is a paradox" (Carter, 2006, p. 1). The manager carries more responsibility, while the player might be torn between recognition of their individual skills and loyalty to the team; managers might earn more respect, but players have the bigger potential to be revered as stars; managers generally can base their authority on experience which the players do not yet have, at least to the same extent. And, maybe most importantly, underachieving players might be dropped from the team, but "few occupations are as volatile or as pressurized" as that of the manager where "failure ultimately results in the sack" (Carter, 2006, p. 1). These are just a few instances that show that the manager is oftentimes perceived as the Other of professional players, even though both are on the same team. With the rise of the genre that has been coined New Football Writing in the 1990s (King, 2002, p. 176), football managers have more frequently been represented in football fiction. The exceptional characteristics described above have informed these representations with the manager becoming a central point of reference for negotiations about the role of the individual in modern football.

Given football's status as one of the most popular pastimes in Europe, especially in the UK, it is somewhat surprising that the genre of football fiction has only recently begun to flourish. From J.B. Priestley to Robin

Jenkins or B.S. Johnson,[1] occasional novels with football as a topic would be published from the 1920s onwards, and football would, from time to time, also find its way onto the cinema screen, but in general, the game was underrepresented within the narrative arts until the last decade of the twentieth century. Although popular opinion has it that literature and sports in general do not go together, there are numerous examples from other disciplines where fiction and sports have formed a successful symbiosis: Norman Mailer's *The Fight* (boxing), Don DeLillo's *Underworld* (baseball), Joseph O'Neill's *Netherland* (cricket), and Alan Sillitoe's *The Loneliness of the Long-Distance Runner*, to name but a few. In contrast, it seems as if literary fiction and football did not constitute easy bedfellows for a long time. One of the reasons for this may lie in the fact that football is a team sport, in which the collective surpasses the importance of the individual; in fiction, however, individual heroes and heroines usually serve a much better purpose than a group of 11. That is why sports like boxing or running lend themselves much easier to fictional narratives than team sports, and even narratives about team sports often single out and focus on individual players and their stories, as the abovementioned examples of 'team sports fiction' by O'Neill and DeLillo do. We only have to consider classic Hollywood films about baseball or football to recognize that even stories of successful teams are almost universally grounded in the stories of individuals within the team.

In a similar fashion as media stories about football highlight narratives around the Rooneys and Ibrahimovićs, fictional plots tend to focus on individuals, but the design of the game offers few incentives for that. In this respect, it is no coincidence that football films often arrange their cathartic scenes around a penalty when cameras can slow down and the competition between two teams boils down to the mytheme of the duel. Peter Handke (1970) famously identified the goalkeeper in his generic isolation between the posts as a potential hero. These same narrative qualities apply to the manager as well. He[2] is part of the team, but then again he is not; he is the individual with the most responsibility, but at the same time he depends on the team and often stays in the background behind star players who take the limelight.

The ascent of the manager

In the English tradition, the terms coach and manager have not always overlapped in the way they do nowadays. Managers historically emerged as intermediaries between boards and players: they took over the responsibility for picking the team, for scouting new players and negotiating contracts; they became the 'face', and often the scapegoat, of the club because they were much more knowledgeable about football than the board of directors (Kelly, 2017, p. 19; Carter, 2006, p. 46, p. 95). As an autonomous figure, the manager's centrality was consolidated in the 1920s and 1930s, and this process marked an important stepping stone in the gradual modernization of the game (Taylor, 2008, p. 214). The figure most readily associated with this era is Huddersfield Town and Arsenal's Herbert Chapman, who set an example of how modern managers would both engage in selecting and coaching the players while simultaneously improving the administrative side of club management. Management became a field in which innovative men could leave their mark, and especially after World War II teams were often identified via their manager and his tactical style, as teams' nicknames like the 'Busby Babes' or the 'Greenwood Men' attest to. However, not all boards of directors were willing to yield so much authority and to delegate so much of their own responsibility to this new 'middle man' between them and the team; Aston Villa, for example, did not employ a manager in name until 1958 (Taylor, 2008, p. 215), and the manager's role as a mediator remained a contested issue.

Considering the narratives woven around the game, it is precisely this middling position, this in-between-ness of the manager, which bestows a poetic potential on the figure, akin to a classical hero, an outlaw against adversary forces. This ambiguity, especially in football fiction, has contributed to the establishment of the manager as a projection screen for supporters' utopian sentiments. It seems, however, paradoxical that the fictional manager should become the figure on whom fans' hopes for the preservation of values and sportsmanship are projected, given that in reality he is the one who usually has to take the blame for a team's lack of success (or maybe it is precisely because of this). This seems even more surprising in face of a number of scandals involving corrupt managers, like the case of Terry Venables, or, very recently, that of England manager Sam Allardyce, which shattered the image of the father figure who walks the moral high ground while his young players are tempted by the glamour and the riches that professional football offers.

End-of-season celebration pictures often show players plus manager, but the most iconic photographs of football managers highlight their individuality and their separateness from other actors involved in the game. Steve McClaren will always be remembered for the picture of him taken during his last game as England manager in November 2007, which the *Daily Mail* dubbed "a wally with a brolly" (Ridley, 2012, p. 62) and in which he seemingly cared more about staying dry than about England losing to Croatia. Similarly, Franz Beckenbauer's stint as football manager will primarily be remembered for his introspective pose at the Stadio Olimpico in Rome after West Germany had just won the 1990 World Cup. Although one should assume that team and manager win and lose together, they occupy different spheres in football narratives. David Peace's fictionalization of Liverpool manager Bill Shankly, *Red or Dead* (2013), captures this accurately in a scene after the manager's resignation. Throughout the novel, Shankly is presented as always emphasizing the communal solidarity among team, supporters, manager, board, and in fact the whole city of Liverpool, but when he loses the support of the club board and his former team after his hasty retreat, the text performs a twist on Liverpool's well-known club anthem "You'll Never Walk Alone": "Bill walked. Out of Anfield. Alone. Bill walked alone" (Peace, 2013, p. 555). For Shankly himself, the loss of support and stability that characterized his working life signifies a personal form of tragedy. The fictional character, however, gains more depth through the emphasis that the text puts on his lonesome character. The poetics of football fiction thus activate vaguely romantic connotations inherent in the figure of the outlaw or the loner that are common to other types of genre fiction (e.g., Westerns or hard-boiled detective fiction). A bit more pedestrian, a poem by Mike Jenkins, "The Manager's Chant," also fits this stance:

> At the end of the day/ We should have won/ … At the end of the day/ We just didn't fight/ At the end of the day/ We played like clowns/ At the end of the day/ The sun goes down/ At the end of the day/ I'm the one to blame.
>
> (Jenkins, 2002, p. 94)

In recent years, there has been a minor shift in the characteristics of football managers that clubs seem to be looking for: the Klopps, Tuchels, Monks or Simeones, although far from being a homogeneous group, have pushed the grey-haired eminence of experienced and somewhat authoritarian or fatherly veterans to the sideline (no pun intended). Modernity in tactics and team-building are promoted, and although the average age of football managers has not dropped significantly over the past decades, a pattern of entrusting teams to youngsters who have gone through modern managing courses and academies is discernible. The main reason for this is that football associations have professionalized their standards and come to require coaching qualifications from managers; a new generation of managers has thus come through coaching academies with a different understanding of the subject. In the German Bundesliga, for example, 28-year-old Julian Nagelsmann took over TSG Hoffenheim in 2016, and despite being younger than several players on his team quickly made a name for himself. In fiction, however, this new trope has not yet arrived and the veteran manager prevails. This underlines the deep-seated skepticism in English football towards theoretical training for a practical job (Kelly, 2017, p. 22). Walt Opie (2007) has convincingly argued that the utopian sports film depends on an experienced coach or manager as a substitute father figure to lead the wayward hero back on track; one might even argue that the sporting hero has to be symbolically orphaned and then taken under the wings of a responsible surrogate father from the sporting world to highlight the formulaic rags-to-riches story. With regard to recent football fiction, such old-fashioned father figures gain further significance by standing in for an era that many fans feel has been irretrievably lost.

The Taylor Report and after

Since the early 1990s, modern football has seen changes unparalleled by anything that came before, with England leading the global transformation of the game. Football in the 1980s frequently became the scene for outbursts of hooligan violence, and politicians like Margaret Thatcher consequently regarded football as a social pariah. *The Sunday Times* in a 1985 editorial even called the game "a slum sport watched by slum people" (p. 16a). On top of the regular occurrence of violence around many fan groups, three horrible stadium catastrophes (Bradford 1985, Heysel 1985, Hillsborough 1989) that cost almost 200 lives provided Thatcher's government with cause to act. Lord Justice Taylor was ordered to investigate the causes of the Hillsborough disaster and to suggest measures for improving football in general.

The publication of the second of the so-called Taylor Reports became a hallmark: the most decisive of his propositions were the recommendation to turn all stadiums in the top divisions into all-seated venues, and the suggestion to introduce closed-circuit television (CCTV) at all grounds to monitor spectators' behavior (Home Office, 1990, pp. 12–13). Roughly 30 years later, one can confidently state that Taylor's ideas have eliminated football hooliganism from the highest echelons of English football almost completely, but this has come at a price. Although Taylor explicitly warned against making supporters pay for these large-scale renovations (Home Office, 1990, p. 13), clubs raised their ticket prices in order to refinance the refurbishment of the old or the building of completely new grounds, and in order to make up for the loss of revenue that the significantly lower capacity of all-seaters entailed. This development can certainly not be separated from other interconnected cash flows, like players' wages and transfer fees spiraling out of control, or the immense sums of television and advertising money flowing into the game. Nonetheless, the main effect for supporters was that ticket prices rose enormously. It is difficult to adequately compare price rises but David Conn's calculation that prices at Manchester United rose by more than 700 percent, at Arsenal by more than 900 percent over a 20-year span seems realistic and is alarming, especially when judged against the background of a mere 77.1 percent inflation rate over that period (Conn, 2011). This new pricing policy attracted more affluent supporters and kept those whose class origin was often associated with a propensity for violence away. Football thus became a site for social exclusion, and the changed demographic altered the atmosphere around the game for good. The Premier League, founded in 1992 as a breakaway project from the egalitarian distribution model of money across the four divisions of the Football League, quickly became the richest and the most expensive league in Europe, and its appeal to global markets everywhere underlines this. However, the system with its dependence on massive foreign investment and complex ownership models is highly fragile, as is shown by the number of clubs that have gambled and fallen into severe financial imbalance: Leeds United and Portsmouth F.C., or Glasgow Rangers north of the border, are only the most prominent examples. These developments, together with players' perceived disloyalty regarding clubs and contracts, have alienated many supporters from the sport formerly known as 'the people's game'. In a nutshell, this is the result of the neoliberal excesses of a game that has moved away from the hooligan-ridden climate of the 1980s to the commodified and mediated mainstream version of the Premier League.

New football writing and neoliberalism

A number of commentators quickly voiced their concern over these developments since the 1990s, and the number of books—some of them academic (Hamil et al., 1999; Dempsey and Reilly, 1998), some of them journalistic (Bower, 2007; Conn, 2005), some of them personal pamphlets (Bazell, 2008; Exall, 2007; Horton, 1997), some of them memoirs (Irwin, 2006)—that condemn how football 'sold its soul' after Taylor seems virtually endless. At least as prominent as these investigative descriptions of modern football's reality is the contribution of the genre of football fiction, which, in most instances, constitutes a reaction against these changes employing forms of nostalgia that romanticize the age that has been lost. Football fiction itself paradoxically profited from football's move into the middle-class mainstream during the 1990s: there had, of course, been novels about football before (like Robin Jenkins's 1954 *The Thistle and the Grail*), but in general the underrepresentation of football in British literature before 1990 hints at the anti-intellectualist sentiment that dominated the game for so long. Coupled with the general changes in football described above, it needed the surprise success of Nick Hornby's 1992 debut *Fever Pitch*, a memoir about his life as an Arsenal fan, to show the potential of football writing outside of the sports pages. In the wake of Hornby, the genre of New Football Writing took off, in turn triggering what has become known as New Football Film, which also began to cater towards the increasing appetite for cultural representations of the game. Tellingly, though, in most of these texts one does not find an uncritical celebration of football's new, gentrified status quo, but instead many texts hark back to the 1970s and 1980s (when most authors' football socialization took place) in order to construct an opposition between the innocence of the pre-Taylor days on the terraces and the moral corruption that seems so pervasive in the glitzy Premier League world. Although different media like literature and film have their own intrinsic specificities and depend on their specific media as well as genre conventions, I would suggest placing both fictional literature and feature films together under the heading of 'fictionality', because it is via their fictionality that both kinds of story production position themselves within a specific historical context.

With regard to voices criticizing the commodification and attendant social exclusion in football in general, Carlton Brick has claimed:

> whilst formally oppositional to the new moralities of the football stadiums, the discourses of resistance are an implicit acceptance and appropriation of the new discourses of regulation that have been a feature of the policing and regulation of post-Hillsborough football fandom.
>
> (Brick, 2000, p. 161)

Brick criticizes that a book market which has only been able to thrive because of football's move upmarket latches onto the inauthentic discourses that it denounces. Instead, "fandoms of resistance ... are entirely consistent with, and compliant in, the development of new discursive and legislative regimes of regulation" (Brick, 2000, p. 161). Admittedly, the role of a genre which has only been brought about by the changes it now challenges is ambiguous. Still, the plurality of emergent voices that condemn the dominance of neoliberal developments in football can inform discussions and discourses about the direction that football has taken over the past decades. Moreover, many fictional texts make their point as much by means of what they do not say as by what they do say; a contemporary text about fan cultures in former decades will, in its omissions, always comment on current issues as well (e.g., a twenty-first-century novel about hooliganism in the 1970s needs to be read against the background of the virtual elimination of organized violence from top-flight football today). The texts thus do not even need to describe explicitly the social exclusion from the 1990s onward. Instead, fiction can symptomatically narrate fans' discontent with such phenomena via the idealization of a bygone age. In this regard, the representation of fictional managers is highly significant, because the emphasis on experienced and old-fashioned managers posited as heroic figures hints at how conservative football fiction as a genre actually is—as it tries to grant stability where it is lacking in the real world.

An old-fashioned prototype

Gordon McLeod in Michael Corrente's 2000 film *A Shot at Glory* is the prototype of such a veteran manager. The resemblance in terms of clothing and physiognomy with Bill Shankly, a fellow Scot, seems intentional, and McLeod's character also harks back to the days of Shanklyite management. McLeod is not the easiest of characters for his next of kin: he is stubborn, does not speak too much, and represents a world of football that is about to vanish. In fact, he himself has left the Scottish Premier League behind to manage Second Division side Kilnockie, located in a fictitious sleepy fishing village. This stylized backwardness, both with respect to the setting and to the protagonist, is, however, precisely what makes McLeod stand out and shine against his antagonists in the film, most importantly his misbehaved star player and son-in-law Jackie McQuillan and American club owner Peter Cameron. Cameron paradoxically sees Kilnockie as a grand business investment and has plans to relocate the team to Dublin if McLeod and his team fail to win the cup. The tweed-wearing McLeod hears about the chairman's various strategies for the first time when the gum-chewing, casually clad American grants the manager an audience at his lavish retreat in the woods (*A Shot at Glory*, 2000, 00:31:40–00:34:58). The binary opposition between the residuum of an innocent and honest version of football and foreign investment's colonization of this world could hardly be more blatant, and the film's emphasis on the distinct and generic underdog status of Scots latches onto that.

Cameron's relocation plans are an implicit reference to the remarkable story of Wimbledon F.C.'s forced move to Milton Keynes, brought about by the foreign takeover of the London club by businessmen who regarded the club as nothing but an object for speculation (Conn, 2005, pp. 234–255). McLeod's opposition to the club owner's plans posits the fair sportsman and his antiquated beliefs as the stronghold against the foreign takeover of Scottish (and British) football. In a central scene, the manager gives a short speech at a club banquet during which he repeatedly highlights the concept of the football club as a home (*A Shot at Glory*, 2000, 01:11:14–01:14:33); the film's moral can easily be identified as claiming that football clubs are no business assets but anchor points for fans' identification, and if no one else is willing to defend these values one can always rely on the manager to stand his ground. *A Shot at Glory* thus stands in a long line of Hollywood-inspired films centered on a utopian trajectory which suggests that sports can challenge all adversary social circumstances (Crosson, 2013, p. 136). Manager McLeod represents residual structures of feeling which the film interprets as a form of resistance against the hypercommodification of football.

Although much less serious, a similar role is performed by Mike Bassett, the manager in Steve Barron's eponymous film from 2001. This satire sees the unlikely figure of Second Division coach Mike Bassett take over the job as England manager after all likely contenders have refused. At his first press conference Bassett astonishes the skeptical journalists when he claims that he wants to win the World Cup, since the country that invented football, parliament, and the singing telegram, that bred Shakespeare and Wordsworth, and that beat Hitler, should aspire to always be world champions (*Mike Bassett: England Manager*, 2001, 00:10:21–00:10:54). This is an accurate comment on the paradoxical expectations before big tournaments, with the press, first and foremost the tabloids, writing off English chances while claiming that England have to win the title for tradition's sake. It also lays bare the paradoxical nature of a nation caught between its allegedly glorious past and its urge to adapt to modern circumstances in order to preserve at least traces of its role as a hegemonic power.

Bassett's appointment also speaks of the FA's "general spirit of amateurism" (Elley, 2001, p. 36), and fittingly it is the manager's most characteristic feature that he is "old-fashioned," as he tells people again and again. This involves playing a traditional 4-4-2 formation and "[writing] the team down on the back of a fag packet" (*Mike Bassett: England Manager*, 2001, 00:17:38–00:17:45), which leads Bassett's secretary to invite Third Division players Benson and Hedges for the next international call-up (2001, 00:30:53–00:31:21). Accordingly, when results fail to show, he is quickly accused of stubbornness because of his reliance on traditional tactics. Public pressure forces him to change tactics, with the result that England luckily manage a goalless draw in the final qualifier and narrowly book their ticket to the World Cup. Bassett and his team are then invited to a futuristic institute which promises to improve his players' fitness and tactical understanding, but this turns out to be a disaster, leaving seven of his players injured. This episode hints explicitly at the anti-intellectualism and distrust of theoretical learning in English football (Kelly, 2017, p. 22). Moreover, the pointlessness and even deleteriousness of modern—often foreign-inspired—tactics is crucial: at the World Cup England draw with Egypt and lose to Mexico, and when a frustrated Bassett is caught dancing half-naked in a bar, the public calls for his resignation. In the cathartic scene of the film, the manager responds by reciting Rudyard Kipling's poem "If" (1963, pp. 273–274) in full length at a press conference (*Mike Bassett: England Manager*, 2001, 01:06:52–01:08:37), ending with an ultimately stubborn, "Ladies and gentlemen, England will be playing four-four-fucking-two!" (2001, 01:08:41–01:08:47). Through a mix of luck and dilettantism, England manage to beat Argentina and make it to the semi-finals, and Bassett returns home as a hero. Even as a satire, it is telling that in the film's rendition of the nation's obsession with international success it is backwardness that triumphs over innovation. Bassett's qualities as a manager are surely limited, but the promises of modernity are ridiculed to at least the same extent as Bassett's old-fashioned limitations, which carry the day in the end. As farcical as Bassett's eventual victory and glorification seem, it is an obvious comment on England's infatuation with its footballing past, which seems to circle endlessly around the triumph of 1966.

Fictionalizing Clough and Shankly: the people's managers

The two most serious novels about football managers so far have been written by David Peace, a novelist who made his mark with the publication of a tetralogy about the Yorkshire Ripper (1999; 2000; 2001; 2002) and a novel about the Miners' Strike (2004). Sticking to the fictionalization of historical events, settings and figures, Peace then published two novels about iconic football managers from the 1960s and 1970s: *The Damned Utd* in 2006, exploring Brian Clough's disastrous spell as manager of Leeds United, a stint that lasted only 44 days, and *Red or Dead* in 2013, focusing on Bill Shankly's career at Liverpool and his subsequent way into retirement. As both texts are set in the pre-Taylor age of the 1970s, these examples are further evidence for New Football Writing's infatuation with football's past, especially when it comes to the representation of managers (see David Kilpatrick's contribution to this volume for a future-oriented, messianic reading of Peace's novels). However, in line with Peace's characteristically bleak and violent style of writing, *Red or Dead* and *The Damned Utd* stray far away from the rose-tinted nostalgia which *A Shot at Glory* or *Mike Bassett: England Manager* employ.

The crucial question with regard to this essay's overall scope is why the fictionalization of two managers from the 1960s and 1970s touches such an important chord with audiences. Jarred Keyes has noted that "the judgment of the present is always implicit in Peace's work and is key to understanding the contemporary relevance of its images" (2011, p. 20); and Katy Shaw writes that the "past continues to assert itself in Peace's work through a half-presence" (2011, p. 3). *The Damned Utd* and *Red or Dead* are thus neither texts that are exclusively about today or about yesterday, but instead explore how the present state of football is still embedded in the residual structures of feeling of a pre-Taylor age. Both novels then put fan cultures' current discontent with many football matters into a historical perspective. This is all the more striking since Peace's texts are no idealized bouts of nostalgia, but texts about men driven by obsession and trauma, one of them living in exile and paranoid (Clough), the other displaying a socialist missionary zeal and fervor (Shankly). Nothing is being romanticized, there is no glorification or metaphorical interpretation of football, and it is difficult to find any character readers can truly identify with. Instead, the texts present professional football as a lion's den, a "tribalistic, macho, introverted and inherently unstable world" (Maguire, 2011, p. 16).

Nonetheless, these texts' protagonists, despite their deep-rooted personal instability, function precisely as the foil to contemporary football because the football world they have to navigate is demarcated by much stricter hierarchies and certainties. *Red or Dead*, for example, derives most of its depth from the disorientation that Bill Shankly faces after having retired from the job. While this is mostly due to the personal catastrophe that the loss of the routines that previously defined him signifies, the protagonist loses his footing also when facing the wider changes that affect professional football. One of the most devastating blows for Shankly comes when he overhears some of his former players ridiculing local rivals Everton while actually celebrating their own triumph in the European Cup (Peace, 2013, p. 626). For their former coach, this marks a watershed move away from his ethos of dignified sportsmanship to an individualist competition in which loyalties and reverence for the dignity of the competition fade into the background.

Unsurprisingly, in the novel, this is mirrored by Margaret Thatcher's 1979 ascent to power. Thatcher's election victory is a recurring moment in all of Peace's works, the watershed event that tipped an already stumbling UK over the edge, away from a basis of socialist principles and towards the abyss of neoliberal individualism. The fictional Shankly himself is a committed socialist, which is why he feels a strong connection to Prime Minister Harold Wilson. The novel makes its take on the rift between political ideologies even more explicit when both politicians are described via their relation to football: at the 1970 election Harold Wilson is introduced as "the Member of Parliament for Huyton in Liverpool, who had been born in Huddersfield and who supported Huddersfield Town Football Club" (Peace, 2013, p. 322) and his opponent Edward Heath as "the Member of Parliament for Bexley in Kent, who had been born in Broadstairs and who supported Burnley Football Club" (Peace, 2013, p. 322). Thatcher, on the other hand, later gets an explicit retort, foreshadowing her feud with football in the 1980s:

> That night, Margaret Thatcher, the Member of Parliament for Finchley in London, who had been born in Grantham and who supported no one, became the Prime Minister of the United Kingdom.
>
> (Peace, 2013, p. 673)

Thatcher's government of course did not cause the three stadium catastrophes of the 1980s, but she was quick to adopt those measures suggested by the Taylor Report that would pave the way for the liberalization of markets, and thus the Premier League. It is telling that Peace's novel implicitly highlights how the reverberations of Thatcher's election in 1979 and the reverberations of the Taylor Report in 1989/90 cannot be separated from one another, and how intertwined football and politics are. Moreover, Peace's two works about Clough and Shankly posit the football manager as a special figure of interest after the ascent of neoliberalism, because their singular status within a club, on the one hand, ties in with neoliberal doctrines about individual responsibility and success, while, on the other hand, it highlights managers' dependence on their squads and players' individualist aims. Clough, for example, fails so tremendously at Leeds United because his players do not follow him, which makes it all the clearer that it was the collective at his former club Derby County that allowed his ego to shine. For the same reason, his predecessor Don Revie succeeded at Leeds, but most Leeds players are not willing to switch their allegiance and loyalties from Revie to Clough, who constantly ranted against Leeds's dirty way of playing while at Derby. This close-knit collective spirit that characterized both Leeds United and Derby County is, somewhat paradoxically, precisely what bars the exiled Clough from bonding with his new team.

If Thatcherism is thus a central backdrop to both novels, one should not overlook that both Shankly and Clough perform roles that are not that different from that of a politician, as one of the protagonists mentions himself: "You are Cloughie. You can do what you want—Football manager one week, prime minister the next" (Peace, 2006, p. 134). Both men are populists of a sort, and they know how to play the media and the fans. Clough is in a constant clinch with the board at Derby County, but he can only afford to keep up this struggle because he knows he has the backing of the people. Repeatedly, he threatens to resign from his post and is stunned when the board finally accepts this. Too proud to simply apologize, Clough then initiates a desperate campaign in which he wants the people of Derby to protest for his reinstallation as manager (Peace, 2006, pp. 252–255). For Shankly, in turn, there is hardly a term that he uses as frequently as 'the people', and his whole working ethos rests on the close bond between himself and the people of Liverpool. Early on, he wants the club directors to repair the toilets at Anfield Road: "The ones the people who pay to watch Liverpool Football Club have to use. Those people who pay my wages. Those people, their toilets" (Peace, 2013, p. 21). This closing of ranks is significant because both managers stand in such obvious opposition to the board of directors. Clough is always at odds with club chairmen, and Shankly feels alienated by the Liverpool board as well. Both characters, with their own problems and weaknesses, thus become 'outlaws' and their moral detachment from chairmen's and players' misbehavior turns them into anchoring devices for a general discontent with the game. The minute explorations of the managers' characters present both of them as flawed, the one almost too saintly and self-righteous, the other eaten up by a self-destructive combination of a giant ego and an enormous inferiority complex. But, most importantly, the novels also emphasize the individuality and particularity of the managing position as such, the struggles of the individual within a game ridden by vanities, and the near-impossible task of the manager to reconcile players', chairmen's, and fans' sensibilities.

The manager as detective

Following from this pattern of fictional managers as potential outlaws fighting against the forces of modern football, it seems logical and fitting that a character would blend the qualities of the manager with those of a related literary model, the private detective. In Philip Kerr's football trilogy, consisting of the books *January Window* (2014), *Hand of God* (2015a), and *False Nine* (2015b), protagonist Scott Manson fulfils precisely that role of manager-turned-detective. In the first instalment, Manson is assistant manager at London City F.C. when his boss João Zarco is found dead. Manson takes over the job as caretaker manager, but is also hired by the wealthy Russian club owner, who does not trust the police, to investigate the murder. Manson succeeds and wins himself such a reputation that in the sequels *Hand of God* and *False Nine* he is again hired by people from the football establishment to solve the suspicious death of a player, and the disappearance of a talented striker, respectively. Manson's character and his style of investigation stand in the tradition of American hard-boiled fiction: he is a loner and a cynic, but also a womanizer. Most importantly, these characteristics lend him a high level of authority both with players on his team and with the people he investigates in his newly-won profession.

Neither as crime novels nor as football novels do Kerr's texts stand out from the mass of genre and formula fiction; the depiction of Manson is nonetheless noteworthy for what it tells us about generic features of the fictional manager. Manson's hypermasculine sexuality hardly helps the three plots, but it highlights the virility of the former athlete who is capable of reconciling the physicality of the football world and the intellect needed for his investigations. The texts are culturally insensitive, especially when it comes to non-English players: the blond German midfielder is called Hörst [sic] Daxenberger, Caribbean people are lazy, and whenever Italian, Russian or black people are represented, the one-dimensional descriptions are steeped in clichés. This worldview mirrors the clear-cut boundaries between two rivalling teams on the pitch. Still, Kerr's texts assign the manager Manson a transgressive role. In all three cases, he is hired because he provides the link between those who run football and those on whom they depend—chairmen or club owners and players. Manson is chosen because as a middle man he knows all sides of the footballing world and because he speaks the players' language. The authority of the manager and his credibility with all groups in the microcosm of football single him out as the one person who can mediate between opposing interests and restore order.

Interestingly enough, Manson is no outspoken traditionalist who detests the commercialization of the game, as so many other fictional heroes like *A Shot at Glory*'s Gordon McLeod do. He is critical of the worst excesses of football's commodification and "thinks nearly everything about the game was better before Sky TV, instant replays and the 2005 IFAB change to the offside rule" (Kerr, 2014, p. 2), but he himself moves with ease among the rich and famous, and although he evades the pitfalls of corruption he encounters, he is no outsider to the glamor of the football circuit. In fact, Manson likes to stylize himself as a sober realist who holds no illusions about the game; the fact that he works at a team called London F.C., which with a name that defies the regional particularities of the capital's different boroughs can only be a franchise or a merger club without tradition, speaks volumes as well. The manager's attitude towards the cash flow involved in modern football seems to be mostly one of tacit acceptance, as this is the hand that feeds him.

However, the immoral and corrupt excesses of the game that he encounters during his investigations increasingly challenge Manson's realism. In *False Nine*, temporarily without a managing job and more and more cynical about clubs' policies, he puts an aspiring young player to the test and confronts him with the following choice of binary oppositions:

> Is it football you really like or the prospect of being the black Beckham? Is it the dressing room that's important to you or the photographic studio? The sports pages or a spread in G fucking Q? Liniment or hair gel? Vaseline or aftershave? A jockstrap or an Armani suit? Some dolly birds or your team mates? The roar of the crowd or the squeal of some totty you're banging up the arse in a nightclub? Playing keepie-uppie or footsie with a hooker?
>
> (Kerr, 2015b, p. 335)

What Manson ridicules in this rant is the stereotype of young and immature but overpaid footballers whom the system has taught to think of themselves as trademarks rather than as athletes, and who care more about the marketable simulacrum of themselves than about the essentials of the game. Manson may start out as an uninvolved cynic, but in his position as private investigator righting the wrongs within the football world he is led to advocate traditional values rather than the neoliberal doctrines of modern football. In other words: the glamor of the modern game cannot push traditional football from its moral pedestal. For that reason, Manson even helps cover up breaches of the law in the overregulated Premier League and encourages a young talent to skip medicals required by insurance companies (Kerr, 2015b, pp. 341–353).

Conclusion

This small selection of examples provides us with some insights into the poetics of the fictional football manager. It is the individuality of the man in the dugout that distinguishes the manager from the players on the pitch; this aesthetics of solitude bestows depth on the inner struggles and outward competitions that these characters are faced with. Moreover, the middling or mediating position of the manager between various interest groups—players, chairmen, agents, fans, journalists—is far more prominent than in other professions. This opens spaces for football fiction to explore the negotiations between different factions within the game, and the figure of the manager stands at the center of many of these negotiations. Interestingly enough, and different from many instances within 'real' football, the manager is the one who can claim moral superiority over most other actors and serves as an anchor point for fans' identification. Especially against the background of greedy players and corrupt club owners the fictional manager's profile gains depth. It comes as no surprise then, that the discourses of resistance, which have become so central in New Football Writing since the watershed changes of the 1990s, should identify the manager as an ideal projection screen for disillusion with the way that football is being run. In turn, traditional fans and managers are depicted as equally betrayed and sharing a similar value system that has come under threat. It is in this regard that the poetics of the football manager become political, since discontent with the state of neoliberal football is projected onto the role of the manager, who with his experience and authority is called upon to grant stability in an age of insecurity.

Notes

1 J.B. Priestley *The Good Companions* (1929), Robin Jenkins *The Thistle and the Grail* (1954), B.S. Johnson *The Unfortunates* (1969).
2 With very few exceptions, like Karren Brady's novel *United*, women do not yet fill leading positions in football fiction.

References

A Shot at Glory. 2002. [Film]. Michael Corrente. dir. UK: Butcher's Run Films, Eagle Beach Productions.
Bazell, M. 2008. Theatre of silence: The lost soul of football. Cambridge, UK: Pegasus.
Bower, T. 2007. Broken dreams: Vanity, greed and the souring of British football. Rev. and updated ed. London: Pocket Books.
Brady, K. 1996. United. London: Little Brown.
Brick, C. 2000. Taking offence: Modern moralities and the perception of the football fan. In: Garland, J., Malcolm, D. and Rowe, M. eds. The future of football: Challenges for the twenty-first century. London: Cass, pp. 158–172.
Carter, N. 2006. The football manager: A history. Abingdon: Routledge.
Conn, D. 2005. The beautiful game? Searching for the soul of football. London: Yellow Jersey Press.

124 Cyprian Piskurek

Conn, D. 2011. The Premier League has priced out fans, young and old. The Guardian. [Online]. August 16. [Accessed October 25, 2017]. Available from: www.theguardian.com/sport/david-conn-inside-sport-blog/2011/aug/16/premier-league-football-ticket-prices.

Crosson, S. 2013. Sport on film. Abingdon: Routledge.

DeLillo, D. 1998. Underworld. New York: Scribner.

Dempsey, P. and Reilly, K. 1998. Big money, beautiful game: Saving football from itself. London: Nicholas Brealey.

Elley, D. 2001. Mike Bassett: England manager. Variety. 39, p. 36.

Exall, K.P.C. 2007. Who killed English football? An analysis of the state of English football. Milton Keynes: Author House.

Hamil, S., Michie, J. and Oughton, C. eds. 1999. A game of two halves? The business of football. Edinburgh: Mainstream.

Handke, P. 1970. Die Angst des Tormanns beim Elfmeter. Frankfurt: Suhrkamp.

Home Office. 1990. The Hillsborough stadium disaster. April 15, 1989. Inquiry by the Rt Hon Lord Justice Taylor. Final report. London: HMSO.

Hornby, N. 1992. Fever pitch. London: Gollancz.

Horton, E. 1997. Moving the goalposts: Football's exploitation. Edinburgh: Mainstream.

Irwin, C. 2006. Sing when you're winning: Football fans, terrace songs and a search for the soul of soccer. London: Deutsch.

Jenkins, M. 2002. The manager's chant. In: Smith-Orr, T. ed. Football: Pure poetry 2. The return match. London: Creative Energy, p. 94.

Jenkins, R. 2006. The thistle and the grail. Edinburgh: Polygon.

Johnson, B.S. 2007. The unfortunates. New York: New Directions.

Kelly, S. 2017. The role of the professional football manager. Abingdon: Routledge.

Kerr, P. 2014. January window. London: Head of Zeus.

Kerr, P. 2015a. Hand of god. London: Head of Zeus.

Kerr, P. 2015b. False nine. London: Head of Zeus.

Keyes, J. 2011. "No redemption": The death of the city in the work of David Peace. In: Shaw, K. ed. Analysing David Peace. Newcastle upon Tyne: Cambridge Scholars, pp. 19–40.

King, A. 2002. The end of the terraces: The transformation of English football in the 1990s. Rev. ed. London: Leicester University Press.

Kipling, R. 1963. If. In: Eliot, T.S. A choice of Kipling's verse. London: Faber & Faber, pp. 273–274.

Maguire, P. 2011. Politics, class and the 1970s/80s. In: Shaw, K. ed. Analysing David Peace. Newcastle upon Tyne: Cambridge Scholars, pp. 11–18.

Mailer, N. 1994. The fight. New York: Vintage.

Mike Bassett: England Manager. 2001. [Film]. Steve Barron. dir. UK: Artists Independent Productions, Film Council, Hallmark Entertainment.

O'Neill, J. 2009. Netherland. London: Harper Perennial.

Opie, W. 2007. Sports films. [Online]. [Accessed August 30, 2013]. Available from: www.greencine.com/central/guide/sportfilms?page=0%2C3.

Peace, D. 1999. Nineteen seventy four. London: Serpent's Tail.

Peace, D. 2000. Nineteen seventy seven. London: Serpent's Tail.

Peace, D. 2001. Nineteen eighty. London: Serpent's Tail.

Peace, D. 2002. Nineteen eighty three. London: Serpent's Tail.

Peace, D. 2004. GB84. London: Faber & Faber.

Peace, D. 2006. The Damned Utd. London: Faber & Faber.

Peace, D. 2013. Red or dead. London: Faber & Faber.

Priestley, J.B. 1966. The good companions. London: Heinemann.

Ridley, I. 2012. There's a golden sky: How twenty years of the Premier League have changed football forever. London: Bloomsbury.

Shaw, K. 2011. David Peace: Texts and contexts. Eastbourne: Sussex Academic Press.

Shindler, C. 2013. The boss: A very British convention. In: Steen, R., Novick, J. and Richards, H. eds. The Cambridge companion to football. New York: Cambridge University Press, pp. 143–155.

Sillitoe, A. 1961. The loneliness of the long-distance runner. London: Pan.

The Sunday Times. 1985. Editorial. May 19, p. 16a.

Taylor, M. 2008. The association game: A history of British football. Abingdon: Routledge.

Chapter 6

The importance of trivial oppositions in football fandom

The narcissism of minor differences in derby games[1]

Kristof K.P. Vanhoutte

Demarcating the playing field

"This city has two great teams, Liverpool ... and Liverpool reserves." Beginning this chapter with a one-liner by Liverpool's one and only Bill Shankly is not intended simply to win the reader from the very first line by means of a well-known witticism. In fact, apart from the typically enjoyable Shankly style of this *boutade*, Shankly's wisecrack is of particular interest with respect to the main topic of this text. As most probably know, the city of Liverpool—in contrast to Shankly's claim—has, besides Liverpool (and Liverpool reserves), one more successful (Premier League) football club: Everton F.C. Shankly's remark, or rather, his cynical omission, perfectly hits the spot regarding what is at stake in the lines that will follow. However, without running ahead of the facts, let me begin by delineating the 'playing field' of this text by addressing what will be discussed and what will not be touched upon.

As the title of this chapter already reveals, fandom is at the center of this essay. Or, to be more precise, the crux of this chapter is fandom accompanied by opposition, contrast, and conflict in conjunction with the occasional and sometimes repeated presence of violence. It is, however, not fandom and its potential violence in general that is at stake. Rather, I will present a close reading of a special type of football game with a very specific type of fandom attached to it: the derby.

It is quite surprising how little attention this type of game has received in academic research on football in general. And the few cases in which academic writing about football has addressed the derby, the discussion usually focuses on its dubious origin. Was the derby, that highly loaded football match between two teams (usually) from the same city[2] born with the derby horse-race? Does it derive from the first football game held in the city of Derby? Or did it come down to us from the Shrovetide football game that was played in Ashbourne, Derbyshire? Nobody knows for sure.

It is still more remarkable to see how little has been written about the derby in academic research on football specifically dedicated to fandom, to which the derby surely is central. For example, to start with some of the more recent scholarship, in Steve Redhead's,[3] Richard Giulianotti's,[4] and Adam Brown's[5] work on fandom the derby is not, or only rarely, present and never treated thematically. Similarly, in Sean Brown's important book *Football Fans around the World: From Supporters to Fanatics* (2007)—a title that, as can be seen quite easily, cries for a little bit of derby attention—the word derby is only mentioned nine times, mostly referring to the city of Derby and the football club Derby County.

In less recent literature on football and fandom the term is equally rare and proper discussions of the phenomenon are entirely missing. The classic *Sport, Culture and Ideology* by Jennifer Hargreaves (1982) features the term just three times without any particular discussion. Similarly, Eric Dunning's work on fandom and violence barely refers to these peculiar games and their fandom.[6] And, to conclude this short survey, even in the often derided *The Soccer Tribe* by Desmond Morris (1981), a book that clearly strives (but fails) to reach exhaustiveness, the word 'derby' is only mentioned five times, and four times it is in reference to the city of Derby or its club Derby County and only once (in a book of more than 300 pages that intends to study the remnants of tribalism (!!) in world-football) does it refer to the derby game.

There appears to be some sort of blind-spot in the academic football literature regarding the derby. This blind-spot is, however, difficult to grasp, especially as these games are usually considered by fans to be not simply another game, but rather the quintessential and definitive moment of the entire season ("it is our reason for existence," as a Turkish fan describes Istanbul's derby [Mitten, 2008, ch. 11]). In fact, as the main character in John King's *The Football Factory* correctly remarks: most games are extremely boring but you turn up anyway, because what else are you going to do on a Saturday or Sunday? (King, 1996, p. 7). But on the day of the derby, on these special occasions, the fans excel in the irony and cynicism of their chants and in their display of special flag- and banner-choreography. And as every true derby fan will admit, and as the hooligan brothers Brimson express rather flamboyantly, even if your team is 15 points adrift at the bottom of the league table, heading straight for relegation and the scum you hate more than life are 10 points clear at the top, winning the derby will have made your season worthwhile— or, vice versa, and, worst case scenario, the scum up the road can ruin your entire season in just 90 gut-wrenching minutes (Brimson and Brimson, 1998).

In what follows, I will not just discuss the derby and its fandom, but I will also consider the derby game as a team's and its fandom's paradigm.[7] Derby football games and derby fandom, are, in fact, hardly ever reducible to the effective derby games. The rivalry remains and pertains throughout the whole season, and teams that do not have a 'natural' derby rival resort to sometimes rather remarkable strategies in the creation or location of one. As the brothers Brimson correctly remark:

> [W]hile every game has some degree of importance, within those lie fixtures that are more significant than others. Games that mean everything and for which the phrase "I don't give a shit what happens this year, but we have to beat those bastards!" was invented.
>
> (Brimson and Brimson, 1998, Introduction)

Or, as a fan of one of the sides of Rome's derby defined the details of derby fandom to me personally: "I hate them, and I do not use the word hate lightly; I wish them ill and I want them to be humiliated in *every* game" (my italics).

This is the derby, and this is its fandom, and it is what football is all about, albeit, as I will attempt to demonstrate, exactly in the opposite way than is attempted to bring home by the fans. The 'hated bastards', the 'scum' are loathed so much not because they are different, but because they are almost exactly the same. The extremely enlarged and exaggerated tiny differences merely function to hide the similarities and the common ground shared by the rivals. What is at stake, then, is a form of what Freud called the narcissism of minor differences.[8]

Before turning to Freud one final theoretical delineation is necessary. As we have already been able to discover in our brief overview of some of the academic football literature from the past decades, much has been written on the concept of fandom and its relation to conflict and violence (generally considered under the umbrella or cover-all denominator of 'hooliganism'). And, astonishing as it might seem, a very large variety of possible explanations have been offered over the past years for this violence. Quite interestingly, the variety of explanations offered for fan violence seems to retrace almost all the scholarly tendencies to sectarian subdivision typical of contemporary academic philosophy.[9]

One thus finds Marxist explanations of fandom and hooliganism, where fan-related violence is considered the result, or the reaction, of the alienated working-class fan to the 'bourgeoisification' of the game. Hostility and violence is explained (away) as the result of the different social and economic backgrounds and histories of the teams in question. This mythology of working-class club vs posh-club works surprisingly well (even if in a rather limited way, as if a club's history could be reduced to socio-economic reasons) for derby teams. It suffices here to think of, for example, AC vs Inter in Milan, where Berlusconi's team was originally considered to have been a working-class club. Other examples consist of Boca Juniors vs River Plate in Argentina, Portsmouth vs Southampton in England, to name just a few.

This Marxist approach was followed by what was called the 'figurational' or more sociological approach, or, as it is also known, the 'Leicester

Trivial oppositions in football fandom   129

school' approach. Drawing on Norbert Elias's theory of civilizing processes, this approach basically claims that 'civilized' behavior has not yet fully penetrated the lower strata of the population, to which, according to the proponents of the Leicester school, the majority of football fans belong. Derby hostility and violence is then simply explicable in terms of this universally applicable theory.

In the rough genealogy of the more general theories of fandom and fan violence presented here, the final turn of explanation was enacted by the post-modern approach. The post-modern approach claims, as should have been expected, the decline of traditional fandom and even the end of hooliganism. In return, one is offered a fandom that amounts to some sort of an amalgam of media and pop culture: post-fandom.

In what follows, I will avoid discussing any of these approaches in detail, for a variety of reasons. First of all (and I will just state my main contention with each of the three grand theories listed), I consider it highly dubious that there should be a specific social class (if one should still speak of social classes at all) from which most let alone all football fans are recruited. As has been demonstrated over and over again, fans, and even hooligans, are never just working-class disillusioned youths; they also consist of middle-class and upper-class people. Quite simply, football fans hail from all social strata. Even though social aspects should not be ignored, socially based (as much as politically and economically based) explanations not only always leave much unexplained, but above all, what they leave unexplained is simply that which they cannot explain. Second, reducing violence or un-civilized behavior to one specific type or class of people is similarly dubious if not just plain wrong. There are in fact numerous different modalities in which violence and related behavior find expression. Finally, I do not see any profound revelation in the fact that, for example, Derrida dreamt of being a professional football player when he was a little boy. I truly cannot see how this in any way confirms the breaking down of the binary division between high and low culture, which, in turn, allegedly proves the transformation of football fandom into some sort of new paradigm, post-modern post-fandom (Redhead, 1997, p. 31).

Besides these big-theory approaches, a plethora of further theorists have been used in order to explain football fandom and its violence. For example, and I do not dare to aim for exhaustiveness here, there are Bakhtin-based carnivalesque and Foucault-like carceral-style interpretations of football and fandom; there are also geographical and sociological investigations of fandom that base themselves on the work of scholars such as Marc Augé, Paul Virilio, Jean Baudrillard, and Pierre Bourdieu.[10] Although I hold all of these thinkers in high esteem and find some of the applications of their theories to fandom and fan violence indeed interesting, I also believe that reverting to their theories for explanations of football fandom is tantamount to taking another *boutade* by Shankly over the top: "Some people think football is a matter of life and death. I assure you, it's much more serious than that." I will try not to take Shankly by the word, as I believe this should not be done. And not just because, in the words of the Brimson brothers, doing so would reduce what we do to yet another bracketed "studies" concocted by academic "poofs," whom the hooligan literate continuously "slag off" (Brimson and Brimson, 1998, Preface).

So much for the demarcation of the playing field. Even though, as already affirmed, all these theories are interesting, Freud's 'theory' of the narcissism of minor differences offers a much more promising and provocative approach in talking about football fandom. If, as already proclaimed, derby-style fandom is indeed the paradigm of football fandom in general, then one needs to begin with the derbies to explain all other instances of fandom and not the other way around. In contrast to the three grand theories just covered, Freud allows us to do just that. Let us now zoom in on derby fandom and Freud.

The game—first half: derby mythology

Often conflict is explained by means of or attributed to elements of strong contrast between the groups in question. It suffices here to mention American political scientist Samuel P. Huntington's highly influential "The Clash of Civilizations" (1993), which predicted that the most serious conflicts of the coming era would be between factions that differ radically from each other in every thinkable way (religious, cultural, linguistic, political, and so on). Derbies and their conflicts do not constitute an exception to this all-comprehensive argumentation. In fact, all sorts of similarly great oppositions have been offered to explain the high stakes and the conflicts before, during, and after derby games.

We all know the 'Old Firm', the derby between Celtic and Rangers, the two strongest teams of Glasgow.[11] This derby and its enduring and explosive rivalry is often explained (away) with reference to their different religious orientations—Catholic and Protestant—that allegedly formed the basis of both team's birth. At least, this is what the legend tells us. But this is just a myth. A similar derby also fueled by the same different religious orientations is found in Northern Ireland's Belfast, where, besides a non-denominational derby between "Belfast's Big Two" Linfield and Glentoran, a religious derby exists between Protestant Linfield and the smaller Catholic club Cliftonville.

But of course, religion is not the only source of possible conflict regarding derby fandom opposition. I have already referred to socio-economic divergences (the working-class-rooted AC vs posh Inter in Milan, Argentina's Boca Juniors vs River Plate), but oppositional political commitments, too, have been claimed as the cause of derby fandom rivalries.

Thus, Lazio Roma's fascist background is contrasted with the leftist origins of AS Roma and monarchist Zamalek is pitted against military republican Al Ahly in the Cairo derby. Many more derbies in this vein could be added here: the inter-city derbies of Sunderland vs Newcastle and Real Madrid vs Barcelona, for example. And even geography has been brought forth as a possible cause of derby hatred. The battle between Europe and Asia, or the battle of the Bosporus as it is better known, between Istanbul's clubs Fenerbahçe and Galatasaray is a good example here. As can be seen, all the elements of Huntington's "The Clash of Civilizations" are present in this short list of some of the more famous derbies.

But what if all these grand oppositions are just effects akin to those of magicians' tricks? What if these grand oppositions merely exist in order to divert, to lead our attention away from what is actually happening? Maybe we should follow and generalize the comment made by a die-hard fan in Andy Mitten's discussion of the Southampton–Portsmouth derby, that although the working-class-divide myth—typically considered to be *the* characteristic feature of this derby—seems to be a popular way of looking at this derby, especially by the more violent fans who actually use it as an excuse for their violence, it cannot be considered the actual cause of the derby opposition, and one simply should not buy into it (Mitten, 2008, ch. 6). These socio-politico-economic or even religious-geographical oppositions can, again, in part be used and do, up to a certain point, actually play a certain part in the derby. However, their role is mainly important in the creation of the derby's mythology.[12] What is actually the case, and what can be found at the 'bottom' of the derby rivalries (maybe even of all great rivalries in general) is, in the end, the involved parties' common ground. It is what they share, what they have in common that divides the most.

In fact, if we look more closely at some of the explanations of the rivalries mentioned above, we can discern how the alleged grand oppositions do not actually comply with reality, and in many cases, are quite irrelevant to the teams' shared histories. For example, and beginning with one of the all-time toughest derbies already mentioned, the opposition in the Eternal City's derby between SS Lazio and AS Roma is said to be a clash between the fascist regionals of Lazio and the leftist urbanites of AS Roma. However, this story is not very accurate. In fact, Lazio existed well before Mussolini gained political power in Italy. In turn, AS Roma *is* actually a fascist construct, created by fascist leader Italo Foschi, who initiated and oversaw a merger between four small city clubs which initially was also supposed to include Lazio. The goal was to create a big Roman fascist team that could compete with the country's more prominent northern teams. Ironically, only Lazio resisted this fascist merger.

A similar story can be told about the Madrid–Barcelona inter-city derby, the so-called *classico*. Legend has it that this rivalry at least partly originates in the stand-off between a decidedly Francoist Madrid over the

132 Kristof K.P. Vanhoutte

anti-nationalist and resistant Barcelona. But the true fascist team, in origins obviously, of the Spanish capital is Atletico, not Real, which actually was on the verge of extinction due to the purges conducted by the victorious Falangist regime as recounted so well by Sid Lowe in his *Fear and Loathing in La Liga: Barcelona vs. Real* (2013, pp. 65–67). True, just like Lazio in Rome, Real were backed up by the fascist leader eventually and this did lead to both Real's and Lazio's surrender to a certain partisan following in the end (obligatory by the way). The origins of both these clubs, however, were not related to geopolitical issues let alone were they fascist creations.

One of the many London derbies, the one between West Ham and Millwall, offers yet another good example of what is at stake. Millwall's fans hate the Hammers, as West Ham are known, and their fans because they are supposedly not 'cockney' enough. And this shows, still according to the reasoning of the members of the Millwall firm, in their being too 'cockney'.[13] Consequently, West Ham supporters are hated for not being enough of what they are supposed to be, which is exactly what Millwall fans are.

It is thus not some unbridgeable difference that is responsible for all these rivalries, but rather a small difference with respect to what the involved parties otherwise share. Or, as Freud, to whom we now turn, would have written: what is at stake are minor differences, which, when cherished narcissistically, become the cause of often very violent antagonisms.

The game—second half: Freud's 'narcissism of minor differences'

Let us now take a closer look at what Freud had to say about these small differences and the narcissism with which they are often maintained and fostered and which often enough leads to so much violence.[14]

Freud introduces the notion of the narcissism of minor differences in his 1917 presentation entitled *The Taboo of Virginity* (Freud, 1991a). Discussing Ernest Crawley's 1902 study *The Mystic Rose: A Study in Primitive Marriage*, Freud transforms Crawley's notion of a 'taboo of personal isolation' into an indicator of minor differences that form the basis of strangeness and hostility between people otherwise alike. Freud writes:

> It would be tempting to pursue this [that is Crawley's] idea and to derive from this 'narcissism of minor differences' the hostility which in every human relation we see fighting against feelings of fellowship and overpowering the commandment that all men should love one another.
>
> (Freud, 1991a, p. 272)

He comes back to the topic of the narcissism of minor differences in 1921, in his *Group Psychology and the Analysis of the Ego*. Here, Freud extends the effects of this narcissism to antagonisms between groups, more specifically to town or regional rivalry:

> Of two neighbouring towns each is the other's most jealous rival: every little canton looks down upon the others with contempt. Closely related races keep one another at arm's length; the South German cannot endure the North German, the Englishman casts every kind of aspersion upon the Scot, [and] the Spaniard despises the Portuguese.
> (Freud, 1991b, pp. 130–131)

Almost ten years later Freud turns his attention once more to this form of narcissism. This time, it is in his famous *Civilization and Its Discontents* from 1930. Nothing new is, however, added by Freud to what he had already said previously—even the same examples of South vs North Germans and English vs Scots are re-proposed. We can thus read:

> It is always possible to bind together a considerable number of people in love, so long as there are other people left over to receive the manifestations of their aggressiveness. I once discussed the phenomenon that it is precisely communities with adjoining territories, and related to each other in other ways as well, who are engaged in constant feuds and in ridiculing each other—Germans and South Germans, the English and the Scotch, and so on.
> (Freud, 1991c, pp. 304–305)

Finally, the topic returns once more in his last essay, *Moses and Monotheism* from 1939, although not under its explicit denominator of the narcissism of minor differences. This time, the context is antisemitism: Having claimed that Jews are not fundamentally different from their 'host' nations, Freud writes that "they are none the less different, often in an indefinable way, ... and the intolerance of groups is often, *strangely enough*, exhibited more strongly against small differences than against fundamental ones" (Freud, 1991d, p. 335, my italics).

Despite Freud's repeated returns to the narcissism of minor differences, its explanation and understanding still leaves much to be desired. In fact, as Anton Blok has correctly remarked, it seems as if Freud himself failed to recognize the importance of his discovery (Blok, 1998, pp. 33–36). He even tried, in his 1921 discussion in *Group Psychology*, to play down its heuristic value. And although he definitely remained intrigued by this form of narcissism he, in the end, simply could not explain it and, as we witness in the passage from *Moses and Monotheism* quoted above, its explicatory power remained *strange* for Freud himself. But Freud's ambiguity does not leave us stranded. In fact, we can derive much about the narcissism of minor differences from other, at times seemingly unrelated, observations by Freud himself as much as by later research conducted in the Freudian tradition.

Let me cite one more fundamental observation by Freud himself that will immediately help us on our way. In *Instincts and Their Vicissitudes* Freud quite interestingly observes that the opposite of love is not hate but indifference, an observation that Freud makes frequently throughout the whole corpus of his work (Freud, 1991e, p. 134). There is more to this observation than the possible common-sense awareness of this non-opposition between love and hate—which indeed seems to confirm on an intuitive level the fact that the hatred felt by derby-rival fans is not necessarily related to grand oppositions as the appropriate response in such an oppositional relation would be indifference and thus ignorance. Obviously, that is not what the fans feel. In addition, as has been demonstrated so well by Sara Ahmed, this observation tells us something quite important about group formation, a process of high interest for what is at stake for us.[15] In her *The Cultural Politics of Emotion* (2004), Ahmed remarks that "hate structures the emotional life of narcissism as a fantastic investment in the continuation of the image of the self in the faces that together *make up* the 'we'" (2004, p. 52, my italics). In fact, love and hate do not pre-exist as such but love, for example, only emerges "through forms of identification that align this subject with this other" and in which "the *character* of the loved is produced as 'likeness' in the first place" (Ahmed, 2004, p. 52, italics in original). Conversely, hatred is produced through forms of "dis-identification" (Ahmed, 2004, p. 52).

So what can we deduce from this? First, there is nothing in the other(s) that would warrant our hatred. The demarcations between the 'we' and the 'they', as Ahmed (2004, p. 51) again accurately remarks, only "come[s] into existence through hate" and love. "Boundary formations ... are the effect of this ongoing constitution of the 'apartness' of a subject as a group" (Ahmed, 2004, p. 51). Second, the construction of the hated group is simultaneous to the construction of the loved one, and since this is, as we just claimed, an ongoing process, the love and hate have to be confirmed and re-confirmed over and over again.

This, to make a quick incursion into the translation of all this into derby language already here, explains the bizarre behavior of fans who so often instead of attending the game of their own team, go booing and causing trouble at the game of the derby rival. Their hatred needs to be re-confirmed, and the boundaries need to be maintained even, and probably especially, when they are not facing each other directly—and this explains why the Roma fan quoted further above said that he wanted their rivals to lose *every single* game, not just the derby match.

To recapitulate: there is no pre-existing content of hate (or love, for that matter); the construction of the hated group is simultaneous to the construction of the loved one; these constructions consist of a process of repeated confirmation and re-confirmation. What we can deduce from all this is that the material out of which the loved and hated groups will be constituted are in fact the 'same'. That is, they are made out of the same 'substance' and the difference between love and hate boils down to a tiny difference *in* this common ground.

Conclusion—third half

Before I conclude by retelling the genealogy of the most mythological of all derbies, the Scottish derby between Rangers and Celtic, let me first attempt to bring together all the theoretical aspects we have considered so far. It is essential to acknowledge that a football club is formed out of the desire to play the game of football by a group of people. The identity of this team is, in the first stages, almost inexistent (a sum of single elements). Some initial, but largely and mainly embryonic, creation of identity is formed with the arrival of a fan-base. But it will only be with the appearance of some sort of antagonism—originally generated almost solely by the football game—that the necessity of a genuine identity arises. The closer and the more similar the opposition is or becomes the more the need to create a 'surplus' of identity.[16] This surplus helps not only to define the 'we', but also, and simultaneously so, a specifically disliked and hated 'them' meet at eye level—simulated antagonism will only produce parodic derbies. In fact, only when the two teams are actually playing at the same level, thus attaining the required vicinity in terms of competitiveness, will this nearness be able to produce the surplus identity in the double sense just mentioned that is typical of derby rivalries. The creation of such a surplus identity (constituting and constituted by a loved 'we' and a hated 'them') is founded on sources and topoi that, as we discovered discussing Ahmed, are shared by both groups. Finally, the narcissistically cherished small differences in otherwise shared elements are translated and transposed into a mythological genesis-story that, from then onwards, will be handed down as a tradition (and a tradition, as its etymology already reveals, is always also a sort of treachery and treason).

This is the building plan of any derby rivalry. And although one needs to take into account that this building plan can be realized both successively and instantaneously and that the mythological deformations and diversions of these special games need to be uncovered and undone— something that might turn out to be rather difficult as not only do these deformations often operate on different levels and thus differ from derby rivalry to derby rivalry, but also because some of these derby mythologies have become self-fulfilling prophecies, mostly gathering fans from the stated background around a club—the same structures will return time and again. We already unveiled, directly or indirectly, some of the operations of deformation at work in some of the more spectacular derbies of the world. We discovered how, to return only to the Roman intra-city derby here, both AS Roma and Lazio share a city, a geographical fan and player base (though the latter no longer really holds in times of almost unchecked globalization), and they share a joint history with both teams' legacy marred by fascism. Lazio, however, happens to be the team cheered by Mussolini himself. It is exactly because of this small difference (a personal preference by Mussolini) that the whole legend of Rome's derby was 'constructed'—the surplus/double identity of both teams was, in fact, constructed along the same political lines (fascist/anti-fascist) and this by means of the misdirection typical for mythologies. Similar stories, with necessary variations and adjustments of course, can be told for pretty much any derby rivalry with the Millwall vs West Ham cockney vs not-cockney-enough difference as arguably the most paradigmatic case for the narcissistic cherishing of a (very) small difference.

In conclusion, it seems that a final test is in order: If our theory wishes to be accurate, it needs to stand the ultimate test, namely being applicable to the derby of all derbies, the Glasgow derby between Catholic Celtic and Protestant Rangers. Only when we are able to demonstrate that all that has been claimed about Freud's narcissism of minor differences, and the minor developments added afterwards, also holds for this titanic clash, can the explanations offered become acceptable.

Only very little effort is needed in order to establish that the Old Firm, too, follows the pattern of the narcissism of minor differences. Contrary to what could be expected, in neither of the two clubs' foundation did religious denomination play a decisive role. Rangers were founded by a group of rowing enthusiasts who had seen other youngsters play (so there was no denomination at stake here at all) and Celtic was founded by a Catholic priest who modelled the club after Edinburgh's Hibernian. At the outset, the two clubs were not related at all, let alone was there any antagonism between them. Furthermore, the first games between the two teams are described as having been extremely friendly in both teams' annals—in fact, according to one of the many extant interpretations, the name 'old firm' derives from the expression 'old and firm friends'.[17]

The religious-political rivalry that was to become the *raison d'être* of this derby was not part of the original encounters between the good old friends. It only arose in the years immediately preceding World War I.[18] And the only thing that seemed to separate Rangers from Celtic at the time was a different religious denomination. When *emotions* started to run high, these two teams began to feel a strong need to create a group identity by means of a strong antagonism. The rather small religious difference within the greater field of otherwise strong similarities started to become 'armed' as a source of hatred and, simultaneously, love. In the end, this difference in denomination became the cipher of opposition—charged and over-loaded with affect. The religious element, which up until then had never played a significant role in their gatherings—and let us remember that for Rangers, it had not even played any particular role at all—instantly became the main element of differentiation and narcissistically posited as the main stake. It was no longer two teams from Glasgow that sought to win a game of football. Suddenly, true religion was at stake at the Old Firm. Despite the fact that both Celtic and Rangers have had Catholic and Protestant players over the past 30 years, myth and legend remain, fueled, just like in all other derbies, not by some great and original difference, but by a narcissistically cherished minor difference.

Notes

1 Some elements in this text are further, more technical, elaborations on some of the themes I addressed in a previous essay (Vanhoutte, 2010). I would like to express my gratitude to Victoria Claire Allen for proofreading this text so carefully and diligently.
2 Some clarifications concerning the very term derby are in order here. While the most common understanding of a derby is that of a game between two teams from the same city (this is the intra-city derby), sometimes games between two different cities are classified as derbies as well (these are the so-called inter-city derbies—for example Real Madrid against Barcelona in Spain or Juventus against Inter in Italy). At times, games between different national teams are also named derbies (these are the international derbies—for example the derby of the low-countries, my own Belgium against the Netherlands, or Argentina against Brazil).
3 In Redhead's two main volumes on football, *Post-fandom and the Millennial Blues* (1997) and *Football and Accelerated Culture* (2015) the term 'derby' is simply absent.
4 In the many books (co-)edited by Giulianotti, the term is mainly present in a mere sporadic way. And, for as much as I have been able to discover, it is never treated thematically. Judging from the titles of some of the more promising volumes edited by Giulianotti, such as *Football Culture: Local Conflicts, Global Visions* (Finn and Giulianotti, 2000) and *Football, Violence and Social Identity* (Giulianotti et al., 1994), one might think that they should allow for thematizations of the derby and its fandom. However, in these volumes, the derby is only conspicuous by its absence. It has to be stressed, though, that Giulianotti's co-edited volume *Fear and Loathing in World Football* (Armstrong and Giulianotti, 2001) is somewhat of an exception here, having more than one chapter dedicated to the discussion of derbies and their effects.
5 Brown's *Fanatics! Power Identity and Fandom in Football* (1998) features the term 'derby' on only six pages and the term is not even deemed worthy of being a lemma in the index. It is, I believe, very telling that in a book on fandom and identity in football the term 'derby' does not even make it into the index.
6 Dunning's co-edited volume *Football on Trial: Spectator Violence and Development in the Football World* (Murphy et al., 1990) features the term only four times with only one of them referring to the game. The same holds true for a previous volume entitled *The Roots of Football Hooliganism: An Historical and Sociological Study* (Dunning et al., 1988). Another co-edited volume, *Fighting Fans: Football Hooliganism as a World Phenomenon* (Dunning et al.,

2002) features the term eight times (and it does not always refer to the game). His monograph on the sociology of sport shows no greater interest in the derby: *Sport Matters: Sociological Studies of Sport, Violence and Civilisation* (Dunning, 1999) features only the city of Derby (and only once). Although these books only represent a small number of Dunning's publications, the quick scrolling over most of his other work did not produce any peculiar change in frequency of references to the derby game.

7 Although I will exclusively focus on fandom demonstrated in derby cities and during derby matches, I do believe the aspects discussed are true for football fandom in general. I will, however, not go any further in my generalization. I will, in fact, not claim that football is or could be considered as some sort of reflection or representation of our everyday life, let alone will I claim that football is some sort of mirror or hermeneutical tool that allows us to understand the world (in line with Franklin Foer's *How Soccer Explains the World* [2004] or Tamir Bar-On's more recent *The World through Soccer: The Cultural Impact of a Global Sport* [2014]). If anything, I think there is more truth in Jean Baudrillard's claim that football is a sign of pure and simple disinterest in the 'reality' of everyday life. Or, if a certain direct link with reality does need to be established, one could say football forms a sort of parody of everyday life. Contrary claims smack too much of ideology.

8 To avoid all possible misunderstandings from the very beginning, although I draw on Freud, I do not draw on Freud because of the following three reasons. First, I do not draw on Freud because fandom has something to do with fanaticism or fanatics. Second, I do not draw on Freud because, as the Italian sociologist Alessandro Del Lago wrote—in the Preface to Nanni Balestrini's epic tale on Italian 'ultras' entitled *I furiosi* (2004)—fandom is some sort or form of fixation, a fixation that arises in childhood (Balestrini, 2004, p. 5). And finally, I do not draw on Freud because derby fandom consists of some sort of enlarged homosexual repression that can be found in the strong almost exclusively male bonding, singing, and hugging (and yes, this has been claimed, interestingly enough, also by a rather large number of hard-core fans).

9 The following three-tiered subdivision is largely based (in a rather free, interpretive way) on Ramón Spaaij's first (historical) chapter in his book *Understanding Football Hooliganism* (2006).

10 And just for curiosity's sake, there have even been Manichean interpretations (based on the second-century heretical teacher Mani who considered the Old and the New Testament as deriving from an evil and a good divinity, respectively).

11 It is worth mentioning that Glasgow is also the home of other professional football teams such as Clyde (though they relocated to Cumbernauld in 1994) and Partick Thistle. The fans of these two clubs thoroughly hate both Rangers and Celtic.

12 In this context, it is illuminating to consider Roland Barthes's 'definition' of myth. A "myth hides nothing," Barthes claims, "its function is to distort, not to make disappear" (1991, p. 120, p. 128). What is at stake in any given mythology is thus a sort of diversion, of deformation, or, to return to an analogy already used, a mythology is almost exactly like a magician's trick.

13 'Cockney' in this context denotes a working-class Londoner.

14 A plethora of scholars have, since Freud, acknowledged the importance of minor differences in the uprising of violence. Listing them all would be an almost impossible feat. It is also not the task of this chapter. As a particularly interesting example, let me thus just refer to René Girard and his 'appropriation' of Freud's original musings. In *Violence and the Sacred* we find Girard

claiming: "[I]t is not the differences but the loss of them that gives rise to violence and chaos" (Girard, 1979, p. 51).

15 It should not go unnoticed here that the second time Freud mentions the notion of the narcissism of minor differences it is in a text on group psychology.

16 Already Ernest Crawley, the author of the book that inspired Freud's coinage of the term 'narcissism of minor differences' indicated that it was one's "coming too close" that stood at the basis of the "taboo of personal isolation" (Crawley, 1902, cited in Freud, 1991a, p. 272).

17 A very similar story can be told about another of the titanic derby clashes that seems to be concerned with large geopolitical differences: the derby of the Bosporus. Fenerbahçe and Galatasaray both rose out of football-loving youngsters' passion for the game, and both clubs' origins are unrelated. More important, the first two decades of encounters between the clubs were extremely friendly. There was no talk of a continental clash whatsoever, even though the teams were from the very beginning situated on two different continents. This small difference (just the crossing of a river) was not yet cherished in a narcissistic way.

18 Rangers were founded in 1872 and Celtic in 1887, 40 and almost 30 years before World War I broke out.

References

Ahmed, S. 2004. The cultural politics of emotion. Edinburgh: Edinburgh University Press.

Armstrong, G. and Giulianotti, R. eds. 2001. Fear and loathing in world football. Oxford: Berg.

Balestrini, N. 2004. I furiosi. Roma: DeriveApprodi.

Bar-On, T. 2014. The world through soccer: The cultural impact of a global sport. Lanham: Rowman & Littlefield.

Barthes, R. 1991. Mythologies. New York: The Noonday Press.

Blok, A. 1998. The narcissism of minor differences. European Journal of Social Theory. 1(1), pp. 33–56.

Brimson, D. and Brimson, E. 1998. Derby days: The games we love to hate. Local football rivalries and feuds. [Kindle e-book]. London: Headline Publishing.

Brown, A. ed. 1998. Fanatics! Power, identity and fandom in football. London: Routledge.

Brown, S. ed. 2007. Football fans around the world: From supporters to fanatics. London: Routledge.

Crawley, A.E. 1902. The mystic rose: A study of primitive marriage. London: Macmillan.

Dunning, E. 1999. Sport matters: Sociological studies of sport, violence and civilisation. London: Routledge.

Dunning, E., Murphy, P. and Williams, J. 1988. The roots of football hooliganism: An historical and sociological study. London: Routledge and Kegan Paul.

Dunning, E., Murphy, P., Waddington, I. and Astrinakis, A.E. eds. 2002. Fighting fans: Football hooliganism as a world phenomenon. Dublin: University College Dublin Press.

Finn, G.P.T. and Giulianotti, R. eds. 2000. Football culture: Local contests, global visions. London: Frank Cass.

Foer, F. 2004. How soccer explains the world. New York: HarperCollins.

Freud, S. 1991a. The taboo of virginity. In: Richards, A. ed. The Penguin Freud library, Vol. 7: On sexuality. Harmondsworth: Penguin Books, pp. 261–283.

Freud, S. 1991b. Group psychology and the analysis of the ego. In: Dickson, A. ed. The Penguin Freud library, Vol. 12: Civilization, society and religion. Harmondsworth: Penguin Books, pp. 91–178.

Freud, S. 1991c. Civilization and its discontents. In: Dickson, A. ed. The Penguin Freud library, Vol. 12: Civilization, society and religion. Harmondsworth: Penguin Books, pp. 243–340.

Freud, S. 1991d. Moses and monotheism. In: Dickson, A. ed. The Penguin Freud library, Vol. 13: The origins of religion. Harmondsworth: Penguin Books, pp. 237–386.

Freud, S. 1991e. Instincts and their vicissitudes. In Dickson, A. ed. The Penguin Freud library, Vol. 11: On metapsychology: The theory of psychoanalysis. Harmondsworth: Penguin Books, pp. 113–138.

Girard, R. 1979. Violence and the sacred. Baltimore: Johns Hopkins University Press.

Giulianotti, R., Bonney, N. and Hepworth, M. eds. 1994. Football, violence and social identity. London: Routledge.

Hargreaves, J. ed. 1982. Sport, culture and ideology. London: Routledge and Kegan Paul.

Huntington, S.P. 1993. The clash of civilizations. Foreign Affairs. 72(3), pp. 22–49.

King, J. 1996. The football factory. London: Jonathan Cape.

Lowe, S. 2013. Fear and loathing in La Liga: Barcelona vs. Real. London: Yellow Jersey Press.

Mitten, A. 2008. Mad for it: From Blackpool to Barcelona, football's greatest rivalries. [HarperCollins e-book]. New York: HarperCollins.

Morris, D. 1981. The soccer tribe. London: Jonathan Cape.

Murphy, P., Williams, J. and Dunning, D. eds. 1990. Football on trial: Spectator violence and development in the football world. London: Routledge.

Redhead, S. 1997. Post-fandom and the millennial blues: The transformation of soccer culture. London: Routledge.

Redhead, S. 2015. Football and accelerated culture: This modern sporting life. London: Routledge.

Spaaij, R. 2006. Understanding football hooliganism. A comparison of six western European football clubs. Amsterdam: Vossiuspers Amsterdam University Press.

Vanhoutte, K.K.P. 2010. Playing the derby. In: Richards, T. ed. Soccer and philosophy: Beautiful thoughts on the beautiful game. Chicago: Open Court, pp. 231–240.

Chapter 7

Stupidity in football

Philip Schauss

Introduction

Stupidity alone is an impossible topic. Avital Ronell (2002, p. 71) calls it "a matter of presentation," that is, stupidity requires a context or background against which to appear. That context will on this occasion be the world of football (or soccer). I have also enlisted the help of Desiderius Erasmus, whose *Praise of Folly* will serve not only as a catalogue of stupidities, but also as a model of how to approach a topic as slippery as stupidity. Its praise is famously sung by the mock-goddess Folly, whose ambivalence towards stupidity I think is exemplary, since to position oneself outside its sphere of influence, as a neutral observer of sorts, is a wholly untenable position. No one is beyond stupidity: it is situational, a hallmark of human finitude, and, therefore, inevitable. It is impossible, too, to consider stupidity in football without simultaneously referring to knowledge, astuteness, or intelligence, the display of which, too, is a matter of situation (which, in turn, can quickly devolve into the stupid). On the field, the line between the magical and the downright daft is thin and shifting, resistant to measurement or regularity.

Cleverness on or off the field does not necessarily lead to a moment of beauty in football. It may result in ugliness, much like extreme stupidity can produce something brilliant.[1] However, beauty in football is not therefore only in the proverbial eye of the beholder, nor is it something we must all unequivocally agree on. Notwithstanding the fact that the experience of a game of football is a communal and, in most cases (if not always), partial affair, there is space not only for the coexistence of various points of view, but also for their correction or gradual convergence. This essay is a contribution to the spirit of openness that, in my opinion, defines the sport.

I begin, in the first section, by considering many of the stupid things said in football, which can be broken down into the emptily obvious, the deliberately misleading, or the overly honest. This is both the result of the content the media solicit, and of the level of professionalism demanded of

142   Philip Schauss

players and coaches in their role as brand representatives (of their clubs, on their own behalf etc.). Next, I consider to what extent the promise of extreme wealth and recognition propagates stupidity in football. The fact that football is a game, played from childhood into adulthood, only partially isolates it from the rigors of professionalism, which are largely extraneous to matters on the field. Then, I examine what sorts of knowledge can be applied to football, and derived from it. Although the game can be measured in almost every of its aspects, how meaningful are the products of such methodologies? I conclude that the richest form of knowledge concerning football is situational, based on our involved observation and practical knowledge. The final section deals with the fanaticism of supporters both from its benign, obsessive side, and from its altogether less attractive, violent aspect, both of which further exemplify how events off the pitch can spill onto it (and vice versa).

Non-sequiturs

The fun or, depending on your experience, the frustration in encounters between the sporting media and footballers or managers lies in the amount of empty words spoken day in, day out—in vast quantities. Most often, a catalogue of flat questions and statements is rattled off before and after every game, leaving all none the wiser.

For instance, after Germany's last-16 2016 European Championship game against Slovakia, Manuel Neuer, the otherwise excellent German goalkeeper, was asked what his team had done to win by three goals to nil. Neuer answered:

> We took our chances well and were leading early on. Then there was the missed penalty, but it was important to go into the break with a two-nil lead. After that, things took their course. We could have scored another goal or two.
>
> (Focus, 2016)[2]

That is a pretty classic example of a dumb answer to a lazy question—fair enough, one might say. Were Neuer not so exceedingly and boringly professional, his answer might even have been quite clever. He does, after all, at first seem to expose the journalist's complacency, but then immediately settles into a comfortable rattling down of bare match facts and football truisms, e.g., that it is good to score before halftime and so on.

Folly, Erasmus's goddess, states that in contrast to rhetoricians, who "[labor] over a speech for thirty whole years (and plagiarized some of it at that)," she prefers "simply *'to blurt out whatever pops into* [her] *head'*" (2003, p. 12, italics in original). If we apply this to Manuel Neuer's post-match interview, footballers fall into the role of the overly prepared, repetitious, and boring rhetorician whom Folly mocks. They have memorized their lines far too well and all too visibly.

Stupidity is then to speak one's mind, with no regard for the unintended consequences of a foul mood. Rudi Völler, when he was Germany's national coach, gave a good example of such disregard after a cringeworthy nil-nil draw away to Iceland in September of 2003. His team's performance was described as "an absolute, new low point" on German state TV (Caoimhín Peterson, 2009), whereupon Völler, in his post-match interview, retaliated in the following manner:

> I can't hear this rubbish anymore! So now every game in which we don't score is a lower low-point than the one we actually already hit. What crap! ... It's really out of order. ... What kind of world are you all living in? You've got to get off your high horses. All the stuff you people dream up, the sort of football we should be playing in Germany.
>
> (Gartenschläger, 2013)

History, of course, has been quite unkind to him: the demands made at the time by journalists and the public at large were soon met by Jürgen Klinsmann and Jogi Löw, who replaced Völler after a lackluster group-stage exit at Euro 2004. And yet his tirade was also understood as a noble gesture, whereby the coach protects his players by deflecting attention onto himself, an oft-employed strategy among managers.[3] Whether or not Völler genuinely thought a scoreless draw away to Iceland deserved no criticism, Erasmus knew that seemingly deluded behavior can indeed be a useful form of deception:

> If a rock falls on your head, that is certainly bad for you. But shame, disgrace, reproaches, curses do harm only insofar as they are perceived. If they are not noticed, they are not harmful. "What harm if all the crowd should hiss and boo; you're safe as long as you can clap for you." But this is made possible only by Folly.
>
> (Erasmus, 2003, p. 49)

Football fans tend to resent evasiveness from footballers or managers, though at the same time they also seem to understand that such behavior is part of a larger media-handling strategy.

Modern managers arrive with a 'philosophy', that is, with a fundamental approach to the game that determines their teams' style of play. Zlatan Ibrahimović famously attempted to insult his former manager, Pep Guardiola, by calling him "the philosopher" (Marca, 2011). Indeed, a conceptual approach to football can easily become the target of ridicule, especially in the Premier League, where it is often seen as a form of continental

European rhetorical showmanship, largely devoid of substance.[4] Folly, too, derides philosophers, emphasizing the gulf between their ideal constructs and the world of everyday experience:

> Though they know nothing at all, they profess to know everything; and though they do not know themselves, and sometimes can't see a ditch or a stone in their path (either because most of them are blear-eyed or because their minds are wool-gathering), nevertheless they claim they can see ideas, universals, separate forms, prime matter, quiddities, ecceities, formalities, instants—things so fine-spun that no one, however 'eagle-eyed', would be able, I think, to perceive them.
>
> (Erasmus, 2003, p. 86)

Only a fine line distinguishes the manager-philosopher from the charlatan. That line's slenderness has to do with the position assumed by the philosopher in Folly's depiction, which promises to provide a view of the whole. Managers, in order to be effective, must bring their own, more enlightened outlook to bear on the world of mere appearances that most players and supporters inhabit. Their success hinges on their work in both these realms—the finite and the ideal. Where ideality is unsuccessful, where it lacks traction on the pitch, the manager's conception of the game suddenly becomes as pedestrian as the lowly fan's. The spell has been broken, the fragile divide between life on the stands and the professionalism at pitch level has been breached, and the manager must go:

> If someone should try to strip away the costumes and makeup from the actors performing a play on the stage and to display them to the spectators in their own natural appearance, wouldn't he ruin the whole play? Wouldn't all the spectators be right to throw rocks at such a madman and drive him out the theater? Everything would suddenly look different: the actor just now playing a woman would be seen to be a man; the one who had just now been playing a young man would look old; the man who played the king only a moment ago would become a pauper, the actor who played god would be revealed as a wretched human being.
>
> (Erasmus, 2003, p. 43)

Spiegel Online, the web outlet of the German weekly magazine *Der Spiegel*, recently published a piece entitled "Das Pep-Guardiola-Experiment: Lassen Sie uns über Fußball reden" [The Pep Guardiola experiment: Let's talk about football]. The so-called experiment was conducted in response to a statement in which Guardiola specifically addressed his dislike of press conferences. He stated:

I love to talk about football, about tactics. But there are newspapers here that haven't managed to ask me a single question about football in three years.

(Montazeri and Gödecke, 2016)

Thereupon and over the next three months, the *Spiegel* journalists attempted to engage Guardiola during press conferences on tactical matters exclusively. So that he would recognize them, they wore red jumpers (perhaps a little silly).

Guardiola, understandably, would only answer questions concerning the opposition team's tactics, as any comment on his own strategy might have given away the plot of the upcoming game. The experiment began in March, in the run-up to a Bundesliga game against mighty Mainz 05. The article describes the situation in the following way: just a dozen journalists had made their way into the Bayern media center for Guardiola's pre-match press conference. The coach seemed bored, would rather have been elsewhere. A journalist in a red jumper rose from his chair and formulated a tactical question. Here is a translation of the journalist's account of Guardiola's reaction to the exchange:

While Mainz's strengths are being laid out, the Catalan begins to nod. His frown disappears, his eyes begin to sparkle. As he answers the question, Guardiola's open left hand becomes the pitch, the fingers of his right hand turn into players. He does this intuitively and so rapidly and matter-of-factly that one begins to grasp how often he must explain his ideas. His lesson in football lasts 76 seconds and for the first time during this press conference he doesn't appear tense. Then the frown returns.

(Montazeri and Gödecke, 2016)

Guardiola's frown seems a protective mechanism against the flood of petty, nosy, and sometimes humiliating questions a Bayern Munich manager must put up with, concerning transfer stories, lederhosen, *Weizenbier* and Oktoberfest, contract renewals, player unrest, or imprisoned board members. Indeed, apart from match reports and a few opinion columns, newspapers' sports pages tend to be filled with gossip, which is great from a fan's perspective: no matter how vapid, it allows you to have a laugh at your rivals' expense, to dream of the star striker that will change your team's fortunes, to while away the ever-shorter period when no football is being played, and so on.[5]

Man-child

I have played and followed football since childhood, but I no longer build cities out of Lego or throw chestnuts at passing cars. Sport is a respectable form of adult play. My obsession with Lego might have turned into a degree in architecture or an interest in DIY (it did not).[6] Footballers just stick to the football. Schoolwork, we assume, is of secondary importance to the youth player. Those footballers who do read books on the team bus are quickly branded 'intellectuals', which in football, as in everyday life, is not always meant to be flattering.[7] At the very least, the implication is that the 'intellectual' footballer is a rarity.[8]

Conversely, there are those footballers who never quite seem to grow up, like Mario Balotelli, who blew up one of his many bathrooms with a box of fireworks (Taylor, 2011). "Too young, too much money, too stupid," tends to be the way the tabloids frame it. And yet, it seems, the game feeds off figures whose stupidity and recklessness can produce moments of sparkling brilliance. As a player, this requires a strong disinterest in whatever knock-on effect your words and deeds might have, in addition to utter fearlessness in the face of the devastating force of public shaming. Folly, Erasmus's goddess, spreads a delightfully ambiguous and truthful message on the stifling effect of virtue and fear on one's self-expression and talent:

> For there are two main obstacles to gaining knowledge of affairs: modesty, which throws the mind into confusion; and fear, which keeps people from undertaking noble exploits once the danger becomes apparent. But folly removes these hindrances in fine fashion. Few mortals understand how very advantageous it is in other ways as well, never to feel modest and to be so bold as to stick to nothing.
>
> (Erasmus, 2003, p. 42)

Folly here resorts to hyperbole in order to show that absolute freedom from commonly held values is akin to nihilism, that is, to being bound by nothing, not even by self-interest. While it is true, at least since Nietzsche, that traditional Christian morality is culturally decadent and stifling for the individual, we know that nihilism poses a far greater threat. Some value or other must be upheld if we are to avoid the point of no return that is the last human being, who is utterly content with the fulfilment of only their bodily desires.[9] To remove the "hindrances" Erasmus speaks of, i.e., virtue and fear, is to be radically alone.

However, solitude is not merely the lot of the fool but also of so-called intellectuals, who thus feel compelled to live apart from humanity's foolish ball games. Folly allows the lonely objectivism of the purist intellectual to lock arms with the moribund subjectivism of the last human. Foolish jokers, still in a Nietzschean vein, may indeed be popular with the crowd,

Stupidity in football   147

but are helpless on their own, with only their ignorance for company, while hermits' path to wisdom requires so reclusive a course of study that they end up unable to convey their learning to others. As is to be expected, Erasmus infuses the fool–hermit dialectic with a great deal of irony, verging on the absurd, but never ascribing inherent good to one position or the other:

> [If] a man acquires more pleasure for himself and more admiration from others according to the depth of his ignorance, why on earth should he choose real learning? First of all it costs a great deal, and then it will make him more disagreeable and timid, and finally it pleases far fewer people.
>
> (Erasmus, 2003, p. 69)

It is many a child's dream to become a footballer (or, for that matter, a star of any popular sport). After all, what could be greater than to seal a famous cup win for your hometown club with a last-minute volley in front of 40,000 of your own? The fool's way to achieve this form of bliss, Folly tells us, is simply to rely on their God-given talent:

> After all, don't you see that, among all the other kinds of living creatures, those which remain at the furthest remove from any formal learning and take Nature for their only teacher lead the happiest lives?
>
> (Erasmus, 2003, p. 52)

While *wunderkinder*, it seems, are best advised, for the sake of ease and happiness, to rely on talent in lieu of training, they ought also to be aware of the resentment their effortless precocity will spark. "[A] child wise beyond his years," Folly tells us, "is a pest" (Erasmus, 2003, p. 21). By the same token, an old man whose mental faculties are not manifestly on the wane is nothing but a giant pain: old age, we are told, ought to bring us closer to childhood, notwithstanding the wealth of experience we amass over a lifetime (Erasmus, 2003, p. 21). This does not quite hold in the world of football, where experience tends to be of great benefit, though it is usual for our star players also to have been much-hyped youngsters.[10]

For a variety of reasons (having to do with agents, marketing, rising transfer fees, etc.), the appetite for prodigies appears to have increased over the past two decades or so.[11] Folly's speculation on what might occur if the Catholic Church elite led Jesus's frugal life, in which she enumerates the many intermediaries who live off the institution's bloated shape, bears some semblance to the game as we now know it:

> [S]o many scribes, copyists, notaries, advocates, ecclesiastical prosecutors, so many secretaries, mule-curriers, stableboys, official bankers,

pimps (I had almost added something more delicate, but I am afraid it might sound indelicate to some ears), in short, the huge mass of humanity which weighs down—pardon me, I meant "waits on"—the see of Rome would be turned out to starve.

(Erasmus, 2003, p. 112)

The same, I think, could be said of football, where intermediaries and player agents, in particular, like Mino Raiola and José Mendes, constitute a novel and rather opaque elite. Their management companies represent a large pool of players, ranging from schoolboys to veterans, on behalf of which they negotiate transfers and contracts, taking a cut from each deal. The ethical problems resulting, for example, from kick-backs paid to managers, bloated transfer fees and salaries, and the dubious practices with which youths are lured to clubs have led to calls for stronger regulation.[12]

Given how few players actually do establish themselves in the game, efforts resembling public awareness campaigns have been made to highlight the importance of education and, therewith, of an alternative path in life, should the football not work out.[13] Folly, still with a good deal of irony, continues to insist that we cultivate the body rather than the mind:

You see, don't you, how these grave and sober personages who devote themselves to philosophical studies or to serious and difficult tasks seem to enjoy hardly any youthful years at all; they grow old before their time because they are forever worrying and beating their brains out about knotty problems, so that their vital spirits gradually dry up, leaving them exhausted and juiceless, as it were. My fools, on the other hand, are plump and rosy, with a very well-preserved complexion; they are as fit as a fiddle, as the saying goes. In fact, they would never feel the slightest discomfort of old age, except that they are occasionally infected with a bit of wisdom by contagion. So it is that nothing in man's life can be absolutely flawless.

(Erasmus, 2003, pp. 21–22)

Professional football, to be sure, comes with mental and physical rigors that prevent most players from fully experiencing adolescence. Some footballers even confess to not liking football at all (Dart and Bandini, 2007), due mostly, one assumes, to matters off the pitch, such as the media circus surrounding professional sport. After all, how could you be part of a game you do not really like, let alone be any good at it?

Hans-Georg Gadamer's brilliant phenomenological account of play in *Truth and Method* shows that a player of any game must combine seriousness and levity for the game to be at all viable. These qualities, seriousness and levity, might at first seem contradictory, but, in order to play with any serious intent, players must willingly lose themselves in the concerted movement that is play. If I, a player, only halfheartedly play my part, the game is no good (Gadamer, 2004, p. 111). If, conversely, everyone is seriously engaged in the game, there is no end in sight, that is, there is no one who will make the sensible decision to drop out for the sake of more serious pursuits. You will want to play again and again, as Gadamer shows:

> It is part of play that the movement is not only without goal or purpose but also without effort. It happens, as it were, by itself. The ease of play—which naturally does not mean that there is any real absence of effort but refers phenomenologically only to the absence of strain—is experienced subjectively as relaxation. The structure of play absorbs the player into itself, and thus frees him from the burden of taking the initiative, which constitutes the actual strain of existence. This is also seen in the spontaneous tendency to repetition that emerges in the player and in the constant self-renewal of play, which affects its form (e.g., the refrain).
>
> (Gadamer, 2004, p. 109)

It is the seductive lightness of effortless repetition (not repetitiveness) that carries and renews play. A good game brings with it this 'addictive' tendency, that is, the strong temptation to reprise the experience. Every new game will be familiar in terms of the game's overall framework, but things will always play out differently. Gadamer, I suspect, might have excluded professional football from his account of play, given nasty practices like diving and time wasting, all of which are attempts to stifle a game, to have it break down or end more quickly.[14] In Erasmus's day, as we shall see in the section "Madness," below, such cheating was met with violence.

Knowledge

Now that we know Gadamer's thoughts on what it takes for a game to be viable, that is, for it to be fun, what does it take to be good at it? A short answer is that it takes mastery of the field of play to the extent that the rules governing the game allow it (or to the extent that you can bend those rules). This requires acute spatio-temporal awareness and kinetic ability.

Additionally, in professional football, particular roles on the pitch tend to be identified with particular bodily characteristics and technical abilities, notwithstanding Jonathan Wilson's finding that players, regardless of their position, are now increasingly coached to be universally skilled all-rounders (Wilson, 2008, p. 352). For most positions on the field, however, it is fairly easy to establish which attributes are essential, but there are notable exceptions, some of which are due to differing footballing cultures. Thus, in the English Premier League the assumption is that goalkeepers and defenders must be exceptionally tall and strong, but that they need not be the most skilled players on the ball. Fabio Cannavaro, Italy's 2006 World Cup and Ballon d'Or-winning center-back was plenty strong, but measures only 1.76 m.

Physical imperatives do not apply so much to teams' creative minds, whose range of influence runs all the way from defensive to attacking central midfield. These are roaming positions that can be "played while you walk," to borrow a Spanish footballing phrase (*jugar andando*), as long as you have a keen sense of the field's dimensions and the speed at which the game is (or should be) moving. This is maybe the part of the field where Gadamer's account of play works best, given that his is a phenomenology of play in general and not of professional sport, with all its ancillary demands.

In attacking positions, too, intelligence and astuteness can more than make up for any physical inferiority to opposition defenders. The infamously crafty Filippo Inzaghi is a good example of this, as is the Germany and Bayern Munich forward Thomas Müller, whose tactical role it is simply to lurk in or around the opposition box. Müller does this so well that he is now referred to as a "Raumdeuter," an interpreter of space, a term Müller himself coined in an interview (Hesse, 2016).

Football, unlike many other sports, is barely understandable with recourse to the statistics commonly provided on TV. Indeed, to measure the sport in this way verges on the stupid: a team's amount of possession or shots on target, or, in a position and role like Müller's, the distance run or the amount of passes successfully completed is no safe indicator of a good performance. It is possible to score highly on all these counts and not only to lose the match, but also to appear greatly inferior to the opposition team. When Germany thumped Brazil 7–1 at the 2014 World Cup, the post-match statistics suggested a tight affair: for instance, Brazil edged ball possession at 52:48, had 18 attempts on goal against Germany's 14, and had a pass completion rate of 79 percent (with 547 passes played) against Germany's 82 percent (with 592 passes played) (FIFA, 2014). Anybody who saw the match would know that, in fact, it was completely one-sided.

A new metric, called the Packing Rate, has been developed by a sports data analysis company and trialed on the German state broadcaster ARD. It promises to better reflect a team's effectiveness and superiority.[15] The Packing Rate is premised on the fact that a team is more likely to score the fewer defenders stand between a player and the opposition goal (so far, so dumb). The measure of a successful pass is the number of opposition players taken out of the game, that is, how many of these are at a greater distance from their own goal than the intended recipient, who has successfully controlled the forward pass. The metric accounts for a team's perceived technical superiority and is well suited to the aesthetics of the modern game, which, broadly speaking, can be described either as long sequences of patient possession play or as shorter, more energetic counter-attacking bursts. The Packing Rate subscribes to a particular conception of superiority, whereby other factors, such as the spirited defending of a scrappy single-goal lead over 70 minutes, are somewhat opaque to it.[16] Such forms of spiritual superiority—an unshakeable belief in the team—allowed Iceland to advance into the quarterfinals of the 2016 European Championships.

On the role of information technology in football, Jonathan Wilson writes that the game has seen so much tactical thought applied to it over the past century that we are unlikely to witness any computer-driven tactical revolutions in future decades (2008, p. 353). Instead, it is likely that tactics will be refined and adapted to individual circumstances with technological means (Wilson, 2008, p. 355). Such advances, however, will have to contend with the importance of individualism to the game (Wilson, 2008, p. 355). The egotist who stands out even from the most perfectly functioning team is, as we have seen, a substantial part of the sport's appeal. Wilson chalks this up to fans' inherent conservatism, which surely is a polite way of referring to their rather basic understanding of the game (Wilson, 2008, p. 355).[17]

Folly identifies a surplus of passion in humans, which, while no hallmark of intelligence, is football's *prima* and *ultima ratio* (Erasmus, 2003, p. 28). The first thing fans expect from their players, if all else fails, is that they appear to be working hard on the pitch. That is stupid to the extent that chasing after every ball may only achieve your players' premature exhaustion. Seen in a different light, however, it is a sure sign of the seriousness Gadamer deems a necessity for play. It shows that play can also be work, putting fans and players on the same plane, as workers who, as it were, 'put in a shift'. This is yet another sign of the porosity of the boundary between pitch and stands.

Despite all this talk about effort, fans, I think, know that there is no justice in football, that there is no definitive measure of who deserves to win a match.[18] This unpredictability is no hindrance to the cultivation of knowledge about football, that is, to the ability to pick up clues on a team's morale or an individual player's physical condition, and to understand finer points of technique or tactics. In doing so, it undoubtedly also helps to have felt, controlled, and hit a ball with your body, and to have played as part of a team, in no matter which sport. And yet, in seeming contrast to such practical and theoretical knowledge of the game, there remains the expectant wait for a mad flash of brilliance or of unimaginable foolishness (the two are sometimes hard to tell apart). No matter which of the two it is, Folly proclaims, it "brings no small delight to those who are mad to a lesser degree" (Erasmus, 2003, p. 59).

Madness

The goddess Folly invites the reader to consider the absurdity of our situation, the disastrous things that continuously happen to people, and how, ultimately, we are at our own bodies' mercy. The invitation is extended in the following terms: "Just think, if a person could look down from a watchtower, as Jupiter sometimes does according to the poets" (Erasmus, 2003, p. 46). Bringing this to bear on football, one might think of helicopter or drone footage of a nighttime kickoff: a packed floodlit stadium at the center of which lies the pitch, with its characteristic shape, on which stand 22 players, discernible only as uniformed blobs, arranged in the formation their coaches determined, with three referees scattered in between, according to their responsibilities. Such images are part of the imagery of the modern game, as stadiums are now built to accommodate the intricate lighting design that adds to the more traditional iconography of the green of the pitch, bordered by white lines of chalk. While, on the one hand, such images are an impressive way of conveying the magnitude of the spectacle, there is also something distinctly stupid and flatly objective about them. It is the sort of image that could make someone—someone daft, who does not like football—say: "Ah, 22 players and just one ball to play with." Obviously, as we have already seen, things are far more complex and interesting than that.

And yet I have come to sympathize just a little with those who resent the constant background noise of football, much discussed recently due to the expanded 24-team, three-games-daily format of the European Championship.[19] It is a debate that will soon enough resurface, in time for the expanded 48-team World Cup, beginning in 2026. A parody by David Mitchell and Robert Webb (2008) of a football trailer for Sky Sports, the television channel that holds the live broadcasting rights for the Premier League in Britain, makes the case for the sometimes overbearing presence of football in the media and, indeed, in our lives. Mitchell, dressed up as a British football reporter (that is, in an ill-fitting suit paired with an improbably short and wide tie), announces in a frightening crescendo of enthusiasm the upcoming month's televised fixtures (e.g., "Meanwhile, there are old scores to be settled at The Dell, scores like 1–0 and 2–2 that have happened in previous years"), backed by hyperbolic sound effects and shifting camera angles. The sketch comes to the following frenzied climax:

> Thousands and thousands of hours of football, each more climactic than the last! Constant, dizzying, 24-hour, yearlong, endless football! Every kick of it massively mattering to someone, presumably. Watch it all here, all here, all the time, forever, it will never stop, the football is officially going on forever! It will never be decided who has won the football! There is still everything to play for, and forever to play it in!

So that's the football! Coming up! Watch it! Watch the football! Watch it! Watch it! It's gonna move ... Watch the football! It's football!

(Mitchell and Webb, 2008)

Stupidity or folly has a long-standing and very close relationship to madness (most suggestively, *folie* in French means madness). Fanaticism and obsession are common conditions in followers of football. The two stand somewhere in between madness and stupidity, without necessarily spilling over into either. The football club I follow and pay a visit to several times a year is Real Mallorca.[20] Its fan base has by now dwindled down to a hard core, following the glory years of 1997–2003. The 6000 or so souls that have hung around to witness the dark days of Spanish third-tier football are thoroughly fed up. They come to the ground, it seems, only to make fun of the (admittedly terrible) group of players. And yet somehow, year in, year out, 50 or so stupidly enthusiastic young supporters (ultras, in Spanish and in many other languages) come together to create at least the semblance of support at Son Moix, the stadium named after a farm (which in turn was named after a cat).[21] Ultras, of course, are not only known for their ability to animate a crowd, but also for their oftentimes violent streak. Fittingly, the goddess Folly speaks of:

> two types of madness: one which is sent up from the underworld by the avenging Furies whenever they dart forth their serpents and inspire in the breasts of mortals a burning desire for war, or unquenchable thirst for gold, or disgraceful and wicked lust, or parricide, incest, sacrilege, or some other such plague, or when they afflict the guilty thoughts of some criminal with the maddening firebrands of terror. There is another kind far different from the first, namely the kind which takes its origin from me and is most desirable. It occurs whenever a certain pleasant mental distraction relieves the heart from its anxieties and cares and at the same time soothes it with the balm of manifold pleasures.
>
> (Erasmus, 2003, p. 112)

The second type of madness, a hypnotic fascination maybe, I would apply to myself as a more or less passive fan and, to a greater degree, to my club's ultras. No matter how hopeless the team, every weekend is a welcome distraction. Regardless also of the running track between the stands and the pitch, no matter how many times the naming rights to the stadium have been sold,[22] every game played at Son Moix is a homecoming.

In this sense, Gadamer did well in insisting on the contrast between *Anstrengung*, in terms of involvement and concentration, with *Angest-rengtheit* [tedium or irritation]. He makes the distinction clearer still when he claims that to inhabit the field of play is to lose contact with the world we habitually inhabit, "the world of aims" [die Welt der Zwecke] (Gadamer, 2004, p. 112).[23] Obviously, the immersion of a television spectator differs hugely from that of a player on the field, but it is an immersion nevertheless. When watching my team, the experience comes close to Folly's ecstatic account of love, borrowed from Plato:

> For a person who loves intensely no longer lives in himself but rather in that which he loves, and the farther he gets from himself and the closer to it, the happier he is. ... Otherwise what is the meaning of such common expressions as 'he is out of his wits', 'come to your senses', and 'he is himself once more'. Also, the more perfect the love, the greater and happier is the madness.
>
> (Erasmus, 2003, p. 136)

It is only in this ecstatic sense that the fan can be said to inhabit the field of play.

The topic of betting is best discussed now, in between the two forms of madness Folly names: the vicious and the pleasurable. To this day, attitudes and laws on betting differ from country to country (although, legislatively speaking, the tendency has been towards liberalization). This has forced teams sponsored by bookmakers to play certain continental away games without their main sponsor on display. Folly briefly hesitates whether to see gambling as a form of crowd-pleasing madness, or whether to attribute it to the realm of vicious violence. She considers it a daft pastime, an addiction even, which enters the realm of violence once debt is due:

> As to gamblers, I am in some doubt whether they should be admitted to our fellowship. But still it is a foolish and altogether absurd spectacle to see some of them so addicted to it that their hearts leap up and throb as soon as they hear the clatter of the dice. Finally, when the hope of winning has kept luring them onward until they suffer the shipwreck of all their resources, splitting the ship of their fortune against the dice-reef (hardly less fearful than the coast of Malea), and when they have barely escaped from the winner of their money, lest anyone should think they are not men of honor. What shall we say when even old men who are already half-blind go on playing with the aid of eye-glasses? Or when they pay good money to hire a stand-in to roll the dice for them because their own finger-joints have been crippled by a well-earned attack of gout? A pleasant spectacle indeed, except that sometimes such gambling ends in violent quarrels and hence falls into the province of the Furies, not in mine.
>
> (Erasmus, 2003, p. 62)

William Gass, in his afterword to the Yale edition of *The Praise of Folly*, reminds us of the prohibition of games and sporting events during Erasmus's age:

> [B]ecause of the violence they provoked, men were murdered for cheating at chess; and though we now sometimes play bingo at the behest of the church, the casino is as common as the cold, and the state runs the numbers racket for the sake of the public schools; over time only what has been enjoined changed, not its practice, for we beat up our umpires and upbraid our opponents as we have in all the so-called golden ages.[24]
>
> (Gass, 2003, p. 188)

Whether such violence is the result of sore losers' anger at their bad luck, or of hooligans' sadomasochistic quest for satisfaction, games are known to be potential venues of violence.

This leads us to the first type of madness identified by Folly, "furious madness," on vivid display in Marseille during the run-up to the 2016 European Championship group-stage game between England and Russia. Such events add a grain of truth to the otherwise far too casual sociopsychological dictum that "football is a substitute for war," a sort of vent for repressed nationalistic sentiments.[25] Hooliganism certainly is one of the many ugly faces of the sport, always lurking in the background, threatening to surface.

Resentful, non-violent *schadenfreude*, however, is common to all football fans. On the rare occasions when things are going well for the English against the German national side, their supporters tend to taunt their archrivals by singing "Two world wars and one world cup." The Germans, for obvious reasons, do not have an answer to that chant—"Zero world wars and four world cups" does not quite work. Instead, they cultivate a rather contrived dislike for the Dutch, which, despite my best efforts, I still struggle to fully understand.[26]

Conclusion

I began by considering many of the stupid things said in football, and there emerged a tension between the types of content solicited by the media and the level of professionalism demanded of players and coaches in their role as so-called "brand ambassadors" (of their clubs, of themselves, and so on). Then, I considered the compatibility of Gadamer's notion of play with the apparently seamless transition footballers make from childhood to extreme fame and wealth. Even though such pressures and incentives corrupt the self-contained dynamism of the game, play proves to be robust and continues uninterrupted. Thereupon, I described the limitations of statistical analysis, which, it emerged, can only be subservient to the situational nature of footballing knowledge. The final section dealt with the effects of fanaticism, benign as well as violent, on the field of play. When the outside world comes flooding onto the pitch, the game suddenly comes to a halt and we are thrown back into real life. That is the moment the cops storm the field, and one of their German Shepherd dogs bites your favorite player.

Moments of beauty or ugliness in football are obvious *and* ambiguous: their recognition depends on the position from which the game is experienced, and, as such, is immediately subject to reevaluation based on the lively and ongoing exchange between the many careful observers of the game.

Notes

1 The back-heel assist that Real Madrid's Guti provided for Karim Benzema in 2010 is a good example of this: Guti, running more or less straight at the opposition goalkeeper, was expected to finish or to cross the ball to a teammate. Instead, he chose to execute a back-heel pass while running at speed—a risky choice, even for a technically gifted player. Had he failed, he would not only have squandered a clear scoring opportunity during a difficult outing at La Coruña; he would also have been subjected to public ridicule for this display of narcissism, that is, the foolish wish to shine individually when playing a team sport. To let the team down is to set yourself apart from the group as a result of your own actions, for example, by receiving an unnecessary red card, or by over-indulging in your own skill. As things turned out, Guti—brilliantly and unselfishly—assisted Benzema for a tap-in.
2 All translations into English are by the author of this chapter.
3 See, for example, Hathaway (2015).
4 See, for example and only by implication, Whitwell (2012).
5 For a detailed analysis of why and how tabloids use language to create gossip about certain football celebrities, see Jan Chovanec's contribution to this volume.
6 As a matter of fact, there is a budding body of literature premised on the fact that many famous architects discovered their later vocation during their infancy, by playing with some form of building block. See, for instance, Vale and Vale (2013) or Bordes (2012).
7 See, for example, Corazón Rural (2012).
8 Taking things further, the 'intellectual' footballer might be seen as a withdrawn and somewhat lonely figure. Aloofness, too, is a common accusation.
9 See, for instance, Nietzsche (2006, p. 9).
10 It is true that the careers of those players who rely mainly on their pace and acceleration—typically, full backs, wingers, or strikers—will decline earlier than those of players with a more balanced skill set.
11 See, for example, Barlow (2011). An extreme case of this was the expectation generated around Freddy Adu, who in 2003, aged 14, contracted with Nike to the tune of $1 million, but never established himself at any of the European clubs he joined (see Mohammed, 2015).
12 See, for example, Riach (2015).
13 See, for example, Conn (2009).
14 See Emily Ryall's contribution to this volume where she discusses timewasting in terms of spectacle and drama.

15 See Impect (2016).

16 The BBC recently introduced an 'expected goals' metric (xG) to its football broadcasts. It calculates the number of goals a team ought to have scored in a given match based on the shooting player's distance from goal, the angle of the shot, the body part employed, the amount of defenders present, the type of assist (e.g., long ball, cross, through ball, pull-back), the passage of play (e.g., open play, direct free-kick, corner kick), whether the player has just beaten an opponent, whether the ball has just rebounded off something or someone, etc. It is surprising that no valuation of the shooting player's skill factors into the metric, although the amount and quality of additional data required would arguably do more harm than good to any claims to accuracy. See Stanton (2017).

17 See Blanka Blagojevic, this volume, for a detailed discussion of Jonathan Wilson's *Behind the Curtain: Travels in Eastern European Football* (2006).

18 As for mistakes made by the first official and his team, the introduction of the video assistant referee (VAR) can only rectify more or less flagrant mistakes. It ought to be clear that subjectivity cannot fully be removed from refereeing, with the exception of decisions concerning the relative position of the ball (e.g., whether or not it has crossed the goal line), which can be made by systems like Hawk-Eye with minimal disruption to the flow of the game.

19 See, for example, Wilson (2016).

20 Yes, a German who not only likes to travel to Mallorca, but who also supports the team—to be clear, footballing allegiances are not chosen, they befall one.

21 The Catalan *moix* translates as "cat."

22 In 2006, Mallorca became the first major club in Spain to sell the naming rights to its stadium.

23 In allusion to Kant's "kingdom of ends" [Reich der Zwecke] from *The Groundwork of the Metaphysics of Morals* (2012, pp. 45–46).

24 You get a further sense for this aversion to play when Folly exposes the lifestyle of supposedly virtuous noblemen, whose days consists of "dice, chess, drawing lots, buffoons, fools, strumpets, games, crude jokes" (Erasmus, 2003, p. 109).

25 George Orwell famously called sport "war minus the shooting" (1945).

26 See Critchley (2002, p. 11), where he refers to this sort of humor as the "comedy of recognition," without passing negative judgment.

References

Barlow, M. 2011. Mind the age gap! Chelsea and United set the trend as top clubs invest in youth. The Daily Mail. [Online]. August 24. [Accessed January 28, 2017]. Available from: www.dailymail.co.uk/sport/football/article-2029349/Premier-League-clubs-buying-young-Old-unwanted.html.

Bordes, J. 2012. Historia de los juguetes de construcción. Madrid: Cátedra.

Caoimhín Peterson. 2009. Rudi Völler drückt "Waldi" seine Meinung. [Online]. [Accessed September 17, 2017]. Available from: www.youtube.com/watch?v=KjOy6SXcze0&t.

Conn, D. 2009. Clubs leave lost youth behind as academies fail English talent. The Guardian. [Online]. September 9. [Accessed January 28, 2017]. Available from: www.theguardian.com/football/david-conn-inside-sport-blog/2009/sep/09/chelsea-fifa-premier-league-academies.

Corazón Rural, A. 2012. Esteban Granero: "Los jóvenes prefieren Twitter o la Play, yo soy más de leer un libro." Jot Down. [Online]. August. [Accessed

January 28, 2017]. Available from: www.jotdown.es/2012/08/esteban-granero-los-jovenes-en-su-tiempo-libre-prefieren-twitter-o-jugar-a-la-play-yo-soy-mas-de-leer-un-libro.

Critchley, S. 2002. On humour. London: Routledge.

Dart, J. and Bandini, P. 2007. The footballers that don't really like football. The Guardian. [Online]. April 25. [Accessed January 28, 2017]. Available from: www.theguardian.com/football/2007/apr/25/theknowledge.sport.

Erasmus, D. 2003. The praise of Folly. New Haven: Yale University Press.

FIFA. 2014. 2014 FIFA World Cup Brazil. [Online]. [Accessed January 28, 2017]. Available from: www.fifa.com/worldcup/matches/round=255955/match=300186 474/statistics.html.

Focus. 2016. Deutschland gegen Slowakei: Stimmen von Löw, Boateng, Draxler, Gomez, Neuer. [Online]. June 26. [Accessed January 28, 2017]. Available from: www.focus.de/sport/fussball/em-2016/em-2016-deutschland-gegen-slowakei-stimmen-und-reaktionen-zum-achtelfinale_id_5671195.html.

Gadamer, H.-G. 2004. Truth and method. London: Bloomsbury.

Gartenschläger, L. 2013. Völlers Ausraster machte Hartmann glücklich. Die Welt. [Online]. June 9. [Accessed January 28, 2017]. Available from: www.welt.de/sport/fussball/article119579600/Voellers-Ausraster-machte-Hartmann-gluecklich.html.

Gass, W. 2003. Afterword. In: Erasmus, D. The praise of Folly. New Haven: Yale University Press, pp. 175–188.

Hathaway, D. 2015. Chelsea and José Mourinho's rough start to Premier League title defense. Playing for 90. [Online]. August 21. [Accessed May 8, 2017]. Available from: http://playingfor90.com/2015/08/21/chelsea-jose-mourinhos-rough-start-premier-league-title-defense.

Hesse, U. 2016. Thomas Müller: The modest assassin. The Guardian. [Online]. February 23. [Accessed January 28, 2017]. Available from: www.theguardian.com/football/2016/feb/23/thomas-muller-modest-assassin-bayern-munich-germany.

Impect. 2016. Home—impect. [Online]. [Accessed September 1, 2017]. Available from: www.impect.com/en/#idea.

Kant, I. 2012. The groundworks for the metaphysics of morals. Cambridge, UK: Cambridge University Press.

Marca. 2011. Ibrahimovic: "Mi problema en el Barça fue el filósofo." [Online]. February 2. [Accessed January 8, 2017]. Available from: www.marca.com/2011/02/24/futbol/futbol_internacional/calcio/1298554825.html.

Mitchell, D. and Webb, R. 2008. Watch the football! [Online]. [Accessed January 28, 2017]. Available from: www.youtube.com/watch?v=MusyO7J2inM.

Mohammed, O. 2015. The pressure to become the face of US soccer ruined Freddy Adu's career. Quartz. [Online]. July 17. [Accessed January 28, 2017]. Available from: https://qz.com/455847/the-pressure-to-become-the-face-of-us-soccer-ruined-freddy-adus-career.

Montazeri, D. and Gödecke, C. 2016. Das Pep-Guardiola-Experiment: Lassen Sie uns über Fußball reden. Spiegel Online. [Online]. March 13. [Accessed January 28, 2017]. Available from: www.spiegel.de/sport/fussball/pep-guardiola-schweigen-als-taktik-a-1093866.html.

Nietzsche, F. 2006. Thus spoke Zarathustra. Cambridge, UK: Cambridge University Press.

Orwell, G. 1945. The sporting spirit. The Tribune. December.

Riach, J. 2015. Football agents fear "Wild West" as Fifa reforms seek to cap fees. The Guardian. [Online]. March 31. [Accessed January 28, 2017]. Available from: www.theguardian.com/football/2015/mar/31/football-agents-fifa-reforms.

Ronell, A. 2002. Stupidity. Chicago: University of Illinois Press.

Stanton, J. 2017. Premier League: "Expected goals" tells us whether a player really should have scored. BBC. [Online]. August 10. [Accessed August 31, 2017]. Available from: www.bbc.com/sport/football/4069943.

Taylor, D. 2011. Mario Balotelli's house set on fire as he shoots fireworks from window. The Guardian. [Online]. October 22. [Accessed January 28, 2017]. Available from: www.theguardian.com/football/2011/oct/22/mario-balotelli-house-fire-fireworks.

Vale, B. and Vale, R. 2013. Architecture on the carpet: The curious tale of construction toys and the genesis of modern buildings. New York: Thames and Hudson.

Whitwell, L. 2012. If my name was Allardici I'd be a top four boss, jokes West Ham boss. The Daily Mail. [Online]. November 2. [Accessed May 8, 2017]. Available from: www.dailymail.co.uk/sport/football/article-2227155/Sam-Allardyce-If-Allardici-Id-boss.html.

Wilson, J. 2006. Behind the curtain: Travels in Eastern European football. London: Orion.

Wilson, J. 2008. Inverting the pyramid: The history of football tactics. London: Orion.

Wilson, P. 2016. Euro 2016: Will it be a mouth-watering banquet or an over-stocked buffet? The Guardian. [Online]. June 4. [Accessed January 28, 2017]. Available from: www.theguardian.com/football/blog/2016/jun/04/euro-2016-preview-england-wales-iceland.

Second half
Rhetoric

Chapter 8

"Caveman stuff"

Ireland's soccer struggle with identity, style, and success

Michael O'Hara and Connell Vaughan

Introduction

In October 2015, Ireland hosted the world champions, Germany, in a crucial home qualifier for Euro 2016. In the pre-match analysis on national television (RTÉ), the problem of Ireland's playing style was yet again adjudged by the nation's premier soccer pundit as an approach that limits the possibility of success and even football itself. Success and soccer, by their very definition, require a commitment to ideals of beauty. The ontology of the game has been aestheticized through television and its punditry. This aestheticization elevates a culture of passing and possession as the ultimate expression of 'the beautiful game'. In order to identify the only path to victory for Ireland, Eamon Dunphy, in his analysis, traced the terms of failure:

> With respect, I think that's caveman stuff against a very, very good team, which they are undoubtedly and they have got a strong team out tonight. We have to play football. We can't go in for that 'lumping it forward' … Where they're weak is at the back and we've got to get there. You won't get there by lumping it forward in my opinion; you'll just give the ball back to them. To get at their back four, Wes Hoolihan has to be on the ball, making the play, bringing [Robbie] Brady into it. Brady is a good footballer. Set-pieces gives [sic] us a chance with Brady. Again, you won't get set-pieces unless you are putting the other team under pressure. You won't get your corners, your free kicks outside the box. So there isn't a way outside this problem without playing football.
> (Euro 2016 qualifiers: Republic of Ireland v Germany, 2015)

Despite his repeated pleas for Ireland to realize a cultured style, a continental sensibility, predicated on passing and control of the ball, Irish soccer persists in valuing passion and energy at the expense of utilizing 'a good footballing brain'. This identification of the problematic relationship of style and success in Irish soccer is a constant refrain led by Eamon Dunphy and others and is revealing of the struggle for aesthetic recognition at the heart of the nation's identity. This assessment of the Irish soccer team includes the nous of previous generations and unlike continental European countries the best of other codes, such as Munster and Leinster in Rugby Union, Dublin and Kerry Gaelic Football teams, and the Kilkenny Hurling team. By situating these experiences in the broader complex history of Irish soccer, we argue that to view such reductive style of play as authentically Irish is to repeat a mistaken narrative.

In the Irish context, the use of the words 'football' and 'soccer' are complicated by the central role the competition between footballing codes plays in national identity. While the term 'soccer' is commonly and incorrectly derided as an offensive Americanism that fails to respect association football as the 'authentic' code, in Irish sporting vernacular it is often necessary to distinguish between 'soccer' and 'football'. In practice, the differentiation remains casual and ambiguous. It is in this context that Dunphy's invocation of the term 'football' denotes and is reserved for an ideal approach to playing sport.

For Dunphy, this philosophy is grounded in fair play, guile, creativity on the ball, and honest labor. In the aforementioned qualifier with 20 minutes remaining, Ireland scored the only goal of the game. With a goal described at the time as "just a long ball played downfield" by co-commentator Ray Houghton (Euro 2016 qualifiers: Republic of Ireland v Germany, 2015), goal-scorer Shane Long characterized the qualities of the apparently typical Irish international player. By anticipating a direct aerial 'long ball' delivered by the goalkeeper to a space behind the German defensive back four, Long outpaced his opponents to smash the ball past the German goalkeeper. The manner of this victorious goal forces a deeper consideration of style and its complicated relationship to success in Irish soccer. This goal is emblematic of how Irish soccer is understood as only spirited and incapable of honoring the beauty of the game. This interpretation fails to recognize as legitimate such playing style.

In this chapter, we argue that no longer is success measured in participation at international tournaments in itself but rather the terms of such participation. The latter entails the recognition of one's style as legitimate 'football'. Central to this distinction, we argue is the defining victory of apparent 'pragmatism' over accepted ideals of beauty in the Charlton era. Trapattoni stubbornly returns to this script in his convictions of the limitations of Irish soccer identity. Trapattoni's management is exemplary of how Irish soccer has been defined as reducible to a direct and ugly vernacular style. Rather than the spectacle of the beautiful game, Ireland's play is deemed uncultured, un-continental, and unwatchable. Taking a longer view of the course of Irish soccer and its mediation, we argue that questions of identity and style are inseparable. In doing so we also argue for the beauty of direct styles of play.

Two Irelands: the complexity of Irish soccer identity

The national soccer team (in a way that other sports are not[1]) is normally an international signifier of the contemporary nation state. It is a clear marker of independence and governance. In the context of British and Irish politics, the complications and compromises of interdependence are written into the exceptional scenario that these islands comprising two states (Ireland and UK) contain five international soccer teams with overlapping jurisdictions. Both national soccer teams of Ireland are a constant challenge to state identity and the legacies of empire. As the other codes remain organized on an all-island basis post-partition, they can skirt around these issues. In claiming all-Ireland positions the GAA and rugby teams can claim a pre-modern legitimacy, and therefore cultivate a mythology of a pre-partitioned Ireland. Soccer in contrast is bound to the messy, modern post-colonial and *real-politik* of partitioned Ireland. This is evident even in the titular challenge of state identity and branding, i.e., naming. Both teams, to this day, carry the legacy of this unclear status.

In the decade from 1912 to 1922, Ireland underwent a political revolution that had existential repercussions for soccer in Ireland. Since partition and independence[2] the jurisdiction has been officially named Irish Republic (1919–1922), Southern Ireland (1921–1922), Irish Free State/Saorstát Éireann (1922–1937), and Ireland/Éire (1937–present). In addition, since the declaration of a republic on April 18, 1949, the state can also be described as Republic of Ireland. The evolution of this naming is testament to the ongoing struggle of the state to articulate its own independence from its colonial past through international recognition. The naming of the national soccer team has followed these names to the peculiar situation where the description 'Republic of' is almost exclusively synonymous with the national team, nationally and internationally. The complications of this soccer identity are a product of how the game was problematized in the national discourse during the Gaelic revival in the late nineteenth century and later compounded in soccer's unique experience of Irish partition. Coinciding with the broader leisure revolution that developed across Europe in the late nineteenth century, Irish sporting organizations were born into a turbulent era of cultural revival and social unrest. The Great Famine of the 1840s cast a long shadow over the island with land agitation marking a more strident nationalism in politics, language, culture, and sport.

In the decade from 1874 to 1884 Ireland underwent a sporting revolution in two stages. The first stage was the importation of the English modernization of football by codification. The establishment of the two major Irish sporting organizations, the Irish Rugby Football Union (1879)[3] and the Irish Football Association (1880), appealed to a burgeoning urban middle class. With the formation of the Football Association in England in 1863, soccer soon spread across the 'Home Nations'. At the invitation of Belfast merchant John McAlery, two teams from Scotland, Queens Park and Caledonians, played an exhibition game at the Ulster Cricket Grounds in Ballynafeigh on the October 24, 1878. On November 18, 1880, the Irish Football Association (IFA) was established in Queens Hotel in Belfast. The popularity of soccer spread beyond the British garrison but crucially not beyond the town. The initial growth of the game in the north-east of the country contrasted with its difficult development in the capital city of Dublin, where it struggled to gain a foothold.[4] The game in Dublin owed its origins less to garrison forces and more to settled Britons and educational institutions that "interpreted the arrival of the new code as an opportunity to foster the physical wellbeing of students" (Byrne, 2012, p. 15). Educational institutions and the garrison were apparatuses of colonial power, and outside the north-east soccer was perceived as a symbol of British rule. This was significant in distinguishing the basis of soccer in Belfast and Dublin as industrial and colonial.

The second stage of this revolution saw the Gaelic Athletic Association (GAA)[5] established in 1884. As a response to these foreign codes and as a means to stake out an independent 'Irish' identity in opposition to an encroaching Britishness, it grew its base from rural Catholic Ireland. The GAA was founded through the patronage of nationalist and religious figures such as Charles Stewart Parnell, Michael Davitt, and Archbishop Thomas Croke. As such, from its inception, the GAA was wedded to a particular politics of Gaelic identity that built on the struggle for land ownership. This struggle became the defining struggle of Irish nationalism. Soccer, in contrast and in competition, arrived loaded with the struggles of the international working class, more commonly concerned with the alienating effects of an industrial, urban society. This counter revolution brought social, economic, religious, and most importantly national divisions to the sporting field. The GAA, from its inception, positioned itself as custodian of Irish sporting identity and cultural history. Hurling, for example, was promoted as the defining Irish game.

Almost paradoxically, the GAA were able to translate the Victorian spirit of Corinthian amateurism and 'fair play' derived from the public-schooled gentleman into a mythical component of Irish sporting identity. This ideal is unavailable to the commercialized game of soccer. The quintessential example of this difference between the professional and the amateur is the formulation of the idea of the penalty kick by William McCrum while goalkeeper for Milford FC, a founding member of the Irish Football League, in the late 1880s. The existence of the penalty kick legislates for the deliberate 'professional' foul. In contrast, the figure of the Gaelic player is constructed as a modern day Cú Chulainn,[6] a loyal and passionate representative of his parish.[7] The cult of amateurism is about an attitude to playing the game, not just about remuneration. In the case of the GAA player this is framed through the virtues of commitment, courage, and resilience.

Urban Ireland is the exception to this GAA narrative that splits the amateur and the professional, the Gael and Briton. Despite the GAA's claim for Irish independence and exceptionalism, international recognition and participation is only viable for sports organized at international level. Significantly, at this stage, this required an acceptance of imperial structures. The establishment of Association Football in Belfast was thus the first team iteration of Irish sporting representation on the international stage (albeit, within the confines of the 'Home Nations').[8]

Within Ireland the competition from the GAA manifested itself through an often pernicious rivalry where the 'garrison game' and those who played it were subject to denouncement and recrimination. This culminated in the banning of participation, playing, and even attendance of 'imported', 'foreign' games, especially soccer and rugby but also cricket and field hockey. The language of the GAA "was virulently anti-British: soccer players were derided as 'Orange Catholics' and 'West-Britons'; the game they played was condemned as 'English' and, by extension, Protestant" (Rouse, 2015, p. 210).

Despite its colonial associations, by 1892, soccer's spread in the Dublin region led to the establishment of the Leinster Football Association (LFA). The LFA quickly began to demand a say about the development of the game and the structure of the national association (IFA). Differences were compounded by a perception of a northern bias in terms of match fixtures, player selection for the national team, board members, and later sectarian clashes at matches. The continued staging of 'home' games in the city of Belfast was another controversy that highlighted the power of the Belfast based IFA. Although the game began to grow across urban Ireland in the first decade of the twentieth century, the antagonism between provincial associations and tensions between northern and southern clubs continued to fester. Soccer grounds became flashpoints of religious identity and difference, highlighting the polarization of a country that was heading towards both war and revolution.

By 1921, at the height of the Irish War of Independence (1919–1921), the grievances between the IFA and the LFA reflected the growing turmoil in the country. The gathering momentum and opposition towards national independence resonated on and off the field. Sectarian tensions were rehearsed between north-eastern and southern clubs through controversies over match fixtures and cup replays that eventually led the LFA on June 8, 1921 to draft a new constitution for a new Dublin-based association. Ten days later, the draft rules of the new association were ratified and the Football Association of Ireland (FAI) was established. After an uneasy 41 years of co-existence, the fracture specifically of soccer on the island expressed the new reality of a partitioned Ireland and an emerging independent state. The result and timing of the split meant that from Belfast and indeed London, the FAI was viewed with suspicion, a tool of the new political power in Dublin. Ironically, the GAA, which had positioned itself as the sporting heart of the new Saorstát (Free State), viewed the FAI as a "partitionist body which had sold out on the notion of a united Ireland" (Byrne, 2012, p. 70). But this was to diminish the hugely important role the new FAI and soccer, the so-called 'garrison game', had in representing and promoting the new Irish State on the international stage:

> For many thousands of people across Europe, the playing of the Irish national anthem, and the tricolour on display at international games, was very often the first manifestation of the birth of a nation.
>
> (Byrne, 2012, p. 71)

The result was that by the mid-1920s only the perceived less Irish of the codes, soccer, now reflected the partitioned nature of the island. A peculiar twist of this unresolved outcome was that both the FAI and the IFA claimed jurisdiction over the entire island. In practice, this meant that there were two teams competing under the name 'Ireland'. This conflicted situation was fueled by the 'dominion status clause' granted to the FAI by the British International board in 1923. Under such status it allowed the IFA to claim players south of the border, much to the annoyance of the FAI.

The most famous example of the complexity of this situation came in 1946 when England finally agreed to play in Dublin for the first time since partition. However, they were forced to play (Northern) Ireland two days earlier as an act of appeasement. The respective claims on players from both associations once again created tensions as the IFA were blamed for leaning on English clubs in an attempt to withhold players for the second match in Dublin. However, to the FA in London it demonstrated the almost farcical nature of identity politics with two players lining up twice against England in the space of 48 hours, on two different teams, notionally representing the same island.[9] Further complicating this was the sectarian divide that affected not only the associations and clubs but encouraged active bigotry against both fans and players alike. Against this backdrop the playing of soccer in Ireland was firmly established as a political act, indicative of religious, social, and political difference. Initially estranged from the Home Countries, England, Scotland, Wales, and (IFA) Ireland, legitimacy for the FAI[10] proved to be hard earned and it would be 1934 before World Cup soccer finally arrived in Dublin. More frustrating for the fledging organization was the battle to legitimately title the new international team 'Ireland'. Due to persistent tension with the IFA, the national team continued to be recognized by London and Belfast as the 'Irish Free State'.

The dilemma of two 'Ireland' soccer teams was not only illustrative of the conflicted question of sovereign identity but impinged upon the role and identity of the player. The case of dual representation remained a constant source of tension between both associations but itself revealed the very complex nature of the Irish problem. Irish identity has routinely been connected to religious difference alone but the fact that players from both traditions sought to represent both 'Irelands' speaks of players' desire to play and willingness to represent such complexity on the international stage. Despite the FAI's continued appeals to both London and FIFA headquarters, it was not until the introduction of the Republic of Ireland Act (1948) that the issue began to be addressed. The 1948 Act, which took Ireland out of the Commonwealth, was quickly followed by the British Government's Ireland Act (1949), which ensured the future of Northern Ireland with the UK.

Simultaneously, independence was symbolically achieved on the field of play. In a forgotten memory for both sides, the game at Goodison Park on September 21, 1949, a historic victory was recorded for Ireland. The Irish soccer team (FAI) had finally come of age and its success demonstrated a deep truth about the recognition of independence and that national representation demands the international stage:

> It's a great day for the Irish. At Goodison Park, 50,000 see the soccer sensation of the season. England's first defeat on home soil by a foreign team ... eleven men for Éire upset the white shirts of England ... Brilliant players that we know them to be [England], they shed their skill with the sun and turn a vital international into a kick and rush hurly-burly. Man of the match is veteran Johnny Carey whose shrewd pass signals Éire's first goal ... Inspired by their one goal lead, Éire profit from some lucky escapes and draw still further ahead when Everton's Peter Farrell slams in number two! The England forwards keep plugging away but Lady Luck favours the Irish.
>
> (southerndiskumfort, 2007)

By the summer of 1950 the soft border between both Irish teams was beginning to harden. Dual representation in international soccer by Irish players was becoming more difficult with 'southern' clubs instructed to sanction players who attempted to play for 'both' Irelands. The problem of two Irelands persisted, with the IFA continuing to claim to be the true representative body of Irish soccer. Although clearly the smaller organization, they cited their history, recognition, and legitimacy from the other Home Nation associations. To clarify matters FIFA ruled, in 1953, that two teams in the same competition could not use the same name. They proposed that the FAI team be described as the 'Republic of Ireland' and the team selected by the IFA be described as 'Northern Ireland'.[11]

After 32 years of claim and counter-claim, the battle for identity and recognition, at least internationally, had been resolved in terms of description at least. However, it would be another 44 years of acrimony and violence before a more normalized relationship between the 'Republic' and the 'North' would fix, without repairing, the question of identity both on and off the field by the Good Friday Agreement (1998). A feature of this arrangement, in granting Irish citizenship to people born in Northern Ireland, was that it controversially enabled players born in Northern Ireland to play for the Republic of Ireland and not vice versa.

"Put 'em under pressure": the manager and the crisis of style

The post-colonial challenge to prove oneself as not only legitimate but capable governors of independence has been a constant theme in the discourse of Irish soccer. From the association's control of its finances to the player's control of alcohol, let alone the ball, Irish soccer is marked by the struggle to be professional. It is in this context that the role of the manager of the national team must be understood. Ireland's first managers were employed from within the association on a part time basis and denied the authority of team selection. Decades after its neighbors, Ireland did not appoint its first manager with ability to select players until 1969. "The lack of a full-time manager definitely cost Ireland" (Keane, 2010, p. 17). Even when managers were given this authority, the challenge of professionalism persisted. In addition to a catalogue of bad luck and near misses the Irish team's ongoing failure was due to constant issues with transport, equipment, facilities, and remuneration. As the axis between the players and the association, the figure of the manager is central to the articulation of professional practice and a sophisticated style. Given the paltry resources available, such as limited access to players, resources, and facilities, the efforts of managers from Jack Carey in 1955 to Eoin Hand in 1985 to inculcate professional standards and a 'good playing style', can be characterized as well-meaning, belated, and doomed to limited success. Years later Niall Quinn would describe the Irish teams of this period as "beautiful, skilled losers" (Malone, 2016).

A key element to this failure was the effect of televised soccer from England during the late 1960s that served to destroy the popular success that the League of Ireland experienced in the previous two decades. It has yet to recover. Furthermore, television made the GAA's prohibition on the viewing of foreign games unenforceable and this ban was abolished in 1971. In relation to the controversial ban "television effectively ended the debate with RTÉ showing rugby and soccer internationals" (Rouse, 2015, p. 302).

Ireland's soccer identity, north and south, came to be dominated by the soft power of the English league. From its inception, the English League was a magnet for Irish players and fans. Irish players could only achieve a career in soccer in England and were therefore drawn abroad. Furthermore, from the 1950s, emigration became the hallmark of the Irish state. Central to this experience was emigration to urban England for employment. In this context, certain clubs such as Liverpool, Everton, Manchester United, and Celtic were claimed as honorary 'Irish' clubs producing great Irish players.

For three decades, the Republic of Ireland national team, however, was considered little more than an adjunct in Irish sport, a "hit the post team" (Keane, 2010, p. 169) managed part-time by former players. John Giles, a championship-winning player with the great Leeds side of the 1970s, attempted to professionalize and modernize the game but continued to be hampered by the ad hoc nature of the association's approach to the game.[12] Despite a few significant victories, the team's continued failure to qualify for a major international tournament exemplified a greater malaise afflicting the state.

It was not until the advent of the Charlton era (1986–1995) that the issue of style and identity became fully invested in the team. This identity and style coalesced around a particularly direct way of playing the game, exemplified by the use of the 'long ball'. Crucially, this era marked the first period of international success for the team and the first appointment of a full-time manager. Charlton's appointment was initially controversial. As the first non-Irish and furthermore English manager, Charlton brought the paradoxical issues of national identity, representation, and style to the fore:

> Despite the presence of ... talented players in his squad, Charlton adopted a style of play that suited him. It was his crude convictions about football rather than the gifts of his players that determined the way Ireland would play.
>
> (Keane and Dunphy, 2002, p. 75)

While criticism of style had existed in previous times, the debate about playing style is to this day grounded in the formative experience of the Charlton reign where the Republic of Ireland team came to symbolize a confident, emerging, modern European nation. Furthermore, success created a broader national identification with the team beyond its traditional urban centers into GAA strongholds in rural Ireland and immigrant communities:

> When Charlton took charge of Ireland, soccer in the country was at a low ebb. The Hand era, although unlucky, had once again failed to popularity. However, Charlton, with a little luck, some tactics never-before-seen at international level, strong team organization, and

the crafty and imaginative stretching of the eligibility rules, managed to change that.

(Keane, 2010, p. 197)

Even at the height of its success, the Charlton approach was always controversial. Essential to the broadcasting of the games in Ireland was RTÉ's commentary and studio analysis that persistently bemoaned the stylistic poverty of the play as "embarrassing and shameful." Charlton's style was evident in team selection, player recruitment, and the emphasis on pragmatism and 'team players'. Driven by risk management, Charlton's commands reduced the game, sacrificing Ireland's creativity to a set of repeatable actions to suffocate the opposition's creativity. Paradoxically, while steadfast in his emphasis on system over player he established an aggressive policy of mining the Irish diaspora in Britain for the recruitment of quality players. Although Eoin Hand began to utilize the so-called 'Granny Rule',[13] Charlton exploited it. Of the 34 players he capped, 21 were English born. Mark Lawrenson was one example of such a player:

[Former Ireland goalkeeper] Alan Kelly (Senior) was assistant manager at Preston and he found out about that [Irish] link. When you're in the middle of the old third division in front of crowds of 5,000 or 6,000 you do not hold any thoughts of playing international football I can assure you, so I was only delighted to say yes. We applied for a passport, got it straight away and I was picked and played. It was as simple as that ... I think Liverpool signed me on the back of playing for Ireland so it was a win, win situation. They obviously felt if I could do it at that level I was good enough.

(Hynes, 2015)

Lawrenson's experience demonstrates how the mechanics of the 'Granny Rule' operated and how the team also became an opportunity to further players' careers. Players such as Ray Houghton illustrate the complexity and pride of representing Ireland:

Not being born there was never a problem. Others might have mentioned the fact that I wasn't born in Ireland but it was never a problem for me. My dad was from Donegal so I never really thought of it as a big issue. Even now, when I hear the Irish national anthem being played the hairs on the back of my neck stand up. It's a really passionate song and always makes me think of my father.

(Hynes, 2015)

As a result, the identity of the team itself then came to represent something beyond an authentic Gaelic Irishness. For the fan, a key feature of the team's and players' identity became the cultivation of the narratives of Irishness beyond Ireland. The soccer team thus came to exemplify the changing nature of the relationship of the state to its emigrants in a way that rugby and the GAA never could. From the ultimate unspeakable figure of shame as proof of the independent Republic's failure, the diaspora became a resource to be engaged, championed and exploited by the modern confident state. At this time 'The Boys in Green' (the players) and 'Jackie's Army' (the fans) became labels owned by the fans who assumed the ambassadorial responsibility of the nation. The fans successfully positioned themselves internationally as fun loving, resilient, and an antidote to (English) hooliganism.

Questions of progeny dominated the discourse surrounding Charlton's teams. With no players from the domestic league the team were labelled 'England B' and 'Plastic Paddies'. Only six of the 22 players that travelled to Italy in 1990 were born in the Republic. At USA '94 only seven of the players were born in the Republic. The rest were born in England (13) and Scotland (2). Furthermore, none of these players were playing for League of Ireland teams. The sense of *ersatz* Irishness was reinforced by the fact that these players were second- and third-generation emigrants:[14]

> every player we brought into the squad considered himself Irish ... Had it not been for the economic circumstances which forced their parents or grandparents to emigrate, they would have been born and reared in Ireland. Should they now be victimized and denied their heritage because of the whims of journalists? I think not.
>
> (Charlton and Byrne, 1996, p. 221)

Integral to this style of management was the aesthetic figure and character of Charlton. The image of 'Big Jack' is of a limited but hard, working-class, combative player who forced his way out of the coal pits of the north-east of England to have a successful career.[15] These characteristics of his playing style became a doctrine for him to apply as a manager. His philosophy was derived from Charles Hughes, 'Director of Coaching of the FA', and his concept of 'Positions of Maximum Opportunity' (POMO), which emphasizes the value of direct play and the use of the 'long ball' over passing:

> Hughes claim[ed] that 85% of goals are scored from moves of five consecutive passes or fewer. A quarter of goals in his study involved no passes at all, being scored directly from set plays, defensive rebounds or interceptions.
>
> (Menary, 2014, p. 60)

Building on POMO, Charlton's approach brought a clearly defined style characterized by the immortal phrase "Put 'em under pressure!"

This involved the repeated and sustained testing of the opposition's defense with long, direct, and high balls into the box. This was achieved by bypassing from above the creative space of midfield, ideally from the goal kick. Through such design, the inventiveness of the midfield and attacking players on the ball for both sides was denied.

The strategy was initiated by the goalkeeper and fullbacks whose task was to launch the ball into the opposition's half. The disorientating effect of high aerial balls disrupts and effaces the advantage of the passing team. A core element of this doctrine was the elimination of perceived risky raids by fullbacks in the service of maintaining a solid defensive shape to frustrate the opposition's creativity. The offensive threat of the team was directed towards a big 'target man' (e.g., Niall Quinn or Tony Cascarino) who was the primary creative agent. The function of this player was to physically impose and force this style of play on the opposition through his persistent pressing and harrying of the opposition's two center-backs and goalkeeper. The success of the striker was measured in more than just goals. The striker was now tasked with defending from the front and winning and defending set-pieces.

The logic of this approach subscribes to the principles of POMO. When "faced with technically superior opponents, Hughes did all he could to win, embracing a more physical, direct approach that eschewed comfort on the ball" (Menary, 2014, p. 62). The resistance to this approach, as exemplified by Dunphy, argues that it is reactionary and anti-football, particularly because in its suspicion it sacrifices the mercurial skill of the cultured footballer, specifically the creative 'midfield playmaker'[16] (Liam Brady, Ronnie Whelan, Andy Reid, and Wes Hoolihan). In Charlton's approach, midfielders such as Andy Townsend, Roy Keane, Ronnie Whelan, and John Sheridan were entrusted with the responsibility of breaking down the play and recycling the ball. This recycling entailed passing the ball back to the defense, including the goalkeeper, to restart the process. In Keane's words:

> My job is to close down the opposition and if possible win the ball. Having gained possession, passing to an Irish colleague seemed the obvious next move. But that was not what Charlton wanted. His fear of Ireland giving the ball away—especially in our own half of the field—caused real inhibitions for me and most of the other players, who were forced to adapt our own games to the Charlton Method. "Don't give the fucking ball away," Charlton would shout in the dressing room if by chance you had lost possession trying to start a move in your own half of the pitch or in midfield. "Hit the front men" was his slogan.
>
> (Keane and Dunphy, 2002, p. 52)

In this system, the field of play is one of physical pressing where the tactic is to disrupt the opposition's capacity to pass the ball. Instead of trusting the spontaneous ability of the player, Charlton's approach to risk management privileged the players who subscribed to his style. The extreme example of Charlton's suppression of midfield creativity came in the selection of the defender Paul McGrath in midfield. He was not deployed as a sweeper, nor as an orthodox defensive midfielder but operated as an auxiliary defender in midfield. However, beyond his formation, Charlton was sure to retain 'creative midfield players' in his squads and team selection on the understanding that his system was paramount. This flexibility meant that his system could accommodate limited creativity once the system was not compromised.

In addition to the goalkeeper offering a reset, the set piece became the privileged route of offensive play. Free kicks, corners, and throw-ins were rehearsed to exploit the physical, direct, and aerial nature of the game plan. The set piece became a short circuit that nullified the difference in quality between two teams. Charlton's teams valorized these moments of reset. These occasions of structured pressure were designed to create chances so players did not have to. Straightforward directions relieved the players of the cognitive and creative demands of fashioning a chance with the ball. The labor of the game was about pressuring the opposition who had the ball. In this context, the game was transformed into a test of the opposition's ability to cope with Ireland's resistance to playing with the ball, especially on the ground.

For Ireland, Charlton's reign was an era of unprecedented and tangible success, qualifying for its first three international tournaments. This success is essential in Charlton's style becoming tied to the image and self-image of the team as peddling an unsophisticated, vernacular style. Other labels routinely used to describe Ireland's 'route one' style include: workmanlike, pragmatic, ugly, negative, limited, etc. Despite different styles, management philosophies, and varying success in the following decade, this identity persisted.

Ireland's stylistic reputation is essential to understanding the disappointments of the Trapattoni era (2008–2013). Upon his appointment, there was great hope among pundits, players, and fans alike, that this internationally heralded forensic Italian coach would bring a sophisticated continental approach to Irish soccer. Trapattoni's approach, however, was marked by a greater distrust of the Irish player to be anything more than workmanlike. The rigidness of his system went further than Charlton. Where Charlton was sure to retain 'creative players', Trapattoni was quick to ostracize any suggestion of midfield invention and ball retention. Risk was to be avoided at all cost. He eschewed new players and had an unbending loyalty to senior players and excused such resistance by repeatedly emphasizing that Ireland was a small country.

If the success of Charlton's teams heralded a 'Celtic Tiger' confidence, then Trapattoni's approach echoed an era of austerity. The question of style instigated a veritable crisis under the Italian coach. Trapattoni subscribed to the cultural stereotype of the technical and tactical limitations of the Irish team and player. His failure to attempt or move beyond such a stereotype belied an inability or unwillingness to import the best of his own coaching record and pedigree to the Irish job. In terms of legitimacy, the challenge for Ireland had moved from one of *participation* (politics) to *style* (aesthetics). Although Trapattoni secured qualification to the European Championship Finals in 2012, his Ireland team was cruelly and embarrassingly exposed by the sophisticated passing styles of elite European nations. Success now demanded stylistic validation.

Trapattoni's "late style," as O'Dea (2016, p. 135) has argued, was an untrusting and "intransigent approach" that ceded all attempts to foster a nuanced and developed style. Specifically "once he had found a way of consolidating a highly structured, technically indifferent defensive unit ... he did not appear too concerned with what may naturally be assumed to be the next obvious destination for thought: attack" (O'Dea, 2016, p. 135). Ultimately, the disappointment of the Trapattoni era was his refusal to inculcate what is commonly seen as an Italian sensibility. This sensibility emphasizes the 'art of defending' that provides the springboard for a more 'cultured' approach to using the ball. Trapattoni's conviction was that continental sophistication could not be translated into Irish soccer and to expect so was unreasonable, given the proven success of direct play. The cliché of the 'direct' style of the Charlton era had become the default blueprint for success at international level. Trapattoni's inflexible approach, convinced that a limited stylistic approach defined the Irish psyche and "apparent acceptance to *remain* misunderstood" (O'Dea, 2016, p. 136, italics in original), blinded him from a potential route to success and eventually alienated him from the Irish soccer community. The poverty of Trapattoni's conservatism was emphasized by the aesthetic context of soccer in this era.

Style as ontological distinction in soccer

Style functions as an ontological distinction in soccer, especially in its aesthetic appreciation. In the British and Irish context, the distinction operates by separating technical excellence on the ball from physical prowess. The former is associated with a continental way of being; the latter signifies an island mentality. This island discourse continually emphasizes the specific 'continental' European aesthetic heritage of Total Football, the disciplining and professional developments of sports science, and the cultivation of the cerebral player. The British[17] and Irish game, in contrast, is routinely defined by the absence of technique and style.

The mark of the 'cultured' team is what they do on the ball. Possession, ball retention and short quick incisive passing on the ground have become the defining metric for stylistic success in the contemporary game. The commentary surrounding the game champions 'The Barcelona Way' as the refined culmination of the beautiful game (see Hunter, 2012). We do not dispute the aesthetic achievements of this playing style. Rather, we challenge the accompanying British and Irish discourse which not only equates style with national identity but valorizes the continental sensibility as the only true way to play and appreciate the game. When elevated to an ontological truth so-called 'European sophistication' condemns a direct style of play as worse than uncultured and vernacular, it is embarrassingly anti-football. Style is in short paradoxically a marker for its opposite, substance. Style, however, is not the preserve of sophistication. There is beauty to the passing game *and* the pressing game. The skilled execution of a simple and direct football (so-called 'route one') has its own aesthetic. This is a beauty recognizable in Shane Long's goal versus Germany. What is this beauty?

We contend that this is a beauty that is transparent in its honesty and directness from Darren Randolph's (the goalkeeper) assist to Shane Long's well-placed shot. In soccer discourse, as seen in Dunphy's quote, such a move has been denied the status of even 'football', being nothing more than "lumping it forward" (Euro 2016 qualifiers: Republic of Ireland v Germany, 2015). This is a beauty, however, that recognizes that the type of scoring used in soccer is discrete and therefore embraces the element of chance that can unlock the best defenses. This is a beauty born of planning not panic. The team knows that Shane Long, using his pace, will repeatedly run into the space behind the German back line. Critical to this is the movement of the rest of the team, especially Jonathan Walters, whose decoy run momentarily misdirects the German defense. This is a well-rehearsed tactic known to both teams yet remains difficult to defend against when executed properly. This is a rare beauty, especially at the elite level of the game. Finally, this is a beauty that can never be entirely framed through the medium of television. It requires vision of the entire field of play, something only available to those present in the stadium.

It could be argued that, more than a marker, the substance of soccer *is* style. If so, then soccer is inherently an aesthetic game. This position is increasingly privileged by the framing medium that is television. Aspects of the undeniable contemporary aestheticization of the game include the video replay, slow motion, live pause, multiple camera angles, and live commentary. These elements combine to reduce the game to a set of peak aesthetic moments. The less directed experience of the spectator in the stadium, in contrast, is sensitive to the collective and individual labor of play, such as decoy movement, feints, and the organization of defending and is exposed to the general material conditions of the game such as the state of the pitch, the weather conditions, and the spectacle of the crowd itself. These elements are denied to the television viewer whose interpretation of the game is experienced as a forensic analysis of a digital product. Even the repeated viewing offered by television cannot fully capture and appreciate the tactical vision inherent in the game.

The Shane Long goal demonstrates the limitations of the screen to represent the beauty and the sophistication of certain passages of play. Its sophistication is difficult to see but its lack of apparent stylization is not a lack of style. This is a concrete style. It is more than skill and ability. This goal demonstrates how the spectacle of modern soccer still evades the complete mediation of the screen and is a quintessential example of a beauty that can be successful.

The denial of the long, high ball as legitimate soccer unfairly equates the Irish footballing psyche as best suited to GAA and rugby.[18] Ireland's style was played without the ball, thus misidentifying them as footballers devoid of guile, craft, and creative style. However, the mark of the cultured team is in fact game management. To focus exclusively on passing and technical ability is a limited perspective. It overlooks all of the play that happens without the ball. To be a refined footballing nation requires embracing both sets of professional practices. Where the direct style seeks to disrupt and deny, the continental passing game is associated, in British and Irish discourse, with deception and denial. Denial in the former limits the opposition's ability to play with the ball; in the latter, the indirectness of play and domination of possession limits the opposition's access to the ball.

Conclusion

In 1990, at the height of Charlton's international success, the Irish team was seen as the most egregious case of a cynical infection afflicting the beautiful game. The perceived cynicism of that style required intervention, and after the World Cup the back-pass rule was introduced, diminishing the keeper's ability to control the ball and influence the tempo of the game. A distinguishing feature of this model which is often overlooked, however, is the key role of pressing that deploys facets of Charlton's management. Indeed, Charlton himself is forthright in his claim that Ireland created and perfected this aspect of the game, way back in 1986:

> It amazes me that teams like Milan and many of the European teams now [are credited with this style], there's a terminology called 'pressing'. We were doing that in 1986, but now it is considered a good thing in the game of football to press. The Irish were pressing teams in '86. We invented the game.
>
> (Desert Island Discs, 1996)

The figure of the European coach is celebrated for his genius, in contrast to the British and Irish manager who is framed in terms of shrewdness and pragmatism. Ironically, Trapattoni's contemporary, Arigo Sacchi, successfully incorporated this tactic. Like the Charlton team of the mid 1980s, Sacchi's famous AC Milan side utilized a high defensive line to close space and frustrate opposition possession. Sacchi's team successfully combined the best of disruptive pressing while maintaining a commitment to the passing game. Unlike Charlton's Irish teams, AC Milan's disciplined pressure was recognized for its variation and flexibility, as Sacchi explains:

> [W]e had several types of pressing, that we would vary throughout the game. There was partial pressing, where it was more about jockeying; there was total pressing which was more about the ball; there was fake pressing, when we pretended to press, but, in fact, used the time to recuperate.
>
> (Wilson, 2014, p. 315)

In current discourse the pressing game is heralded as the new European way, the consummate example being Jürgen Klopp's now infamous *Gegenpressing* ('counter pressing').[19] However, this emphasis on the pressing game is little more than a repackaged and rebranded Sacchi/Charlton hybrid.

In the immediate aftermath of Ireland's surprisingly comfortable play-off qualification (at the expense of Bosnia-Herzegovina) for the European Championship Finals 2016, Roy Keane, in his role of Assistant Manager, presented the figure of a man broken by the Irish aesthetic and its relationship to professionalism. "Attitude is more important than ability," he conceded to RTÉ soccer correspondent Tony O'Donoghue (Euro 2016 qualifiers: Republic of Ireland v Bosnia-Herzegovina, 2015). This shattered, tragic figure perhaps realized 'on mature reflection' that it was a statement that could also apply to him. Keane as Ireland's most famously successful player epitomized all character but fought for an unattainable professionalism. There is in Keane's concession a realization of a *different path* to success in soccer. In doing so this reckoning requires recognition that Keane is not abandoning a commitment to technique. The commentary by Eamon Dunphy on Ireland's current style appears to acknowledge this progression: "We are playing a *bit* of ball now ... we are passing the ball ... that old caveman stuff is over" (Today with Sean O'Rourke, 2016, our italics). The recognition that the identity of the national team, and by extension the country itself, is no longer bound to the clichéd narrative of 'the long ball'. In short, in terms of success, participation has been supplemented by the question of style and its management.

Notes

1 The teams that compete in international soccer, with some exceptions such as the four UK nations, are independent states. The national team in rugby and cricket for example is less wedded to the contemporary nation state.
2 An unclear date, but depending on one's political view it could be any one of several dates between 1916 and 1949 or not yet achieved.
3 Initially, two separate rugby associations arose in Dublin and Belfast, but they quickly bridged their differences and amalgamated in 1879.
4 Significantly, the north-east was the only area of the island to experience the industrial revolution and contained a majority of the Unionist community.
5 Its full name is the Gaelic Athletic Association for the Preservation of Cultivation of National Pastimes.
6 Cú Chulainn is a mythical Irish heroic warrior, defined by his fierceness in battle and his loyalty.
7 The teams are organized around the network of Catholic parishes.
8 The British Home Championship 1884–1984 was an annual soccer competition contested between England, Scotland, Wales, and Ireland. It was the oldest international football tournament.
9 Until FIFA's ruling in 1954, over 40 players lined up for both Irelands at international level.
10 FAIFS or Football Association of the Irish Free State was the new title of the FAI from 1923 when the new association sought legitimacy and membership from the IFAB (International Football Association Board) and then FIFA. It was not until the drafting of a new Irish constitution in 1937 when the Irish Free State became Éire (Ireland in the Irish language) that FAIFS returned to its earlier title of the FAI. The Belfast-based team represented Ireland in the British Home Championship after partition.
11 "the IFA tabl[ed] a motion at FIFA's annual Congress at Lisbon in 1954, calling on the authorities to instruct the FAI to refrain from misrepresenting themselves as Ireland in international competition" (Byrne, 2012, p. 198). Although the IFA's claim was rejected, they continued to pointedly play as 'Ireland' in the British Home Nations championship until the tournament's demise in 1981.
12 In 1969, Giles, then a player, led a player's convention to the FAI demanding that the manager be allowed to pick the team. The FAI relented, and for the first time the manager was now tasked with selecting his squad and starting eleven.
13 The 'Granny Rule' refers to the FIFA statute that permits a player to play for a given national team as long as at least "[H]is grandmother or grandfather was born on the territory of the relevant association" (FIFA, 2016).
14 The first-generation emigrant has tended to congregate around the GAA.
15 This image is in immediate contrast to and overshadowed by his more skillful brother Bobby who played his way out.
16 Internationally the midfield playmaker (*regista* or *meia-armador*) is a player who controls the tempo of the game and is the fulcrum of possession and the creative locus for attack. Contemporary examples include: Luka Modric, Xabi Alonso, Andrea Pirlo.
17 While we have focused on the Irish context the same question of style clearly haunts the English national team as well. See Jonathan Wilson's excellent analysis of 'English pragmatism' and the adoption of a direct style at coaching level of the FA during the 1980s in contrast to the more possession-based play of continental European teams (Wilson, 2014). See also David Kilpatrick's contribution to this volume.

18 The German coach, Joachim Löw, for example, has made that connection: "They can defend really well. It's part of their tradition, to defend their own goal, like in Gaelic football or rugby" (RTÉ, 2013).

19 See Simon Critchley's contribution to this volume on "Klopp's Heideggerianism."

References

Byrne, P. 2012. Green is the colour: The story of Irish football. London: Carlton Books.

Charlton, J. and Byrne, P. 1996. The autobiography. London: Partridge Press.

Desert Island Discs, Jackie Charlton. 1996. BBC Radio4. October 25, 09:05. Available from: www.bbc.co.uk/programmes/p0093n6w.

Euro 2016 qualifiers: Republic of Ireland v Bosnia-Herzegovina. 2015. RTÉ2. November 16, 19:00.

Euro 2016 qualifiers: Republic of Ireland v Germany. 2015. RTÉ2. October 8, 19:00.

FIFA. 2016. FIFA statutes. [Online]. [Accessed September 12, 2017]. Available from: www.fifa.com/mm/document/affederation/generic/02/58/14/48/2015fifasta tutesen_neutral.pdf.

Hunter, G. 2012. Barca: The making of the greatest team in the world. London: Backpage Press.

Hynes, J. 2015. Why I chose to play for Ireland: Former internationals explain their decisions. Irish Independent. [Online]. May 7. [Accessed September 12, 2017]. Available from: www.independent.ie/sport/soccer/international-soccer/why-i-chose-to-play-for-ireland-former-internationals-explain-their-decisions-31202072.html.

Keane, R. and Dunphy, E. 2002. Keane: The autobiography. London: Michael Joseph.

Keane, T. 2010. Gaffers: 50 years of Irish football managers. Dublin: Mercier.

Malone, E. 2016. Euro '88: Jack Charlton points Ireland's "beautiful, skilled losers" on path to glory. The Irish Times. [Online]. May 28. [Accessed September 12, 2017]. Available from: www.irishtimes.com/sport/soccer/international/euro-88-jack-charlton-points-ireland-s-beautiful-skilled-losers-on-path-to-glory-1.2663602.

Menary, S. 2014. Maximum opportunity. The Blizzard. **12**, pp. 57–62.

O'Dea, A. 2016. Late style. The Blizzard. **19**, pp. 133–141.

Rouse, P. 2015. Sport in Ireland: A history. London: Oxford University Press.

RTÉ. 2013. Joachim Loew praises Ireland's defending tradition "like in Gaelic football or rugby." [Online]. October 9. [Accessed September 12, 2017]. Available from: www.rte.ie/sport/soccer/2013/1009/479364-loew-ireland-will-be-no-pushovers/.

southerndiskumfort. 2007. Football: Ireland v England 1949. [Online]. [Accessed September 12, 2017]. Available from: www.youtube.com/watch?v=09jvRjdHFwE.

Today with Sean O'Rourke, Weekend Sports. 2016. RTÉ Radio 1. June 27, 10:00.

Wilson, J. 2014. Inverting the pyramid: The history of soccer tactics. London: Orion.

Chapter 9

The beautiful and the grim

British cultural discourses of the Eastern European game

Blanka Blagojevic

In the preface to his book *The World through Soccer*, Canadian-Israeli scholar and avid soccer fan, Tamir Bar-On posits:

> If we examine the world through soccer, we learn lessons about human nature, leadership, discipline and hard work, talent, luck, time, rules, values, ethics, passion and reason, individuality and teamwork, ... culture, politics, business and marketing, violence, spirituality, life meaning, ... and social struggle.
>
> (Bar-On, 2014, p. xiii)

With a similar faith in soccer's ability to uncover the secret of other nations' mentalities and cultures, two sports journalists and travel authors, Simon Kuper in 1994 and Jonathan Wilson in 2006, set off from Great Britain to learn about the world through the soccer lens.

In the introductory section of his book, Simon Kuper explains that his nine-month long soccer journey into 22 countries around the world would be guided by the following two questions: "How [does] football affect ... the life of a country?"; and "how [does] the life of a country affect ... its football?" (Kuper, 1996, p. 2). In contrast, Jonathan Wilson proclaims that his travel book "is a testament to the extraordinary cultural fact of football, its universality, its ability to draw people together from utterly different backgrounds," but also that "it is the story of how Eastern Europe has changed since the Berlin Wall came down" (2006b, pp. 4–5).[1] Unlike Kuper, whose framing of the game's relationship with the countries he visits is of a more general nature due to his more global itinerary, Wilson is more precise with respect to the subject matter which he is to explore in the course of his journey. He points out that one of his journey's and the book's goals is to analyze how the countries of the former Eastern Bloc are now coping with the new capitalist order and how the economic and political transition after the fall of the Iron Curtain has affected the soccer game (Wilson, 2006b, p. 5).

My analysis of the way Eastern European soccer is depicted in the two narratives—Kuper's *Football against the Enemy* (1996) and Wilson's

Behind the Curtain: Travels in Eastern European Football (2006b)—seeks to identify representations of both the beautiful and the grim aspects of the Eastern European game, and, more generally, to answer the question as to how these authors perceive Eastern European cultural spaces in the first place. Both narratives are written post-1989 and thus make many references to both the Communist period and Cold War era and to the often painful and unstable aftermath in the transition period of the 1990s.

Following David Spurr's analysis of the basic rhetorical features of colonial discourse in his classic *The Rhetoric of the Empire*, where he identifies a number of "rhetorical modes, or ways of writing about non-Western peoples" (1994, p. 3), I borrow the concept of 'debasement' to identify the grim and the concept of 'idealization' to discuss the beautiful elements of the Eastern European game as depicted in the soccer narratives under scrutiny here. I argue that although both narratives contain many instances of representing Eastern European soccer spaces as marred by the grim picture of the Cold War tensions between the East and the West and by the negative image of the East due to its legacy of Communism and isolation, they manage to produce a fairly balanced picture of soccer culture in the European East by applying the rhetorical mode of 'idealization' in their accounts of individual players' performances as well as particular teams' playing styles. The rhetorical mode of 'debasement', as David Spurr contends, reads as a fairly straightforward "projection of anxiety onto the … cultural Other" where the focus is on "images inspired by … fear and loathing" (1994, p. 77). The trope of 'idealization' is more ambiguous, because alongside the positive images of the Other on which it focuses, this trope always carries 'the subtext' of romanticized images of the Other in conjunction with the authors' moralizing stance towards their own culture and the need to distance themselves from it. This romanticized imagery has the potential of doing a disservice towards the Other because it treats the Other as "a *construct*" and "an abstract ideal" filled with "symbolic value" rather than real people in real contexts (Spurr, 1994, p. 126, italics in original). David Spurr claims that the strategy of idealization "always takes place *in relation* to Western culture itself" and that it uses the cultural Other "to expand the territory of the Western imagination," transforming "the Other into yet one more term of Western culture's dialogue with itself" (1994, p. 128, italics in original). Oddly enough, idealization strategies go hand in hand with debasement strategies as they strive to domesticate and commodify "the more bizarre and threatening aspects of the cultural Other" (Spurr, 1994, p. 129). The fact that these idealized descriptions appear in travel narratives in relation to sports and sports journalism does not come as a surprise given that the mentioned rhetorical proclivities are inherent to both of these genres at large.[2]

Spurr draws his examples from "nonfiction writing, and literary journalism" and related genres such as travel writing (1994, p. 3). Kuper and

Wilson's texts fit squarely here as they constitute hybrids between sports journalism and travel writing. Spurr notes that the rhetorical modes he identifies "are part of the landscape in which relations of power manifest themselves" (1994, p. 3). Furthermore, he maintains that "[t]hese rhetorical modes ... are the tropes that come into play with the establishment and maintenance of colonial authority, or, as sometimes happens, those that register the loss of such authority" (1994, p. 3). It is precisely this *loss of power* which becomes visible in the two narratives I analyze.

I have already mentioned that these rhetorical modes are "ways of writing about non-Western peoples" (Spurr, 1994, p. 3). To which extent, then, does the colonialist rhetoric play out in discourses about Eastern Europe? Eastern Europe, as Maria Todorova (2009, p. xi) reminds us, "came to be identified more often, and often exclusively, with industrial backwardness, lack of advanced social relations and institutions typical for the developed capitalist West" thus being constructed as yet another non-Western Other. Although Todorova's work focuses primarily on the image of the Balkans in the Western cultural imaginary, she maintains that there is a strong similarity between the Western perception of the Balkans and that of Eastern Europe as a whole, which, in her words, has "become a synonym for a reversion to the tribal, the backward, the primitive, the barbarian" (2009, p. 3). The period of the Cold War and the 'political technology'[3] of the Iron Curtain helped to reinforce this East–West division of Europe, which remains vivid in the cultural memory as "a crucial structural boundary in the mind and on the map" (Wolff, 1994, p. 1). German literary and cultural discourses have recognized this phenomenon as "the wall in the head" or "die Mauer im Kopf,"[4] which suggests that even after the physical obstacles of the Cold War divisions have been dismantled, the mental divisions and cultural stereotypes still remain. However, as Larry Wolff reminds us in the aftermath of the dismantling of the Iron Curtain, the idea of Eastern Europe is much older than the Cold War divisions of the twentieth century (1994, p. 3).

Wolff (1994, p. 4) claims that "[i]t was Western Europe that invented Eastern Europe as its complementary other half in the eighteenth century, the age of Enlightenment" when, according to Wolff, Western Europe invented the term 'civilization'. Western European intellectuals then used the term to describe the European West as the center of civilization while the construction of Eastern Europe as the West's

> ... complement, within the same continent, in shadowed lands of backwardness, even barbarism ... flourished as an idea of extraordinary potency ... neatly dovetailing in our own times with the rhetoric and realities of the Cold War.
>
> (Wolff, 1994, p. 4)

The biased rhetoric surrounding Eastern European cultural spaces has out-lived the fall of the Iron Curtain just as British colonial discourse and imperialism have survived "the formal ending of colonial rule" (Spurr, 1994, p. 5).

In this vein, Wilson adds that his soccer travel narrative is also "the story of how Eastern Europe has changed since the Berlin Wall came down"—presumably leaving behind that Communist backwardness and starting to resemble more and more its Western counterpart (2006b, p. 5). This is a recurrent narrative feature as post-Wall travel narratives about Eastern Europe constantly refer to the watershed year of 1989 as well as to the period before the fall of the Wall in order to observe changes in Eastern Europe's cultural landscapes and people.[5]

Apart from confirming and cementing Eastern Europe's subaltern status of the non-Western Other, there is another key element which symbolizes British imperial power in Wilson's and Kuper's texts—the heritage of the soccer game itself. In her study of stereotyping in soccer, Sybille Frank reiterates Christiane Eisenberg's claim that "the British conquered the world a second time with the help of football" and that "[t]he globalisa-tion of the game ... was accompanied by an increasing national codifica-tion of football" (Eisenberg, 2004, p. 44, cited in Frank, 2011, p. 72). Drawing on the studies of Richard Holt and Barrie Houlihan on sports, politics, and nationalism, Athena S. Leoussi (2001, p. 280) concludes that "[g]lobalized sport ... legitimized British imperialism and nationalism in the nineteenth century" and that it helps "foist Western values upon the non-West today."

The fact that Britain is the cradle of the sport and *the* one place to come to play it in order to be perceived as a respectable opponent is noted by both Kuper and Wilson. Kuper, in his description of the efforts of the Croatian national team in the mid-1990s to become recognized and taken seriously by the West, suggests that they see it as the legitimation ritual not only of their sporting qualities but also of the then young and newly inde-pendent state of Croatia. He writes:

> So, Croatia desperately wants to be accepted by the West, and there are few stronger symbols of Western Europe than Wembley. The stadium stands for the old, unchanging Europe. For Croatia, playing at Wembley is as if Tudjman [the then President of the State] were asked to address the House of Commons. To play at Wembley is to be accepted.
>
> (Kuper, 1996, p. 234)

Leoussi (2001, p. 282) confirms this tendency "to gain legitimacy inter-nationally" through sports as she argues that sport becomes a means to legitimize or promote the political interests of a country as there is little risk involved in doing so. In addition, this often happens in such a way as to appear unrelated to the pursuit of national(istic) interests. This argument is clearly reflected in Kuper's view of Croatian politics using soccer as a legitimization platform.

Similarly, Wilson, describing the memorable 1953 game between England and Hungary, which was in his words "billed as the 'Match of the Century'" (2006b, p. 70), notes that what made the game particularly memorable for the Hungarian team was the fact that it was played in England against the English national side. "Wembley was like a holy place for footballers, so there was a certain nervousness in going out there," Wilson (2006b, p. 77) writes, and the side which displayed this "nervousness" was the Hungarian 'Golden Squad' led by the legendary Ferenc Puskas, whose team in the end and despite the awe they felt in having to play the British on their home turf, still won the match.

The British assuredness of their top status as well as England's self-perception as *the* soccer power comes out in both travel narratives, albeit admittedly not without a slight critical tinge. This tendency reflects what Spurr defines as 'the colonial condition', which entails:

> [a] set of relations [which] is put into place between two different cultures: one fast-moving, technologically advanced, and economically powerful; the other slow-moving and without advanced technology or a complex economy.
>
> (1994, p. 6)

Kuper, whose narrative displays a more dismissive view of non-Western cultures than Wilson's, notes down in detail his conversation with Danish soccer manager Richard Moeller-Nielsen, just because, or so it seems, the manager is full of praise for "England and English football" (1996, p. 32). He quotes Moeller-Nielsen:

> "I like the long-ball game," ... "It gets the balls in front of goal. Football should not be played in midfield. English football has a class, a decency to it which does not exist anywhere else in the world ... I am often at Manchester United and Liverpool, and I see how well organized these clubs are, how fair the fans are."
>
> (Kuper, 1996, p. 32)

While Wilson fails to find an interlocutor who would admit to admiring English soccer culture as openly as Moeller-Nielsen, he takes notice of the English confidence in their own superiority even on the eve of some of the greatest soccer failures. Thus, returning to the 'Match of the Century' against Hungary in 1953, Wilson observes that the English fans' faith in their athletic and general superiority was palpable on the eve of the match:

Britain was still great. The war was over, and won, the rationing was coming to an end ... and there was a young queen newly crowned—her place in the divine order of things seemingly confirmed, as news broke on the day of the Coronation that the Empire had conquered Everest, And, of course, in popular opinion, England were still the best in the world in football, unbeaten at home against foreign opposition—as the joke of the time had it—since 1066.

(Wilson, 2006b, p. 70)

These lines seem to suggest what Spurr (1994, p. 3) perceives as "latent crisis," a term he borrows from Georges Balandier, and "the fear of 'the loss of ... authority'" (Spurr, 1994, p. 6): England is lulled into the illusion of their invincibility on the eve of the game they are going to lose, forgetting that their long row of victories had in fact been interrupted recently when they lost to the Republic of Ireland in 1949 (Wilson, 2006b, p. 70).[6]

Another team which came close to challenging the English at Wembley despite their underdog status was the Polish national team in 1973. The star of the evening was their goalkeeper Jan Tomaszewski, who was mocked by the British press as "a 'clown'" looking "disheveled" with a "mop of gingery hair held in place by a length of twine," as Wilson remembers the moment, "but he kept goal like a brick wall" and "produced a series of unorthodox blocks to earn Poland the draw that saw them to the World Cup finals at England's expense" (2006b, p. 43). The awe before Wembley and England is present once again. Wilson writes that the Polish team went "to Wembley in a state of approaching terror" and that "Wembley was hell" (2006b, p. 44) because of its size, its noise, and its construction, none of which the Polish team had experienced before. Moreover, the imperial aura of the place is firmly cemented when both Polish and English teams have "a presentation to the queen" during which "[t]he Polish players all stood to attention, but the England players were used to it, very casual" and "chewing gum" (2006b, p. 44). This episode once again recalls Spurr's "fear of the loss of [colonial] authority" (1994, p. 6), at least by hindsight, as Wilson actually admits that the draw of 1973 "remains one of those landmarks in the perceived decline of English football, the first time England had failed to qualify for a World Cup" (2006b, p. 45).

Wilson also notes that the fans in Eastern Europe are inspired by various aspects of the "British disease"—hooliganism. Thus, when writing about one of Red Star Belgrade's subgroups of supporters—the so-called Red Devils—he notes that they describe themselves as a group "who 'adopted Serbian habits mixed with English habits', ... 'drinking to death, beating rivals and consuming marijuana'" and adds that "[a]s with their English counterparts, the general violent nihilism coexisted with an extreme right-wing philosophy" (2006b, pp. 105–106). A couple of pages further on, Wilson observes again, in a slightly mocking tone, that the Ultras of Dinamo Zagreb[7] call themselves "the Bad Blue Boys," explaining that they "took their name … from the Sean Penn film *Bad Boys*," the name "always written in English, of course, for all the best hooligans are English" (2006b, p. 154). Similarly, Kuper notices the pervasive influence of English soccer culture on the Eastern European game, even if at times it is only detectable in its pale symbolic traces. While observing a game between the Estonian and Swiss national teams playing each other at the Estonian capital of Tallinn, Kuper notes how the Swiss fans behave more creatively and freely, even singing in English "Always Look on the Bright Side of Life," while the Estonians "had only one chant—'Esti, Esti'—though they painted a flag in the shape of the Union Jack, but in Estonian colours" (1996, p. 33).

The legacy of the game born in England and brought to Eastern Europe by the English is emphasized time and again. Thus, Kuper reminds the readers that the English played an active and founding role in the historical heritage of Russian soccer culture. Kuper tells us that the club that later in the Soviet period became Dynamo Moscow—the "team of [KGB]—one of the most privileged sectors of society under Joseph Stalin"—"was founded by Englishmen," the Charnock brothers, to be more precise (Edelman, 2002, p. 1445). This is, according to Kuper, "[h]ardly surprising, … because Englishmen founded clubs all over the world, but not, one would have thought, Dynamo Moscow" (1996, p. 48). Although the club's initial name Orekhovo Sport Club was changed later, Kuper notes contently that "one Charnock tradition survived, and does to this day: Dynamo still play in the blue and white of the Orekhovo Sport club" because the founders were fans of the Blackburn Rovers (1996, p. 48).

However, in the contemporary globalized world, the symbolic power struggle over who owns whom complicates the old paradigm of association football as the British game. Not only are British teams enhanced by Eastern European soccer talent, they are sometimes owned by Eastern European money. Thus, in a subtly subversive antipode to the symbolic victory of one old Empire over the other, Wilson (2006b, p. 303) duly remarks that the "Chelsea" of the 2000s became a "symbol of the new Russia," and as can be inferred from the narrative, the fact that its owner is a Russian attracts a new wave of Russian fans to cheer for Chelsea in Moscow bars and pubs these days.

The examples above indicate the tendency of both narratives' attempt to establish the notion that in the British cultural imaginary Britain, which more often than not means England, saw itself as the rarely disputed soccer world power and an ultimate authority when it came to the quality of soccer and the culture surrounding the game itself. Moreover, they do not fail to emphasize their country's role in spreading the game into the

The beautiful and the grim 189

European East—a 'civilizing mission' so to speak. But neither do they, or at least Jonathan Wilson, fail to recognize that Eastern Europe has the power to exert some organizational and economic influence on the game's home turf.

In order to identify the elements of the beautiful and the grim in the two narratives, I would like to return to Spurr's two rhetorical modes of colonial discourse—'idealization' and 'debasement'. Spurr defines 'debasement' as "a form of negation [as] it negates the value of the other" (1994, p. 43). This 'negation' of the Other also encompasses those discursive strategies which depict the non-Western Others as the ones who fail to change and hence remain technologically and culturally immobile (Spurr, 1994, p. 99). This strategy, continues Spurr, "of defining [the Other] as without history and without progress, make[s] way for the moral necessity of cultural transformation" (1994, p. 99). Furthermore, the discourse of debasement avails itself of the well-known themes of the Other's "lack of self-discipline," including a remarked tendency to be corrupt and the inability "to govern themselves" (Spurr, 1994, p. 76).

In the narratives I discuss, the rhetorical modes elaborated by Spurr surface as issues of poor management, lack of soccer tradition, corruption, and technological stasis. For example, Wilson's impressions of Poland and Polish soccer seem to be colored by these very themes: Poland and Polish soccer culture emerge as without history and without progress, in need of the moral necessity of cultural transformation. In other words, all the discursive qualities which Spurr assigns to the colonial discourse of the 'debasement' of the Other are detectable in Wilson's text. Wilson remarks that "Polish football ... had become stuck in the ways of the seventies, and unthinkingly persisted with a libero," that compared to the English soccer tradition, Poland does not have "grass-roots" (2006b, p. 66) and that the passive quality of "[d]efeatism is a common Polish trait" (2006b, p. 58). The passive qualities of the 'othered' Polish soccer culture are further emphasized by noting that this is a wider cultural issue. Quoting one of the local insiders of Polish soccer, Wilson reports:

> It's a problem beyond sport. We are all the children of the Communist regime, even if we were against it or born after the collapse of the system; it still is very, very much inside us. It's in the mentality.
>
> (Wilson, 2006b, p. 59)

These ruminations about the causality of the political regime and Polish mentality echo Spurr's examination of 'debasement' discourses, particularly his observation that in such "discourse every individual weakness has its political counterpart" (1994, p. 76). Spurr also notes that 'debasement' is reflected on the occasions "when the natives [Eastern Europeans, in this case] take on the manners and values of the [Western] European colonizer" and, as Spurr further notes, are then, paradoxically, "ridiculed for their attempts to imitate the forms of the West" (1994, p. 77).

On his trip to Poland, Wilson visits the soccer grounds of one of, as he dubs it, "Poland's so-called 'big four' ... Groclin Grodzisk" whose "floodlights ... dominate the skyline, but the ground itself is modest, quaint even, resembling, oddly, a provincial English cricket club" (2006b, p. 63). The incongruence of the size of the floodlights and the modest size of the actual soccer pitch seem to suggest the narrative undercurrent of debasement which, of all the other aspects of the author's visit to the town, foregrounds little else but the failed attempt to imitate Western standards. Even the pronouncement that "[t]his is a business club run on robustly business lines" (Wilson, 2006b, p. 63) does not seem to do the club much justice as it will, as Wilson regrets, only erase the traces of the old architectural traditions.

Kuper's narrative contains similar examples as well. His visit to Dynamo Moscow's club grounds triggers a flashback of Dynamo's beginnings and especially the past glory days where at "the height of Stalin's purges" the club's stadium was "the only place where a gathering could express its hatred" (Kuper, 1996, p. 49) towards the loathed regime. In comparison with those g(l)ory days of rabid Communism, today's club "ha[s] very few spectators, and few of those are fans" (Kuper, 1996, p. 49). Although the author initially seems to sympathize with the club's and fans' turbulent past, the text quickly takes a turn towards the discourse of 'debasement' when Kuper reports on the present-day situation—the laziness of contemporary fans whose loyalties have faltered and waned, while the club's A team's "car park" is filled with "Audis, Mercedes, Volvos and Fords, almost all without number-plates as they had not been registered" (1996, p. 49), thus suggesting a corrupt system.

Besides highlighting corruption and immobility or backwardness, the text also presents us with a ridiculed attempt at imitating the West. A touch of mockery can be detected in Kuper's description of Dynamo Moscow's stadium, which "was oversized, grey and uncovered with a running track" (1996, p. 49). The debasement is continued as the words of "the club's chairman, the cheerless Nikolai Tolstich" (1996, p. 49) are related through Kuper's somewhat contemptuous filter. Kuper skeptically comments that the chairman's attempt to "give the ground an 'English atmosphere'," to "get rid of the running track and to build a roof" (1996, p. 49), might never come to fruition or at least will not be really successful in turning it into a place that is apt to evoke anything like the atmosphere of English stadia. Furthermore, by exclaiming in dismay that "Dynamo were painting their stadium brown!" (Kuper, 1996, p. 49) he confirms his disbelief that the East is able to successfully imitate Western-style attractiveness and sophistication and that the closest it can get is to attempt a drab copy of the Western glitz, despite the fact that one of Kuper's friends later "pointed out" that "the undercoat of paint is always brown" (1996, p. 49). But even so, Kuper, in his own words, was "still not convinced" (1996, p. 49).

Spurr (1994, p. 77) further maintains that the "active production of images inspired by ... fear and loathing" dominates the discursive mode of 'debasement'. In this vein, Kuper frames his narrative with the theme of soccer equaling war by discussing the links between Croatian and Serbian soccer fans' involvement not only in violent hooliganism following the good old traditions of the 'British disease',[8] but also in the war crimes in the former Yugoslavia. Thus, "[t]he Bad Blue Boys, the Dynamo[9] fans," as Kuper writes:

> come from Zagreb suburbs so depressing that the blocks of flats daily surprise you by not falling down. When Yugoslavia was still one country, the BBB—as they are usually called—would follow Dynamo Zagreb to Sarajevo or Belgrade to fight Bosnian or Serbian fans. When war broke out, they put on army uniforms and went to fight Serbian fans in uniform.
>
> (Kuper, 1996, p. 228)

The discourse of 'fear and loathing' similarly pervades the descriptions of Slovak and Hungarian rivalries and Ukrainian and Russian soccer cultures. Both texts discuss at length the biographies of Russian soccer players Eduard Streltsov, also known as "Russian Pele"—a Torpedo player—and Nikolai Starostin and his three brothers, the founders of Spartak Moscow, who all suffered at the hands of the Communist regime and were deported to gulag camps in Siberia where they spent years in imprisonment and humiliation (Kuper, 1996, p. 39).

The case of the Hungarian–Slovak rivalry depicted in Kuper's narrative is a brief four-page sketch of some of the ethnic and political complexities of Eastern Europe. Here, too, the author picks up details from the various local attempts at copying the British soccer culture, such as in the case of stadium spaces, which are described as "[a]ll quite British" with "the fans ... trying to be Britons too" (1996, p. 68). However, the locals are said to "have never quite mastered our style" (Kuper, 1996, p. 68) because they kiss on the cheeks and sing English songs in heavy Hungarian accents—all very un-British. In passages like this, the narratives once more display what Spurr calls "colonizing gestures in language" (1994, p. 68). Kuper admits, though, that the British disease of hooliganism "may have hurt Britain's image abroad," not without adding that "to one section of every society they are heroes" (1996, p. 68), by which he means, of course, the hooligan subcultures around the world. However, it seems that even Eastern European-style hooliganism is a perverted borrowing from the great British original for Kuper, because he claims that "English fans enjoy their rivalries; [while] this [Hungarian] crowd *loathed* Slovaks" (1996, pp. 68–69, italics in original). Kuper is a weathered sports reporter, however, the behavior he witnesses at the stadium prompts him to confess to a Hungarian fellow journalist that he has " 'never seen an atmosphere like it' " (1996, pp. 68–69). In depicting the Hungarian–Slovak rivalry, Kuper enters an unsettling terrain that reveals many layers of cultural borrowing from British soccer culture—both as enrichment of other nations' sporting cultures and as a new platform for "spectators," as Sybille Frank argues, "to demonstrate national unity and national differences by means of flags and anthems" in a time in which "national affiliation be[comes] an essential part of media reporting" (2011, p. 72). The travel narratives analyzed here show that these Eastern European cultural borrowings from the English game are transformed by local flavors often coinciding with the nationalization of soccer, a tendency confirmed by recent scholarship. Thus, Sybille Frank notes that "[t]he globalisation of the game ... [is] accompanied by an increasing national codification of football"[10] (2011, p. 72).

Finally, both authors notice the fact that the warring parties in the Yugoslavian wars manned their fighting troops from the ranks of the most loyal soccer fans, something that comes across as an extreme example of Eastern European grimness. Both Wilson and Kuper dedicate a chapter each to the case of the Yugoslavian wars and its soccer fans.[11] "Nowhere was football so entwined with the disintegration of the Communist regime, and nowhere was the disintegration so prolonged and bloody" as in the case of former Yugoslavia, Wilson maintains (2006b, p. 103). Both Wilson and Kuper go on to provide details about the involvement of Dinamo Zagreb's Bad Blue Boys and Red Star Belgrade's Delije or Heroes in the Yugoslavian wars where they supported Croatian and Serbian efforts, respectively. In fact, both authors note that in both former-Yugoslav clubs as well as among their fans it is believed that the wars began at the Dinamo Zagreb soccer stadium. Thus, Wilson writes:

> In the eyes of the Delije, it was they who fought the war's first battle, during a league game against Dinamo Zagreb. Dinamo's ultras, the Bad Blue Boys (BBB), seem to agree. Outside the Maksimir Stadium in Zagreb there is a statue of a group of soldiers, and on its plinth is written: "To the fans of this club, who started the war with Serbia at this ground on 15 May 1990."
>
> (Wilson, 2006b, p. 109)

Another statue at another Eastern European club ground commemorates another act of rebellion against an opponent team. The event being commemorated has grown to mythical proportions due to appropriation and distortion during the Communist era, as both authors agree. It is the case

The beautiful and the grim 193

of several 1940s Dynamo Kiev players who participated in a match against a German team called "Flakelf, representing the Luftwaffe" during the Nazi occupation (2006b, p. 11). The " 'official' [Communist] version" of the event, as Wilson relates, is that since the Ukrainian team were winning towards the end of the game, "the Luftwaffe ... responded to losing by having every Ukrainian player summarily shot at the final whistle" (2006b, p. 11).

While Kuper refuses to go into historical details and simply dismisses the story as a propaganda "myth concocted after the War by the local Communist Party" (1996, p. 64), Wilson delves a little further into the story explaining that the truth was less wild, yet still dramatic. He maintains that the Ukrainian players were not shot on the spot but "rounded up for interrogation" during which one player died of torture while the others were then "sent to the prison camp where some were executed" (2006b, p. 12).

These examples from both narratives show the tendency of both authors, despite their considerable differences in approach and attendance to detail, to look for extreme grimness in Eastern European soccer and soccer culture. Such use of at times even traumatic examples contributes to the formation of a negative image of Eastern Europe, which is seen, in Bruno Naarden's words, as "Europe's Asiatic backyard" (2007, p. 238) in which the beautiful game is marred by the barbarity inherent in Eastern European soccer.

There is yet another staple trope of Eastern European grimness—the assumption that its soccer is pervaded by corruption. Kuper, for example, is quick to dub it "ancient Russian custom" (1996, p. 35) and he persistently notes its occurrence in every Eastern European country he visits. Kuper provides an example, related to him by a local journalist, of how the system works. He quotes:

> Recently, three contracts have appeared for the sale of one player from Torpedo Moscow to Olympiakos Piraeus. One contract is for the Greek tax inspectors, one they show to the player, and the third is the real contract, but no one knows which is which.
>
> (Kuper, 1996, p. 36)

Another equally fascinating grim subject is the influence of the mafia, which is discussed in some detail in Kuper's account of Dynamo Kiev's club history. Although he admits that "Dynamo were good to me: along with Barcelona, Cape Town Hellenic, and the USA team, they were the nicest club I dealt with that year," he brings up the issue of mafia involvement in the very first interview he conducts with the club's officials (Kuper, 1996, p. 63). In the course of his visit, the grim story is unraveled. Dynamo Kiev apparently set up joint ventures for which profit was tax-free, and in order to "safeguard the joint ventures, Dynamo invited leaders of the mafia to join" (Kuper, 1996, p. 56). Ironically, as it turns out, one of the companies involved in the joint venture business is "the British firm Securitas" (Kuper, 1996, p. 64). As Kuper does not provide any further details about the legality of the British company's business dealings, the extent and type of the British involvement remain ambiguous for the reader. The place where this comment appears in the text is, however, telling, because it reads as a subversive innuendo suggesting that the British, too, and not only Eastern Europeans, might be involved in illegal activities. This somewhat unexpected side remark undermines the otherwise high moral ground from which the West operates in sports compared to the East whose clubs' corrupt practices are regularly seen as very un-Western economic phenomena.

Despite this abundance of grim elements in their representations of Eastern European soccer, both texts—Kuper's to a lesser and Wilson's to a greater extent—manage to produce positive images about the Eastern European game. These positive images sometimes struggle with the tendency to fall into another rhetorical mode which comes out of colonial and postcolonial discourse—that of 'idealization', which, as I have argued above, is ambivalent at its core. Spurr theorizes that the idealization of the cultural Other "is invariably produced by a rhetorical situation in which the writer takes an ethical position in regard to his or her own culture" (1994, p. 125). He maintains that the Other "is less a real and living presence than an abstract ideal whose purpose lies in the symbolic value for the social and political configurations" of present-day Britain and the West (1994, p. 126).

At the very beginning of his book, Wilson acknowledges his genuine interest and admiration for soccer in Eastern Europe, but his discourse lingers on the border between an abstract idealization and realities at home, which he is not sure are equally romantic. He writes:

> something in me warms to eastern Europe, and I rather suspect it's related to my affection for the classic thrillers of post-war espionage. There is, to my mind at least, just something plain romantic about taking a rattling old night-train from Ljubljana through Zagreb to Belgrade, about sipping thick Russian coffee in a St Petersburg café. ... There is magic even in the names: Odesa, Tbilisi, Szombathely. I fear that sounds frivolous, almost condescending: I hope not. I hope there is a Serb version of me, delighting in his journeys from London to Ipswich to Blackburn, smacking his lips at the thought of another lukewarm station pastry and revelling in the poetry of the Tyne-Wear Metro as it ploughs through Brockley Whins, East Boldon and Seaburn before finally pulling into the Stadium of Light.
>
> (Wilson, 2006b, p. 2)

This ambivalent imagery notwithstanding, Wilson exercises a certain dosage of self-criticism by expressing awareness that his reasons for liking the European East could, at worst, be read as potential arrogance. Further in the text Wilson is more concrete about his reasons for appreciating the soccer style of the region. He professes what seems to be a genuine affection for the playing style of Eastern Europe:

> I'm not sure there is any particularly good reason for this, but I just prefer precise, technical football ... my benchmarks were Valeriy Lobanovskyi and Dragan Stojkovic. I suppose, my brain having always been more adept than my body, I naturally look to those who try to make football a cerebral pursuit.
>
> (Wilson, 2006b, p. 3)

Another description of an Eastern European soccer team provides further insight into Wilson's reasoning for his admiration. The team which, in his own words, "remains the apogee of football" is "that Red Star team of 1991" (Wilson, 2006b, p. 100). On the same page, Wilson admits that they were a combination of "virtues and vices" and:

> not the best side I have ever seen, ... but the one that best combined the elements I would most want to see in a team I supported: technical brilliance, fluidity, a capacity for moments of staggering flair, supreme organization, cynicism, and a pervading sense of mental fragility.
>
> (Wilson, 2006b, p. 100)

The descriptions of individual players' qualities are consistently positive and contain fewer rhetorical interventions which ascribe flawed personality factors to a perceived Eastern mentality. This kind of respectful rhetoric praising the Eastern European style can also be found in theoretical texts. Thus, Tamir Bar-On, in theorizing about the stature and legacy of Dragan Dzajic, a Yugoslavian soccer star from the 1960s and 1970s, posits that individual players' achievements "arguably helped to transform mentalities about his country and the Balkans" (2014, p. 126). This fact seems to come into play in Kuper and Wilson's narratives when they focus on individual success stories. Only then do biases about Eastern Europe seem to ease and the authors are fairly generous with their praise. Kuper writes with unusual reverence about Nikolai Starostin and his trials and tribulations under the Soviet regime. In his journalistic work outside the scope of the travel book Wilson is more poignant and more generous in his descriptions. For example, he proclaims that the Hungarian player Ferenc Puskas, "along with Johan Cruyff [was] one of the two greatest European footballers of all time" (Wilson, 2006a).

Stars like Puskas or Starostin and others are granted the greatness they deserve. At the same time, however, each of them is admired as an Eastern European star phenomenon of the past era, as both are deceased now. As such, they "constitute" what Spurr calls "an object to be admired in the abstract," ultimately inhabiting "a realm outside of time" (1994, p. 127).

Both Kuper's and Wilson's narratives display tendencies towards adopting the rhetorical mode of 'idealization' in the passages containing genuine admiration for the skills and achievements of Eastern European soccer legends. Both texts remain tinged with an air of ambiguous nostalgic fascination for the great foreign players of the bygone era. The authors seem to maintain the distance between now and then in order to create a symbolic safety which cannot be disturbed as these potentially dangerous soccer rivals all belong to the past and pose no threat of competition in the present.

While such instances of a more positive depiction of Eastern European soccer despite their idealization provide a somewhat more balanced view of the entire region, they tend to underestimate and downplay Eastern Europe's complexity with its diversity of cultures and ethnicities. The legacy of isolation behind the Iron Curtain still helps maintain Eastern Europe's image of the more obscure or even, to borrow Francis Tapon's term, "hidden" part of the European continent.[12] With this obscurity comes the so-called "myth of uniformity," as Eva Hoffman puts it. Contrary to this myth, Hoffman makes clear that the countries of Eastern Europe are "a mélange of ethnic groups, classes, and subcultures" (2010, pp. xii–xiii).

In this vein, it can be argued that Wilson's affection for the "technical brilliance" of Eastern European soccer combined with its "mental fragility" constitutes, in fact, but another myth of uniformity because scholarship actually suggests that "the playing styles change regularly as players and coaches come and go or modify their tactics" (Lanfranchi and Taylor, 2001, p. 191). Interestingly, though, national teams *qua* representatives of a nation are generally regarded as employing a distinct and "constant style" (Lanfranchi and Taylor, 2001, pp. 191–192).

At the same time, the very fact that Kuper and Wilson in particular travel through each country carefully examining the playing styles and characteristics, the similarities and differences between regional rival clubs, makes them able to provide further insight into the complexities of Eastern Europe's cultures. Thus, we learn about the details of and reasons for the hatred between Slovakian and Hungarian teams, the differences between the fans of Spartak Moscow and Dynamo Moscow, the background story behind the rivalry between the Bad Blue Boys of Zagreb and the Delije (or Heroes) supporting Red Star Belgrade, and a plethora of other intricacies. All these details, as much as they might be blighted with the prejudiced discursive elements elaborated in this chapter, still paint an unmistakably vivid and memorable picture of Eastern European soccer and the region as a whole.

I would like to conclude by saying that although both narratives are imbued, whether consciously or unconsciously, with the standard repertoire of 'topoi' traditionally attached to Eastern Europe—backwardness, primitivism, and barbarism—they manage to produce instances of earnest admiration for the Eastern European soccer game and thus help, to a certain extent, balance out the beautiful and the grim impressions of the region. This very phrase, 'the beautiful and the grim', coined by Wilson to describe the Romanian leg of his soccer journey, is applicable to both authors' vision of Eastern Europe at large, and it succinctly suggests the complexity and ambivalence of British depictions of Eastern Europe.

Notes

1 Prior to writing his book, Jonathan Wilson had covered Eastern European soccer as a journalist visiting Eastern European countries over a number of years while working for the now defunct soccer website onefootball.com both as a freelancer and privately (see "Prologue" in *Behind the Curtain*). Wilson's itinerary covers 13 Eastern European countries making it twice as large as that of Simon Kuper's book. Wilson visited Ukraine, Poland, Hungary, Serbia, Slovenia, Croatia, Bosnia, Bulgaria, Romania, Georgia, Armenia, Azerbaijan, and Russia. Kuper is less specific but he does list and/or discuss the Baltics, Russia, Ukraine, Czech Republic, Hungary, and Croatia.

2 In addition to Spurr, see Holland and Huggan (1998) for a detailed account of the rhetoric of travel writing.

3 The term 'political technology' has been discussed at length by Stuart Elden in *The Birth of Territory* (2013). Elden examines space in terms of territorial divisions made and maintained by political, military, cultural, and technical actors and means of control (see Elden, 2013, pp. 10–18, as well as "Coda").

4 The term "Mauer in den Köpfen" [a wall in people's heads] first appeared in the novel *Der Mauerspringer* published in 1982 by West German author Peter Schneider, and has since become a commonplace expression, according to Katja Neller (2006).

5 Compare travelogues about Eastern Europe by Rory Maclean, Eva Hoffman, Nick Hunt, Tom Fort, Michael Palin, Jonathan Dimbleby, Anne Applebaum, Robert D. Kaplan, Dervla Murphy, Francis Tapon, Jan Morris, Giles Whittell, Andrew Meier, Tony Hawks, Victoria Clark, Andrew Eames, and Nick Thorpe, to name but a few.

6 For the fraught relations between English and Irish soccer see Michael O'Hara and Connell Vaughan's contribution to this volume.

7 Note that there are spelling variations in the two authors' spelling choices of various Eastern European clubs named Dynamo. While Jonathan Wilson uses the "Dinamo" spelling for Dinamo Zagreb, and "Dynamo" for both Dynamo Moscow and Dynamo Kyiv, Simon Kuper spells all three clubs' names with a 'y', i.e., "Dynamo." The English versions on the clubs' websites use the following spellings: "Dinamo Zagreb," "Dynamo Kyiv," and "Dynamo Moscow," confirming Jonathan Wilson's use. When not quoting directly from the authors' texts, I follow the spelling suggested by the respective clubs' websites.

8 According to Tamir Bar-On: "In the mid-1960s soccer hooliganism was seen as an 'English' or 'British disease', but ... has since spread like wildfire" (2014, p. xxii).
9 Simon Kuper keeps misspelling Dinamo Zagreb's name.
10 See also Chapter 7 on "National Styles, International Stars" in Lanfranchi and Taylor (2001, pp. 191–211).
11 See Kuper "The President and the Bad Blue Boys" (1996, pp. 227–235); Wilson "The Former Yugoslavia: Ever Decreasing Circles" (2006b, pp. 98–182).
12 Francis Tapon's 2012 travel book about Eastern Europe is titled *The Hidden Europe* and argues that although "businesses and tourists have poured into the region ever since the Wall came down ... the world is still far more familiar with Western Europe than Eastern Europe" (2012, p. 14).

References

Auster, P. 2001. The best substitute for war. Conjunctions. **37**(20th anniversary issue), pp. 355–358.

Bar-On, T. 2014. The world through soccer: The cultural impact of a global sport. Lanham: Rowman & Littlefield.

Edelman, R. 2002. A small way of saying "no": Moscow working men, Spartak soccer, and the Communist Party, 1900–1945. The American Historical Review. **107**(5), pp. 1441–1474.

Elden, S. 2013. The birth of territory. Chicago: University of Chicago Press.

Frank, S. 2011. From England to the world: Ethnic, national and gender-based stereotyping in professional football. Journal for the Study of British Cultures. **18**(1), pp. 69–81.

Hoffman, E. 2010. Exit into history: A journey through the new Eastern Europe. London: Faber & Faber.

Holland, P. and Huggan, G. 1998. Tourists with typewriters: Critical reflections on contemporary travel writing. Ann Arbor: University of Michigan Press.

Kuper, Simon. 1996. Football against the enemy. 2nd ed. London: Orion.

Lanfranchi, P. and Taylor, M. 2001. Moving with the ball: The migration of professional footballers. Oxford: Oxford University Press.

Leoussi, A.S. ed. 2001. Encyclopaedia of nationalism. New Brunswick: Transaction Publishers.

Naarden, B. 2007. Slavs. In: Beller, M. and Leerssen, J. eds. Imagology: The cultural construction and literary representation of national characters. Amsterdam: Rodopi, pp. 237–242.

Neller, K. 2006. Getrennt vereint? Ost-West-Identitäten, Stereotypen und Fremdheitsgefühle nach 15 Jahren deutscher Einheit. In: Falter, J.W., Gabriel O.W., Rattinger, H. and Schoen, H. eds. Sind wir ein Volk?: Ost- und Westdeutschland im Vergleich. Munich: Verlag C.H. Beck. pp. 13–36.

Schneider, P. 1982. Der Mauerspringer: Erzählung. Darmstadt: Luchterhand.

Spurr, D. 1994. The rhetoric of the empire: Colonial discourse in journalism, travel writing, and imperial administration. 2nd ed. Durham: Duke University Press.

Tapon, Francis. 2012. The hidden Europe: What Eastern Europeans can teach us. Kolkata: Thompson Press India.

Todorova, M. 2009. Imagining the Balkans. Oxford: Oxford University Press.

Wilson, J. 2006a. Best, Beckenbauer, Platini, Zidane: Puskas topped them all. The Guardian. [Online]. November 17. [Accessed June 1, 2017]. Available from: www.theguardian.com/football/2006/nov/17/sport.comment2.

Wilson, J. 2006b. Behind the curtain: Travels in Eastern European football. London: Orion.

Wolff, L. 1994. Inventing Eastern Europe: The map of civilization on the mind of the enlightenment. Stanford: Stanford University Press.

Chapter 10

"Text sex with Becks"
Football celebrities, popular press, and the spectacle of language

Jan Chovanec

Introduction

On April 6, 2004, the British broadsheet paper *The Telegraph* published its daily cartoon, Matt. Under the caption *Last golden eagle in England*, the picture showed an eagle holding a mobile phone and composing a text message that read "*Where R U? I'm feeling really * * * * * !*" (see Appendix 1). The cartoon combined a reference to two unrelated events: a serious environmental news story published on the same day (headlined LAST GOLDEN EAGLE MALE IN ENGLAND FAILS TO FIND MATE), and a sexting scandal involving the British football player David Beckham. The scandal broke in the tabloid media only two days earlier. Thanks to the asterisked taboo word, the intertextual reference to the Beckham case was instantly recognizable to the national audience, with the obvious incongruity between the two news stories giving rise to the intended humorous effect of the cartoon.

This humorous artefact was one of the many instantiations of play found across the British media in connection with the event. In this chapter, I am interested in how the popular press makes a spectacle of the language it uses in cases of scandalous, sensational news stories that involve football celebrities. While the whole culture of modern sport, and particularly football, is defined around the notion of spectacle, I argue that this aspect is also significantly present in the media coverage of the salacious acts that football players are sometimes alleged to have committed off the pitch. On the one hand, this reflects the shift of modern sport towards celebrity culture (Boyle, 2006) and, on the other, it stems from the popular media's trend towards infotainment aimed at amusing their readers at the expense of celebrities.

As regards its theoretical underpinnings, the chapter is positioned at the intersection between media discourse analysis and cultural studies. It traces the systematic use of certain micro-level linguistic phenomena and poetic strategies, connects them with the established journalistic practices of the British popular media, and interprets them with reference to the current status of football stars as media celebrities. As Conboy (2006, p. 12) points out, the language of popular journalism is characterized by "sensationalism, emotive language, the bizarre, the lewd, sex, suppression fees, checkbook journalism, gossip, police news, marriage and divorce, royal news, celebrities, political bias and any form of prurience which can be included under the general heading of human interest." It is therefore the aim of this chapter to increase our understanding of the role of language in the operation of popular journalism.

The cultural context: celebrities and the media

This section outlines the broader cultural context in which my analysis of the media coverage of the Beckham affair by the British popular press is set. First, I note the existence of the 'Beckham phenomenon' as an instantiation of the trend of the modern media to treat (select) football players as celebrities, thanks to which they become the centerpieces of the media's attention much beyond their sporting pursuits. Then I discuss the role of the topic of sex in tabloids, suggesting some ways in which media reports on sexual misconduct of football players can be seen to counterbalance how the same football players are treated as positive national heroes. Finally, in order to show the continuity and appeal of sex scandals in the British media, I discuss some of the most (in)famous cases involving sexual transgressions by British football players.

Football stars and celebrity culture

Outside of the sports field, football players are treated as celebrities, with their personal lives covered extensively in the lifestyle sections of the media. Some of these individuals achieve a cult status, promoted through increasing commercialization of sport and 'celebritification' of its heroes, as manifested by such metrosexual idols as David Beckham in the 2000s, Cristiano Ronaldo in the 2010s, and other legends of the past (e.g., the notorious Northern Irish football icon George Best). Much of their presence in the media is related to various gendered performances of their identities in the public (cf. Cashmore and Parker, 2003). Their masculinities are articulated through the cult of the body and an exaggerated focus on diverse aspects of their physical appearance (e.g., tattoos, hairdos, etc.). Football players are, thus, significantly objectified. As argued by Schirato (2013, p. 73), the identities and representations of the modern "metrosexual bodies" of such "iconic male sports stars ... [are] ... highly sexualized and eroticized: [George] Best was fashionable and [Muhammad] Ali was controversial, but Beckham, Ronaldo and Nadal are first and foremost erotic objects."[1]

In a different context, Schirato (2007, p. 18) suggests that the "Beckham phenomenon" is an outcome of "the colonization of a working-class sport by advertising and the media, leading to its incorporation into commodity culture." He notes that David Beckham's career is exemplary in this respect, with football initially triggering his celebrity career and then the media heavily pursuing that dimension. The media attention enjoyed by Beckham has led to the situation that:

> when stories appear about him in the media, they are more likely to have a business (Real Madrid marketing new Beckham gear in Asia), fashion (his latest haircut), gossip (stories about his relationship with his wife, or his affairs), pop culture (his autobiography) or lifestyle (Beckham the metrosexual) focus than be reporting something about his sporting activities.
>
> (Schirato, 2007, p. 18)

The reason for this lies in the fact that top football players have become 'stars' who turn their "cultural or symbolic value into economic or capital value" (Boyle and Haynes, 2004, p. 73). The celebrity status of the top players means that they constitute significant financial assets to their teams and their names are turned into marketable brands. Pursuing the idea of likening football to 'the new rock-'n'-roll', Boyle and Haynes point out that "for some in the game a footballer is as much a performer as an actor or pop singer. We can certainly agree in this context that David Beckham, the star, has probably more in common with singer Robbie Williams than he does with fellow professional Robbie Fowler" (2004, p. 73).

Thanks to this 'wider cultural capital', football celebrities have moved out of the sports pages of newspapers and started increasingly to colonize other sections of newspapers' content. As noted by Boyle and Haynes (2004, p. 87), "Beckham may occupy the front, back and even the centre pages of daily tabloid newspapers," which can be read as an attestation to the football star's economic, cultural and social roles within the national as well as the global communities. At the same time, all media representations of Beckham, and other major football stars, are subject to extensive scrutiny from their PR agents, lawyers, advertisers, team managers, and other stakeholders, who control the rights to the foot-ballers' images and help to preserve and extend the economic value of the 'brand'.

However, while the intensity of the football stars' presence in the media has increased, it seems that they are also under a closer view that is not necessarily always sympathetic. Referencing some football-related scandals caused by "young English males," Boyle and Haynes argue that while those problems had always been there in the pre-digital media:

> [w]hat is different in the new media age is the levels of wealth involved, the more intense media scrutiny from a larger and more

complex commercially focused industry and a complicit popular press who are happy to both help create and condemn aspects of celebrity culture.

(Boyle and Haynes, 2004, p. 162)

The dependence of the media on celebrities thus does not prevent the media from taking a high moral stance and evaluating, with varying degrees of explicitness, the off-pitch behavior of star footballers.

Sex, scandals and the tabloid agenda

The attention of the media to celebrities' negative behavior, whether public or private, is particularly poignant when describing any problems that football stars experience in the area of their private sex lives. Arguably, this is related to the popular media's interest in topics that lend themselves well to adopting moralizing stances and judgments, particularly where it serves to affirm social and cultural stereotypes associated with certain groups (such as football players).

There is, of course, a close co-existence between the media and the celebrities. While the press is free to pursue various stories in accordance with its norms of newsworthiness, it faces numerous constraints when bringing soft news on football mega-stars and other celebrities. In this compliant co-existence, the media rely on the supply of the copy and images from the stars and their representatives, but their freedom is tied up by legal regulations, contracts, and sanctions (Boyle and Haynes, 2004). Arguably, the focus on the celebrities' misconduct means that the media can pursue their soft news agenda under the aegis of the avowed journalistic ideal of providing news coverage, while simultaneously freeing themselves from the various constraints that regulate material provided by the celebrities themselves.

Thus, the moral transgressions of football stars enable the media to juxtapose the sanitized versions of the celebrities' lives, found in their conscious media appearances, with those negative aspects of their personalities that are likely to have never been meant as performances for the media and are more indicative of the football celebrities' private selves. In other words, the controlled acts staged for and served to the media are thus complemented with behavior that appears to have a stronger claim to authenticity: frontstage performance becomes juxtaposed with the alleged reality of backstage behavior (Chovanec, 2016; Goffman, 1981). Another contrast comes from the almost uncritical veneration of football players at the times of major international tournaments such as the World Cup or the Euro Soccer Championship, when the media recycle various long-term national narratives and myths that involve not only historical references, particularly to military conflicts and engagements such as the two world wars, D-Day, etc. (Chovanec, 2017; Bishop and Jaworski, 2003), but also the assumed superiority of national playing styles and feelings of past injustices (Tudor, 2006; Alabarces et al., 2001). By widely reporting on their extramarital affairs and other scandals, these national representatives are brought down from the pedestal, with the readers getting the chance to assert their own moral superiority over the 'fallen super-heroes'.

As regards the link between sex and the media, sex-related scandals have, of course, featured among some of the most salient topics in the popular press, with the last couple of decades seeing a gradual shift towards a 'sexualization' of content even in sex-unrelated domains (Conboy, 2006, p. 123; Holland, 1998). Stories with some sexual content, particularly when they concern celebrities, form staple editorial content because they satisfy multiple news values, such as entertainment, appeal to the elites, and negativity (Bell, 1991). Any reference to sex, as argued by Harcup and O'Neill (2001, p. 274), is often emphasized in order to highlight the entertainment potential of news stories, even where it plays only a tangential role.

It is stories about sex, particularly when combined with (sports) celebrities and crime, i.e., other components of the 'tabloid agenda' (cf. Conboy, 2006; Franklin, 1997), that may even achieve epic proportions and pass into shared cultural knowledge. This concerns, for instance, the widely known cases of the US boxer Mike Tyson, who was convicted in 1992 for the rape of Miss Black Rhode Island, and the golf champion Tiger Woods, whose infidelity scandals, revealed and acknowledged by him in 2009, proved a major set-back to his professional career, apart from ruining his personal life.

Football stars in non-footballing scandals

As noted by Sunderland (2013) "[u]nfortunately, personal lives—and romantic escapades in particular—have become among the most frequently discussed aspects of English football." Thus, over the past few years, there has been a steady flow of sex-related stories involving footballers and other football-related individuals in the British media. To refer to just a few of the most memorable cases, these included the reports on the then England national team manager Sven-Göran Eriksson's relationship with an FA secretary in 2004 (*The Telegraph*, 2004). The same year, Stan Collymore lost his job as a BBC Radio 5 commentator after accusations of dogging were made public in the *News of the World*, and Wayne Rooney became subject to much media ridicule for his alleged sexual encounters with an old-age prostitute (cf. Hills, 2004). Rooney made the headlines again in 2010, when the media indulged in reporting claims of his sex with two prostitutes during the pregnancy of his wife Coleen (Moore, 2010; Wright, 2010).

"Text sex with Becks" 205

Two recent major cases have shifted from the prurient interest in football celebrities' sometimes unusual sex lives towards more political issues, namely the ultimate power of these individuals over the media and their collusion with administrative/political elites. Thus, in 2010, a High Court judge issued a super-injunction, banning the media from reporting the allegations that footballer John Terry had an affair with Vanessa Perroncel, a former girlfriend of his Chelsea teammate Wayne Bridge (Greenhill, 2010). The injunction, protecting his privacy but not that of Perroncel, was lifted only one week later. Owing to the scandal, Terry was removed from the captaincy of the national team. A similar case occurred in 2011, with Ryan Giggs availing himself of a super-injunction against the British press to block *The Sun* newspaper from reporting on his alleged extramarital affair with the model Imogen Thomas (Beckford, 2012). However, the story broke on Twitter and was covered in non-UK media (including the Scottish newspaper the *Sunday Herald*, which was outside the jurisdiction of the injunction). The media interest was only exacerbated when Giggs took legal action against Twitter (Halliday, 2011). The case exposed the contrast between the right to privacy and freedom of expression and even led to appeals for a legal reform after MP John Hemming confirmed Giggs's identity in the House of Commons (*BBC News*, 2011). So far the latest in the long list of English football figures' acts of sexual misbehavior is the case of sexual abuse of young football players by coaches, as broken in the British media at the end of 2016.

While the British media seem to churn out a constant supply of sex-related stories on football players in the UK, this is not an exclusively British phenomenon. In the Czech media, for instance, a similar level of notoriety was achieved in 2007 with an otherwise relatively isolated case. This involved a story published in the tabloid newspaper *Šíp*, reporting on a birthday celebration during which four football players (after losing a World Cup qualifying match to Germany 1-2) ordered escort service to their hotel room (*iDnes*, 2007). When asked about the payment for the female companions' service, the player Tomáš Ujfaluši simultaneously refuted and confirmed the allegations by commenting: "It's not true. I was at the reception, that's right, but I did not pay for anything like that. And the amount is absolutely wrong" (*iDnes*, 2007). Unsurprisingly, his last utterance reached almost epic proportions, becoming a well-known one-liner even among people not interested in football.

Data and analysis

This section is based on an analysis of a data set collected from the mainstream British media (with a focus on the popular press) in April and May 2004 on the issue of the alleged infidelity of the British football icon David Beckham. The data consist of a set of over 50 media texts retrieved from the online versions of the popular daily papers *The Sun*, *Daily Mail*, *Daily Mirror*, and *News of the World*. The data include news reports, headlines, and front pages that were accessed on the internet at the time of the case. Alongside this material, headlines and articles were also collected from several broadsheet newspapers (reports of the case appeared, among others, in *The Telegraph*), and some additional data were obtained from the Czech and German popular press (the *Blesk* and *Bild* newspapers, respectively) in order to document the mutual interrelatedness of media reports and the spread of some creative word formations across language boundaries.

All of the articles in the data set deal with the same news event: the alleged extramarital affair between Beckham, who played for Real Madrid at that time, and his Spanish-Dutch personal assistant Rebecca Loos. When the 28-year-old lost her job after being spotted with Beckham in a club, she sold her story to the British tabloid *News of the World* (Harrison, 2016). Loos became an instant celebrity, eventually going public in a famous TV interview where she presented text messages between her and Beckham.[2] Only a few days later, another woman, the Malaysian-born model Sarah Marbeck, came up with similar allegations dating from 2001, though it was later suggested that her claims were lies (*Daily Mirror*, 2004). The Loos story, only exacerbated by the co-opted allegations from Marbeck, was in the prime focus of the media for weeks, and eventually damaged Beckham's reputation as a dedicated family man.

The analysis of the data has identified several stylistic features that are characteristic of the tabloids' linguistic treatment of the news event as a 'spectacle of language'. These features include the use of poetic forms, such as assonance, word play and creative coinages, and the handling of linguistic taboo, where certain lexical forms are expunged from the papers despite their presence being constantly evoked through asterisks. The poetic forms and the presence of linguistic taboo are linked to the sensationalizing strategy of the press (cf. Molek-Kozakowska, 2013), whereby a news event of whatever triviality may be capitalized on for its entertainment value, particularly as long as it involves a celebrity.

Poetic forms

A very prominent characteristic feature of popular journalism is the use of poetic forms and structures, i.e., devices that draw attention to themselves. In Roman Jakobson's famous dictum, "the poetic function projects the principle of equivalence from the axis of selection into the axis of combination" (1960, p. 358). In the analyzed data, these devices include phonological parallelism and orthographical foregrounding, and are complemented with word play and ad hoc word formations. As noted by the critical linguist Roger Fowler, such devices are very commonplace in the British popular press:

The Sun indulges in 'poetic' structures in places where it is being at its most outrageous about politics or sex. Cues are foregrounded to the point of self-parody. Deplorable values are openly displayed, pointedly highlighted; even a critical reader can be disarmed by pleasure in the awfulness of the discourse.

(Fowler, 1991, p. 45)

In the sections to follow, I trace how micro-level linguistic elements are deployed in poetic ways and how they contribute towards the creation of the disarming pleasure that the readers may find in such texts.

Text sex, assonance, and phonological parallelism

One of the most noticeable forms in the entire media coverage of the Beckham saga included the very substance of the news story: the compound *sex text*. The phrase refers to the exchange of sexually explicit messages via mobile phones, a practice that has since become lexicalized in the English language as 'sexting'.[3] The use of the phrase can be illustrated with the following example:

1 The Madrid temptress who says she slept with David Beckham claims he swapped <u>sex texts</u> with a second girl.

(*The Sun*, April 7, 2004)

The subject matter of the scandal was referred to with an extensive range of expressions. The over-lexicalization of this field (cf. Fowler et al., 1979) attests to the tabloids' preoccupation with this topic. Consequently, its meaning becomes intensified (Mayr and Machin, 2012, p. 123). Moreover, the list of expressions found in the data set indicates that the adjectives collocating with the key words 'text' or 'message' actually serve to increase the news value by heightening the sexualized nature of the story and, frequently, adding a morally evaluative dimension to it (Conboy, 2006, p. 18). Thus, the expressions range from the almost surgically precise "explicit mobile phone txt messages" (*The Sun*, April 5, 2004) to "(those) explicit texts," "red-hot phone messages," and "sexy texts." Among the later references in *The Sun* were "steamy texts" and "lewd text messages" (April 23, 2004), and some synonyms such as "dirty talk" and "text flirting." The *News of the World* newspaper used the following forms of reference: "graphic texts," "raunchiest texts," "raunchy no-holds-barred sex texts," "dirty texts," "hot text," "(they texted) erotic love messages" (April 15, 2004), "lust-filled txt sex," "sexually explicit txt messages," and "dirty txts" (April 18, 2004). Interestingly, the combination 'text sex' was also attested, though it was rather infrequent, essentially being limited to a couple of examples. These include "(she admits she clung on to) text sex with Beckham" and even "his last text sex session" (*News of the World*, April 15, 2004), which suggest more physicality than was actually the case on account of the word 'session' appearing as the head noun in the nominal phrase.

The expressions 'sex text'/'text sex' appear to have been limited to the tabloids. The coverage of this news story in the other papers indicates that the broadsheets avoided this monosyllabic catchphrase, opting for a more restrained form of reference. Thus, *The Telegraph*, for instance, refers to "lurid text messages" (April 6, 2004), "explicit text messages" (April 11, 2004), "raunchy text messages" (April 12, 2004) or simply "texts," clearly avoiding the combination of the words 'sex' and 'text' that became so dominant in the tabloids. However, the adjectives 'lurid', and 'raunchy' also indicate that *The Telegraph* adopted an evaluative stance whereby it communicates a similar degree of moral condemnation as the tabloids. On the other hand, the paper also used several creative phrases, such as "text lovers" (*The Telegraph*, April 15, 2004), "kiss-and-text story"[4] and the headline "Texts, lies and audiotapes" (April 11, 2004). The latter, while alluding to the name of a famous 1989 film *Sex, Lies, and Videotapes*[5] is illustrative of the more sophisticated creative and playful attitude that the broadsheets take to the reported content. As demonstrated by Lennon (2004), this kind of playfulness is found across all the British mainstream media. However, the broadsheets—as is the case with *The Telegraph*'s allusive headline "Texts, lies and audiotapes"—resort to more sophistic-ated puns and allusions that cater to their more educated readership. In other words, the popular v. quality press dichotomy is not distinguished through the presence versus absence of word play but, rather, the gradient extent and nature of this phenomenon.

The phrase 'sex text' became a shortcut for the media to designate the whole story. On the syntagmatic axis of combination, the phrase combined with 'Becks', the popular name of the footballer David Beckham, resulting in assonance consisting of not only two but as many as three lexemes. This is apparent, for instance, in the following headlines:[6]

2 BECKS AND THE SEX TEXTS.

(April 5, 2004)[7]

3 REBECCA: "I WASN'T THE ONLY GIRL WHO HAD TEXT SEX WITH BECKS."

(*The Sun*, April 7, 2004)

Subsequently, the three words have appeared in immediate proximity in such combinations as 'Becks sex texts' and 'Becks text sex', with the latter being more frequent. Arguably, it is these forms that realize the poetic treatment of the story in the popular press to the maximum extent. While the phrase contains a repetition of identical vowels and consonants, the monosyllabic nature of the three words adds a distinct rhythm to the entire phrase. The transcription of the pronunciation [beks seks teksts] reveals the crucial sound group [eks], which is repeated verbatim in all three words. It is only the initial sounds [b], [s], and [t] (also used as a final consonant in one case) which differentiate between the words. There is, thus, only a very minimal degree of variation (except for the final [s] used as a plural marker but this is absent once 'text' is used as a modifier of the head noun 'sex' in *text sex*). This kind of triple repetition with such minimal, yet meaningful variation is a modern-day tabloid parallel to the election campaign slogan 'I like Ike' (used by Dwight Eisenhower in his presidential election campaign), the classic example of a poetic structure mentioned by Jakobson (1960). Needless to say, both of these phrases are so powerful precisely because their referential meaning is complemented with a clever and noticeable use of linguistic forms that direct the recipient's attention from the meaning to the form itself (cf. also Chovanec, 2008).

Funnily enough, as indicated by the second of the two headlines above, the name of the woman who claimed to be involved in the text affair with Beckham (Rebecca Loos) also contains the sound [bek], as does the surname of Sarah Marbeck, the second woman who followed up with similar allegations. The poetic potential of the women's names in connection with the whole case was pointed out by the *Scotsman* newspaper (2004), which noted:

> [t]here have been some very ironic twists to the whole saga. For example, the names of the two women at the centre of the allegations could not have been better tabloid fodder. Thanks to the inclusion of the letters 'B-E-C' in their names, Rebecca Loos and Sarah Marbeck could both have been called 'Becks'.
>
> (*Scotsman*, 2004)

And indeed they were: my data include the following examples where abbreviated forms refer to Rebecca Loos:

4 BECKS, <u>BECCS</u> AND SEX.

(*Sky News*, April 16, 2004)

5 <u>Becca</u> and her Becks could not stop themselves from bonding for Britain.

(*The Telegraph*, April 16, 2004)

The abbreviation of Rebecca to "Beccs" in example (4) (a headline) and "Becca" in (5) (an in-text reference from an opinion piece in *The Telegraph*) establishes a parallelism between the monosyllabic composition of both names. In the case of 'Becks' and 'Beccs', moreover, there is total phonological identity, with the names being distinguished visually only thanks to their slightly different spellings.

Orthographical parallelism

The phonological parallelism between the sounds, observed in the examples above, is also mirrored on the orthographic level. This kind of parallelism takes the form of modifying the spelling of words so that they either include the grapheme 'x' or contain some feature of spelling that is visually representative of "textspeak" (Crystal, 2008). This kind of spelling alteration constitutes a form of language play because it highlights the identity of different pronunciations by manipulating the standard forms and instituting a similar parallelism on the visual level of the language as well.

This kind of play that emphasizes the identity of pronunciation through playful spelling is found in the following front page headline:

> 6 I'VE GOT PHONE <u>PIX</u> OF SEX WITH BECKS.
>
> (*Daily Star*, April 16, 2004)

The spelling of 'pics' as "pix" uses the salient visual grapheme that is also present in the word 'sex'. Thus, a visual connection is established between the two lexemes. Interestingly enough, there is no attested case of Beckham's nickname "Becks" being changed into 'Bex', as might be expected. It seems that there are limits to the play. Beckham's abbreviated nickname is, in itself, sufficiently informal. Its further modification may be avoided in order to prevent the name from being less recognizable.

More common, however, is the second strategy through which the conventions of textspeak can be evoked, namely the omission of vowels and the condensation of spelling of some words. Thus, by abbreviating the word 'text' into 'txt', the newspapers imbue their news texts with "heterography" (Shortis, 2016, p. 491), which is associated with personal and informal genres. In this particular case, the formal transformation of 'text' into 'txt' achieves two results: first, the paper indicates that it consciously taps into the genre conventions of the text messages, which are in fact the main subject matter of the entire news story; and second, it makes the words 'txt' and 'sex' visually equivalent in length, with each consisting of three letters only. Arguably, this equivalence of length is particularly efficient when the two words are juxtaposed and placed in mutual combinations, cf. the following examples (7) to (9):

> 7 he ... fought back tears as he confessed to sending his lover lust-filled <u>txt sex</u>.
>
> (*News of the World*—"I'm so sorry," April 18, 2004)

8 ... as their <u>sex-txt</u> affair continued.
(*News of the World*—"Beckham and his Pretty Woman 'hookers',"
April 18, 2004)

9 BECKS <u>SEX TXTS</u>: THE UNSEEN MESSAGES
(*News of the World*, homepage headline, April 18, 2004)

Interestingly enough, this form of abbreviation also occurs in textual segments that provide a discursive representation of reported speech, i.e., in what appear to be direct speech quotes. As a result, these segments are evidence of the linguistic stylization that the popular press resorts to in order to achieve a maximum effect on its readers:[8]

10 "Yes, I did have the affair and I did send Rebecca the <u>txts</u>."
(*News of the World*—"I'm so sorry," April 18, 2004)

11 "But the <u>txt sex</u> continued. And we eventually made love one last time in December."
(*News of the World*—"Where the XXXX is he?,"
April 18, 2004)

On the basis of all of these examples, it seems that the popular press will use orthographical parallelism and the conventions of textspeak to modify words that are syntactically brought into some kind of relationship with the word 'sex'. This tendency might also motivate the choice of words that contain the sound group [eks] or [ks] and contain the grapheme 'x', e.g., the verb "axed" in example (12) below, and which may thus become linked to the three key words of the story, namely *Becks*, *sex*, and *text*. As a result, chains of phonological parallelisms appear not only in short discourse segments (on the phrase level) but also within sentences and between larger stretches of text:

12 The messages ... are said to have been sent after Rebecca was <u>axed</u> as Beckham's assistant.
(April 5, 2004)[9]

13 The story ... also included details of <u>explicit text</u> messages allegedly <u>exchanged</u> between the pair last month.
(*Daily Mirror*, April 7, 2004)

14 They referred to a variety of <u>sex</u> acts and the language was so strong that many of the words were <u>asterisked</u>.
(*The Sun*, April 5, 2004)

15 Spanish-born Rebecca, revealed to be <u>bisexual</u> in yesterday's Sun, was fired when <u>Becks</u> quit the <u>SFX</u> management company last year to sign up with <u>Victoria</u>'s firm.

(April 7, 2004)

16 <u>Beck's</u> sister Joanne's secret affair with Blue star Antony Costa was <u>exposed</u> ... when his <u>ex</u> found their <u>sexy</u> texts.

(*News of the World*, April 18, 2004)

All of these words (*explicit, axed, asterisked, bisexual, SFX, exposed, ex, sexy*) are closely related with the three key lexemes *Becks, sex*, and *text*. It is thus not only on the level of sound on which they can be connected with them but also on the level of meaning and syntactic combinations.[10]

Word play

The propensity for word play is among the most typical rhetorical devices of the popular press. As with the other strategies, word play and punning "call upon a very active involvement from their readers" (Conboy, 2006, p. 18). In the data set, the punning tends to occur mostly in the headlines, where the constrained space and the need to appeal to the readers predispose this structural element of news stories to become the prime discursive space where word play and humor are conventionally deployed (for a more systematic treatment of the different forms of humorous word play related to football in the popular press, see Chovanec, 2005a, 2005b; for a case study, see Conboy, 2013).

Several punning headlines illustrate this phenomenon. The first example plays with the juxtaposition of the words 'posh' and 'Posh',[11] i.e., the nickname of Victoria, David Beckham's wife:

17 SHE IS REALLY <u>POSH</u>, POSH.

(*The Sun*, April 17, 2004)

The following headline uses the surname of Rebecca Loos in a syntactic position where it simultaneously functions as a complement of the copular verb 'be'. In this position, the name becomes a homophone of the adjective 'loose', which can be read as a description of her character:

18 UMA: REBECCA IS <u>LOOS</u>.

(*The Sun*, April 22, 2004)

19 LOCK UP YOUR HUSBANDS ... REBECCA'S ON THE <u>LOOS</u>(E).

(*The Sun*, May 21, 2004)

> 20 The Loos woman sold her story for an estimated £500,000—a Lottery win for you and me but that's a couple of weeks' wages to Beckham.
>
> (*The Sun*—"Beckham spins out of control," April 17, 2004)

Unsurprisingly, the phonological identity between Rebecca's name and the adjective 'loose' became the source of much word play in the media around the time of the incident and thereafter. Thus, for instance, the following half-page headline that capitalizes on this form of humor was used by *The Sun* on its front page, re-activating the scandal a month later:

> 21 BECKS LOOS-ES IT.
>
> (*The Sun*, May 26, 2004)

> 22 I DON'T WANT TO LOOS YOU.
>
> (*Daily Mirror*, May 21, 2004)

In this case, the weak pun consists of the similar pronunciation of the verb 'lose' and the name 'Loos', with the latter inserted in the grammatical position of a verb. Thanks to this kind of punning, the headline condenses an additional layer of semantic complexity into the sentence: the meaning of the substituted and alluded verb 'lose' is quite evident to the readers, but the inclusion of Rebecca Loos's name adds the reason for that action, and provides an intertextual link to the text sex scandal. The modified spelling of 'lose' as 'loos' thus triggers the whole scenario, with the headline achieving a maximum condensation of meaning into a minimal space.[12]

An identical strategy occurs in puns substituting the spelling 'Beck' for the adverb 'back', also in compounds:

> 23 THE BECKLASH BEGINS.
>
> (*Daily Mirror*, June 30, 2004)

> 24 BECK-LASH OF VANDAL.
>
> (*The Sun*, June 30, 2004)

Some further word play involves creative modification of names and nicknames, and alliteration:

> 25 Even from their early days, it was more Pecks than Becks.
>
> (*The Sun*, April 21, 2004)

> 26 QUICK BUCK ON BECKS.
>
> (*The Sun*, April 17, 2004)

27 BORED OF THE BECKHAMS™.
   (*The Sun*, a T-shirt in the Sun commercial section, April 24, 2004)

The general propensity of the popular press for entertainment takes the shape of not only making up content and quotes (see the currently hot topic of 'fake' or 'hoax' news) but also manipulating and creatively appropriating linguistic forms. In one of its later articles, for instance, *The Sun* newspaper re-activated the topic of the text sex scandals by reporting on an alleged change affecting the English language. The article, headlined TIME FOR POSH & BECKS (May 6, 2004), suggested that the binominal phrase 'Posh and Becks' had become lexicalized in modern British slang: "Apparently, the couple's names have become a rhyming euphemism for sex." The article supported the claim with a reference to a book called *Brit Slang* by Ray Puxley (2004), giving examples of many other similar humorous coinages.

Creative coinages

Another aspect of the treatment of the Beckham scandal in the popular press concerns linguistic creativity, whereby new linguistic forms are coined on the spur of the moment. This phenomenon is, understandably, closely linked to some of the examples of word play mentioned in the previous section, even though the creative coinages need not be intended to have a humorous effect. In any case, they constitute a manipulation of the linguistic form and, hence, qualify as falling within the scope of the poetic function.

In this section, I want to address the label 'Sexham' which was used for a brief period of time in reference to David Beckham at the time of the most intensive media attention. The expression, unattested from English-language sources, appears to have originated in the German popular press and been confined to Continental/Central Europe. The first documented occurrence is from the German tabloid *Bild*, who most likely coined the creative blend formation 'Sexham' in its headline on April 17, 2004, and used the label in two different articles on the same day. Interestingly enough, when the main news actors are identified in the text, the article keeps the made-up surname, thus ending up contrasting 'David Sexham' with 'Victoria Beckham':

28 SEXHAM TRÄGT JETZT EINE BÜSSER-GLATZE
   In demonstrativ trauter, verkuschelter Wir-sind-grenzenlos-happy-Zweisamkeit tauchten David Sexham (28) und seine schamlos betrogene Gattin Victoria Beckham (30) in der „Royal Albert Hall" auf. Der 1. offizielle Auftritt nach den Sex-Enthüllungen!
   (*Bild*, April 17, 2004)[13]

[SEXHAM SHOWS A REGRETFUL FACE
Demonstrating trust and familiarity in a 'we're a boundlessly happy couple' manner, David Sexham (28) and his shamelessly deceived wife Victoria Beckham (30) attended the Royal Albert Hall in their first official appearance after the sex revelations!][14]

While the first headline indicates the ad hoc lexical formation by italicizing a part of the blend ('*Sex*ham'), thereby helping readers to analyze its meaning as composed of the two constituents ('Sex' + '[Beck]ham'), the second headline and article already use this designation in a matter-of-fact way, see example (29):

29 DAVID SEXHAM—WAS MACHT DEN FUSSBALL-GOTT ZUM FRAUENSTÜRMER?
Die Liebestricks des David Beckham. Seine angebliche Sexgespielin Rebecca Loos (26) schwärmte im englischen TV von ihrer Kurz-Affäre mit dem Freistoß-Genie—und machte Millionen Frauen neidisch. Was ist dran an David <u>Sexham</u>?

(Bild, April 17, 2004)[15]

[DAVID SEXHAM—WHAT MAKES THIS FOOTBALL GOD A WOMEN'S STRIKER?
David Beckham's love tricks. His alleged sex playmate Rebecca Loos (26) spoke on an English TV channel about her short affair with the free kick-genius—making millions of women envious. What is it about David Sexham?]

The new designation was apparently picked up by some other media. Example (30) illustrates how an online sports news site references the original source (the German *Bild*) by means of a relative clause that includes the creative nickname 'Sexham':

30 Der 28-Jährige, <u>dem die "Bild" den Spitznamen "Sexham" verpasst hatte</u>, soll laut dem "Sunday Mirror" seiner Frau tränenreich den Seitensprung gebeichtet haben.

(Tennismagazin—"Beckham beichtet Sexabenteuer,"
April 18, 2004)[16]

[According to the "Sunday Mirror," the 28-year-old, who was given the nickname "Sexham" by the "Bild," tearfully admitted the affair to his wife.]

Since the expression 'Sexham' is an entirely new coinage, it is also possible to trace how it spreads across other media and other countries, attesting to the

216 Jan Chovanec

way the popular press in Europe 'piggybacks' on each other's stories, monitoring their content and taking over whatever may be deemed of interest for local audiences. Based on an internet search at the time, it was attested from Dutch, Czech, and Slovak sources. This indicates how the tabloid media in these countries monitor and draw on the German mediaspace. Thus, for instance, the Czech tabloid newspaper *Blesk* published the following story only three days after the expression 'Sexham' was coined by *Bild*:

31 DAVID SEXHAM:
Ostříhal se a přiznal nevěru! Fotbalový mág David Beckham (28) kápnul božskou.

(*Blesk*, April 21, 2004)

[DAVID SEXHAM:
He had a haircut and admitted infidelity. The football wizard David Beckham (28) has come clean.]

A rather more interesting situation occurred in the online report by the Slovak private TV channel *Markýza* (April 29, 2004), which stated that Beckham is referred to with the new coinage 'Sexham' in Spain, but the text actually included a reference to the German tabloid newspaper *Bild*. It is therefore probable that, while the paper did take the new coinage over from the German source (and acknowledged it correctly), it enhanced the actual story by taking the liberty of localizing the expression to the country where Beckham was currently playing. In this way, it contributed to the elaboration of a fictional scenario in a rather 'post-truth' manner.

Playing with linguistic taboo

Since references to sex and private body parts represent the most frequent example of taboo (Allan and Burridge, 2006), they tend to be avoided in public discourse. However, there is a whole range of avoidance strategies whereby the offending expressions are replaced by euphemisms or allusions. One of the most typical ways of dealing with taboo in the press is to edit out the offending words: by beeping them out in spoken broadcasts and replacing them with asterisks in the written press.

Once the flirting text messages became available to the media, they were quite extensively republished in the popular press. However, the texts were not reprinted in their full, unedited versions. Instead, the media represented the linguistic taboo as a form of puzzle for the readers. The analysis of the data has revealed three strategies of how the popular press handles the offending expressions. The strategies consist of: entirely withholding the taboo word; implying the word through initial letters or inflectional morphemes; and supplying an alternative, non-offending word instead.

The first strategy, i.e., of 'not mentioning the unmentionable', consists of using words that are completely asterisked. The verbal context helps to disambiguate the message since it enables the readers to correctly infer the word class of the missing expression. Together with the number of asterisks indicating the length of the taboo word, this narrows down the list of candidates considerably, allowing readers to make relatively informed guesses:

> 32 DB: Now I am doing something, thinking about your ****.
> RL: What sort of stuff? Why, u at hotel? What do u need? I haven't **** yet, u bastard.

In some cases, this strategy is taken to extreme ends when the tabloids use asterisks even for words that are evidently not taboo at all, including such grammatical words as articles, prepositions, and auxiliaries. This boosts the sensationalist nature of the story by stimulating additional titillation of the readers, who may embark upon a guessing game to determine which words are actually missing.[17] Arguably, what the replacement of taboo (and even non-taboo) words with asterisks achieves is the activation of readers, who are led to engage with the semantically vague and indeterminate texts in search of the missing lexemes. That is the case in the following examples:

> 33 RL: Your tongue ** **** ** **** ***** then softly on my **** **** *** **** ** ** mouth and u choose from there.
> DB: Can just imagine how *** *** **** u are.[18]

In these extracts, the correct identification of the missing words is rather difficult, if not impossible. In addition, there appears to be some indication that veracity is not the media's goal at all. In fact, the number of asterisks may be quite arbitrary and unrelated to the actual text that the media censor for the readers. By leaving out relatively inoffensive words and longer stretches of connected text, the tabloids increase the news value of their stories, inviting the readers to partake in a voyeuristic quest to discover the allegedly offensive and missing content. As a result of the general trend towards tabloidization and familiarization of language in the media, some research indicates that there is a trend in the modern media to use fewer asterisked versions of taboo words (Clark, 2013). However, in this particular case the papers reprinted entire text conversations in which they deleted up to 30 words, almost having a field day blotting out this and that.

The second strategy—'implying the unmentionable'—is characterized by some kind of formal indication of what the missing word actually is. This can take two forms: the retention of initial letters or the use of inflectional morphemes, typically at the ends of the asterisked words. The latter strategy makes instantly clear the word class of the taboo word but, as there is no trace of the lexical form of the taboo, the bound morphemes do not violate the taboo. Occasionally, an initial and final letter/morpheme are also provided (e.g., *t**t, sh***ed, a**e*). These strategies can be illustrated with the following examples:

> 34 DB: Someone just came in my room. S*** I was looking forward to that. Have u any of my stuff you (sic) need bring round to me?
> 35 DB: Next time it will be ****er and **tter and all ****** you.
> 36 DB: Baby i know it's a ****er but keep that flight on hold cause someones ****ed up my diary and September could be a problem, don't worry they got the sack.
> 37 DB: u sound like you need to get ***ed!
>
> (*News of the World*, April 18, 2004)

Finally, there is the third strategy. This involves 'mentioning the unmentionable', albeit in a rather modified form. The taboo is entertained here entirely for humorous purposes. Thus, for instance, *The Sun* published an article speculating on the expression that had been edited out from one of the text messages ("You need to save all your energy for ****," allegedly texted by Beckham to Loos). The story, headlined IS BECKS PECKER A SVEN OR PELE? (April 7, 2004), was based on the (possibly spoof) report that the bookmakers Paddy Power opened betting on the missing expression (understood as Beckham's reference to his private parts), offering a range of odds for the various possibilities:

> 38 And the betting is that the mystery word is Becks' pet name for, well, every bloke's closest mate. ... Favourite is Dave at 8–1 and second favourite is Beck at 10–1. Other odds on offer include Pele 16–1; Mate 16–1; José 20–1; Posh 20–1; Sven 33–1; Dude 33–1; Eric 50–1; Geri 50–1; Gary 50–1; Phil 66–1; Raul 80–1; Nike 100–1; Alex 100–1 and Figo 100–1.
>
> (*The Sun*, April 7, 2004)

With this kind of fictionalized coverage, the popular press turns the entire event into a welcome opportunity to engage in risqué humor at the expense of Beckham. Needless to say, however, the use of asterisks in this 'national guessing game' quickly became part of the shared cultural knowledge in the UK. As shown at the very beginning of this chapter with *The Telegraph* cartoon, the strategy could be (and was) drawn on for the sake of humor also in non-footballing contexts, with the asterisks indexing an intertextual link to the text sex scandal.

Conclusions

The findings of the analysis of the 'Becks text sex' scandal in the media can be generalized to make several conclusions concerning language, the media, and football celebrities. First, the popular press systematically draws on a range of poetic strategies (e.g., alliteration, assonance, word play, homophony) whereby it directs the readers' attention to aspects of the linguistic form. Since the strategies are inherently playful, this kind of treatment of the events adds to their entertainment potential and their perception as non-serious gossip, available for the amusement of the mass readership. In other words, the entertaining form of presentation can turn the presented content into entertainment (Chovanec, 2008). Second, the preoccupation with taboo, particularly where it concerns sex and related issues, attests to the popular papers' aim to titillate the readers and draw them into the complicit co-construction of the missing links in the narrative. By censoring and playing with taboo in various ways, the media simultaneously present the readers with a semantic puzzle—some information is provided but the salient expressions are withheld on account of the media flaunting their blatant moralistic attitudes.

It seems that the attention paid by the popular media to the non-footballing pursuits of football celebrities reflects an increasing level of public scrutiny over sportspeople beyond the sports arena. As suggested by Boyle (2006, p. 121), the coverage of these scandals is partly related to the changing nature of the media, where people in the sports industry are increasingly subject to similar media treatment as other people in public life, such as pop culture celebrities and political figures. It appears that "there is a growing parallel not simply between sports and more general entertainment journalism, but with areas of 'hard news' such as politics" (Boyle, 2006, p. 122). When sportspeople and other celebrities do not live up to the idealized norms of behavior, they are easily turned into butts of humor and sometimes viciously ridiculed and laughed at by the press (cf. Dakhlia, 2012). In this way, they are delegitimized as society's role models. Thus, football celebrities are not only venerated as national icons and heroes at times of key international championships: they see this positive coverage counterbalanced with the vicious bad press they receive at other times, particularly if some real or assumed moral failure is involved.

As a result of all of this, readers may find a disarming pleasure in the spectacularly playful—and playfully spectacular—tabloid discourse about morally questionable non-footballing acts committed by football celebrities. Often contrasting the celebrities' open frontstage performance with their actual backstage behavior, this kind of discourse relativizes the distinctions between reality and fiction, seriousness and non-seriousness, and the private and public spheres.

Appendix 1

Figure 10.1 Humorous treatment of taboo in the Matt cartoon. *The Telegraph*, 6 April 2004. © Telegraph Media Group Limited 2004, published with permission.

"Text sex with Becks" 221

Appendix 2

Figure 10.2 A parody of the taboo guessing in the Matt cartoon. *The Telegraph*, 23 April 2004. © Telegraph Media Group Limited 2004, published with permission.

Notes

1 In the case of David Beckham, the general attention to his metrosexual body has even found its representation in Beckham's notorious nickname "Goldenballs" (revealed accidentally by his wife Victoria in an interview; see Hewett, 2014). Presently, the label refers simultaneously to his footballing achievements and his exaggerated manliness, associated with his appearance in male underwear advertising campaigns.

2 After a brief career in the media and a participation in several reality shows, Loos moved out of the public eye.

3 The *Oxford English Dictionary* dates its earliest example of 'sext' to 2001, 'sexting' to 2005, and 'to sext' to 2007.

4 The "kiss-and-tell story" is a phrase used by *The Telegraph* to refer to the coverage of the story in the tabloids, attesting to the mutual preoccupation of the papers with each other.

5 This is an independent drama film directed by Steven Soderbergh, which attracted strong critical acclaim and won the Palme d'Or award at the 1989 Cannes Film Festival.

6 Capital letters in the examples indicate headlines.

7 Original news text available online at http://sgforums.com/forums/12/topics/ 74895 [accessed May 17, 2017].

8 Rather than being truthful representations of reported speech, direct quotes in the print media conventionally serve to construct the impression of authenticity and immediacy, particularly in headlines (Chovanec, 2014). In such cases, stylization overrules veracity.

9 Original news text available online at http://sgforums.com/forums/12/topics/ 74895 [accessed May 17, 2017].

10 This kind of phonological parallelism appears to have been omnipresent in the media coverage throughout Beckham's sporting and celebrity careers, cf. the monosyllabic headline "Becks sex pics shock," published by the *Daily Star* at a later time and in a different context (April 18, 2007). Needless to say, however, a similar phenomenon may be observed in some broadsheet papers as well. *The Telegraph*, for instance, included the following assonant combination in one of its reports: "she flashed her excellent teeth at all the right moments. 'I'm a woman, I'm single and I'm bisexual', she said, revealing just three of the reasons why the excitable men of middle Britain have reared up" (*The Telegraph*, April 16). Whether intentional or not, the recurrence of the [eks] sound constitutes a poetic effect that underlies the aesthetic effect of the language forms.

11 The nickname 'Posh' is a shortened version of 'Posh Spice', a name under which Victoria had been known when she sang in the women's pop group Spice Girls, hugely popular in the 1990s. Her professional history also provided the cultural background for some articles during Beckham's 'sex text scandal'. This is evident, for instance, in the headline "Spice up your text life" (May 21, 2004), under which *The Sun* advertised its new SMS service for readers ahead of the 2004 Euro Football Championship.

12 In this connection, it is worth mentioning that the same kind of punning actually became the subject of some media coverage. On June 30, 2004, a large David Beckham photo-poster shown at an exhibition in the Royal Academy of Arts in London was vandalized by an anonymous individual with the words "Beckham and Meier, you loosers" written all over it. The reference here was to the referee Urs Meier, who disallowed a last-minute goal in the Euro 2004 quarterfinal between England and Portugal, and to Beckham's failure to score two penalties at the same championship. The media speculated that the spelling

of 'loosers' may also have been a reference to the recent affair with Rebecca Loos. When asked about this particular issue, the curator of the exhibition said "I don't know if it was a pun. Knowing football hooligans, they probably just couldn't spell" (Moyes, 2004).

13 www.bild.t-online.de/BTO/showpromis/2004/04/17/beckham/beckham__sex__koerper.html, retrieved on April 21, 2004, link no longer functional.

14 All translations into English are by the author of this chapter.

15 www.bild.t-online.de/BTO/showpromis/2004/04/17/beckham/beckham__sex__koerper.html, retrieved on April 21, 2004, link no longer functional.

16 www.tennismagazin.de/nncs/fussball/2004/04/18/52241.html, retrieved on April 21, 2004, link no longer functional.

17 *The Guardian* called the situation "a nationwide guessing game over what naughty words have been blotted out" (Smith and Campbell, 2004). This attests to the significance the whole case had for British popular culture at that time and for the way the broadsheet papers have approached the case differently, namely adding a metaperspective from which the 'spectacle of language' in the other papers was described. Interestingly, in *The Telegraph* newspaper the asterisking game was taken up in another of its Matt cartoons, this time in a jocular reference to the mysteriousness of the missing words (see Appendix 2; April 23, 2004).

18 These transcripts ([32] and [33]) were originally published in *News of the World* and *The Sun*. They remain accessible in various non-media sites, such as blogs and discussion groups. For a humorous treatment of one of these texts, see also a feature column from *The Guardian*, reprinted in Mangan (2009, ch. 3).

References

Alabarces, P., Tomlinson, A. and Young, C. 2001. Argentina versus England at the France '98 World Cup: Narratives of nation and the mythologizing of the popular. Media, Culture & Society. 23(5), pp. 547–566.

Allan, K. and Burridge, K. 2006. Forbidden words: Taboo and the censoring of language. Cambridge, UK: Cambridge University Press.

BBC News. 2011. Ryan Giggs named by MP as injunction footballer. [Online]. May 23. [Accessed September 6, 2017]. Available from: www.bbc.com/news/uk-13503847.

Beckford, M. 2012. Ryan Giggs named in court for first time over injunction. The Telegraph. [Online]. February 22. [Accessed September 7, 2017]. Available from: www.telegraph.co.uk/news/newstopics/lawreports/9096152/Ryan-Giggs-named-in-court-for-first-time-over-injunction.html.

Bell, A. 1991. The language of news media. Oxford: Blackwell.

Bishop, H. and Jaworski, A. 2003. "We beat 'em": Nationalism and the hegemony of homogeneity in the British press reportage of Germany versus England during Euro 2000. Discourse & Society. 14(3), pp. 243–271.

Boyle, R. 2006. Sports journalism: Context and issues. London: Sage.

Boyle, R. and Haynes, R. 2004. Football in the new media age. Abingdon: Routledge.

Cashmore, E. and Parker, A. 2003. One David Beckham? Celebrity, masculinity, and the soccerati. Sociology of Sport Journal. 20(3), pp. 214–231.

Chovanec, J. 2005a. Czeching out puns and clichés in football reporting. Theory and Practice in English Studies. 3, pp. 61–67.

Chovanec, J. 2005b. From zeroo to heroo: Word play and Wayne Rooney in the British Press. In: Slovak Studies in English I. The Proceedings of the conference organized on the occasion of the 80th anniversary of the opening of British and American Studies at the Faculty of Arts, Comenius University, Bratislava. Bratislava: Comenius University, pp. 85–99.

Chovanec, J. 2008. Focus on form: Foregrounding devices in football reporting. Discourse & Communication. 2(3), pp. 219–242.

Chovanec, J. 2014. Pragmatics of tense and time: From canonical headlines to online news texts. Amsterdam: John Benjamins.

Chovanec, J. 2016. Eavesdropping on media talk: Microphone gaffes and unintended humour in sports broadcasts. Journal of Pragmatics. 95, pp. 93–106.

Chovanec, J. 2017. Wordplay and football: Humor in the discourse of written sports reporting. In: Chłopicki, W. and Brzozowska, D. eds. Humorous discourse. Berlin: Mouton de Gruyter, pp. 131–154.

Clark, C. 2013. It's always the same old news! A diachronic analysis of shifting newspaper language style, 1993–2005. In: Bamford, J., Cavalieri, S. and Diani, G. eds. Variation and change in spoken and written discourse. Amsterdam: John Benjamins, pp. 269–282.

Conboy, M. 2006. Tabloid Britain: Constructing a community through language. London: Routledge.

Conboy, M. 2013. Geoff Hurst's ball. In: Korte, B. and Lechner, D. eds. History and humour: British and American perspectives. Bielefeld: Transcript Verlag, pp. 193–210.

Crystal, D. 2008. Txtng: The Gr8 Db8. Oxford: Oxford University Press.

Daily Mirror. 2004. Becks sex was a lie. [Online]. July 25. [Accessed September 7, 2017]. Available from: www.mirror.co.uk/news/world-news/becks-sex-was-a-big-lie-1600826.

Dakhlia, J. 2012. Humour as a means of popular empowerment: The discourse of the French gossip magazines. In: Chovanec, J. and Ermida, I. eds. Language and humour in the media. Newcastle upon Tyne: Cambridge Scholars, pp. 231–248.

Fowler, R. 1991. Language in the news. London: Routledge.

Fowler, R., Hodge, B., Kress, G. and Trew, T. 1979. Language and control. London: Routledge.

Franklin, B. 1997. Newszak and news media. London: Arnold.

Goffman, E. 1981. Forms of talk. Philadelphia: University of Pennsylvania Press.

Greenhill, S. 2010. England captain John Terry jeered on the pitch as affair with team mate's girlfriend is revealed. Daily Mail. [Online]. January 30. [Accessed September 7, 2017]. Available from: www.dailymail.co.uk/news/article-1247042/John-Terry-Married-England-captain-affair-team-mate-Wayne-Bridges-partner-launched-legal-cover-up.html.

Halliday, J. 2011. Twitter faces legal action by footballer over privacy. The Guardian. [Online]. May 20. [Accessed September 6, 2017]. Available from: www.theguardian.com/media/2011/may/20/twitter-sued-by-footballer-over-privacy.

Harcup, T. and O'Neill, D. 2001. What is news? Galtung and Ruge revisited. Journalism Studies. 2(2), pp. 261–280.

Harrison, G. 2016. "I have no regrets": Glamour girl-turned-housewife Rebecca Loos is living a new life after the "David Beckham affair" storm, moving to a remote Nordic ski village to raise her children. The Sun. [Online]. September 6. [Accessed September 6, 2017]. Available from: www.thesun.co.uk/living/1734 569/glamour-girl-turned-housewife-rebecca-loos-is-living-a-new-life-after-the-david-beckham-affair-storm-moving-to-a-remote-nordic-ski-village-to-raise-her-children/.

Hewett, E. 2014. Victoria Beckham at her finest: Why is David Beckham affectionately known as Golden Balls? Metro. [Online]. March 22. [Accessed September 7, 2017]. Available from: http://metro.co.uk/2014/03/22/victoria-beckham-at-her-finest-why-is-david-beckham-affectionately-known-as-golden-balls-4673059/.

Hills, S. 2004. Rooney admits "sex with a granny." Evening Standard. [Online]. August 23. [Accessed September 7, 2017]. Available from: www.standard.co.uk/news/rooney-admits-sex-with-a-granny-6952363.html.

Holland, P. 1998. The politics of the smile: "Soft news" and the sexualization of the popular press. In: Carter, C., Branston, G. and Allen, S. eds. News, gender and power. London: Routledge, pp. 17–32.

iDnes. 2007. Výpověď je jasná: Byly to prostitutky. [The statement is clear: They were prostitutes]. [Online]. March 27. [Accessed August 23, 2017]. Available from: http://fotbal.idnes.cz/vypoved-je-jasna-byly-to-prostitutky-d8c-/fot_reprez.aspx?c=A070326_224315_fot_reprez_no.

Jakobson, R. 1960. Linguistics and poetics. In: Sebeok, T.A. ed. Style in language. Cambridge, MA: The MIT Press, pp. 350–377.

Lennon, P. 2004. Allusions in the press. An applied linguistic study. Berlin: Mouton de Gruyter.

Mangan, L. 2009. My family and other disasters. [Kindle e-book]. London: Guardianbooks.

Mayr, A. and Machin, D. 2012. The language of crime and deviance: An introduction to critical linguistic analysis in media and popular culture. London: Continuum.

Molek-Kozakowska, K. 2013. Towards a pragma-linguistic framework for the study of sensationalism in news headlines. Discourse & Communication. 7(2), pp. 173–197.

Moore, M. 2010. Wayne Rooney "slept with prostitute while wife Coleen was pregnant." The Telegraph. [Online]. September 5. [Accessed September 6, 2017]. Available from: www.telegraph.co.uk/sport/football/teams/england/7982734/Wayne-Rooney-slept-with-prostitute-while-wife-Coleen-was-pregnant.html.

Moyes, S. 2004. Becklash: Beckham portrait defaced with the words "You loosers." Daily Mirror. [Online]. June 30. [Accessed September 6, 2017]. Available from: www.thefreelibrary.com/BECKLASH%3B+Beckham+portrait+defaced+with+the+words+'You+loosers'.-a0118777227.

Puxley, R. 2004. BritSlang: An uncensored A–Z of the peoples' language, rhyming slang. London: Robson.

Schirato, T. 2007. Understanding sports culture. London: Sage.

Schirato, T. 2013. Sports discourse. London: Bloomsbury.

Scotsman. 2004. Becks text sex? Keep on taking the tabloids. [Online]. April 16. [Accessed September 6, 2017]. Available from: www.scotsman.com/news/becks-text-sex-keep-on-taking-the-tabloids-1-1008790.

Sex, Lies, and Videotapes. 1989. [Film]. Steven Soderbergh. dir. USA: Outlaw Productions, Virgin.

Shortis, T. 2016. Texting and other messaging: Written system in digitally mediated vernaculars. In: Cook, V. and Ryan, D. eds. The Routledge handbook of the English writing system. London: Routledge, pp. 487–516.

Smith, D. and Campbell, D. 2004. The great Becks orgy. The Guardian. [Online]. April 11. [Accessed September 7, 2017]. Available from: www.theguardian.com/media/2004/apr/11/pressandpublishing.comment.

Sunderland, T. 2013. 10 biggest English Premier League scandals of all time. Bleacher Report. [Online]. February 19. [Accessed September 6, 2017]. Available from: http://bleacherreport.com/articles/1535094-10-biggest-english-premier-league-scandals-of-all-time.

The Telegraph. 2004. FA chief and Eriksson had affair with secretary. [Online]. July 25. [Accessed September 7, 2017]. Available from: www.telegraph.co.uk/news/1467822/FA-chief-and-Eriksson-had-affair-with-secretary.html.

Tudor, A. 2006. World Cup worlds: Media coverage of the soccer World Cup 1972 to 2002. In: Raney, A.A. and Bryant, J. eds. Handbook of sports and media. Mahwah: Lawrence Erlbaum, pp. 232–246.

Wright, Simon. 2010. Wayne Rooney cheats on pregnant wife Coleen with £1k-a-night prostitute. Daily Mirror. [Online]. September 4. [Accessed September 6, 2017]. Available from: www.mirror.co.uk/news/uk-news/wayne-rooney-cheats-on-pregnant-wife-245523.

Chapter 11

Multimodal construction of soccer-related humor on Twitter and Instagram

Thomas Messerli and Di Yu

Introduction

Technology-mediated communication, particularly within popular social media sites, grants users active roles and participatory access to its content (Chovanec and Dynel, 2015). In this chapter, we analyze specialized soccer humor channels on Twitter and Instagram and explore the multimodal construction of soccer-related humor on these sites, and how that humor is taken up in followers' comments. Accordingly, our research questions are: (1) How is humor constructed by original posters (OPs) on soccer-related Twitter and Instagram channels? (2) How do other users/commenters react to humorous tweets and Instagram posts, and what forms of humor support can be observed in this context?

In the analyzed posts, the broadcaster, i.e., the "'followable' party that makes talk available to recipients" (Draucker, 2015, p. 49), uses text, images, videos, audios, and GIFs to construct humorous incongruities and invite their followers to laugh with them about a specific target—usually an individual player or a soccer club. In doing so, broadcasters establish involvement in the sense of Tannen (2007), i.e., they use the specific linguistic and non-linguistic materials at their disposal to create and maintain an emotional connection between their followers and themselves. In our analysis of OPs, we will thus focus on the ways in which visual and textual components are combined and reused by posters to construct soccer-related humor. As the analysis will show, the soccer frame is activated more directly by referring to or combining constituent elements (including participants and events) of the beautiful game, or more indirectly by repurposing aspects from other domains and forcing a shift towards the soccer frame. Encoded in the posts is an assumption by OPs that their common ground with the recipients extends to even minor events in recent soccer games of the major European leagues as well as of European international competitions like the Champions League. While the multimodal construction of humor in itself may well be shared with humor in other domains, the thus constructed soccer-related incongruities are special because they can appeal to a wider audience despite the extensive knowledge they require to be successfully processed as humor.

In a second step, we will then investigate the comments that followers post in response to the OP and establish how reactions more generally and humor support more specifically are encoded in these comments. By demonstrating how original posters construct humor and how other users respond to and support humor, we provide further evidence of the complexity of humor construction and collaborative nature of communication on social media. These comments also support the successful uptake of humor and thus the understanding and appreciation of the soccer-related details that the OPs made use of.

Before presenting the findings of these empirical analyses in the fourth and fifth sections ("Analysis 1: Humor construction in original posts" and "Analysis 2: User responses to humorous soccer-related posts"), we will briefly establish the theoretical framework that informs our understanding of computer-mediated communication (CMC), interaction and of humor therein (second section: "Background"), as well as the data and methodology on which these findings are based (third section: "Data and method").

Background

Communication on social media

Previous research has noted some prominent properties of the interactions occurring on social media in various aspects such as the role of the original poster (OP), the participation framework, the role of media artifacts, and the possibility to engender civil participation. Draucker (2015) for example, in analyzing the structure of interaction and participation on Twitter, identified the role of the 'broadcaster' as one that complements the production roles in the Goffmanian tradition and better captures the complexity of interactions occurring on the medium of Twitter. It is suggested that the broadcaster can not only be distinguished as the animator, the author, or the principle, but can also serve as an accountable party that makes talk available. It has also been noted that, despite participants' spatial separation, interaction on social media enables an "infinite number of potential participants" (Chovanec and Dynel, 2015) to become an automatically ratified audience.[1] As Chovanec and Dynel (2015) point out, instead of being simply a passive recipient, any audience member also has the potential of taking on other participation roles and becoming active producers themselves, which leads to a shift from simply dyadic interaction to dynamic co-creation. Besides the complex roles of participation, social media sites also provide the use of media artifacts, which has also become a noteworthy phenomenon. Typical artifacts, such as memes, pictures, videos, GIFs, Vine video loops, are said to help express one's perspectives and facilitate the dialogue between parties with different opinions, which essentially contributes to creating "a plurality of coexistence and inter-action" (Milner, 2013, p. 2358). Overall, social media as an interactive and democratic platform has been found to be consequential for engaging the public and creating opportunities for civil participation (Butterworth, 2014). More specifically regarding soccer, it has been found that media discourse contributes to normalizing fandom and fanaticism and spectacu-larizing and commercializing soccer events (Lee, 2005). Cleland (2014) also found that soccer-related social media can become platforms for anti-Islamic and anti-multiculturalism racist discourse. As will be seen, our data contains some aspects that may be regarded as conservative or even homo-phobic, but generally is of an entirely more playful nature, bringing together posters and commentators that jointly engage in topical humor about the sport they are interested in.

Theoretical approach to humor

We follow what can be described as an essentialist view of humor in this chapter, which is interested in the mechanisms and affordances the broad-casting party employs in the creation of humor in the original posts, as well as in how followers encode their reactions to humorous posts in their comments. Within the classical three strands of humor—relief, superiority, and incongruity (see e.g., Attardo, 1994)—this study adheres to a defini-tion of humor based on incongruity and resolution, which is informed by Suls's (1972) model of humor processing. Humor is understood first and foremost as a cognitive phenomenon that occurs when a surprising stimu-lus runs against recipient expectations: the stimuli that recipients encounter evoke a particular narrative frame, i.e., knowledge structures that lead to vague expectations as to what events are likely to follow. Subsequent stimuli, e.g., in the form of narrative events, are measured against those expectations, and humor ensues if a stimulus is incongruous with recipient expectations, and if that incongruity can be resolved by finding a rule that explains its presence. While humor processing ultimately takes place in the minds of the recipients—in this case the followers that read and react to the posts—the focus of this study is on the basis of these processes in the stimuli that are encoded in posts on social networks.

Humor in interaction and CMC

The forms of humor in interaction are found to include but are not limited to joke telling, anecdotes, wordplay, and irony (Norrick, 2003). Typical features of conversational humor include overlapping speech, co-constructions of utterances, metaphorical language, teasing, sarcasm, linguistic put-downs, higher pitch or volume, increased speech rate, and significant pauses (Attardo et al., 2011; Coates, 2007). In conversations, it has been found that humor can be accompanied and signaled by paralinguistic cues such as the speaker's or the listener's laughter or smile, change in tone of voice, change in pitch or rhythm (Glenn, 2003; Norrick, 2003; Jefferson, 1979). For conversations within CMC, it has been suggested that humor is used to establish group solidarity and identity as users navigate social life on online platforms (Baym, 1995). Evidently, not all of the mentioned features will be found in humor instances on social media. As our discussion of humor comments will show, however, the posters and commenters use the particular linguistic and paralinguistic cues afforded to them by the respective social media platform in order to encode humor and humor support.

Humor support strategies and responses to humor

Also relevant to this project, particularly the second research question, which addresses the uptake of humorous posts in subsequent comments, is previous work on humor support strategies and responses to various types of humor. Treating humor as an interactive phenomenon, Hay (2001) notes commonly observed humor support practices including laughter and echoing or contributing more humor. Overlap and other involvement strategies can be used to show appreciation and enthusiasm. In the case of self-deprecating humor, often sympathy or contradiction are found as responses. In experimental settings, Bell (2013; 2009) also observes responses to failed or incomprehensible humor, which is particularly interesting for the purpose of this project. She discusses a few typical responses to failed humor including signaling recognition while expressing the lack of appreciation, laughter and fake laughter, metalinguistic comments, interjections, evaluative responses, rhetorical questions, and sarcasm. In the case of incomprehensible humor, she also discovered that typically recipients respond with expressions of non-understanding, smile, laughter, silence, repetition of the punch line, assessment of jokes, and request for explanation.

Soccer as a semantic frame

In order to address the specificity of the humorous incongruities we find in our data for soccer, we will describe it as a semantic frame by using the terminology and existing framework that is implemented in FrameNet (see e.g., Fillmore and Baker, 2009). Understood from this point of view, soccer can be described as a form of competition, which as core elements involves a set of participants, the players, as well as many less central elements that include the venue (the pitch that it is played on), the additional participants that are involved (e.g., referees), and a particular purpose (winning this particular game, winning a competition, etc.). For the particular type of soccer that our tweets and Instagram posts relate to, we can further specify that we talk about the kind of top-tier men's professional soccer that is broadcast on television and seen by a global audience, either because it belongs to a soccer competition that is itself international, or because it is part of a national competition whose appeal goes beyond national borders (e.g., the English Premier League).

When we talk about soccer-related humor in our discussion, we thus mean humor that uses the core and non-core elements of internationally broadcast professional soccer as part of its setting. In particular, we find that both the verbal and visual elements of the individual humorous posts activate particular aspects of the soccer frame and work in relation to expectations based on knowledge of soccer, the domain of professional soccer and the conventions of televisually broadcast soccer. As will be shown, all of these knowledge structures are assumed by original posters to be part of the communal common ground of their recipients, which in turn renders them affordances for humor construction. At the same time, these processes thus also construct a particular audience—we find no traces of explication of any post elements to recipients who may not be familiar with them.

Based on this study alone, it is not possible to decide to what extent the patterns we find here are shared with other semantic frames. However, it is striking that the topicality of the channels we investigate here translates into exclusively topical humor that is either inherently situated entirely within the soccer frame or transferred there with the help of processes that we will discuss in the fourth section ("Analysis 1: Humor construction in original posts"). It can be added that while the mechanisms of humor construction we find here are linked more generally to the affordances offered by Twitter and Instagram, their concrete realization builds on a number of aspects that in their combination are particular to the soccer frame. These aspects include the international popularity of the game that leads to similar televisual representations across the globe; the fact that it is a playful competition that is received as a form of entertainment and therefore requires little work to be made the topic of humor; and the appearance of particular participants (e.g., the player Lionel Messi) as well as more generic roles (e.g., referees), whose typical traits and behavior are known to an international audience.

Data and method

In order to answer our research questions, we collected data from four public soccer-related social media accounts, two each on Twitter and on Instagram, in the first week of June 2016. Our analyses focus on the original posts from each account, as well as on comments by other users in response to each post, which lets us address both humor construction by original posters (OPs) and humor uptake, including humor support, in the subsequent response to these original posts. Given our interest in the multi-modal construction of soccer-related humor and its uptake in the social media, we started by searching for topical Twitter and Instagram accounts and based on their popularity selected *FootyHumour* and *Footy_Jokes02* on Twitter, and *footballjokes* and *perksoffootball* on Instagram. This can be regarded as a form of cluster sampling: We assume that posters on these social platforms do in most cases not create the individual elements that constitute their posts and will instead (re-)assemble pre-existing pictures, GIFs, videos, and even texts in order to create posts they then share with their followers. Thus, the selection of humor we find on each account should be a heterogeneous subset of humorous soccer-related posts that are being shared on each of the two social networks. Indeed, we found that while there were differences between Instagram and Twitter, the two accounts on each platform were very much comparable with regard to the type of posts they contained.

Since this is an exploratory study interested in creating a typology of multimodal humor construction on social networks, we were content with a relatively small data set in our first analysis and accordingly limited the number of posts to a sample of 20 from each account. For the resulting 80 posts, we saved the URL where each of them was accessible, the texts each of the posts contained, and a screenshot of the post as it presented itself in June 2016. We mention this here because a first observation we can make is that these posts have various degrees of fixity. Whereas the majority of posts by three of the four accounts could still be accessed in January 2017, *Footy_Jokes02* has since been closed. Similarly, some of the comments we collected for the second analysis are still publicly available, while others have been removed—mostly because the accounts of the commenters have since been deleted.

Having selected the posts, we analyzed them qualitatively for the ways in which they multimodally create humorous incongruities, which resulted in a non-exhaustive list of humor construction strategies that will be presented and discussed based on illustrative examples in the section "Analysis 1: Humor construction in original posts." Based on the finding of the first analysis that each of the two Instagram and Twitter accounts were comparable clusters of humorous soccer-related posts on the respective platform, we again decided on cluster sampling for the second analysis and limited our study to the 643 comments made in response to the posts of the Twitter account *FootyHumour* and the 1292 comments to *perksoffootball* on Instagram. These comments were analyzed qualitatively and bottom-up, i.e., without preconceived notions about what type of comments we as research-ers expected. The results of the second analysis are presented in the section "Analysis 2: User responses to humorous soccer-related posts."

We want to conclude this section with a brief note on research ethics. First, we agree with Bolander and Locher (2014, pp. 16–17) that ethical issues need to be taken into account by researchers that work with data, which includes data that are publicly available on the internet. The data we analyze here are public not only in terms of their accessibility, but also in terms of their content, and we have found no evidence in posts or comments that would indicate in any way that the poster or commenter would want their message to be understood as private. Moreover, the analyzed data can be described as light-hearted interaction on a public and non-sensitive topic, and it is not conceivable how our research could be disadvantageous in any way to any of the posters and commenters whose contributions appear in our data. We therefore decided that even in the absence of consent, analyzing the data and presenting them in examples as we do here is well within what we deem to be ethically sound research practice. The public nature of the data notwithstanding, all personal information that is not immediately relevant to our analyses has been greyed out in the figures.

Analysis 1: humor construction in original posts[2]

As outlined in the previous section, the initial analysis of soccer-related humor on Twitter and Instagram focused on the original posts by *Footy-Humour* and *Footy_Jokes02* on Twitter, and *footballjokes* and *perksof-football* on Instagram. Since the analyzed posts are multimodal in the sense that they make use of one or several pictures and of short texts, which are present in the form of captions or post texts, we will present the types of incongruities that occur in the data categorized by the primary locus of the incongruity. This can be either in the pictorial content, in the textual content, or in equal parts in each of the two.

Picture-related incongruities

As we have mentioned, the primary mode of Instagram is visual, which is to say that every post will by default contain at least one picture or video. Twitter posts, on the other hand, may consist of text only. However, due to the role that television broadcasts play in the dissemination of the type of soccer we focus on here, we expected only marginally less multimodality on Twitter than on Instagram. This was confirmed by the analysis of our data, with 39 of 40 tweets including a picture or video. The only exception is a tweet that uses only text to emulate a scoreboard and thus nonetheless creates a visual effect. Not only do pictures occur in the data, they are often also the primary locus of the humorous incongruity, and the following five OP-strategies are ways in which pictures are exploited for soccer-related humor.

Strategy 1: incongruities in pictures

When it comes to the work that is involved for the poster, the simplest strategy for constructing a picture-based incongruity is to find pre-existing humor and share it with followers. One or several pictures or videos that contain incongruities are presented either without text, or with a caption or post that highlights the incongruity the target audience is meant to look for in the post.

Figure 11.1 illustrates this by presenting what it labels the "Best kisses in football history": It includes three pictures of soccer players kissing other players or male or female fans, with the poster asking their followers to choose their favorite of the three. The pictorial incongruities in Figure 11.1 can be interpreted on different levels. For starters, the combination of the frames of soccer and romance is untypical and thus surprising. At its core, soccer as a competition is about those actions that allow the group of participants that play for one team to win against the other team using the means that the rule of the game affords them. Including more peripheral activities, celebratory scenes when significant steps towards that goal have been taken are also expected, in which case elements of the frames of celebration as a type of social event and friendship as a type of personal relationship are also evoked. This does not, however, include unambiguously romantic actions. Given the strong heterosexual bias shared by the majority of soccer players (and athletes more generally) and many of their fans, the two pictures displaying kisses between two men may be perceived

Figure 11.1 Incongruities in pictures. Perksoffootball, 1 June 2016. Instagram.

as particularly incongruous with expectations.[3] While comparatively little effort is required for the poster in these cases—they merely *find* rather than *create* incongruities—the inclusion of the third image (a player kissing a woman) and the explicit invitation by the OP for followers to choose between the three images ("Which one is your favourite?") indicate that the inherently incongruous material is carefully positioned in a way that highlights its incongruousness. It has to be added that this strategy is constrained by the availability of pictures and videos that can be found and distributed: In order to be relevant for these accounts that are dedicated to soccer-related humor, postable pictorial content needs to be both humorous and belong to the domain of soccer.

Strategy 2: captions recontextualizing incongruities in pictures

The second strategy apparent in the data is related to the first one insofar as here, too, the posted picture already contains a humorous incongruity and thus can be said to be humorous in and of itself. However, in this case, the incongruity does not or not entirely reside within the domain of soccer, which is why work has to be done by the poster to make it relevant. In Figure 11.2, for instance, the pre-existing incongruity in the picture contrasts the frame of soccer with that of the snowman, an inanimate object that bears some iconic resemblance to a human agent. This contrast is only activated, however, when the poster establishes a metaphorical connection to Atlético Madrid's Slovenian goalkeeper Jan Oblak. In the decisive penalty shoot-out of the UEFA Champions League final, which had taken place three days before this Instagram post was made, Oblak failed to stop

Figure 11.2 Recontextualizing incongruity. Perksoffootball, 31 May 2016. Instagram.

any of his opponents' penalties. The post is thus an attempt to make fun of Oblak, who is made responsible for the resulting defeat against city rivals Real Madrid. The picture and the reference to effectivity on penalties in this case only require generic knowledge of soccer. Recipients need to know that the participant that stands between the goalposts is typically the goalkeeper and that he or she attempts to anticipate the direction of the ball and stop it before it crosses the line. They realize that for a snowman to be called more effective than a goalkeeper, that goalkeeper must do worse than standing still. This instance of hostile humor is then merely linked to the name 'Oblak', which evokes not only the particular goalkeeper, but also his performance in the recent final.

Figure 11.3 from the Twitter account *FootyHumour* follows the same strategy, but uses the caption to liken a video of a dancing boy to the joy Manchester United fans must have experienced when they learned about star player Zlatan Ibrahimović joining their club, which was announced around ten days before this post. Interestingly, the OP accidentally or consciously left a previous caption, "Chelsea fans right now...," in place, which shows that the same video on Vine had previously been used to establish a link to another club, Chelsea, and metaphorically render their reaction to another event.

Strategy 3: reinforcing incongruities in pictures by juxtaposing them with other pictures

Another similar strategy employed by OPs in our data is to find a humorous soccer-related picture or video and then to combine it with new pictorial content in order to reinforce the humorous effect. This strategy can be described as a combination of the first two, since it on the one hand makes use of a pre-existing incongruity from the domain of soccer, and on the other hand uses additional content from a different domain for humorous effect. Figures 11.4 and 11.5 are two stills from a video that was posted by *perksoffootball* and used to create humor in this fashion: The video consists of two parts, each of them around two seconds long. The first part, illustrated by Figure 11.4, is a moment taken from the live broadcast of a recent soccer game, in which the referee is repeatedly sticking his tongue out. The second part (Figure 11.5) simply adds video of a goat doing similar movements with its tongue. As was done in the Snowman/Oblak example (Figure 11.2), the post establishes a connection between soccer and a different semantic frame, in this case that of animal behavior. However, whereas the former example finds pre-existing non-soccer related humor in order to make fun of a soccer event, in this case the pre-existing visual incongruity is already topical and could be posted on its own, and the juxtaposition with another domain merely serves to emphasize the unexpectedness, in this case of the referee's behavior. While our analyses here

Soccer-related humor on Twitter and Instagram   237

Figure 11.3 Reinforcing incongruities in pictures. Footyhumour, 3 June 2016. Twitter.

leave aside aspects of typicality, we would assume this third strategy to be rarer than the first two because it has the same constraints as the first one, i.e., it is limited to pre-existing humorous and soccer-related material, and at the same time requires extra work by the poster like the second strategy.

Strategy 4: incongruous collages

The strategies that were discussed so far have in common that they do not alter the individual images they use to construct humor. This is different in

Figure 11.4 Incongruous action. Perksoffootball, 31 May 2016. Instagram.

Figure 11.5 Juxtaposing incongruities. Perksoffootball, 31 May 2016. Instagram.

the strategy that we have here termed *incongruous collages*. Conceptually, it is again a case of establishing a metaphorical link between different events. However, rather than achieving this effect in a linear fashion, by juxtaposing different elements, the images themselves are manipulated in order to map the two domains. Figure 11.6 presents an example from *footballjokes*, in which the underlying picture shows an Atlético Madrid player running to the sidelines to embrace a female supporter, while a man in a white shirt holds on to the player's arm. This image has been altered by the poster in a very simple fashion, by inserting a logo of the soccer club Real Madrid to cover the Atlético player's head, a picture of the UEFA Champions League cup to cover the female fan's face, and an Atlético logo to cover the face of the man in the white shirt. Without the manipulation, there is of course nothing incongruous about the celebratory scene. However, for those aware of the context of the UEFA Champions League final between Real and Atlético that was already mentioned, a relation of opposites between the two levels of the picture emerges. In the original picture, an Atlético player is about to embrace an Atlético fan, while another fan acts as a bystander desperate to quite literally grab the player's attention; in the collage, the Atlético player becomes a symbolic representation of Real and the female Atlético fan is made the cup Real is about to hold in their hands, the prize they are about to win. It is Atlético that becomes the bystander on this second level established by the collage. However, perhaps because of the simplicity of the way in which the collage is created, it is open to different readings that depend on the mapping between the two levels, i.e., on the individual recipient's inclusion or exclusion of particular elements of the original picture as meaningful constituents of the collage. Thus, another reading of the three-party interaction is a

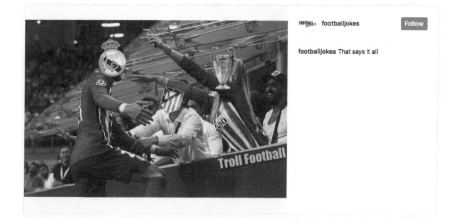

Figure 11.6 Incongruous collage. Footballjokes, 29 May 2016. Instagram.

reinterpretation of the male fan's grab of the player's arm as an attempt to stop Real from reaching the cup; and the collage of the female fan as Champions League cup can both be seen as an attribution of volition to the prize, which is thus consciously partial in the Real/Atlético rivalry, and/ or as a sexist mapping of prize to young woman on which the plausibility of the metaphorical links between the two levels depends.[4]

The collage shows how a simple yet effective manipulation of the picture enables the OP to make a humorous comment about the fact that contrary to the joyous scene of player and fan in the original picture, Atlético lost in the end, whereas Real won the competition. It is interesting to note here that while this humor strategy is clearly visual in nature, the humorous incongruity does not in fact reside either in the original picture or in the layer that the OP superimposed on it: What is incongruous here is the relationship between the two levels, which create a co-existence of two opposites.

Strategy 5: juxtaposition of incongruous pictures

For the final pictorial strategy we want to discuss here, the focus is also on the established relationship between the pictures it juxtaposes. An incongruity is created by combining two pictures that are in contrast with each other. This is the case in Figure 11.7, where—in the context of the young

Figure 11.7 Juxtaposed incongruous pictures. Perksoffootball, 31 May 2016. Instagram.

Soccer-related humor on Twitter and Instagram 241

player Marcus Rashford scoring for the national team of England—two very different reactions by Rashford's team mates are contrasted: A smiling Wayne Rooney on the right faces a less than pleased Daniel Sturridge on the left. As was the case in Strategy 4, humor depends on the work done by the OP, that is, connecting the two pictures by putting them next to each other. Apart from the thus achieved incongruity, humor here can also be related to superiority, which is already present in the post. Essentially, the followers of the OP can laugh with them and the smiling Wayne Rooney about Sturridge who was at that time competing with Rashford for a place in the England squad at the Euro 2016. Thus, the successful communication of humor in this case requires for recipients to be familiar with the particular situation in which each of the depicted players found themselves at the time of posting. This allows recipients to make inferences about which players are in direct competition with each other and would therefore be happy or unhappy to see their teammate succeed.

Text-related incongruities

In the first five strategies, the OP constructed humor mainly in pictures or by establishing new relationships between pictures. Contrary to this, humor in the following two cases depends mostly on the work done in the captions or post texts.

Strategy 6: humorous captions and post texts

Despite the fact that visual materials are central to all four accounts, one strategy for OPs is to construct humorous incongruities linguistically and use imagery for purely illustrative purposes. In Figure 11.8, for instance, the OP pokes fun at Manchester City for spending too much money on an individual player and contrasts this with another successful club, Juventus, who have managed to sign a number of very successful players for free. Instead of listing the names of these players, the OP simply posts a picture of all of them.

Strategy 7: humorous recontextualizations

Another way of creating incongruity within captions or post texts is to present one or several non-humorous pictures and recontextualize them with the text. The post in Figure 11.9, for instance, unites two pictures of Real Madrid player Gareth Bale, one of his hair that appears to show a bald spot, and one where he celebrates the Champions League victory by putting the cup on top of his head. The caption recontextualizes this second picture and jokes that Bale uses the cup to cover up the bald spot shown in the other picture.

242 Thomas Messerli and Di Yu

Figure 11.8 Humorous caption. Footyhumour, 5 June 2016. Twitter.

At first glance, this humor strategy appears to be very similar to Strategy 2, which uses captions to recontextualize non-soccer-related incongruities in pictures. In this case, however, there is no incongruity in the pictures per se, and the humorous effect on the followers depends on the caption providing an unlikely yet plausible interpretation of what the two images represent. While the two pictures are of course still essential to the post, the humorous incongruity is clearly established linguistically, and the caption can thus be identified as the primary mode in this strategy.

Figure 11.9 Humorous recontextualization. Perksoffootball, 31 May 2016. Instagram.

Multimodal construction of incongruities

In all the humor construction strategies we discussed so far, either the visual or the textual mode could be identified as the primary locus for the creation of humorous incongruities. In contrast, the final two patterns entirely depend on the interaction of the two modes.

Strategy 8: juxtaposition of pictures and captions

The first of these two types of truly multimodal humor-construction consists of non-humorous pictures and non-humorous captions. Humor emerges, however, when these are combined by the OP. Figure 11.10 illustrates this and shows three pictures that relate to personnel changes at Manchester United on the left as well as icons and text on the right. The pictures establish a chronology of former coach van Gaal leaving the club, Mourinho arriving as his replacement, and the transfer of Ibrahimović, which was rumored at the point in time of the post. The first two icons on the right seem to be made up of the logo of Nike, but they are used as check marks that identify the illustrated personnel changes as completed. The labels below the two marks specify the respective changes. The third icon, next to Ibrahimović, instead uses an icon that typically signifies within the domain of computers that a program is loading, which is indeed

244 Thomas Messerli and Di Yu

Figure 11.10 Juxtaposed pictures and captions. Perksoffootball, 1 June 2016. Instagram.

confirmed by the label below it. In this case the incongruity is created between the frame of soccer and that of computer programs: Establishing the surprising connection ultimately amounts to a humorous way of representing the wait for the confirmation of the new signing.

Strategy 9: establishing and breaking a pattern

The final strategy that occurred in our data is reminiscent of a prototypical way in which jokes are structured. As Sacks (1974) already established, the pattern of three units—two similar ones and a different one—is one classic way in which jokes construct incongruities (see also Norrick, 1993). Similarly, types of posts on Twitter and Instagram create a sequence of pictures and captions, with two or more establishing a pattern, and the final one running against the expectations that this pattern evokes. In Figure 11.11, the first two pictures and captions establish that the two Champions League finalists, Real (left) and Atlético (right) are ready for the game, and the final, larger picture of the squad of Barcelona establishes in a colloquial register that they, too, are ready for the game. Since all three pictures show soccer teams and captions that state the teams are ready, it may seem at first glance that there is no unexpected element here and thus no incongruity. However, the different,

Figure 11.11 Breaking the pattern. Perksoffootball, 31 May 2016. Instagram.

more colloquial phrasing is a first hint at a clear contrast between Barcelona and the two other teams: As Barcelona was already eliminated from the Champions League competition at that point, they quite simply had nothing to be ready for. Accordingly, the post serves to create humor at the expense of Barcelona and their fans.

Summary of Analysis 1: humor construction in original posts

The qualitative analysis of 80 posts from Twitter and Instagram accounts that focus on soccer-related humor revealed a range of different strategies that are used by OPs to construct humorous incongruities relevant to soccer-fans in their posts. While some of these strategies rely mostly on the finding of imagery that is humorous a priori, in which case the work of the OP mainly consists in finding and distributing the humorous material, in many cases humor only emerges due to the work done by the OP. On the one hand, this may include recontextualization in the sense that humorous materials from different domains are adapted to the soccer frame with the help of captions, or by establishing a connection between different frames by juxtaposing seemingly unrelated imagery. On the other hand, non-humorous soccer-related images may be combined in creative ways to create humorous effects. The analysis furthermore showed that these posts are truly multimodal texts that depend both on linguistic and on visual modes, and allow humor construction in either of them or indeed between them, that is, humor that emerges only when text and image are successfully combined in order to create incongruities.

Analysis 2: User responses to humorous soccer-related posts

For the second part of the analysis, we examined a sample of responses to the Instagram and Twitter posts we have just illustrated in examples. Based on the number of comments, we limited this second analysis to the comments made to just one of the humorous soccer accounts on Twitter and Instagram each. As a result, the following findings are based on 643 comments to the Twitter account *FootyHumour* and 1292 comments to *perksoffootball* on Instagram. Whereas the original posts in the first analysis could be treated as similar across the two platforms, there are some clear differences between the two platforms' presentations of comments that need to be addressed here. In the case of Instagram, comments appear listed under or to the side of the original post and are thus presented as part of that post. On Twitter, however, comments appear in the form of new tweets, which is to say that they—while being linked to the original post—exist independently and require Twitter users to move from comment to comment, in order to read them.[5] While the first four sections of our summary and exemplification of comment patterns will discuss comments that occur on both platforms, the fifth and sixth will discuss phenomena that are exclusive to Twitter comments.

Comments that do not directly relate to humor

When it comes to the comments that are not directly related to the humorous incongruities in the original post, we find that followers first of all react to the OP and other users. In those cases where the OP asks a question in the initial post, this is taken up as a first pair part by many of the commenters, and—as is to be expected—they accordingly comply with a direct answer to the question as a second pair part in their responses.

In those posts where contrasting images are juxtaposed, we find comments that offer an opinion as to which of the two images, perceived as two choices offered by the OP, the commenter prefers. More generally, since most posts contain references to specific soccer players or teams, many comments offer evaluations of these figures and clubs of the sport. These evaluations in turn provide grounds for reactions by followers to other followers, which range from simple agreement or disagreement with the offered opinions to more ad hominem comments that either praise or insult other followers.

As has become clear in the presentation of examples in "Analysis 1," most of the original posts require a significant amount of previous knowledge about soccer in general and recent important events in the soccer world more specifically. Accordingly, commenters do not always understand all references, which results in clarification questions in the comments. Similarly, some of the assertions made by OPs and followers alike lead to disagreements about their factual accuracy, which results in followers correcting one another in the comments.

There are also comments that can be described as purely interactional. These include early commenters simply claiming one of the first few spots in the sequential order of comments, which is done for instance by simply posting "first" or "1" as a first comment. Finally, there are many responses that tag other users, which is done by including an @ symbol followed by the respective user name. These comments serve to make the tagged users aware of the post and potentially trigger further responses by them.

Humor appreciation

When it comes to specifically humor-related comments, a first type of comment signals humor appreciation in some fashion. Often, this occurs in the form of typographic emoticons or image-based emojis, since Twitter and Instagram (as well as most major social networks) offer a wide range of such more elaborate emojis to their users. Based on our analysis, the crying-laughing emoji (Figure 11.12) seems to be particularly popular. Appreciation of humor can also be encoded in language. This is done by transcribing laughter as any variation of "hahaha," by using an acronym such as LOL (laughing out loud), or by explicating humor appreciation, e.g., by asserting "that's funny." Typically, appreciation seems to be only encoded on one of the presented levels, i.e., either by using emoticons/emojis or by any of the linguistic strategies, but not by a combination of both.

Humor construction in comments

Rather than simply reacting appreciatively to humor, comments are also used to construct humorous incongruities. These incongruities may simply be call backs, i.e., repetitions of the humor created by the OP, but they also construct new incongruities, which typically relate to the same teams and/or players to which the OP made reference. In either case, the

Figure 11.12 Crying-laughing emoji. *U+1F602: Face of tears of joy*. Unicode.

constructed humor often makes the presented players and teams the butt of the joke. In reaction to the post presented in Figure 11.10, for instance, one follower offers the following comment:

1 Ibrahimovic don't play on thursdays

First, this comment explicitly mentions Ibrahimović, who is presented in the original post, but the comment cleverly creates humor that targets not only him, but also the club he is at that point rumored to join, Manchester United. On the one hand, refusing to play on a certain day of the week ties in with the arrogance often associated with this player; on the other hand, Thursday is picked by the commenter because that is the day when Europa League games take place. Thus, the commenter also creates a humorous jab at Manchester United, who have not been successful enough to qualify for the superior Champions League, which would mean playing on Tuesdays or Wednesdays.

Finally, there are also some rare cases of simple language-based humor, for instance when a commenter makes fun of the name of Leicester City player Danny Drinkwater:

2 No drinkwater yes drinkchampagne

Humor comment or question

An interesting avenue of humor research is the study of failed and incomprehensible humor. With regard to incomprehensible humor, Bell (2013, p. 187) finds that for the most part, respondents "admit their lack of understanding openly." In the case of Twitter and Instagram comments, however, we would expect there to be much less pressure on followers to acknowledge their lack of comprehension, and we speculate that the default answer to failed and to incomprehensible humor will simply be the absence of a comment. Having said that, there are some responses in our data that explicitly confirm lack of comprehension:

3 Don't get it
4 What does it mean?

While there are only few occurrences of such admissions in our data, response to incomprehensible humor on social media would be an interesting topic for future research.

Stranded conversations

Specifically on Twitter, one common type of response found in comments is stranded conversations in which commenters break into smaller conversations on their own, quite similar to the notion of schisming in face-to-face multi-party interactions (Egbert, 1997; Sacks et al., 1974). The comments in Figure 11.13 are in reaction to an original post that reads, "I said Bale not Bailly you useless idiot..." featuring the photos of José Mourinho and one of Manchester United's scouts on the phone. The first user responds with a laugh token "haha" and commenting that "either way, @ericbailly24 wouldn't be a bad signing," while tagging the OP as well as another user and one of the soccer players discussed. The two users then commence a three-turn conversation on their own regarding the details of the signing.

Although the two users break into a smaller, dyadic conversation, note that the tagged parties are notified of being tagged and have the choice of participating in this particular conversation. Similarly, other recipients of the original post can also view this stranded conversation and have the option of liking and retweeting particular turns, or even joining in. The specific strategies of schisming on social media platforms with such technological affordances, such as Twitter and Facebook, are also an interesting phenomenon that warrants further research.

Multimodal comments

Another unique phenomenon found on Twitter is the use of multimodal comments such as pictures and memes. Figure 11.14 below is an example

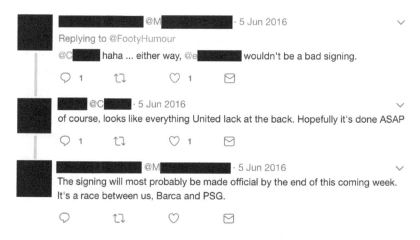

Figure 11.13 Stranded conversation in comments. MoketeMoloantoa and Cobbz6, 5 June 2016. Twitter.

250 Thomas Messerli and Di Yu

Figure 11.14 Multimodal comment. Danielellgam, 5 June 2016. Twitter.

of a multimodal comment responding to an original post that says, "Ronaldinho could nutmeg a mermaid #SoccerAid2016." Responding to the OP, the recipient comments "not that difficult" with two frowning face emojis, accompanied by a picture showing a mermaid with a red line crossing through her tail. This seems to indicate that nutmegging a mermaid is not as challenging as the OP suggests. This comment is potentially critiquing the content of the original post and the use of the picture serves to illustrate the commenter's point.

Another example is the comment in Figure 11.15, which features a single meme with no verbal comment except tagging the OP. The original tweet, illustrated earlier in Figure 11.8, states that "Juventus got all these players for free. Man City paid £49m for Raheem Sterling," while posting the photos of nine soccer players. The comment itself is a meme featuring Spiderman sick in bed with the caption "THIS POST GAVE ME CANCER, EBOLA AND AIDS," which receives 12 likes. The meme serves

Soccer-related humor on Twitter and Instagram 251

Figure 11.15 Multimodal comment (Twitter: Footyhumour). Sambob180, 5 June 2016. Twitter.

to illustrate the strong impact of the original post (i.e., "it kills me"), be it of its humorous effect, or its poignancy, or perhaps the lack of humor.

Although not many instances of multimodal comments are present in our data, they enable the audience to comment in ways more complex than a brief verbal comment, which allows more equal participation and encourages creative use of the comment space.

Summary of Analysis 2: user responses

The second part of the analysis, which addressed user reactions to humorous posts, illustrates first of all that there are a range of response patterns that are not directly linked to humor. Besides offering evaluative comments related to specific players or teams, more importantly for the central questions of this chapter, commenters were shown to signal humor appreciation in different ways and even to construct new humorous incongruities in their comments. In cases where they inferred the intention by the OP to be humorous but did not understand the post's humor, commenters also explicated their lack of comprehension and asked the OP for clarification. We have also observed that there are humor response patterns that are exclusive to Twitter. Twitter commenters have the option to post multimodal comments, which means that they have the option to construct further instances of multimodal incongruities. Finally, the difference in presentation, with responses to tweets being more independent from the OP than those on Instagram, also leads to stranded conversations on Twitter. More generally, we find that Twitter facilitates more discussion and interaction among recipients and enables them to make creative contributions to humor as a type of support strategy.

Conclusion

We analyzed 80 posts on two Twitter and two Instagram accounts dedicated to soccer-related humor as well as just fewer than 2000 comments, in order to establish how posters used the multimodal affordances of the two social networks to construct humorous incongruities, and how commenters reacted to these posts. The analysis of original posts showed that even within this relatively small sample, a range of strategies are employed by posters, which make full use of the multimodal affordances provided by the medium. In particular, posters based the humorous incongruities in their posts on pre-existing humor they found in pictures and videos, but they also creatively constructed humor by juxtaposing visual and textual materials from the domain of soccer as well as from other domains. Often, humor is thus not or not only a product of funny pictures and funny texts, but also the result of a relationship between different stimuli that is only established due to the work done by the broadcasting party.

When it comes to the responses to posts, our data shows that commenters actively engage with OPs by signaling humor appreciation and recognition in different ways, but also by communicating explicitly that they did not understand a particular humorous instance. Furthermore, commenters also interact with each other—sometimes in direct relation to the topical humor of the OP and at other times more independently. On Twitter in particular, responses which appear in the form of new tweets that are linked to the original tweet can lead to separate dyadic conversations, which also indicates that Twitter as a social platform encourages more active participation in humor construction by followers than is the case on Instagram. However, both networks enable not only posters, but also their followership to play an active role in humor construction. Even an action as simple as tagging another user contributes to active participation and multiple authorship of soccer-related CMC humor, since it invites other users to join the interaction and contribute to the humorous event, be it by simply liking or retweeting the original post, by showing their appreciation, criticism or incomprehension, or even by contributing more humor in support of the OP. Thus, the participation role of followers is not limited to that of passive recipients: They are involved as agents who create humorous content by and for themselves, which means that the conversations that ensue can be described as polylogues (Marcoccia, 2004), in which followers encourage other users to co-construct further humorous instances. The resulting humorous polylogues underline that humor in this domain, although managed by broadcasters, is a collaborative effort that involves broadcasters, followers, and other users.

Appendix

Note: some URLs might be inaccessible due to accounts that have since been deleted.

Notes

1 While the number of participants is of course finite at any given moment in time and restricted to those that have the technological means to access the particular form of online communication in question, the claim of a potentially infinite audience includes the fact that interactions on social media are on record, i.e., that it is not foreseeable when or if they cease to be accessible to new audiences.
2 In this section, which focuses on original posts, the figures present the respective post as it appeared on our screen, with comments whited out.
3 Identifying a man kissing another man as incongruous of course in no way reflects the value systems of the authors of this chapter. However, responses to this post such as "Ha gayyy ..." and "The one that is not gay ..." reveal that some of the followers do indeed evaluate the pictures as incongruous because of their representation of male soccer players kissing male colleagues or fans.
4 We would like to thank the editors for pointing out the alternative readings of this collage. They not only show additional potential for this particular post, but also highlight yet again that humor is ultimately constructed by individual recipients. While most of the posts we examine here are fairly unambiguous at least when it comes to the main incongruity that is being constructed, others allow a range of different interpretations for recipients and only encode some cues that allow researchers to infer the OP's intent.
5 There is of course a range of devices and, in the case of Twitter also a range of software, through which posts and comments can be read. The individual choice of soft- and hardware will influence the reading experience and may in some cases relativize the distinctions we made here. However, the differences hold true at least when users access posts through the official Twitter and Instagram apps on their smartphone or computer.

References

Attardo, S. 1994. Linguistic theories of humor. Berlin: Mouton de Gruyter.
Attardo, S., Pickering, L. and Baker, A. 2011. Prosodic and multimodal markers of humor in conversation. Pragmatics & Cognition. 19(2), pp. 224–247.
Baym, N.K. 1995. The performance of humor in computer-mediated communication. Journal of Computer-Mediated Communication. [Online]. 1(2), [no pagination]. [Accessed October 12, 2017]. Available from: https://pdfs.semantic scholar.org/e277/1956aadd617afc48a548c2da50b438c03313.pdf.

Bell, N.D. 2009. Responses to failed humor. Journal of Pragmatics. **41**(9), pp. 1825–1836.

Bell, N.D. 2013. Responses to incomprehensible humor. Journal of Pragmatics. **57**, pp. 176–189.

Bolander, B. and Locher, M.A. 2014. Doing sociolinguistic research on computer-mediated data: A review of four methodological issues. Discourse, Context and Media. **3**(1), pp. 14–26.

Butterworth, M.L. 2014. Social media, sport, and democratic discourse. In: Billing, A.C., Hardin, M. and Brown, N.A. eds. Routledge handbook of sport and new media. New York: Routledge, pp. 32–42.

Chovanec, J. and Dynel, M. 2015. Researching interactional forms and participant structures in public and social media. In: Dynel, M. and Chovanec, J. eds. Participation in public and social media interactions. Amsterdam: John Benjamins, pp. 1–23.

Cleland, J. 2014. Racism, football fans, and online message boards: How social media has added a new dimension to racist discourse in English football. Journal of Sport and Social Issues. **38**(5), pp. 415–431.

Coates, J. 2007. Talk in a play frame: More on laughter and intimacy. Journal of Pragmatics. **39**(1), pp. 29–49.

Draucker, F. 2015. Participation structures in Twitter interaction. In: Dynel, M. and Chovanec, J. eds. Participation in public and social media interactions. Amsterdam: John Benjamins, pp. 49–66.

Egbert, M.M. 1997. Schisming: The collaborative transformation from a single conversation to multiple conversations. Research on Language and Social Interaction. **30**(1), pp. 1–51.

Fillmore, C.J. and Baker, C. 2009. A frames approach to semantic analysis. In: Heine, B. and Narrog, H. eds. The Oxford handbook of linguistic analysis. Oxford: Oxford University Press, pp. 313–340.

Glenn, P. 2003. Laughter in interaction. Cambridge, UK: Cambridge University Press.

Hay, J. 2001. The pragmatics of humor support. Humor. **14**(1), pp. 55–82.

Jefferson, G. 1979. A technique for inviting laughter and its subsequent acceptance/declination. In: Psathas, G. ed. Everyday language: Studies in ethnomethodology. New York: Irvington, pp. 79–96.

Lee, F.L. 2005. Spectacle and fandom: Media discourse in two soccer events in Hong Kong. Sociology of Sport Journal. **22**(2), pp. 194–213.

Marcoccia, M. 2004. On-line polylogues: Conversation structure and participation framework in internet newsgroups. Journal of Pragmatics. **36**(1), pp. 115–145.

Milner, R.M. 2013. Pop polyvocality: Internet memes, public participation, and the Occupy Wall Street movement. International Journal of Communication. **7**, pp. 2357–2390.

Norrick, N.R. 1993. Repetition in canned jokes and spontaneous conversational joking. Humor. **6**(4), pp. 385–402.

Norrick, N.R. 2003. Issues in conversational joking. Journal of Pragmatics, **35**(9), pp. 1333–1359.

Sacks, H. 1974. An analysis of the course of a joke's telling in conversation. In: Bauman, R. and Sherzer, J. eds. Explorations in the ethnography of speaking. Cambridge, UK: Cambridge University Press, pp. 337–353.

Sacks, H., Schegloff, E.A. and Jefferson, G. 1974. A simplest systematics for the organization of turn-taking for conversation. Language. 50(4), pp. 696–735.

Suls, J.M. 1972. A two-stage model for the appreciation of jokes and cartoons: An information-processing analysis. In: Goldstein, J.H. and McGhee, P.E. eds. The psychology of humor: Theoretical perspectives and empirical issues. New York: Academic Press, pp. 81–100.

Tannen, D. 2007. Talking voices: Repetition, dialogue, and imagery in conversational discourse. 2nd ed. Cambridge, UK: Cambridge University Press.

Chapter 12

Multilingualism in football teams

Eva Lavric and Jasmin Steiner

Introduction and research overview[1]

International football teams can be seen as complex linguistic ecosystems in which players and coaches with different mother tongues and cultural backgrounds interact with each other. In particular, mixed international teams with large numbers of foreign players might seem likely to encounter problems caused by language and communication barriers. Despite such linguistic (and cultural) barriers, effective communication within the team is vital for efficient and goal-oriented interaction and cooperation at all times. The Innsbruck Football Research Group[2] at the University of Innsbruck's Faculty of Humanities, has been working on elucidating the issue of multilingualism in football since 2006,[3] starting with the edited volume *The Linguistics of Football* (Lavric et al., 2008) and continuing with a series of other publications,[4] including the *Football and Language Bibliography Online,*[5] and most recently, the organization of the international workshop "Multilingual and multifaceted football," which took place in Innsbruck on June 10, 2016. In this chapter, we want to show the complexity and the beauty of the use of different languages in the realm of football.

To illustrate the relevance of multilingualism in football, let us give three examples where foreign language skills or the lack thereof worked as an asset or as a drawback: Our first example is the German coach Otto Rehhagel, who won the 2004 European Championship with the Greek national team. Since Rehhagel did not speak a word of Greek, this success is at least partly credited to his brilliant interpreter Ioannis Topalidis (see Ehrmann, 2012). Second example: When Pep Guardiola took over Bayern Munich, he spent half a year learning German intensively in order to be able to give his first press conference in the very language of the club (see Bundesliga, 2013). The third example occurred in the semi-finals of the 2002 Champions League, when Bayer 04 Leverkusen was playing against Manchester United. Manchester United was attacking the Leverkusen goal, and goalkeeper Jörg Butt shouted in German at Diego Placente, a newly arrived defender from Argentina, that he should stay on the line. Placente had already received some language training and understood what he was asked to do. He thus stayed on the line and was able to intercept the arriving ball. This scene was decisive for Bayer 04 Leverkusen winning the game and moving on to the Champions League final. "This prevented goal was worth the equivalent of 50 years of language training," Frank Ditgens later commented (interview Ditgens 2016). These are three examples that show how language matters in football—and how research about multilingualism in football teams can provide us with essential insights into how communication on and off the pitch actually works.

From the perspective of a 'linguistics of professional multilingualism', football is first and foremost a multilingual workplace like many others: Just as for political scientists, foreign players are first and foremost a special case of migrant workers (see Liegl and Spitaler, 2008). But football teams are a special kind of multilingual workplace, because their primary interest does certainly not lie in language or verbal interaction. To quote the title of the only relevant study preceding the work of the Innsbruck Football Research Group: "Feet speak louder than the tongue" (Kellermann et al., 2006). A football player will be recruited on account of their motor skills, their tactical abilities, and their cooperative competence, but hardly ever on account of their language competences. And yet, if they play in foreign clubs, they will have to communicate verbally, over time, in different linguistic environments. This also applies to the coach, as well as to international referees.

The fundamental problem in the football-and-languages context might simply be time spans: football with its frequent transfers is much more fast-moving than what would be required for a normal language learning process, and—in contrast to what happens e.g., in business—this problem is not compensated for by a language-focused recruiting policy.

This opens up a vast field for research about multilingualism in football teams, which can shed new light on the well-known 'beautiful game'. We will offer evidence to show that feet *do not* always speak louder than the tongue.

Eleven theses on multilingualism in football

In this section, we will summarize the outcome of our research in a collection of *11* theses. The results that will be presented stem from two Innsbruck project seminars about "Multilingualism in football" (2009 and 2016), where students of Romance linguistics carried out empirical research under supervision of Eva Lavric. The majority of investigations was conducted by means of qualitative interviews, often complemented by field notes and video recordings.[6] These results offer a broad-base study of a research area that has not been in focus before, and that illustrates a type of multilingualism (professional, often "survival" level) which is yet to be investigated.[7]

Without language, nothing works. But with a little bit of language, many things are possible

Fairly often players report serious misunderstandings that occurred during their first time in a new country,[8] and emphasize the problem of arriving and not understanding anything at all.[9] In the case of Austria, this is due to the fact that incoming foreign players often have no competence in German, and often enough a very poor competence in English. In their new team, there might be nobody who speaks their mother tongue or at least a similar language, and in this case, communication problems are inevitable. However, as soon as the player has assimilated the most basic terms like *right, left, forward, backward,* etc., they are able to function on the pitch during the match. In training sessions, they can imitate what the others are doing.[10] If they are not able to follow during tactical meetings, they will know anyway what is expected in their playing position. Moreover, tactical moves are often explained through graphical means (flipchart, blackboard, power point). Also, acceptance within the team usually depends more on the player's performance during the game than on their language skills.[11]

Another problem that is almost as important for the newcomer as the new language is the new culture. Many players report that they experienced a substantial culture shock during their first weeks at a new club. This ranges from adapting to the food, to eating and working hours, to punctuality, to dealing with authorities, and to the climate: A particularly striking example is reported by Austrian coach Heinz Peischl (interview Peischl 2016), who told us about the experience of a player who had newly arrived from Africa. According to Peischl, during a November training session it started snowing, which was such a startling and overwhelming experience for the player in question—who had never seen snow before in his life—that he immediately stopped playing.

The important thing is to convey the message—no matter how

This means that in principle, everything is allowed: You may combine English chunks with pieces of the local language, and complete the whole thing with facial expressions or gestures,[12] or with drawings—everything works, provided communication takes place, i.e., one understands and is understood. There is a kind of beauty in this, a beauty that does not spring from the perfection of language skills, but from getting along as well as possible with the linguistic and communicative resources at hand. Translated into linguistic terminology, this means: In football, one may find lingua franca[13] communication in English. But relying on English as the allegedly universal lingua franca might be less successful in football than in other areas. Incidentally, our interviews and field notes showed that the real lingua franca—i.e., in Myers-Scotton's (1983) terms the "unmarked language choice"—in a multilingual football team is first and foremost the language of the club's home country, e.g., Italian at US Triestina,[14] or German at FC Grödig. Rather surprisingly, Steiner (2014) found that at the Tyrolean club FC Wacker Innsbruck it was not German, but its Tyrolean dialectal variety that functioned as lingua franca—causing considerable problems to newly arrived foreigners.

Players also often report on the mixing of languages ('code switching'), or the mixing of verbal and nonverbal codes (gestures, drawings). For example, Czech player Tomáš Jun spent some time playing for Turkish clubs before coming to Austria, and he characterizes his verbal behavior as follows: Starting a sentence in German, adding a few English words, going on in Czech, and closing everything up in Turkish.[15] This is a clear example of language mixing due to lack of competence (a linguistic 'gap'), because there is no other way to communicate; but even in situations where this is not the case, some players report that they mix languages just out of fun ('ludic function'), switching to another language for small interjections like "schade" [what a pity] or "Scheiße" [shit/fuck] (see interview Voříšek)—which is also confirmed by Steiner (2014, pp. 321–322), who reports about a Spanish player at FC Wacker Innsbruck who resorts to his mother tongue for small particles like *sí* and *no* and when cursing.

We have also collected reports about coaches (by players as well as by coaches themselves) that adapt to their foreign players by switching to their respective mother tongues from time to time, and others that resort to language mixes because they lack the required competence in the local language. As an example, Bolivian player Karl Dusvald parodies his former Swiss coach: "Karl, du musst sofort jugar a la pelota!" or "Auf keinen Fall andar a pasos cortos!" Sentences that start in German end in Spanish—which, in any case, confirms the linguistic adaptability of the coach.

A rather unusual form of code switching is regularly practiced by the Spanish club Athletic Bilbao (where all players are Basque), whose then coach Joaquín Caparrós reports:

> On the pitch, we use the Basque language especially when attacking, in order to surprise our adversaries. Not with encrypted words or secret signs, but with simple commentaries: whether the free kick will go towards the far post, or whether the corner will be short ... Or simply to signal to a team mate that he is free, not under pressure.
>
> (Larrea, 2009)[16]

This means that the players speak Basque to manifest their complicity through insider comments in order to destabilize the opponent (this is what is called the 'cryptic function' of language choices). It is also reported that in Austria, clubs from the Vorarlberg region, where a rather unusual Alemannic dialect is spoken, use this code in a similar way.

Better language skills are important for well-being and integration, and many players make it a personal goal

It seems to be true that a football player can operate on the pitch very well with much reduced skills in the language of their club. But this does not mean that all players are unwilling to learn languages and confine themselves to that strict minimum. In fact, many are highly motivated to learn the new language as well as they can. Therefore, they often engage in self-study, develop a remarkable degree of ambition and strive for accuracy, and are neither afraid of talking freely without thinking twice nor to start anew in each new country. Consequently, many of them acquire a remarkable repertoire of foreign language skills in the course of their professional life (see Soccer Training Info, 2016).

A good example of such a language enthusiast is former Brazilian international Zé Elias, who played mid-field at SCR Altach during the 2008–2009 season just before he retired and who, in the course of his football life, has learned Italian, Spanish, Greek, and German. He had the following to say about language learning:

> I have to do everything in order to learn German. I cannot change the country. So, the quicker I understand the language, the better it is. It is really important. That's something I like. In my view, it is very important to make all possible efforts in order to learn the language quickly. ... For me it is easy to acquire new language skills, because I learned in Germany that one has to listen very carefully. As soon as you are able to listen carefully, you can also start talking. I possess one very important quality: I'm not afraid to speak. For me, learning to speak is very important, because that way people are able to correct me and to help me.
>
> (Interview Zé Elias)

Language learning also has to happen alongside culture learning, getting to know and fitting into the new culture. A positive example in this respect is Guido Buchwald, former German international and former coach of Alemannia Aachen, who spent seven years in Japan with his family (at Urawa Reds) and who succeeded very well in integrating himself (see Okuma, 2007). Other remarkable examples are the Slovak Martin Petráš who played for US Triestina from 2007 to 2009 before moving on to play for other Italian teams and who raises his son to be bilingual, and Samir Occhial, a young Nepalese talent in AC Milan's youth team, who took cultural integration to such a level that he switched from Hinduism to Christianity (interview Krassimirov).

Good language skills are indeed decisive for a person's well-being and long-term satisfaction as the following quote by coach Heinz Peischl (former assistant coach of the Austrian national team) shows:

> Alas, I have to say that most clubs do not care about the integration of their foreign players. They see the player as a commodity which has to function from the beginning, and are not aware of the fact that performance is related to well-being. ... It is logical that a person coming into a new country from abroad needs help and support. They need someone to help them with the administrative procedures and to find a suitable social environment where they are fully accepted. ... Foreign players certainly need a few months in order to feel comfortable in the new country, and the more support they get, the quicker they can settle in and can deliver their sportive performance. This is something clubs still have to learn.
>
> (Interview Peischl)

A more in-depth knowledge of language and culture that goes beyond what is necessary on the pitch thus plays an important role in the integration into the new environment, especially when it comes to organizing private or family matters.

Good clubs will provide newly arrived players with interpreters or, more often, with personal assistants helping them in the beginning

Such a level of individual support financed by the club is unfortunately too expensive for lower league teams, but the higher league clubs can afford hiring an interpreter, or, actually, a personal assistant, for each player or group of players with a new foreign language. Bayern Munich, for instance, did so at the arrival of Luca Toni, as did Bayer 04 Leverkusen at the arrival of Renato Augusto from Brazil and of Theofanis Gekas from Greece, as did Wacker Innsbruck when they hired their first Brazilian player Fabiano. This special category of staff members does not necessarily have to consist of professional interpreters; their function is to take care of the newcomer in a variety of ways: linguistically, e.g., during meetings with the coach and the management, but also administratively and personally, such as helping to find a flat, buy a car, or choose a school for the children.[17]

The club with the highest degree of linguistic awareness in the German language area seems to be Bayer 04 Leverkusen, which has been systematically implementing this concept of individual assistance for a couple of years (combined, though, with language classes, see the section "Language courses are not very popular, but some clubs promote them very much," below):

> [This club] has hired ... graduates of Cologne sports university, who developed a 'support system' as yet unrivalled. From the small worries of everyday life (furniture, car, household appliances) to the compulsory language course, everything has been thought of. ... Top priority is [given to] the non-stop availability of the assistants.
>
> (Wulzinger, 2002)

In many clubs, it is not a specially hired interpreter or a personal assistant but a club manager or a former player who takes over the function of facilitating the newcomers' integration into the new club and the new environment. One example is the Swiss Jörg Stiel, former goalkeeper and physical therapist at Borussia Mönchengladbach, who is fluent in French, Italian, and Spanish and could thus act as a linguistic and general assistant to Venezuelan player Juan Arango as well as Argentinian striker Raúl Bobadilla. Another example is Marco Cernaz, former long-term manager at US Triestina, who, apart from his mother tongue Italian, also speaks Spanish, Romanian, English, and German and thus became a translator, a confidant, and a cultural bridge builder for Austrian player Marko Stanković and for many others.

This kind of solution, however, even though it looks very practical, seems to have one disadvantage in particular, that is, it might lead to linguistic laziness. This becomes evident in the example of Zé Elias, who used to be completely dependent on his personal assistant—until the latter went away and the player realized how lost he was in the foreign environment. It was only then that he decided he had to learn the host country's language:

> In Germany, what happened was that I had been there for three months already and did not speak English. My friend and translator went back to Brazil. ... I spent one month more there, and in that time I had to order in the restaurant using the menu and felt like a child of four or five, as I had to point to the dishes and say, I want this, I want that. At that moment I realized that I had to learn the language as quickly as possible.
>
> (Interview Zé Elias)

Apart from the club manager or the personal assistant or interpreter, there is yet another solution which many clubs tend to apply—it is in some ways ideal but not always possible.

Multilingualism in football teams 263

The most frequent method of integration is translation by a team mate who speaks the same mother tongue

It is evident that the trick with the team mate as interpreter can only function if there really *is* a player that has the required language skills, i.e., the same mother tongue and mastery of the local language due to a longer stay in the club's country.

In translation studies, this is known as 'community interpreting', i.e., interpreting by non-professionals, often in immigration or social work settings, where the interpreter does not only translate but also takes the newcomer under their wings in some way.[18] The team mate with the same mother tongue acts as a facilitator not only in linguistic but also in cultural terms. This is an ideal solution for the club, as it is cost-effective and the fellow player-interpreter will be engaging with the player off and on the field. Furthermore, they are well acquainted with everything, know the context, and will certainly give the correct translation (even if they do not master the local language perfectly). However, Masaki Morass, an international coach who worked in Austria and in Japan, pointed out that one should not forget about the competition between different players in today's football teams (interview Morass 2016). This might result in the translating team mate not being always content with the position of the interpreter, particularly if the newcomer plays in the same position.

Even if, from time to time, clubs venture a bold step by employing their very first Korean, French, Czech, or Latin American player, the presence of another player with a certain mother tongue is an argument that is definitely taken into account when it comes to planning new acquisitions at a club. This kind of language policy certainly has a positive effect on the well-being of the two or three compatriots playing in the team (although it may not be ideal for their motivation to learn the local language). In this context, we want to emphasize the role of long-serving language enthusiasts among the foreign players, who can rely on a large number of years in the same language area and are thus well-integrated. They act as contact persons for new generations of fellow countrymen. This was the case e.g., at Borussia Dortmund with the Brazilian veteran Leonardo di Deus Santos (called "Dedê"), who supplied his newly arrived compatriots not only with linguistic help, but even offered accommodation in his house, which was jokingly referred to as "die WG" [the shared flat]. Another good example to illustrate this kind of community interpreting in football is the Andorran defender Ildefons Lima Solà, formerly at US Triestina. He has a special talent for languages and speaks Spanish, Italian, Greek, and English—and for years, he used to be the integration aide for all new players at Triestina, whether they came from Uruguay, Ireland or elsewhere.

It is not even necessary that the aide and the newcomer share exactly the same language, as thanks to intercomprehension related languages

(Spanish/Portuguese, or Spanish/Italian, or different Slavic languages, especially the languages of the former Yugoslavia[19]) may also be useful for this type of team-internal community interpreting.

Language courses are not very popular, but some clubs promote them very much

We heard many similar reports about players being sent to language classes by their clubs or of a club organizing such a class for its foreign players.[20] These classes, however, seemed to have received very little acceptance among the players and consequently these players lacked the motivation to learn the local language. The main reason players give for this lack of motivation is tiredness; after a demanding training session, there is not much energy and time left to devote to language learning. This lack of motivation for language learning might be due to the fact that very basic skills are sufficient in order to function pretty well on the pitch. Players also struggle with the general character of many language courses, which usually fail to adapt to the professional needs of footballers.[21]

There is one program in the German speaking area that tries to remedy this deficiency, called "Deutsch für Ballkünstler" [German for ball artists] developed by Uwe Wiemann. It is a milestone in didactics for foreign players,[22] as it is the first language course book—in any language—ever developed specifically for football players.[23] Wiemann collaborated with the German Bundesliga club Bayer 04 Leverkusen, which is known to be one of the most language-sensitive clubs and one of the very few that have actually developed a consistent language policy. This means that all foreign players are obliged to learn the local language, and that they are offered optimal conditions for doing so.

Language learning is specifically advocated in many clubs' youth academies, e.g., at Manchester United, where all players—which come from very different backgrounds—have to learn English. The same goes for AC Milan's youth academy, where not only Italian, but also English and French are taught regularly. The prime example of a club with a successful youth development system, not only with respect to languages, is FC Barcelona (interview Díaz 2016). The club is very proud of recruiting a considerable part of its players from its own youth academy. This does not mean that the team has mainly regional roots, as the youth academy itself is already very international (31% Catalans, 31% Spanish, 38% international). The common language in the youth academy as well as in the club is Spanish—which means that FC Barcelona has a language policy that does not insist on their regional identity, but prefers the language of the country to the language of the region—most likely in view of their international players. Each player in the youth academy gets their own individually tailored language courses; and even the coaches and the rest of the staff are offered the possibility to develop their language skills. This policy guarantees the best and quickest possible integration of the young talents.

A club that fosters the language competences of its players ultimately acts in its own best interest. There is, in fact, an undeniable relationship between language skills, integration, and well-being, and from this insight it is only a small step to the quality of the player's performance during the game. As an example, there is AC Milan's former Brazilian goalkeeper Dida (Nélson de Jesus Silva), whom the club had to force to finally learn Italian:

> When Dida came to the club, he spoke no Italian at all and he had communication problems with his fellow players. He did not feel good and his performance was bad. As soon as he learned the language, his performance became much better and he ended up producing very good results.
>
> (Interview Manzoni 2009)

Frank Ditgens, who, for many years, has been holding the position of a 'coordinator for foreign players' at Bayer 04 Leverkusen,[24] boldly addresses this link between language skills and playing performance, underlining the clear advantages for the club:

> If a player speaks [German], he will be a better player. This increases his value. It worked for Jorginho, Emerson, Paulo Sergio, Zé Roberto and lately Lucio. When Bayer 04 Leverkusen transferred these players, either abroad or to Bayern Munich, we made money.
>
> (Repplinger, 2005)

Language, however, is only one part of a package that also includes culture and local playing style, as Massimo Cosentino, Secretary General of UC Sampdoria affirms during the interview. Being asked whether a foreign player can be sold at a higher price to another Italian club after learning the Italian language in Genoa, he answered:

> Yes. This happens, however, not really because he has learned Italian, but because he has already played one season in Italy and therefore he knows not only the language and the Italian way of playing, but also the culture, habits, and traditions.
>
> (Interview Cosentino 2014)

This shows the important things a player learns during their first time in a new team and country. It seems that a club's functioning language and integration policy, together with the individual players' efforts to integrate and adapt themselves, pay off in the end.

The amount of language a player needs will depend on his playing position on the pitch

This is a new, but not unexpected finding of our study: Players need different amounts of verbal interaction to communicate efficiently on the pitch depending on their playing position. The offensive players, who account for a majority in our test group, seem to be the ones needing the least linguistic resources. Among those who communicate most are the goalkeepers, who have to make themselves understood in particular in standard situations, e.g., when they arrange the wall.[25] Midfield players also have high communicative needs, as it is them who have to link offense with defense and vice versa. Regarding the defenders, research in the 2016 project seminar showed that they have a similar amount of verbal communication as midfielders, apparently because they have a good overview of the whole game from the back. In general, we suggest that the relationship between playing position and verbal interaction needs further empirical research.

In any case, one thing seems to be clear: The captain in particular fulfils an important communicative task, especially in tricky situations such as conflicts with the referee—which means that in international teams the captain should at least speak English. This is confirmed by Jocelyn Blanchard, the former French captain of Austria Wien, who compares captaincy with managing a family and underlines the necessity for him to speak English as well as the team's local language. In a similar vein, Petr Voříšek, former Czech midfielder at SCR Altach, emphasizes the need for the captain to keep their calm and remain capable of acting (also linguistically) in very stressful situations.

It is clearly the coach who has the strongest language needs—and there are different ways of providing for them

Whereas players at a pinch can do without complex verbal communication about difficult subjects with some of their team mates, coaches are completely dependent on finding common linguistic and communicational grounds with each single player in their team. And, as we know, these teams are increasingly multilingual these days. In such a situation, basic language skills in at least some of the mother tongues of their players can be very helpful for the coach. Coaches will, of course, try to work with community interpreting, graphical means,[26] facial expressions, and gestures, as well as language mixing. However, the ideal type of contact still runs via the individual players' mother tongue. This means that the coach not only has to speak the language of the country in which they are working, but also a little bit of the languages of their players—and that they have to have good multilingual and multimodal communication skills.[27] For instance, Dietmar Constantini, former coach of several Austrian Bundesliga teams and the Austrian national team, insisted on learning Spanish in order to communicate with some hispanophone players in his team (interview Constantini 2006).

The necessity to speak the language of the country they work in also has to do with the fact that coaches, no less than players, are likely to have an international career and change the country every couple of years. Just like the players, the coach will not be given any acclimatization period, instead they will have to show excellent results right from the beginning. Thus, the coach has to be operational, even if they are Central European and the working language of their team is, for instance, Arabic or Greek. In such cases, the club will usually appoint an interpreter. However, this interpreter, too, is faced with the nearly impossible task of translating not only the content of the coach's instructions, but also their enthusiasm and the psychological and motivational elements of a coach's speech, all of this in real time.[28] This is one of the reasons why in Greece Otto Rehhagel's interpreter Ioannis Topalidis is nearly as famous as Rehhagel himself.

A coach who takes communication with the team seriously will try to learn the basics of the new language as quickly as possible in order not to be completely dependent on their interpreter. This will—in addition—earn them much respect and goodwill among the team.

Referees have to communicate smoothly with their colleagues. They need English, but maybe even more[29]

The average football spectator is certainly not aware of the area where the referee's real communication problems lie. We usually see them holding up the yellow or red card (i.e., practicing highly conventionalized nonverbal communication), or discussing with infuriated players (we may well wonder in which language the discussion unfolds). According to their own statements, the real communicative challenge for the referee arises within their own group. That is, for a referee it is not that important to understand what players are trying to tell them; what really counts is trouble-free communication with their assistant referees. To this end, Champions League matches, for example, are usually preceded by referee meetings, where some additional signs—beyond those conventionally prescribed—are agreed on within the group (interview Plautz 2007). Nevertheless, it seems that communication does not always flow smoothly. How else can the UEFA Champions League's fairly recent introduction of the rule that the entire referee team of a match has to come from the same country be explained? A revolutionary device in this respect was the introduction of the head set in 2006, giving the verbal communication in the referees' team a clear advantage over the nonverbal one.

The referee, however, does not only have to be able to communicate clearly with their colleagues and with the players on the pitch, but also with the public watching the game at the stadium and on TV. Egon Bereuter (together with Konrad Plautz one of the very few FIFA referees/referee assistants coming from Austria) points out that nonverbal communication will always remain important for the referee, because it is the only aspect of communication that the audience can perceive clearly. According to Bereuter, the referee has to "sell" their decisions and therefore their gestures have to be clearly visible to and identifiable for everybody.

Let us now address the question in which language the players, and especially the team captains, carry out discussions with the referee. At least in international games, this will usually take place in the universal lingua franca English, among other reasons because it plays the most significant role in referee-training.[30] This might, however, be short-sighted since most of the referees we interviewed told us that it is very useful to master more languages in order to be able to talk with the players. Some of the languages the referees mentioned as being very useful are above all Spanish, Portuguese, and Italian.

If you really feel the need to insult the referee, you had better choose a language they do not understand

We have just seen in the previous section that referees should actually be able to speak more than only English. For players, however, multilingual referees might not be such a good idea, since a player who, losing his temper in the heat of the moment,[31] insults the referee inevitably sees the red card—except in the case when the player chooses to insult the referee in a language the referee does not understand. Indeed, the referee has to note down in the match report what the player actually said to them, which, of course, they cannot do if they did not understand the words but only inferred the insult from tone and expression.

When asked about this issue, some referees told us that they regularly study lists of common insults in the respective languages before international games. A coach of a German lower league club catering predominantly towards Turkish migrants (see interview Yüksel 2016) even told us that he regularly warns his players not to recur to insults in Turkish, because the German referees have most certainly studied them beforehand. In this context, it is well known that a gesture is worth a thousand words and that players who lack the necessary language competence always find a way to convey their message—even though they might regret the success of that nonverbal insulting act in the end. Interestingly, gestures are not always as international as one might believe, and they, too, can give rise to misunderstandings as the following anecdote by Jocelyn Blanchard makes clear:

Multilingualism in football teams   269

I wanted to show the referee that I had been fouled at the head, with the gesture I would have used in my home country. ... But he interpreted it as an Austrian gesture meaning "you are crazy" and showed me the red card.

(Interview Blanchard)

Eleven players—one goal: team spirit and cooperation are crucial for success

With all its multiculturalism and multilingualism, a football team ultimately constitutes a group that has to stick together and show solidarity not only on the pitch, but also on a linguistic level in order to ensure successful communication. Hence the importance of community interpreting, mutual aid, and team spirit. Here is Tomáš Jun, with a fairly typical remark in this respect:

Players have a common goal. If I explain/translate something to another player, he will help me in the field—he will know what to do, where to run, etc. If he does not know what to do, it will be more difficult for me in the field, too.

(Interview Jun)

Thus, every player has a direct interest in the fact that their fellow players integrate quickly and well—also linguistically—into the new club. Only when its members truly work together, can a multilingual and multicultural team eventually be successful.

Summary and outlook

The football team and the pitch are not multilingual workplaces like so many others, they are a particularly interesting type of multilingual workplace. The two project seminars (2009 and 2016) conducted in Innsbruck showed that the mix of protagonists with different linguistic and cultural backgrounds, together with the obligation to succeed without delay, gives rise to ad hoc solutions that in the first instance emphasize communication at any cost. Nonverbal means like gestures and graphics interact with language mixing and lingua franca communication, while the implicit but well-known specific requirements of the different playing positions have an attenuating effect.

Language and communication may particularly come into focus when a club—provided it has the necessary funds—appoints interpreters, organizes language classes, and hires personal assistants for new players. The easiest and most frequent solution, however, seems to be 'community interpreting', i.e., translation by a team mate sharing the same mother tongue as the newcomer. This becomes possible due to highly motivated players who make it a point to develop—often through self-study—an impressive level of language competence, which is especially helpful for the personal integration into the new environment.

Moreover, coaches, who have to convey their message to every single member of their multilingual team, often display language skills in a variety of languages. During a match, the amount of language needed by a team member will depend on their playing position: Goalkeepers and midfielders use verbal communication much more frequently than forwards. Language also plays an important role for referees, who work in a team and cannot allow misunderstandings to happen.

We hope to have given an impression of the richness of scientific insights to be gained through the empirical study of multilingual football teams. We have seen that communication, and specifically multilingual communication, has a crucial role to play in the process of forming a group of individual players with very different backgrounds into a harmonious, effective, and successful football team.

Let us appreciate, at this point, the beauty of the determination deployed by those players and managers whose international careers have led them through a variety of languages and cultures, and who have started anew and made the effort to learn a new language every single time they arrive in a new country—acquiring thus an incredibly rich repertoire of linguistic competences in the course of their professional lives.

Notes

1 Many thanks to Carmen Konzett, Andrew Skinner, and Gerhard Pisek for proofreading an earlier version of this chapter.
2 Irene Giera, Erika Giorgianni, Eva Lavric, Gerhard Pisek, Andrew Skinner, Wolfgang Stadler, Jasmin Steiner.
3 In the meantime, international research caught up with the subject, see Chovanec and Podhorna-Polická (2009) and Baur (2012).
4 See Lavric (2012), Lavric and Steiner (2017; 2011a; 2011b), Steiner (2014; 2011), and Steiner and Lavric (2013).
5 This bibliography, compiled by Erika Giorgianni, is continuously updated and now contains over 100 pages of references.
6 All players quoted without mentioning the year were interviewed during the 2009 project seminar; in addition, interviews were conducted with Dietmar Constantini (2006), Konrad Plautz (2007), Massimo Cosentino (2014, by Erika Giorgianni), Ziya Yüksel (2016, by Eva Lavric), Francisco Díaz, Frank Ditgens, Masaki Morass, and Heinz Peischl (interviewed by students of the 2016 seminar).
7 Franceschini (2010), for instance, points out that this type of multilingual environment has hardly ever been studied before.
8 Marko Stanković, an Austrian player at US Triestina (Italy) at the time of the interview, tells an anecdote about how he failed to explain to a team mate that he had two dogs—because instead of "due cani" he kept saying "due chiavi" (two keys).

9 The Bulgarian player Antonio Mihaylov Krassimirov reports that when he first joined AC Milan's youth team, he could not communicate at all with his team mates—for him, this was a strong motivation to learn Italian as quickly as possible.

10 The following report by the Bolivian player Karl Dusvald about his time at FC St. Gallen in Switzerland makes this case:

> For our coach, it was very important that every single player could understand what he had to do. Therefore, during the training sessions he always had two players exhibit each of the exercises. So, I had to observe exactly what I was expected to do.
>
> (Translated from German by Eva Lavric)

11 But this is not necessarily true everywhere. For example, Marko Stanković reports about his experiences in Italy at US Triestina that for integration into the group language skills were more important than sporting performances. He told us: "The Italians speak only Italian and BASTA!" (translated by Eva Lavric).

12 For instance, it is very easy to show by facial expression that one has not understood something (interview Mehdi Mahdavikia). Gestures can also be very useful to indicate to a team mate that you want to receive the ball (interview Tomáš Jun), and a goalkeeper is able to organize a wall purely relying on gestures (interview Bartoloměj Kuru). Even coaches can, when needed, resort to gestures and facial expression: Karl Dusvald reports that Ademar Lisboa, the former coach of SV Reutte, spoke only a little bit of German and even less English, but he managed to get his message across with the help of gestures and facial expressions and thus to be understood and respected by his team.

13 A lingua franca is a language that people with different mother tongues use for communication although it is the mother tongue of neither of them (or of an insignificant minority).

14 Surprisingly enough, at Triestina this held true also of Stanković's several Uruguayan team mates when they spoke among themselves. They did not speak in their common mother tongue Spanish out of respect for their fellow players (interview Stanković).

15 The interview with Jun was conducted and then translated into English by Jan Chovanec.

16 If not indicated otherwise, all excerpts have been translated into English by Eva Lavric.

17 Steiner fulfilled this function at FC Wacker Innsbruck for several hispanophone players, which allowed her to include her insights in her Ph.D. thesis (see Steiner, 2014).

18 Examples from FC Wacker Innsbruck would be e.g., Fabiano, the Brazilian player whom we already mentioned, and who later on acted as a linguistic and cultural mentor for a second Brazilian player who was appointed after him; at SV Grödig, Diego Sehnem Viana was the interpreter for two other Brazilian players, Leonardo Ferreira da Silva and Thiago de Lima Silva.

19 Erich Müller reports about his time at FC Dornbirn (in the 1970s) that players of Yugoslavian origin used to translate extensively for each other. It is probable that this implied the languages designated nowadays as Bosnian, Croatian, and Serbian.

20 The concrete cases in our studies include: FC Wacker Innsbruck, US Triestina, SV Reutte, SC Kriens, Manchester United Youth.

21 The following significant anecdote conveys this point: The Brazilian player Lúcio (Lucimar da Silva Ferreira) came to Bayer 04 Leverkusen and was expected to learn German. But as soon as he discovered in his course book terms like 'Waschmaschine' [washing machine] and 'Socken stopfen' [mending one's socks], he categorically refused to continue with his lessons (see Repplinger, 2005). (So much for the link between machismo and language learning motivation.)

22 See Wiemann (2003a; 2003b), Repplinger (2005), Wiemann (2008), and Wiemann et al. (2008). The course works with special football situations and football terms, has a shallow progression, and an emphasis on communication. The astute sense for the target group is visible, e.g., in the fact that the numbers from 1 to 20 are introduced with reference to famous players who used to have these numbers on their jerseys. The program is adapted personally to each new player through references to their club and its history.

23 Since, Redmond and Warren have published their *English for Football* manual (2012).

24 He speaks fluent German, English, and Spanish, and also a little Portuguese, French, and Italian.

25 This is reported e.g., by Bartoloměj Kuru, the former Czech goalkeeper of SV Grödig. Simon Manzoni, the former Italian goalkeeper of the same club, says that you have to coordinate verbally with other players when there is a free kick or a corner.

26 The importance of graphical support for the communication between coaches and players is emphasized e.g., by Martin Petráš, to whom, shortly after his arrival in Italy, the coach used to explain everything with the flipchart. Similar remarks come from Tomáš Jun, who regards tactical instructions via flipchart as extremely useful for foreign players, and Martin Bichl, who at FC Reutte played under a coach that could speak neither English nor German and thus had to communicate all his instructions via graphical means.

27 One might object that for instance Giovanni Trapattoni in all his years as a coach of Bayern Munich, VfB Stuttgart, and Red Bull Salzburg never learned proper German—in spite of this, he must have been very resourceful in his communication, otherwise he would not have been able to motivate his players.

28 Constantini emphasizes furthermore that the interpreter should not know too little about football, but not too much either. If they know too little, they will provide a very poor translation, but if they know too much, they will try to interfere and convey their own contents.

29 Lisa Müller conducted a study on referees in the framework of the 2009 project seminar, distributing 16 questionnaires across all Austrian leagues. In addition, three Austrian referees were interviewed: international referee Konrad Plautz, international assistant referee Egon Bereuter, and Austrian-Ghanaian referee Bella Bello Bitugu.

30 English, French, and German are the official languages of UEFA.

31 In fact, because of the intensity of emotions, insults seem to occur rather frequently during a game, whether between players or between players and referees. The same applies to cursing; interestingly, another study (Steiner, 2014) suggests that players very often curse in their mother tongue, as it is the act of cursing and not the content that counts.

References

Baur, M. 2012. English for foreign Premier League football players: Linguistic needs, tutoring options and support mechanisms. A framework of an ESP course. Saarbrücken: Südwestdeutscher Verlag für Hochschulschriften.

Bundesliga. 2013. Guardiola getting to grips with German. [Online]. June 9. [Accessed May 15, 2017]. Available from: www.bundesliga.com/en/news/Bundesliga/0000256979.jsp.

Chovanec, J. and Podhorná-Polická, A. 2009. Multilingualism in football teams: Methodology of fieldwork. Language and Literature. European Landmarks of Identity. 5(1), pp. 186–196.

Ehrmann, J. 2012. Die Zwei. 11 Freunde. [Online]. June 22. [Accessed May 15, 2017]. Available from: www.11freunde.de/artikel/griechenlands-triumph-2004-das-werk-eines-duos.

The Football and Language Bibliography. [Online]. [Accessed May 16, 2017]. Available from: www.uibk.ac.at/msp/projekte/sprache_fussball/bibliography/.

Franceschini, R. 2010. Zukunftsperspektiven für die Mehrsprachigkeitsforschung. [Lecture]. January 28. Ringvorlesung Mehrsprachigkeit: Interdisziplinäre Ansätze. University of Innsbruck.

The Innsbruck Football Research Group. 2008. The football and language bibliography: In: Lavric et al. eds. The linguistics of football. Tübingen: Gunter Narr, pp. 399–418.

Kellermann, E., Koonen, H. and van der Haagen, M. 2006. Feet speak louder than the tongue: A preliminary analysis of language provisions for foreign professional footballers in the Netherlands. In: Long, M. ed. Second language needs analysis. Cambridge, UK: Cambridge University Press, pp. 200–222.

Larrea, U. 2009. El euskera como táctica. El País. [Online]. March 3. [Accessed July 26, 2017]. Available from: https://elpais.com/diario/2009/03/03/deportes/12 36034808_850215.html.

Lavric, E. 2012. Politiques conscientes et "bricolage" linguistique dans les enterprises et dans les équipes de football. In: Cichon, P., Erhart, S. and Stegu, M. eds. Les politiques linguistiques explicites et implicites en domaine francophone. Berlin: Avinus, pp. 165–186.

Lavric, E. and Steiner, J. 2011a. "Wenn er die Sprache kann, spielt er gleich besser": 11 Thesen zur Mehrsprachigkeit im Fußball. In: Mendoza, I., Pöll, B. and Behensky, S. eds. Sprachkontakt und Mehrsprachigkeit als Herausforderung für Soziolinguistik und Systemlinguistik. Munich: Lincom, pp. 101–120.

Lavric, E. and Steiner, J. 2011b. Football: Le défi de la diversité linguistique. Bulletin VALS/ASLA—Bulletin Suisse de Linguistique Appliquée. 95, pp. 15–33.

Lavric, E. and Steiner, J. 2017. Personal assistants, community interpreting, and other communication strategies in multilingual (European) football teams. In: Caldwell, D., Walsh, J., Vine, E.W. and Jureidini, J. eds. The discourse of sport: Analyses from social linguistics. London: Routledge, pp. 56–70.

Lavric, E., Pisek, G., Skinner, A. and Stadler, W. eds. 2008. The linguistics of football. Tübingen: Gunter Narr.

Liegl, B. and Spitaler, G. 2008. Legionäre am Ball. Migration im österreichischen Fußball nach 1945. Vienna: Braumüller.

Myers-Scotton, C. 1983. The negotiation of identities in conversation: A theory of markedness and code choice. International Journal of the Sociology of Language. 44, pp. 115–136.

Okuma. 2007. Fußball in Japan und in Deutschland: Ein Interview mit Guido Buchwald. Japan-Forum. [Online]. October 9. [Accessed August 4, 2017]. Available from: www.dus.emb-japan.go.jp/profile/deutsch/japan_forum/jf_2007/2007_09-10_jf150_1-3.pdf.

Redmond, A. and Warren, S. 2012. English for football. Oxford: Oxford University Press.

Repplinger, R. 2005. Deutsch für Ballkünstler. Zeit Online. [Online]. December 6. [Accessed May 15, 2017]. Available from www.zeit.de/online/2005/49/49_rund.

Soccer Training Info. 2016. Soccer players speaking foreign languages. [Online]. [Accessed January 8, 2017]. Available from: www.soccer-training-info.com/soccer_players_speaking_foreign_languages.asp.

Steiner, J. 2011. Il plurilinguismo nel calcio: L'analisi delle situazioni e delle strategie comunicative attorno a squadre multilingui. Innsbruck: Innsbruck University Press.

Steiner, J. 2014. "Iñaki, du musch ummi laufen!": Empirische Analyse von Mehrsprachigkeit und Kommunikationsstrategien in einer Fußballmannschaft. Ph.D. thesis, University of Innsbruck.

Steiner, J. and Lavric, E. 2013. Mehrsprachigkeit im Fußball. Fallstudie eines spanischen Legionärs in Österreich. In: Gradoux, X., Jeanneret, T. and Zeiter, A.C. eds. Rôle des pratiques langagières dans la constitution des espaces sociaux pluriels d'aujourd'hui: Actes du colloque VALS/ASLA (Lausanne, 1–3 février 2012) = special number of the Bulletin VALS/ASLA. Winter, pp. 187–213.

Wiemann, U. 2003a. "Wir haben Lehrer, die die Spieler die deutsche Sprache beibringen": Ein Konzept zur sprachlichen Integration ausländischer Fußball-Profis. In: Adelmann, R., Parr, R. and Schwarz, T. eds. Querpässe: Beiträge zur Literatur-, Kultur- und Mediengeschichte des Fußballs. Heidelberg: Synchron Publishers, pp. 139–153.

Wiemann, U. 2003b. Deutsch für Ballkünstler. Lehrmaterial für den Deutsch-Unterricht mit ausländischen Fußballspielern. Private publication.

Wiemann, U. 2008. Idee und Konzept. Deutsch für Ballkünstler—Ein Sprachkurs für Fußballprofis. [Online]. [Accessed June 27, 2016]. Available from: www.deutsch-fuer-ballkuenstler.com/index.php?option=com_content&view=category&id=30&Itemid=156.

Wiemann, U., Auffenberg, T. and Robra, W.G. 2008. Deutsch für Ballkünstler. [Online]. [Accessed June 27, 2016]. Available from: www.deutsch-fuer-ballkuenstler.de/.

Wulzinger, M. 2002. Empfindliche Seele. Spiegel Wissen. [Online]. November 18. [Accessed September 13, 2017]. Available from: www.spiegel.de/spiegel/print/d-25718167.html.

Contributors

Blanka Blagojevic is a Ph.D. student in Anglophone Literary and Cultural Studies at the University of Basel, Switzerland. She started her doctoral thesis as part of the "British Literary and Cultural Discourses of Europe" research project supported by the Swiss National Science Foundation at the English Department of the University of Basel. Her research interests span British and Anglo-American twentieth-century literatures, British literary representations of Eastern Europe in the twentieth and twenty-first centuries, British and American travel writing, and the relationship between literature and geography.

Jan Chovanec is Associate Professor in the Department of English and American Studies, Masaryk University in Brno. He has done research on various written and spoken media discourses including online news, live text commentary, sports broadcasting, and, most recently, TV documentaries. He is the author of the book *Pragmatics of Tense and Time in News: From Canonical Headlines to Online News Texts* (2014) and co-editor of several volumes, including *Representing the Other in European Media Discourses* (with Katarzyna Molek-Kozakowska, 2017), and *The Dynamics of Interactional Humor* (with Villy Tsakona, 2018). His new book on online soccer commentaries in the *Guardian* newspaper is set to be published under the title *The Discourse of Online Sportscasting* with John Benjamins in 2018.

Simon Critchley is Hans Jonas Professor of Philosophy at the New School for Social Research. His books include *Very Little ... Almost Nothing* (1997), *Infinitely Demanding* (2007), *The Book of Dead Philosophers* (2009), and *The Faith of the Faithless* (2012). Recent works include a novella, *Memory Theatre*, a book-length essay, *Notes on Suicide*, and a book on David Bowie. His new book, *What We Think About When We Think About Football* was published in November 2017. He is series moderator of "The Stone," a philosophy column in *The New York Times* and co-editor of *The Stone Reader* (2016). He is also 50 percent of an obscure musical combo called Critchley & Simmons. Their new album, *Moderate or Good, Occasionally Poor*, was recently released.

Daniel Haxall is Professor of Art History at Kutztown University of Pennsylvania. A former fellow at the Smithsonian American Art Museum and Institute for the Arts and Humanities, he earned his Ph.D. from the Pennsylvania State University. He publishes on diverse topics in contemporary art, including abstract expressionism, collage, installation art, and the African diaspora. His recent research investigates the intersection of art and sport, and he is editor of *Picturing the Beautiful Game: A History of Soccer in Visual Culture and Art* (2018).

Adam Kadlac is Associate Teaching Professor of Philosophy at Wake Forest University where he teaches (among other things) a class on sports and society. He works broadly in ethics and political philosophy and has published papers in *American Philosophical Quarterly*, *Journal of Applied Philosophy*, *Philosophical Studies*, and *Public Affairs Quarterly*. A supporter of Tottenham Hotspur and Columbus Crew SC, he coaches a U12 youth team that he hopes will eventually learn to play beautiful soccer.

David Kilpatrick is Associate Professor at Mercy College and Club Historian of the New York Cosmos. He is the author of *Writing with Blood: The Sacrificial Dramatist as Tragic Man* (2011) and *Obrigado: A Futebol Epic* (2015), and editor of *The State of the Field: Ideologies, Identities and Initiatives* (2018). He has coached soccer at the youth, scholastic, college, and adult levels and oversees coaching education in the northeastern United States as the Section 3 Coach Trainer of the American Youth Soccer Organization. The founding former President of Rivertowns United FC and former President of Arsenal America, he remains active with both organizations, as well as the Society for American Soccer History and Football Scholars Forum.

Eva Lavric is a full professor of Romance linguistics at Innsbruck University (since 2003), specializing in French and Spanish. Her academic career started at the Department of Romance Languages at the Vienna University of Economics and Business (Wirtschaftsuniversität Wien) (1983–2003). Her research interests are widespread and include referential semantics, contrastive linguistics, special languages and their didactics, pragmatics, sociolinguistics (code choice and code switching), and gastronomic and sports language. From 2010 to 2013 she directed the VinoLingua-EU-project, designing language teaching materials for winemakers. In 2006 she founded the Innsbruck Football Research Group with a focus on multilingual practices on the soccer pitch. She has been honored with several awards and distinctions for her doctoral thesis, her second thesis, and especially for her work as the director of Innsbruck University's interdisciplinary France Focus.

Contributors   277

Thomas Messerli is a researcher and lecturer in English linguistics at the University of Basel, where he completed his doctoral thesis on repetition and humor in telecinematic discourse. He has an M.A. in English and German Linguistics and Literature from the University of Zurich, and an M.A. in Film Studies from the Réseau Cinéma CH (Universities of Zurich and Lausanne). His current research interests are the pragmatics of fiction, participation structures, humor studies, human–computer interaction, and audiovisual translation.

Michael O'Hara is an artist and writer and lectures in Fine Art at the Dublin School of Creative Arts in Dublin Institute of Technology. He is an associate researcher with the Graduate School of Creative Arts and Media (GradCAM) and committee member of the Aesthetics Research Group and Digital Studies Seminar Group. His work focuses upon the processes of art-making and object relations and his research is concerned with a phenomenological account of digital technologies and computation. He has written on philosophy and aesthetics, from arts policy in Ireland to deconstruction and the avant-garde, and more recently on aesthetics and football in contemporary culture.

Cyprian Piskurek teaches British Cultural Studies at TU Dortmund University. He completed his Ph.D. on fictional representations of soccer fan cultures after the Taylor Report and has published on soccer studies, detective fiction, and Raymond Williams.

Emily Ryall is Senior Lecturer in the Philosophy of Sport and Exercise at the University of Gloucestershire, UK. She has written and published books and articles across a range of issues in the philosophy of sport, including technology, violence, fairness, equality, and aesthetics. She is editing author of the Routledge *Philosophy of Play* book series and author of *Philosophy of Sport: Key Questions* (2016) and *Critical Thinking for Sports Students* (2010). She is also associate editor for the *Journal of the Philosophy of Sport*.

Philip Schauss studied Law with French Law at the London School of Economics (L.L.B.) and holds an L.L.M. from Georgetown University. He is a Ph.D. candidate in Philosophy at the New School for Social Research, where he is writing a thesis on phenomenology of perception and repetition in architecture.

Jasmin Steiner studied Italian and Spanish (teacher training) at the Department of Romance Philology of Innsbruck University, with a semester at the University of Oviedo. She wrote her M.A. thesis in 2009 about "Multilingualism in football: Analysis of communication situations and strategies in multilingual football teams," which was published in 2011 through Innsbruck University Press. She then undertook a Ph.D.

in Linguistics and Media Studies at Innsbruck University, for which she won a doctoral scholarship covered by the University's Young Researchers Fund. At the same time, she worked as an employee in the management section of FC Wacker Innsbruck, offering German courses for Spanish players and translation services for the press, radio, and TV. Her Ph.D. thesis—"'Iñaki, du musch ummi laufen!': An empirical analysis of multilingualism and communication strategies in a football team"—received Innsbruck University's Dr. Otto Seibert Award. Jasmin has since completed a vocational training course for journalism and is currently working as a journalist for Austria's biggest newspaper.

Kristof K.P. Vanhoutte is a Research Fellow at the International Studies Group of the University of the Free State, Bloemfontein, South Africa, and an Invited Professor of Philosophy at the Pontifical University Antonianum, Rome, Italy. He started his studies in Philosophy at the Higher Institute for Philosophy, Catholic University of Leuven, Belgium and obtained his Ph.D. in Philosophy at the Pontifical University Antonianum, Rome, Italy. He studied Spiritual Theology at the Pontifical University Gregoriana and was Postdoctoral Research Fellow at University of Edinburgh's Institute for Advanced Studies in the Humanities. In 2010 he was awarded the European Philosophy from Kant to the Present Prize, issued by the University of Kentucky. He has published on topics in continental philosophy, patristics, theology-philosophy-politics interdependencies, educational theory, and soccer.

Connell Vaughan is a philosopher and a lecturer in Aesthetics and Critical Theory in the Dublin School of Creative Arts (DIT). He is an associate researcher with the Graduate School of Creative Arts and Media (Grad-CAM) and committee member of the European Society for Aesthetics and the Aesthetics Research Group. His research focuses on how challenges to aesthetic, educational, and political institutional norms and narratives gain recognition over time. He has published on the avant-garde, public art, curation, vandalism, the canon, curriculum design, the essay, classroom aesthetics, national identity, soccer, contemporary aesthetic theory, and art practice and policy.

Di Yu is a doctoral student in Applied Linguistics at Teachers College, Columbia University. Her research interests include media discourse, political discourse, humor, and the use of multimodal resources in interaction.

Index

Page numbers in *italics* denote figures.

A Collection of Heroes (Schrank) 71, *72*
A Shot at Glory (Corrente) 17,
    115–116, 118, 121
abbreviation 209–211
actions 29–30, 33, 34, 37, 39, 50, 52,
    53, 55, 56, 58, 90, 156n1, 172, 234;
    human action 36 (*see also* dramatic
    spectacle); intelligible action 45–49,
    57
Adidas 83, *84*
aesthetic experience 38, 50–51, 52–55,
    57, 58
aesthetic judgment 16, 29, 44, 45, 50,
    52, 54, 57, 60n5; *see also* judgment
Aesthetica (Baumgarten) 14, 21n7
aesthetics 13–16, 21n4, 29, 57, 91,
    123, 150, 176; aesthetic judgment *see*
    aesthetic judgment; beauty *see*
    beauty; concept of the aesthetic 13,
    14–15; definition of 14; everyday
    aesthetics 15; genius *see* genius; and
    perception 14, 16, 54 (*see also*
    aísthēsis); and representation 13, 14,
    62, 63, 81, 93, 109, 114, 115, 118,
    183, 194, 201, 202, 222n1, 231,
    239; of soccer 13, 14, 16, 20, 21n4,
    47; of sport 13, 21n4, 27–28, 31, 33,
    36, 37, 42; as theory of art 13, 14;
    see also style
After Virtue (MacIntyre) 45–48
Ahmed, Sara 17, 134, 135
aísthēsis 14–15, 16
alliteration 213, 219; *see also* poetics;
    rhetoric
allusion 84, 157n23, 208, 216; *see also*
    poetics; rhetoric

amateurism 34, 166–167
ambiguity 51, 74, 99, 111, 133, 146,
    156, 164, 183, 194, 196
Aristotle 17, 18–19, 21n10, 21n12,
    59n2, 91, 104n3; *see also Poetics*
    (Aristotle); *Rhetoric* (Aristotle)
assonance 206, 208, 209; *see also*
    poetics; rhetoric
Augenblick see moment, the

Bad Blue Boys 188, 191–192, 196
backstage behavior 203, 219
Bakhramov, Tofik 70
Ballkünstler (Leipzig 2006) 74
Bannister, Roger 31–32
Barthes, Roland 138n12
Baudrillard, Jean 81, 129, 138n7
Baumgarten, Alexander Gottlieb 14–15,
    21n7; and sensuous cognition *see*
    aísthēsis
beautiful game, the 14, 27, 33, 38, *40*,
    42, 42n2, 44, 62, 80, 90, 92, 103,
    104, 163, 164, 177, 178, 193, 227,
    257; *see also* soccer
beauty 14, 16, 27–32, 37, 40, 41, 44,
    45, 49–59, 59n2, 59n3, 59n5, 60n5,
    81, 91, 141, 156, 163, 164, 177–178,
    183, 189, 197, 256, 258, 270
Beckenbauer, Franz 4, 71, 72, 73, 111
Beckham, David 20, 84, 200, 201–202,
    205–216, 218, 222n1, 222n10,
    222n11, 222n12
Behind the Curtain (Wilson) 157n17,
    182–197, 197n1
belief 7, 8, 98, 101, 104, 151; self-belief
    99

280 Index

Bereuter, Egon 268, 272n29
Best, David 20n2, 28
betting 154, 218
Birth of Tragedy, The (Nietzsche) 15, 91
Blanchard, Jocelyn 266, 268–269
bodies 14, 15, 16, 28, 32, 39, 148, 149, 151, 157n16, 195, 216; female 86; masculine 201; metrosexual 222n1; and movement 16, 28, 32, 46, 47, 55, 57
Borge, Steffen 16
Brimson brothers 127–128, 130
British disease, the 187, 191, 198n8; *see also* hooliganism
broadcaster 150, 227, 228, 253
Buchanan, Roderick 62–63
Büttner, Werner 71, 73, 73

Caparrós, Joaquín 259
careers 52, 58, 64, 156n10, 171, 172, 173, 202, 204, 222n2, 222n10, 267, 270; managerial 94, 118
celebrities 156n5, 200, 201–206, 219, 222n10; stars 71, 84, 109, 110, 116, 145, 147, 187, 195, 196, 200–204, 236
Chapman, Herbert 111
Charlton, Jack 164, 171–176, 178–179
Clarke, Stuart Roy 64–67, 65, 87n3
Clough, Brian 90–92, 93–95, 97–104, 118–120
coaches *see* managers
coaching: ability 3; education 92, 102–103, 112; qualifications 112; pedigree 176; staff 6; style *see* style
code switching 259, 266, 269, 276
Cold War, the 76, 183–184
commentary 22n15, 78, 79, 81, 172, 177, 179
comments 227–233, 246–249, 249, 251–252, 253n2, 253n5
commercialization 121, 201
communication: at any cost 269; problems 256, 258, 265, 267; computer-mediated (CMC) 228, 230, 252; intercomprehension 263; lingua franca 259, 268, 269, 271n13; multilingual 270 (*see also* multilingualism); nonverbal 259, 267–268, 269; and soccer *see* soccer; technology-mediated 227; *see also* rhetoric; semiotics

communism 183, 185, 189–193
community interpreting 263–264, 266, 269; *see also* interpreters
Constantini, Dietmar 267, 270n6, 272n28
Cosentino, Massimo 265, 270n6
creative coinage 206, 214; *see also* linguistic creativity
creativity 21n4, 31, 32, 40, 42, 150, 164, 172, 174–175, 180n16; *see also* linguistic creativity; poetics
Critchley, Simon 9n1, 15, 157n26, 181n19
Croatia 185–186, 191, 192
crowds 29, 68, 78–79, 146, 153, 178
Cultural Imperialist Rascals' Trick (Büttner) 71, 73, 73

Damned Utd, The (Peace) 92, 101, 94–102, 118
Davis, Paul 34
debasement 20, 183–184, 189–191; *see also* rhetoric
defeat 4, 6, 8, 34, 236
Delije 192, 196
Dennett, Daniel 54
derbies 17, 21n9, 126–137, 137n2, 137n3, 137n4, 137n5, 137–8n6, 138n7, 138n8, 139n17
Derrida, Jacques 129
Dida 265
Ditgens, Frank 257, 265, 270n6
Dixon, Nicholas 37
dramatic spectacle 21n4, 32, 35–37, 38, 41, 156n14
Dunphy, Eamon 163–164, 174, 177, 179
Dusvald, Karl 259, 271n10, 271n12

Eastern Europe 20, 182–197, 197n1, 197n5, 197n7, 198n12
e-games 33, 35–36, 42; *see also* t-games
Elias, Norbert 129
Elias, Zé 260, 262
Empire Stadium *see* Wembley Stadium
Endless Column (Buchanan) 62
England 62, 63–65, 67–70, 66, 77–80, 86, 87n3, 92, 103–104, 113, 117, 166, 168, 170–171, 173, 186, 188; men's national soccer team 41, 63, 64, 67–69, 79, 87n4, 94, 103, 111, 116–117, 155, 168–169, 180n8, 180n17, 186–187, 204, 222n12, 241

Index   281

England (Steele-Perkins) 66
entertainment 204, 206, 214, 219, 231
Erasmus, Desiderius 17, 141–144, 146–149, 151–155, 157n24
Ersen, Esra 81–83, *82*, 86

FA (Football Association) 63, 64, 87n2, 92, 117, 166, 168, 180n17
faction 91, 97, 100, 101, 103, 104n5; *see also* fiction
FAI (Football Association of Ireland) 167–169, 180n10, 180n11, 180n12
FAIFS (Football Association of the Irish Free State) 180n10
False Nine (Kerr) 17, 121–122
fandom 6, 8, 17, 21n6, 37, 56, 62, 64, 67, 68, 76–77, 78, 83, 86, 111, 113, 115, 123, 126–137, 137n4, 137n5, 138n7, 138n8, 143, 151, 155, 173, 187–188, 190, 191–192, 229; *see also* derbies; hooliganism
fascism 9, 131–132, 136; national socialism 70–71, 73, 77, 193
Feet Ball (Hajjaj) 83
Feezell, Randolph 21n4, 56
fetish 81; *see also* Baudrillard, Jean
fiction 17, 102, 110; football fiction 17–18, 21n11, 90–104, 104n5, 104n6, 104n7, 109–123, 123n2; New Football Writing 109, 114–115, 118, 123; *see also* faction
FIFA 64, 87n4, 169, 180n9, 180n10, 180n11, 180n13; FIFA Men's World Cup 22n15, 41, 62, 63, 64, 68–70, 70–71, 74, 76–81, 83, 86, 87n5, 104n3, 111, 150, 152, 168, 178, 203, 205; FIFA Women's World Cup 58
Folly 141–144, 146–148, 151–155, 157n24
Football against the Enemy (Kuper) 182–197, 197n1, 197n7, 198n9
football *see* soccer
football fiction *see* fiction
football film 110, 114
Freud, Sigmund 17, 128, 130, 132–134, 136, 138n8, 138n14, 139n15, 139n16
Friedlander, Eli 53
frontstage performance 203, 219
fundamental attunement 7–8; *see also* Heidegger, Martin; moment, the

GAA (Gaelic Athletic Association) 165–168, 170, 171, 173, 178, 180n5, 180n14
Gadamer, Hans-Georg 148–151, 153–155
Galeano, Eduardo 81
Gass, William 155
Gegenpressing 4, 179
genius 14, 15, 16, 21n4, 40–42
Germany 62–63, 70–71, 73–74, 76–78, 81–83, 86, 184; Federal Republic of Germany (FRG) 68–71, 73, 74, 197n4; Flakelf 193; German Democratic Republic (GDR) 74, 76; men's national soccer team 68–69, 70–71, 73, 74, 111, 142–143, 150, 155, 163–164, 177, 181n18, 205
Giggs, Ryan 205
Giles, Johnny 102, 171, 180n12
Girard, René 100, 138n14
Golden Squad (Hungary) 186
Good Friday Agreement 170
Granny Rule 172, 180n13
Grösch, Wiebke 74
Guardiola, Pep 109, 143–145, 256
Gumbrecht, Hans Ulrich 21n4, 52–53, 55–56
Guti 156n1

hagiography 101–102
Hajjaj, Hassan 83–86, *84*, *85*
Hand, Eoin 170–172
Hand of God (Kerr) 17, 121
headlines 200, 204, 206, 208–215, 218, 222n8, 222n10, 222n11
Heidegger, Martin 4–7, 8, 15, 36; and resoluteness 5–6; and Situation 5, 7; and *Stimmung see* fundamental attunement; *see also* moment, the
Hesse, Uli 177
Hoepker, Thomas 74, 76, 76
Homes of Football (Clarke) 64–65, *65*
hooliganism 113, 114, 115, 127, 128, 129, 130, 155, 173, 187, 198n8, 223n12; Eastern European 187–188, 191
Hughes, Charles 92, 93, 173
Hume, David 52
Hummel 86
humor 20, 157n26, 200, 212–214, 218, 219, 227–228, 229–232, 252–253; humor construction 227–228, 231, 232, 233–246, 247–248, 252–253,

282 Index

humor *continued*
253n4; humor support 227–228,
230, 232, 246–252, 252–253;
incomprehensible humor 230, 248,
251
Hungary 186, 191–192, 195, 196
Hurst, Geoff 69, 70, 78, 81

idealization 20, 115, 183–184, 189,
194, 196; *see also* rhetoric
IFA (Irish Football Association)
165–169, 180n11
In the Penalty Area (Ersen) 81–83, *82*
incongruity 200, 227, 229–230, 232,
233–244, *234, 235, 237, 238, 239,*
240, 245–247, 251–252, 253n3,
253n4
individualism 119–120, 151
Instagram 20, 227, 231–232, 233, *234,*
235, 235, 238, 239, 240, 243, 244,
244, 245, 245, 246, 247, 248, 252,
253n5
insults 94, 143, 246, 268, 272n31
integration 260–265, 269, 270, 271n11
intellectuals 146, 156n8, 184; anti-
intellectualism 114, 117
intentionality 46–47, 55–57
interaction 18, 228–230, 233, 239,
243, 247, 249, 252, 253n1, 256;
participation roles 227–229, 249,
251–252; verbal 257, 266
interpreters 150, 256, 261–264, 267,
269, 271n18, 272n28; *see also*
community interpreting
interviews 4, 82, 91, 94, 100–101, 102,
142–143, 193, 206; qualitative 257,
259, 268, 270n6, 271n15, 272n29
Ireland 19, 163–179, 180n9, 180n10,
180n11; Northern Ireland 64, 87n4,
130, 168–170, 201; Republic of
Ireland 163–165, 169–171, 187
IRFU (Irish Rugby Football Union) 165
Iron Curtain 182, 184–185, 196

Jakobson, Roman 206, 209
January Window (Kerr) 17, 121
journalism 114, 183–184, 195, 200–201,
203, 206, 219; journalists 123, 142,
143, 145, 182, 192, 193, 197n1
judgment: aesthetic (*see* aesthetic
judgment); moralizing 203; negative
157n26; objective 29, 30; subjective
29

Jun, Tomáš 259, 269, 271n12, 272n26
Just Do It (Hajjaj) 84, *85,* 86

Kant, Immanuel 52–54, 59n4,
59–60n5, 157n23
Keane, Roy 174, 179
Kerr, Philip 17, 121–122
Kilpatrick, David 14, 17–18, 19,
104n3, 104n4, 118
Klopp, Jürgen 3–4, 6–8, 112, 179
Kreft, Lev 14, 15, 21n4, 36
Kretchmar, R.S. 33–41, 42n5
Kuhn, Thomas 30
Kuntz, Paul 31–32
Kuper, Simon 20, 182–197, 197n1,
197n7, 198n9, 198n11

Lacerda, Teresa 21n4, 40–41
language 18–20, 91, 104n3, 156n5,
200–201, 206, 210, 217, 219,
222n10, 223n17, 247, 248, 256–270;
foreign language skills 256, 260;
language barriers 256; language
course book for football players 264,
272n21; language courses 262, 264,
269; language enthusiasts 260, 263;
language learning 256, 257, 260,
264, 265, 267, 272n21; language
mixing *see* code switching; language
policy 263, 264, 265; language skills
256–258, 260–261, 263, 265, 266,
270, 271n11
lexicalization 207, 214, 215, 218
lexis 17, 18–19, 20, 21n12, 91; *see also*
poetics; *Poetics* (Aristotle); rhetoric;
Rhetoric (Aristotle)
LFA (Leinster Football Association) 167
linguistics: linguistic creativity 206,
208, 213, 214, 215; linguistic form
209, 214, 219, 245; linguistic
strategies 18–20, 200, 211, 247; of
professional multilingualism 257;
repertoire of linguistic competences
259, 270; *see also* creative coinages;
poetics; rhetoric
long ball 157n16, 164, 171, 173, 179
Long, Shane 164, 177–178
Loos, Rebecca 206, 209, 212–213, 215,
218, 222n2, 222n12, 223n12

MacIntyre, Alasdair 45–48
McClaren, Steve 111
McNamee, Mike 16

madness 151, 153–155
Magnum Photos 76
managers 3, 14, 17, 90–104, 109–123,
  143–145, 155, 164, 170–173,
  175–176, 179, 180n12, 205, 243,
  256–263, 266–267, 270, 271n10,
  271n12, 272n26, 272n27; as outlaw
  figures 111–112, 120, 121
Maradona, Diego Armando 41
Marbeck, Sarah 206, 209
Mauer im Kopf, die 184, 197
media 19, 20, 22n15, 71, 78, 80–81,
  93, 98, 101, 109, 110, 120, 129,
  141, 142, 143, 145, 148, 152, 155,
  200–208, 213–217, 219, 222n2,
  222n8, 222n10, 222n12, 229; news
  media *see* news media; social media
  see social media
metric 150, 157n16, 177
Mike Bassett: England Manager
  (Barron) 17, 116–118
minor differences 17, 128, 130,
  132–134, 136, 137, 138n14, 139n15,
  139n16; *see also* Freud, Sigmund;
  narcissism
Miracle of Berne 70
Mitchell, David 152–153
Moeller-Nielsen, Richard 186
moment, the 4–5, 7–8; *see also*
  fundamental attunement; Heidegger,
  Martin
Morocco 83–84; women's national
  team 86; Royal Moroccan Football
  Federation 86
mother tongue 256, 258, 259, 262,
  263, 266, 269, 271n13, 271n14,
  272n31
Mourinho, José 4, 7, 109, 243, 249
multilingualism 18, 257–258, 270n7;
  multilingual workplace 18, 257,
  266–267, 269; multilingualism in
  football 256–270
multimodality 19, 20, 227, 232, 233,
  243, 245, 249–252, 266
Müller, Thomas 150
Mumford, Stephen 21n4, 36–37,
  40–41, 59n1
Mussolini, Benito 131, 136
mythology 80, 94, 101–103, 128, 131,
  135–136, 138n12, 165

narcissism 17, 128, 130, 132–137,
  139n15, 139n16, 139n17, 156

narrative 21n10, 32, 37, 41, 46, 48–49,
  51, 52, 54, 58–59, 62, 74, 86, 93,
  110–111, 113, 115, 131, 135, 136,
  139n17, 164, 167, 173, 179,
  182–197, 200, 203–205, 207–208,
  212, 216, 217, 219, 222n4, 229
National Football Museum (England)
  64
Nehamas, Alexander 51
neoliberalism 114–115, 119, 122, 123
Neuer, Manuel 142
New Football Film *see* football film
New Football Writing *see* fiction
news media 20, 66, 71, 76, 80, 86, 145,
  200–219, 223n17, 223n18
news values 204, 207, 217
nicknames 68, 93, 111, 210, 212, 213,
  215, 222n1, 222n11
Nietzsche, Friedrich 15, 91, 104n4, 146
Nike 83, *84*, 86, 156n11, 243
Nike v. *Adidas* (Hajjaj) 83, *84*
nostalgia 67–70, 79, 80, 100, 114, 118,
  196

Oblak, Jan 235–236
Old Firm 130, 136–137

parallelism: orthographic 210, 211;
  phonological 206, 209, 211–212,
  222n10
partisanship 37–38, 41–42
Peace, David 17, 90–104, 104n6,
  104n7, 111–112, 118–120
Peischl, Heinz 258, 261, 270n6
performance 17, 29–31, 37, 40, 45, 47,
  49, 50, 55, 59, 74, 78, 201, 202,
  203; frontstage performance *see*
  frontstage performance; playing
  performance *see* soccer; *see also*
  dramatic spectacle
personal assistants 206, 261–262, 269
Pfeiffer, Paul 77–81, *79*, *80*
phenomenology 8, 15, 150
Philippines 78–80
philosophy 8, 13, 15, 21n4, 41, 45, 92,
  100, 104, 128, 144; of sport 13, 15,
  27, 31, 33
play 14, 21n4, 34, 36, 45, 53–54,
  56–57, 76, 91, 146, 148–151,
  153–154, 155–156, 156n6, 157n24,
  200, 219
playing position *see* soccer
playing style *see* style

284 Index

poetics: concept of the poetic 13; and creativity *see* creativity; of fandom 17; and literature 17–18, 111, 112, 122–123; poetic effect 222n10; poetic forms 206, 208; poetic function 214; poetic potential 209; poetic strategies 200, 207, 219; poetic structure 209; as production 15–16, 18; and soccer 15–16, 17–18, 19, 20, 21n14, 91; *see also* aesthetics; style

Poetics (Aristotle) 17, 18, 21n10, 21n12, 91, 104n3

Poland 189–190; men's national soccer team 187

popular press 200–201, 204, 205, 206, 208, 211, 212, 214, 216, 218, 219; *see also* media; news media; tabloids

Positions of Maximum Opportunity (POMO) 173–174

Premier League (England) 3, 57, 63, 66, 80, 114, 115, 119, 122, 126, 143, 149, 152, 231

professionalism 34, 57, 104n1, 111, 112, 118–119, 141–142, 144, 148, 149–150, 155, 166–167, 170, 171, 176, 178, 179, 231

punning 208, 212–213, 222n12

purism 36, 37–38, 57, 100

Puskas, Ferenc 186, 195–196

Rashford, Marcus 241

recontextualization 235, 241–242, 243, 245

Red or Dead (Peace) 17, 92, 96–99, 100, 102, 111, 118

Reep, Charles 92–93, 100

referees 5, 69, 70, 71, 78, 157, 222n12, 236, 257, 266, 267–269, 270, 272n29, 279n31; referee teams 5, 157n18, 267, 270

Reflections on Poetry (Baumgarten) 14, 21n7

Rehhagel, Otto 256, 267

repetition 8, 101, 143, 149, 209, 230, 247

representation 13, 14, 62, 63, 66, 80, 81, 83, 86, 92, 93, 97, 100, 102, 109, 114, 115, 116, 118, 121, 138n7, 166–169, 171–172, 178, 183, 194, 196, 201, 202, 204, 211, 216, 222n8, 231, 239, 244

Revie, Don 93–98, 100–103, 120

rhetoric: concept of the rhetorical 13; *lexis see lexis*; and the media 20, 78, 212; and multimodality *see* multimodality; as persuasion 18; and politics 19, 63, 73–74; rhetorical strategies 13, 18–20, 183–185, 189, 194–196, 212; and soccer 19–20, 21n14, 142–144; *see also* linguistics; poetics; *Rhetoric* (Aristotle); semiotics; style

Rhetoric (Aristotle) 18, 21n12, 21n13

Rhetoric of the Empire, The (Spurr) 183–187, 189–191, 194, 196

romanticisms 15, 112, 114, 183, 194

Ronay, Barney 93

Ronell, Avital 141

Rooney, Wayne 204, 241

RTÉ (Raidió Teilifís Éireann) 163, 170, 179

Rundlederwelten (Berlin 2006) 71, 81

Russia 188, 191

Sacchi, Arrigo 179

sacred, the 100–101, 103–104, 104n7

St. George's Cross flag 64, 68

Saints, The (Pfeiffer) 77–81, 79, 80

scandals 20, 111, 200–201, 202, 204, 205, 207, 213–214, 218, 219, 222n11

Schrank, Volker 71–74, 72

Sein und Zeit (Heidegger) 4–5, 8

semantics: semantic complexity 213; semantic frames 230–231, 236

semiotics 18, 19, 63

sensationalism 200–201, 206, 217

Serbia 191, 192

settings 45–51, 53, 57–59, 66, 84, 116, 118, 231, 263

sexting 200, 207, 222n3

Shankly, Bill 17, 90–93, 95–100, 102–104, 111–112, 116, 118–120, 126, 129–130

skills 14, 15, 16, 29–31, 33–34, 36–42, 48, 49, 50, 149–150, 156n10, 157n16, 174, 177, 178, 257; closed 39–42, 40; open 39–42, 40; skillful interchanges 33, 36, 37, 38–40, 40

soccer: coaching academies 112; and communication 18, 20, 104n7, 257, 258–259, 266–270, 271n9, 271n13, 272n22, 272n26, (*see also* communication); constitutive elements of 15–16, 17;

as constructive–destructive sport 16; and multilingualism *see* multilingualism; playing performance 6, 7, 8, 57, 58, 143, 150, 183, 236, 258, 265, 271n11; playing position 92, 149–150, 258, 263, 266, 269–270; playing style *see* style; and stupidity 16–17, 141–156; youth soccer 14, 45, 48–49, 57, 59, 261, 271n9; youth academies 264

social media 20, 227–232, 248, 249, 253n1

socialism 93, 96, 97, 100, 102, 104, 118, 119

Sommermärchen 77

Sparwasser, Jürgen 74

spectacle 14, 66, 77, 79, 81, 152, 164, 178, 229; of language 200, 206, 219, 223n17; *see also* dramatic spectacle

Spieler (Tübke) 74, *75*

Spurr, David 183–187, 189–191, 194, 196

stadiums 6, 64, 66, 68, 74, 113, 119, 152, 153, 157n22, 177, 190, 191, 192; *see also* Wembley Stadium

Stankovi , Marko 262, 270n8, 271n11, 271n14

Starostin, Nikolai 191, 195–196

stars *see* celebrities

statistics 7, 150, 155

Steele-Perkins, Chris 66–67, *66*

story *see* narrative

Sturridge, Daniel 8, 241

style 19–20, 31, 37; coaching style 7, 111, 173, 175, 176; playing style 44, 48, 50, 57, 92, 143, 163–164, 170, 171–172, 173–179, 180n17, 183, 195–196, 204, 265; stylistics of soccer 20; writing style 100, 118, 206, 211, 222n8

Sydnor, Synthia 103

tabloids 117, 146, 156n5, 200–209, 214, 216–217, 219, 222n4; tabloid agenda 204; *see also* media; news media; popular press

taboo 132, 200, 206, 216–219, *220, 221*

tactics 18, 19, 50, 91–92, 98, 109, 112, 117, 145, 151, 175, 177, 179, 258, 272n26

talent 146–147

Taylor Report 113–115, 118, 119

textspeak 210–211

t-games 33–36, 38; *see also* e-games

Thatcher, Margaret 70, 95, 99, 113, 119–120

31 Hayes Court (Wallinger) 67, *67*

Three Pillars of Society (Clarke) 65, *65*

time: clock-time 4–5; Klopp-time *see* moment, the; limitedness 33–36; regulatedness 33–35; wasting 34–35, 149, 156n14

Topalidis, Ioannis 256, 267

totaalvoetbal 44, 176

Total Football see *totaalvoetbal*

translation 262–263, 267, 269, 271n19, 272n28

Trapattoni, Giovanni 164, 175–176, 179, 272n27

Tübke, Albrecht 74, *75*

Twitter 20, 205, 227–228, 231–233, 236, *237, 242,* 244–249, *249, 250,* 251–252, *251,* 253n5

UEFA 99, 272n30; Champions League 3, 6, 8, 57, 227, 235, 239–240, 241, 244–245, 248, 256–257, 267; Europa League 3, 8, 82, 248; European Championship 58, 62, 63, 64, 70, 87n4, 104, 142, 143, 151, 152, 155, 163–164, 176, 179, 203, 222n11, 222n12, 241, 256

ugliness 16, 59n1, 141, 156, 30, 44–45, 50, 57, 58, 164, 175

ultras 138n8, 153, 188

UMBRO 68

Union Jack flag 64, 67–68

value 27, 30, 31–32, 35–40, *40,* 78, 111, 116, 122, 123, 146, 173, 202, 206, 253n3; *see also* aesthetics

verbal interaction *see* interaction

videos 62, 77–78, *79, 80,* 81–82, *82,* 157n18, 177, 227, 228, 232–236, 252, 257

violence 87n6, 113, 115, 126, 127, 128–129, 131, 132, 138n14, 153–156, 170, 191

Völler, Rudi 143

Vuitton, Louis 83–84

Wallinger, Mark 67–70, *67, 69,* 87n6

Webb, Robert 152–153

Wembley Stadium 67–68, 77–80, 96, 185–187

When Saturday Comes 68
Wiemann, Uwe 264, 272n22
Wilson, Harold 99, 119
Wilson, Jonathan 20, 91, 149, 151, 157n17, 180n17, 182–197, 197n1, 197n7
Winner, David 92
Wolff, Larry 184
Wolstenholme, Kenneth 69, 78

word play 90, 206, 208, 212–214, 219, 229
world wars 63, 68, 71, 76, 86, 111, 136, 139n18, 155

Yugoslavia 191–192, 195, 264, 271n19

Zatopek, Emil 30–31
Ziff, Paul 27, 31